GOVERNING OREGON

An Inside Look at
Politics in One American State

Thomas L. Mason

 KENDALL/HUNT PUBLISHING COMPANY
4050 Westmark Drive   Dubuque, Iowa 52002

To Jessica, in whose beautiful hands rests the future

TABLE OF CONTENTS

PREFACE

"All politics is local," said Tip O'Neil,[1] and indeed it is. This is a book about "local politics" in one Western American state --Oregon. It is also, however, about "all" politics. Regardless of how "local" it is, political activity is a universal phenomenon, a fundamental part of the human experience. A book is one means to understand part of that experience, a medium to translate an objective reality to knowledge. If a biography is effective, we not only increase our understanding of the individual subject, but of ourselves. An effective volume on one state's politics should resemble a good biography. If we learn about the political life of a particular state we learn about all states. We find commonalties; all states are subject to some of the same general forces and dynamics of political life. If we are fortunate, we can learn about ourselves and even use what we have learned.

This book attempts to accomplish that end in three ways. First, it is a text for use in college level state and local government classes. The history, political culture, economy and Constitution of this one state are considered and analyzed. Then, the background and current use of the initiative, referendum and recall, key aspects of Western political development, are closely examined. These institutions are at the heart of politics and government in Oregon. The work then looks at executive, legislative and judicial functions, and discusses significant local variations. There are also chapters on the media, political parties and interest groups. The section on local government looks at more than the typical structure of cities and counties -- it considers some seemingly mundane items such as tax collection, land-use planning, garbage and welfare. As pedestrian as these functions may seem, they are among the most important tasks that local jurisdictions perform, and there are significant political aspects to each of these activities. School finance and other "perennial issues" are discussed at length in Chapter 11.

Secondly, this is a book about real people and the way in which they govern. It is not a history of Oregon politics per se --that remains to be written --but it does try to relate incidents and insights that portray the participants in their moments of folly as well as their moments of glory. These are the threads that make up the warp and woof of Oregon politics, that give it color and texture.

If there is one necessary caveat to accompany this work, it is that it is written by a participant and not an outside observer. The inescapable irony is that twenty plus years in the public arena allow one to accumulate knowledge as well as prejudice. Be warned, the perspective is that of a card-carrying, liberal Democrat who is not known for his non-partisanship. No matter how insightful the observations or anecdotes may seem, they should be taken with a grain of salt. This caveat especially applies the discussion 1993 Legislative Session. This book is a report from a battlefront, by an out-of-breath participant, more than an objective analysis. Criticisms of the other politicians might well be nothing more then a Democrat pot calling a Republican kettle black. My apologies to anyone I have offended; they are welcome to write their own book.

Finally, this work describes a state whose politics and basic form of government are in transition. While the term "politics" is used in the title and throughout the book, the term "democracy" would have served as well. Indeed, one could argue that in this particular jurisdiction the terms are almost interchangeable. Oregon is a democracy, but the most significant recent political developments in the state have changed the nature of that democracy. The body politic has been wounded by the processes of popular democracy. The death penalty, victims' rights, the tax revolt, term limits, abortion and gay rights have all been the subjects of recent initiatives and referendums. These have been, and continue to be, the bitter political controversies that dominate Oregon politics. At best, these issues are only temporarily resolved.

This is especially true of the gay rights issue. In 1992, Oregon received national attention because of the infamous anti-gay Ballot Measure 9. The proposal was sponsored by the ultra-conservative Oregon Citizens' Alliance which has emerged as a major force, for better or worse, in the state's politics. Ballot Measure 9 failed, but the issue remains at the top of the political agenda. It is a major sub-topic of Chapter 3, "Direct Democracy -- From Populism to Culture Wars."

More importantly, the cumulative effect of almost one hundred years of the initiative and referendum on Oregon's form of government cannot be ignored. Chapter 12 "Who Governs?" concludes by describing recent fundamental changes in the nature of this state's politics. The conclusion is not particularly sanguine. There is no guarantee that this particular state will continue to be governed in an effective manner.

---

1   Speaker of the United States House of Representatives.

ACKNOWLEDGMENTS

There are innumerable people who have made this book possible. Individuals, both in and out of government, have been kind enough to share information and valuable insights with me. I would particularly like to thank those who helped with the writing and production of the final manuscript: Claudia Black, Barrie Herbold and Wayne McFetridge.

Ron Cease and Hans Linde offered advice and perspective.

Finally, there are those people whose support made my participation in the political arena possible. Mary Wendy Roberts, Jeff Campiche, and Renee Bryant were there at the beginning.

CHAPTER 1

HISTORY, ECONOMY, POLITICAL CULTURE

The land was ours before we were the land's.
She was our land more than a hundred years
Before we were her people.

Robert Frost
"The Gift Outright"

Introduction

The purpose of this chapter is to give the reader an understanding of the more fundamental aspects of Oregon. Topics include:

- An examination of the initial question of why any American state is worthy of study as a separate entity.
- Consideration of Oregon's basic geography and how it affects the social institutions of the state.
- Review of the state's history.

- Description of the economy.

- Portrayal of the state's political culture.

A Unique State?

It is a political truism that citizens of each of the American states think that their particular place is unique. This is not unusual; provincialism is a world-wide phenomenon. Bavaria, Wales, Tuscany, Manchuria -- all have a sense of place, an identity and a certain pride. But how really "unique" can any American state be? Objectively, one should find significant characteristics in nations or regions with long histories or strong ethnic groupings. True uniqueness should reside in places with more definable characteristics than American states. How can Oregon really differ from Washington? Why bother looking at this one state? A modern-day de Tocqueville would at best observe subtle variations when comparing the attributes of a New York and a Pennsylvania. The real dissonance should occur when examining a Japan beside an Italy or comparing a Costa Rica with a Russia. Where does the uniqueness of any American state come from?

The answer is this -- American states are somehow more than mere geographical regions of a homogenous large country; they are <u>sovereign</u> entities. This enigmatic "uniqueness" is, to a great extent, a consequence of each individual state being a "state" in the classical sense of the term. Almost all governing in America is done by the states. Aside from defense, Social Security and a few other matters, the great tasks of government (education, roads, sewers, jails and welfare) are either state functions or state-administered federal programs. Americans are governed as Oregonians or Washingtonians; because of this, they perceive themselves in those terms. In addition, all of these sovereign, separate "states" have their own geographies, histories, constitutions, statutes, government institutions, local economies and political cultures. All these factors blend together to create 50 similar yet distinctive entities. Oregon does not really differ from Washington, yet it does. Even so, if we understand politics in this one state, we will inevitably understand politics in other American states.

Basics -- Where on Earth?

Before one looks at politics, the human process of government, it helps to understand geography. Oregon is a moderately large state in the northwest corner of America. It has a land area of 97,073 square miles[1] and is approximately the size of the United Kingdom. It is bordered on the north by Washington, on the south by California and Nevada, on the east by Idaho and on the west by the Pacific Ocean. The Columbia River separates Oregon from Washington. The Pacific is the only other natural boundary.

Three geographical factors color all of the state's history, economics and politics. First, Oregon is very isolated from the rest of the United States. The only major city, indeed the only city of any significant size within easy traveling distance, is Portland, which sits on the confluence of the Columbia and Willamette rivers. Seattle is 140 miles north; most Oregonians see no reason to travel to a city that just resembles Portland. Boise, a relatively small town, is 432 miles east and San Francisco is a 14-hour drive south. Almost all media is local which exacerbates the isolation. In fact, it has been argued that Oregon is so isolated that most of its citizens don't know it is isolated.

The second salient geographical feature is the Cascade Mountains, which run north and south, and divide the state politically as well as spatially. The populated western third with its legendary wet climate[2] is generally more liberal and urban. Eastern Oregon, the remaining two thirds, is basically arid ranch land, and is rural and conservative. Most of the population lives in the western part of the state; 70% of all Oregonians reside in the Willamette Valley which follows the Willamette River north to the Columbia River.

The valley, running north and south, is approximately 100 miles long, and is bordered on the east by the Cascades and on the west by the Coast Range. It was the primary goal, known as "The Eden," of state's forefathers and foremothers who traveled the Oregon Trail starting in 1843. Portland anchors the northern end of the valley, while the city of Eugene sits at the southern tip. Interstate Highway 5 serves as a kind of mainstreet for the valley, connecting most of the major cities and towns.

The final element of significant geography is that Oregon is on the Pacific Rim. It faces the East and has significant trade relationships with Japan, Korea and China. It does more trade with Japan than it does with Canada and 52 percent of all foreign tourists are from Asia.[3] These strong ties to the Orient are ironic as Oregon is so isolated from the rest of the United States. One commentator, James Gardner, has noted that Oregon, as well as the rest of northwest America and Canada, is located half way between two of the major centers of economic activity in the world, the European Economic Community and the Pacific Rim. Gardner thinks that the region is uniquely positioned, but whether it can take advantage of the circumstances remains to be seen.[4]

History -- The Northwest Passage, Fur Traders and Methodists

Saying that a state was "discovered" by anyone, when an indigenous population already existed, is an example of how selective history is. Oregon is no exception. History is written by the prevailing culture and thus this state was "discovered" by Europeans, not by the ancestors of Native Americans who walked across what is now the Bering Strait.[5]

Oregon was "discovered" from the Pacific Ocean as part of the effort to find a Northwest Passage from Europe to the Orient. As best we can tell, the southern coast was first sighted by a Spanish expedition led by Cabrillo in 1543.[6] In 1545, Sir Francis Drake in the Golden Hind also touched the southern coast.[7] Another Spaniard, Martin Aguilar, marked what he thought to be the Columbia River on his charts in 1603.[8] Bruno Heceta found the mouth of the river in 1775, but didn't have the wherewithal to explore upstream.[9] In 1788, American merchant Captain Robert Gray explored the Oregon coast and traded for furs with the natives.[10] Later, in 1792, he returned and at 8:00AM., May 11, 1792, he finally took his ship the *Columbia Rediviva*, up what had been the legendary "Great River of the West."[11] Gray had to wait seven days before he could cross the dangerous bar of the Columbia; even then he followed an Indian canoe for safety![12] The door was open to a new land.

The Lewis and Clark Expedition arrived in Oregon in 1805, and in 1810, John Jacob Astor's Pacific Fur Company established a trading post on the mouth of the Columbia at what is now Astoria.[13] The Astor effort was eventually replaced by the Hudson's Bay Company and Dr. John McLoughlin who, in 1825, founded Fort Vancouver on the northern shore of the Columbia, in what is presently southwest Washington.[14] Fur trapping was the primary industry in the region until 1829, when ex-trappers began farming in the Willamette Valley.

Methodist missionary Jason Lee arrived in Oregon in 1834 and, along with three companions, settled in the Willamette Valley near present day Salem. Lee and his associates published the <u>Oregon and Indian's Advocate,</u> which was filed with extravagant claims meant to sell the new land.[15] The Methodists later established missions at Oregon City on the Willamette, at The Dalles on the Columbia and at Clatsop Plains. Perhaps the most lasting effect of this early missionary activity was the establishment of Oregon's first colleges -- Pacific, Willamette, Linfield and Lewis and Clark. These church-founded schools still thrive today.[16]

Notwithstanding these early efforts, religion seems to have done poorly in the Northwest. According to a recent survey, by the Graduate School of the City University of New York, 17 percent of all Oregonians claim to have *no* religion. This is the highest percentage of non-believers in the United States.[17] It also makes the non-believers the largest "religious" group in Oregon. Given recent events, such as the emergence of the strongly religious Oregon Citizens' Alliance, this seems incredibly anomalous.[18]

And who would eventually control this new land? Who would win the competition between Britain and America? The issue was decided both locally and internationally in favor of the United States. On May 2, 1843, a group of settlers met at Champoeg Landing, in the mid-Willamette Valley, and by a bare margin voted to form a provisional

3

government which was in effect, a step toward American statehood.[19] After intense negotiations and the threat of war ("Fifty-four Forty or Fight"), President Polk signed a treaty with Great Britain in 1846 which established the 49° of latitude as the present U.S.-Canadian border; the issue was settled.[20]

Migration on the Oregon Trail was the major source of population for the state through the middle of the Nineteenth Century. Why did some people take the southern detour to California while others continued north, to Oregon? The recruiting of the more religious to the Willamette Valley played some role in the selection,[21] but two more apocryphal theories give better insight. One theory is that all of the dour, conservative, proper, midwestern burghers went to Oregon while the frontier version of the fast-track yuppies went to California. There is also the story that as the immigrants came to the divide in the road there was only one sign, which said "To Oregon;" those who could read took its advice. Of the 350,000 people who traveled the Oregon Trail between 1843 and 1865, the great majority did not go to Oregon; 250,000 went to California, 50,000 to Utah and only 50,000 went to Oregon itself. More than a hundred years later, between 1985 and 1991, the trend was reversed, with 1,186,000 moving out of California to other western states. Of these, 174,000 came to Oregon, and 294,000 to Washington.[22]

In this century, immigration has furnished most of Oregon's population. Between 1840 and 1860, 53,000 people came to the State, mainly from the Midwest. In 1910, the population was only 400,000; by July of 1991 there were 2,930,000 people in the State.[23] Oregon had the largest growth of any state in the Union -- 49 percent, from 1.3 million to 1.9 million, from 1939 to 1948.[24] It was also during this period that the first significant number of black Americans came to Oregon. Most migrated from the South to work in the Kaiser shipyards in Portland during World War II. Until then, almost all blacks in Oregon had worked for the railroad.[25]

Economy -- The Perpetual Need to Diversify

On January 10, 1949, departing Republican Governor John .Hall gave his farewell speech at the inauguration of Douglas McKay, the man who had defeated him in the primary election. Hall had originally been the Speaker of the House and was thrust into the Governorship by the tragic simultaneous deaths of Governor Earl Snell, Secretary of State Robert Farrell Jr. and Senate President Marshall Cornett. All three died in a single plane crash October 28th, 1947, while traveling to Nevada for a hunting trip.[26] Under the Oregon Constitution, in effect at that time, Hall was the next in line of succession.

Hall's tenure was of little note, except for his final speech which reads like a Cassandrian commentary on the past, present and future of Oregon's economy. Hall stated that the state was too dependent on timber for its economic base and there was an urgent need to diversify. Oregon was, and is, overly sensitive to national economic trends, i.e., in good times people build and buy houses and in bad times they don't. Consumers always buy commodities such as food and gasoline, but they don't always buy houses. For the economist, timber is a classic example of a cyclically sensitive industry. An old cliché says that when the nation catches a cold Oregon gets pneumonia.

In his 1949 speech, Hall went on to say that the way to diversify Oregon's economy was to emphasize tourism, light manufacturing and trade. He also said that good education was crucial to economic development. Has anything changed?[27]

4

Over the 40-plus years since Hall made his speech, the biggest success story has been the emergence of a significant electronics industry in Washington County, west of Portland. This is Hall's "light manufacturing." Oregon's version of Silicon Valley started underground when Howard Vollum, Jack Murdock, Miles Tippery and Glenn McDowell began manufacturing oscilloscopes in Vollum's parents' basement in 1946. The four men called their company Tektronix. At it peak in 1981, "Tek," as it is called locally, employed 24,000 people[28] and eventually spun off other companies such as Floating Point Systems, Mentor Graphics and Planar Systems. In 1976 outside companies such as Hewlett-Packard and Intel opened plants in Oregon, and in 1985 Nippon Electric Company (NEC) started its operations in Washington County as the first Japanese concern. It was followed by Epson in 1985 and Fujitsu in 1986.[29]

Where the electronics industry has grown, the timber industry has gone through an agonizing series of retreats. In 1939, 60 percent of Oregon's economy was based upon timber,[30] but by 1991 timber was the base of less than 10 percent of the economy.[31] At its peak, in the 1950s, the industry employed 85,000 Oregon citizens. By 1991 that number had fallen to approximately 50,000 people.[32] From 1949 to 1991 the percent of Oregon's population employed in the timber industry dropped from 4.7 to 1.9 percent.[33] One of the biggest blows came in 1982 when Georgia-Pacific (GP) moved its headquarters from Portland to Atlanta. GP had originally been the Georgia Hardwood Lumber Co. when it started in Atlanta in 1921.[34]

Not only is the timber industry sensitive to national economic trends, but the actual supply of timber is being reduced due to several other factors. In 1990, Richard Haynes of the Forest Service observed that location of the supply in America changes in approximately 75 year cycles.[35] The Northwest and the South alternate as the primary sources of timber for the country. In retrospect, there was nothing unusual about Georgia Pacific's move back to Atlanta.

The situation is further exacerbated by two other conditions. First, it is more profitable to ship raw logs overseas than to manufacture finished wood products in Oregon. Trite as it sounds, the export of timber is the export of jobs. In 1962, there were 152 plywood mills in the West; in 1990, only 71 were left. In that same period, the South went from three plywood mills to 70.[36]

This timber economy has been further impacted by a small, nocturnal carnivore -- the Northern Spotted Owl. The Portland Audubon Society filed its first lawsuit to preserve old-growth timber as habitat for the owl in 1987. The Spotted Owl battle continues to be fought to this day. Regardless, the overall effect of all these elements has been less timber and fewer timber jobs. The necessity to diversify the state's economic base is probably more evident today than it ever has been.

Oregon's economy differs in more than size from its two large neighbors, Washington and California. Washington has everything that Oregon has, but it also has Boeing, a $30 billion year giant. California has innumerable Boeings and other industries to drive an economy that was more than ten times larger than Oregon's in 1989, $697 billion verses $52 billion in gross state product.[37] Even the very climate conspires against Oregon. Sun falls on California, rain falls on Oregon. Sun grows oranges and rain grows trees, but oranges grow faster. Basically, Oregon's resource-based economy is in a state of flux.

Another peculiarity of the Oregon economy is the relatively few federal defense spending dollars which are expended in the state. Oregon is 49th out of the 50 states in military spending; only West Virginia gets fewer defense dollars. In 1993, Washington state received $1,064 per capita while Oregon received $193 for each citizen.[38]

Political Culture -- Coalitions, Innovations, Couples and Carmen

To begin, the outside observer needs to appreciate the smallness of Oregon's "political culture." There has never been a "census" taken, but the number of people actually involved in Oregon politics is probably less than two or three thousand. It is a very limited group; in many ways it resembles a small town with its neighborhoods, families and human conflicts. Everybody knows everybody and there are very few secrets. In Oregon, even the socioeconomic profile of the politically active resembles a small town. These people are not an "elite" in a sociological sense. Most people that participate in Oregon politics are solidly middle class. There are very few blue collar workers and even fewer people who could be considered wealthy. Only a few full-time elected positions exist which pay enough to support someone. At the same time, the size of the state makes it possible for any hardworking individual to have significant impact without being personally wealthy.

Oregon's political culture is the natural result of all of the previously mentioned geography, history, economics and more. The most prominent feature of this culture, or "small town," is the constant conflict between urban and rural interests. Like provincialism, this is a common phenomenon -- urban-rural political battles are universal. Cities are always cesspools of corruption; the country is always home to narrow-minded bumpkins, or so it seems to the other side.

In the legislative arena, this conflict usually emerges as a competition for limited state resources. Urban lawmakers tend to favor education, human resources (welfare) and mass transit. The more rural legislators support agriculture and highways. Republicans who represent cities tend to be more "liberal" than their fellow party members from the country. The same is true for Democratic lawmakers: rural members of the party are inevitably more "conservative" than their city counterparts.

Historically this urban-rural tension has created an opportunity for coalition politics; i.e., members from two parties joining forces to control a house of the Legislature. The last overt coalition occurred in 1977 in the Oregon House. Two thirds of the way through the session Republicans and conservative Democrats formed a coalition to strip Democratic Speaker Phil Lang of his powers. The State Senate was controlled by a coalition of conservative Democrats and Republicans from 1957 to 1971.

This urban-rural clash also comes into play during elections. In 1986, gubernatorial election, former Mayor of Portland and U.S. Transportation Secretary Neil Goldschmidt, Democrat, was running against ex-Secretary of State Norma Paulus, the Republican nominee. On August 5, 1986, during a television interview about the negotiations over debate locations, Goldschmidt said that he didn't want the debates to take place in a "nowhere" location like Bend (then a modest ski resort town in eastern Oregon)(emphasis added). Rural people were already suspicious that he would only care about urban issues; his remark seemed to confirm that view. Demonstrations were held in Bend, and the locals demanded an explanation. Two weeks later Goldschmidt made a very contrite appearance in the city and apologized for his remark.[39] He won the election and served one term as Governor.

Politically the rural areas seem more sensitive to the issue than urban areas. The tiff over the Goldschmidt "nowhere" remark was not atypical. Rural candidates will frequently campaign using the rhetoric that they won't be pushed around by the people from the Portland area. Urban candidates, on the other hand, will rarely mention rural issues. Obviously Portland is a much better political target.

The Populist tradition from the turn of the century continues to be strong in Oregon. This is not only found in the initiative, referendum and recall, known as the "Oregon System," but in an attitude that the people should have the last say on any matter of public policy. Political parties have never been strong in Oregon, and there is no real history of "machine" politics; there never has been a "Tammany Hall" in Oregon. Oregonians love to vote on everything -- the initiative, referendum and recall apply at all levels of government and are used frequently. There are innumerable locally elected governing bodies, including 340 school boards, 36 county commissions and 242 city councils.

Some of the state's perennial issues add to this Populist feeling. Oregonians have been fighting about fish for most of their history, and they have rejected a sales tax nine times. Access to beaches, government organization, death penalty, liquor, gambling, women's suffrage and dozens of other issues appear on the ballot year after year. The voters almost expect it. Because of this constant process of public discussion, the general public seems to assume that this is the norm for all states. Thus, "Populism" is part of the political psychology and the political culture of the state.

Related to Populism is a perceived tradition of innovation. It is hard to say when this became part of the Oregon psyche, but it definitely exists. In 1967, after a long series of political battles, a policy of free access to all public beaches was adopted, and this continues to be an article of faith for Oregon politicians today. In 1971 the bottle bill was passed, requiring deposits on all soft drink containers. Also in 1971, an innovative bike path law was adopted. In 1973, marijuana was decriminalized and the most extensive land use planing system in the United States was adopted. Fluorocarbons were banned in 1975. Most of this progressive legislation came out of the 1971-1978 era of the colorful Governor Tom McCall.

Oregonians perceive themselves as being innovative, regardless of whether they are more or less progressive than any other group. This is an important part of the political culture. Politicians talk to the voters with pride in their voices about the glorious past when Oregon showed the country how it could be done. Almost every campaign speech contains a litany of the state's brilliant accomplishments, along with the requisite allusion to beaches, mountains and abundant forests. This perception of "innovation" can also be a political tool. Innovation is a big selling point for a bill in the Legislature, especially if it ensures that Oregon will again be the first in the nation to do something. This sometimes goes to an extreme, as in 1985 when the first "state wine cellar" in the United States was established. This legislation, introduced by a pseudo-sophisticated Portland Democrat, was first roundly criticized, then adopted!

Layered on top of these feelings of Populism and innovation is an almost overt xenophobia directed at migrants from other states, especially California. In 1971, Governor McCall made his infamous remark to tourists, "Come to visit, please don't stay." This attitude was picked up by the national press and quickly became a kind of mythology.' The myth has been fed by Ken Kesey's novels and movies One Flew Over the Cuckoos Nest and Sometimes a Great Notion. William Staffords fine poetry also contributed to the Oregon image as have Ursula le Guin's science fiction books. In 1975, Ernest Callenbach wrote a fanciful futurist work about the Northwest seceding from the rest of America and forming a country called Ecotopia, a kind of politically correct, environmental version of the Confederacy.[40] Also in 1975, the James G. Blaine Society, a tongue-in-cheek group, threatened to erect a 10 foot fence around Oregon to keep people out.

Oregon's political culture also has some unusual traditions. One of the most unusual is that of husbands and wives serving in the Legislature together; one in the House and one in the Senate. This started in 1950 when Maurine Neuberger, the wife of State Senator Richard Neuberger, was elected to the Oregon House. Both husband and wife were Democrats from Portland. Dick Neuberger was a nationally known author and the press loved the couple. The Neubergers made the most of the situation with such notorious comments that they could "caucus in bed." Neuberger was elected to the United States Senate in 1954, then tragically died of cancer in 1960. Maurine was elected to fill his unfinished term, then served a full six years of her own.[41]

Since the Neubergers, there have been numerous couples, as well as other family combinations, in Oregon politics. Ben Musa was in the Senate and Katherine Musa was in the House. Marva Graham was in the House and her husband assumed her seat after retirement. Martin and Curt Wolfer were a father-son combination in the House in the 1970s. Steven Kafoury was in the House in 1973 and when he moved on to the Senate his ex-wife Gretchen took his seat. Gretchen is now a member of the Portland City Council. Kafoury's next wife Marge was also elected to the Metropolitan Service District, and now works as the lobbyist for Portland.[42] Ed Fadeley served in the Senate and his wife Nancy served in the House. Robin Lindquist succeeded her husband Ed in the House in 1983. Jane Cease preceded Ron Cease in both the House and Senate.

Betty Roberts was elected to the State House in 1964 and her husband Frank was elected to the House in 1966. Frank's daughter by a previous marriage, Mary Wendy Roberts, was elected to the House in 1972, the same year Frank was defeated for re-election. Frank and Betty were divorced, Betty went on to the State Senate, ran for governor in 1974 and lost, was appointed to the Court of Appeals and eventually retired while on the Oregon Supreme Court. In 1974, Frank was elected to the State Senate, and in 1978 Mary Wendy was elected Labor Commissioner. Frank then married Barbara Sanders, who was elected State Representative in 1980, Secretary of State in 1984, and Governor in 1990.

The author would be less than candid if he didn't reveal his own affiliations. He managed Mary Roberts' first campaign for the House, and his ex-wife Renee Bryant, a former Deputy Attorney General, is now Chairperson of the Employment Appeals Board. Political names are almost considered community property in Oregon.

Political vaudeville, beyond the standard repartee and posturing, is also another Oregon tradition. A Democratic political club known as the "Campaigners" puts on a review as a biennial fund-raiser in Portland. The show usually parodies a musical or TV sitcom and is known for its off-color, sarcastic comments on the foibles of public figures. In 1985 the author appeared as Carmen Miranda in a dance number. In the same show, future Governor Barbara Roberts came on stage in a spangled bathing suit and starred as a grinning beauty queen being fawned over by her campaign workers.

Not to be outdone, the counterpart Republican Club "The Trumpeters," puts on its "Tent Show" at a party conference held every two years at the Oregon Coast. Secretary of State Norma Paulus earned herself a piece of political immortality by doing a belly dance during one performance.

Immediately after the final gavel comes down at the end of each legislative session, the "Turkey Awards" are held. This gathering of staff, legislators, press and political groupies is traditionally put on in one of the two chambers. "Turkeys" are ridiculous bills. Other awards given out are for devious political maneuvering and for romantic involvement of legislators and staff.

The legislative staff itself gets its revenge with skits at the end-of-session "Staff Sine Die Party." Secretaries and administrative assistants wear large signs identifying themselves as various law makers in less than flattering situations. A particularly amorous Democrat was once portrayed as being so drunk that he tried to talk a parking meter into going home with him. A somewhat dense Senator asked whether the cost of a program was half a million or $500,000. No prisoners are taken at any of these gatherings.

"Filing day" is the February deadline for candidates to get in their filing forms and fees to the secretary of state, Oregon's chief elections officer. Clerical operations are set up in the House chamber and a large board with the various offices and names of aspirants is placed on one wall. These offices include state and federal slots as well as judicial positions. This is a kind of Witch's Sabbath for politicians. Several hundred law makers, candidates, hangers on, lobbyists, judges, journalists and other nefarious characters mill about on the House floor and watch the big board like some kind of pre-horse race lineup. The room resembles a huge book-making operation.

Last minute filings are not unusual, and rumors run rampant as people go through the filing line. Well-known politicians such as the late Governor McCall were known to walk through the line without filing, just to make one or two hearts stop. McCall did this in 1980 when he was rumored to be considering a race against U.S. Senator Bob Packwood, a fellow Republican. At five o'clock, the Secretary of State steps to the end of the line with a State Police Officer at his or her shoulder, and that is the end of the process. Deadlines are deadlines, after all.

First names also play a role in the way Oregon politicians interact with each other. Given names are the usual second person form of address in the Capitol. The governor is casually referred to as "Barb," or "Neil" instead of Governor Roberts or Governor Goldschmidt. This familiarity gives the impression of inside access which may be totally unmerited. Members of Oregon's capitol gang love to sound like they are well connected with what is a very small community in Salem.

The ultimate venue for this type of camaraderie is the center table in the Capitol Coffee Shop. This is the place where the heavy hitters hold court in the morning over coffee and the shop's traditional large and gooey cinnamon rolls. Rumors are traded, stories are leaked and deals cut. A few reporters, such as Ron Blankenbaker (the political columnist for the Capitol's newspaper the Statesman-Journal), will also spend their mornings in the shop, looking for leads and exchanging banter. The governor is always welcome, as his or her State Police bodyguards will discreetly blend into the woodwork while the pols bond with each other.

Another interesting aspect of Oregon politics is the relative lack of corruption. Lobbyists, and other political operatives who have worked in other states, constantly comment on how squeaky clean Oregon politics is. It is a common comment that what would be the normal greasing of political wheels will get you five to ten years in Oregon. Most Oregon politicians wouldn't know a bribe unless it had a label on it.

Conclusion -- Everything is related

Environmentalists like to say that "Everything is related to everything." And so it is. Everything is related to everything, in politics and everywhere else. Our description of Oregon's history, economy and political culture is, in this sense, artificial. Throughout this book, as in most works, we have separated and labeled things for convenience of description, not as a means to duplicate what is in the real world. As we continue to look at how Oregon is governed, let us always keep in mind how complex, subtle and interrelated the elements are which make up our topic.

---

[1] Oregon, Secretary of State, Oregon Blue Book 1991-1992, (Salem: Secretary of State, 1991), 8.

[2] "You must go through a winter to understand....You must go through at least a year of it to have some notion....Fog is draped over the low branches of vine maple like torn remnants of gossamer bunting. Fog ravels down from the pine needles. Above, up, through rain in the branches, the sky is blue and still and very clear, but fog is on the land. It creeps down the river and winds around the base of the house, eating the yellow-grained planks with a soft white mouth. There is a quiet hiss, not unpleasant, as of something pensively sucking..." Ken Kesey, Sometimes a Great Notion, (New York: Penguin, 1964), 21,22. Kesey was writing about the rain in the Oregon Coast Range, but the same somewhat depressing weather can be found in the Willamette Valley.

[3] The West Comes of Age: Hard Times, Hard Choices, (Lexington: The Council of State Governments, 1993), 46, 52.

[4] James Gardner, "The Competitive Advantage of Cascadia," The New Pacific, Winter 1992/1993, 12-13.

[5] Recent studies have debunked some cherished myths about the settlement of the West. There were relatively few battles between the Indians and the settlers on the Oregon Trail; approximately 360 migrants were killed, as opposed to 400 Indians. Disease killed more natives than anything because of lack of immunity. Some tribes lost 90% of their population to smallpox, cholera, measles and such. The settlers' attitude was anything but benevolent, as illustrated by the comment of Gustavus Hines a Methodist historian -- "The doom of extinction is over this wretched nation. The hand of Providence is removing them to give place to a people more worthy of a fertile country." Both quote and figures from; Timothy Egan, "150

Years Later, Indians Cope With Bitter Results of White's Arrival," <u>The New York Times</u>, 1 June 1993, A11.

6   John B. Horner, <u>Oregon</u>, (Corvallis: Press of the Gazette Times, 1919), 25.

7   <u>Oregon Blue Book 1991-1992</u>, 394.

8   Charles H. Carey, <u>A General History of Oregon</u>, (Portland: Metropolitan Press, 1935), vol. 1, 25.

9   William L. Lang, "Creating the Columbia: Historians and the Great River of the West," <u>Oregon Historical Quarterly</u>, 93 (Fall 1992), 237.

10 Horner, <u>Oregon</u>, 30. Gray traded with the Indians for sea-otter furs and paid them "less than one shilling" each. He then sailed to China and sold the furs for $200 a piece, purchased tea and returned to Boston as the first American ship to circumnavigate the globe. He made history, and a 4000% profit. Ibid.

11 Lang, "Creating the Columbia: Historians and the Great River of the West," 237.

12 That Grey had Indian help in the initial exploration of the river is a little known historical fact pregnant with symbolism. The author's source is an interview with Sandy Brown, Captain of the Lady Washington, a modern day replica of the companion ship to the <u>Columbia Rediviva</u> . As part of the Lady Washington project, Brown examined all journals kept by the officers of both the <u>Columbia</u> and Lady Washington. In one of these journals, mention of the canoe is made.

13 Terrence E. O'Donnell, <u>That Balance So Rare --The Story of Oregon</u>, (Portland: Oregon Historical Society Press, 1988), 18-19.

14 Ibid. 23.

15 Samuel Elliot Morrison, <u>The Oxford History of the American People</u>, (New York: Oxford University Press, 1965), 542.

16 Oregon, Secretary of State, <u>Oregon Blue Book 1993-1994</u>, (Salem: Secretary of State, 1993), 371.

17 Barry A. Kosmin and Seymour P. Lachman, <u>One Nation Under God</u>, (New York: Harmony Books, 1993), cited in Kenneth L. Woodward, "The Rites of Americans," <u>Newsweek</u>, 29 November 1993, 80-82.

18 An initial query might be in order -- if there are so many non-believers in this state why are the "believers" having such an impact? The answer is probably more obvious than one might realize and it deserves some reflection before we discuss it in detail later. In a contest between believers and non-believers, the believers will almost always prevail for the exact reason they believe in <u>something</u>. The greater motivation will always be with those who have beliefs as opposed to those who have doubts.

19 The vote was 52 to 50, divided between Canadians and the Americans except for two Canadians, F. X. Matthieu and Etienne Lucier, who voted for the proposal to become part of the United States. Carey, <u>A General History of Oregon</u>, 330-331.

20 Ibid., 455, 460.

21 Ibid.

22 Timothy Egan, "Eastward Ho! The Great Move Reverses - Forsaken Frontier," <u>The New York Times</u>, 30 May 1993, 1, 12.

23 <u>Oregon Blue Book 1993-1994</u>, 373, 385.

24 Oregon, Secretary of State, <u>Oregon Blue Book 1949-1950</u>, (Salem: Secretary of State, 1949), 187.

25 Elizabeth McLagagan, <u>A Peculiar Paradise</u>, (Portland: The Georgian Press, 1980), 116.

26 <u>Oregon Blue Book 1993-1994</u>, 344. What they were hunting in Nevada remains unclear.

[27] Joanne Bockelman, 'The 45th Legislative Session," unpublished paper, Portland State University, 1987.

[28] Julie Nusom, Tektronix, Inc., Corporate Public relations, Facsimile to author, 16 March 1994.

[29] Gordon B. Dodds and Craig Wollner, <u>The Silicon Forest</u>, (Portland: The Oregon Historical Society Press, 1990), 28..

[30] <u>Oregon Blue Book 1949-1950,</u> 188.

[31] Ken Hamburg, "Forecast," <u>The Sunday Oregonian</u>, 2 May 1993, K-1

[32] <u>Oregon Blue Book 1993-1994,</u> 211.

[33] Arthur Ayre, Oregon Economic Development Department, Facsimile to author, 28 February 1992.

[34] Alan Ota, "South emerges as No. 1 wood-products region," <u>The Oregonian</u>, 18 December 1991, A1, B1.

[35] Richard W. Haynes, <u>An analysis of the timber situation in the United States 1989 -2040</u>, Gen. Tech. Rep. RM-199 (Ft. Collins: U.S. Department of Agriculture, Forest Service, Rocky Mountain Forest and range Experiment Station, 1990).

[36] Ibid.

[37] <u>The West Comes of Age: Hard Times, Hard Choices</u>, 60.

[38] Don Hamilton and Alan Ota, "Oregon Remains in basement for military spending," <u>The Sunday Oregonian</u>, 27 June 1993, A18.

[39] Foster Church, "Goldschmidt apologizes to Bend for his 'nowhere' remark," <u>The Oregonian</u>, 22 August 1986, C 12.

[40] See Elizabeth Godley, "View from the edge," <u>The New Pacific</u>, Issue # 9, 12-15.

[41] See Richard Neuberger, <u>Adventures in Politics</u>, New York: Oxford University Press, 1954).

[42] Common political names and divorce sometimes don't mix well. U.S. Senator Mark Hatfield returned to Oregon for an event in July of 1993, walked up to Marge Kafoury, the lobbyist, and greeted her in his best political style, "Gretchen, good to see you." Marge was not amused. "Upfront -Verbatim," <u>The Oregonian</u>, 12 July 1993, B-1.

CHAPTER 2

CONSTITUTION, ETHICS AND OPEN GOVERNMENT

When Dr. Johnson defined patriotism as the last
refuge of the scoundrel, he ignored the enormous
possibilities of the word "reform."

U.S. Senator Roscoe Conkling

This guy came from California and asked me 'Who
do I pay off?' I told him that most of what's good
lobbying in other states is a felony in Oregon.

Anonymous Lobbyist

Introduction

This chapter will examine the basic structures of Oregon government, including:

- A discussion of the role of a state constitution.

- How the Oregon Constitution was written.
- Civil liberties and state constitutions.

- The Oregon Bill of Rights.

- Structural provisions of the Oregon Constitution.

- The impact of certain Constitutional provisions on government's taxing power.
- The "clean government" atmosphere in Oregon.
- The Government Standards and Practices Commission.
- "Open" government and sunshine laws.

The Forgotten States

There are fifty-one constitutions used by governments in America. "Constitutional law" is not just that which is expounded by the United States Supreme Court; it is the law of state constitutions as well. The relationship between the states and the federal government is complex and is usually discussed under the heading of "federalism." The basic functions of the states are set by the federal Constitution; it leaves little doubt about its supremacy both theoretically or politically.[1] Some things, such as coining money, maintaining an army or navy, and conducting foreign relations are completely forbidden to the states. Additional fields of governance, such as commerce, are the purview of both the states and the central government. Other things such as domestic relations and alcohol regulation, are left almost totally to the states.[2]

To a great extent, state constitutions are variations on a theme; they all tend to look and sound like the federal Constitution, three branches of government, separation of powers, checks and balances and the usual other provisions. Except for a few anomalies, such as the unicameral legislature in Nebraska, these documents are remarkably similar, the subject matter of Political Science 101. Regardless, specific detail is important and the details of state constitutions have a tremendous impact on how we are governed. The average citizen in Oregon knows little or nothing about his or her state constitution, but knows a goodly amount about the federal Constitution. Even so, most government activity remains state government activity. The United States Supreme Court may have abolished school segregation in 1954,[3] but the schools are still run by Oregon and the other states in America. The states spend approximately as much money on schools as the Federal government spends on defense.[4] Schools, prisons and roads are just a few of the functions that are controlled by state constitutions.

Writing the Oregon Constitution -- The Slave Question

One might think that Oregon's pioneers unanimously supported statehood. Nothing could be further from the truth. Settlement of the Oregon Territory, writing and adoption of the Constitution, and eventual statehood were all inextricably involved with the most burning American issue of the nineteenth century --slavery. Some say it is amazing Oregon even became a state.[5]

Until the arrival of the transcontinental railroad, the majority of Oregonians were Democrats with Southern sympathies. Before the Civil War, there was a substantial question whether Oregon would be a slave or free state. The slogan "The Union" on the Oregon flag is as much a rewrite of history as a political statement.

The writing of the Oregon Constitution and the process of becoming a state were both played out against the backdrop of pre-Civil War politics, a complex series of maneuvers by slavery advocates and abolitionists. The "Oregon Question" --whether the Northwest would be part of Great Britain or the United States --was decided by treaty in 1846. The Territory was organized by Congress on August 14, 1848.[6] Abraham Lincoln was offered the post of governor, but he turned it down and it was accepted by General Joseph Lane, a pro-slavery, slave-owning Democrat from Indiana who arrived in the Territory in 1849. The first Territorial Assembly met in August of the same year and debated statehood, but the question was not submitted to the people for a vote.

The Democratic Party held its first convention in May, 1850. Statehood became one of its early principles. The minority Whigs continued to oppose the idea until the mid-1850s when they and the anti-Catholic, anti-foreigner "Know-Nothings" evolved into the Republican Party. The question of calling a constitutional convention and applying to Congress for statehood was submitted to the people for a vote in 1854, 1855 and 1856. Finally, in 1857, the proposal passed. Throughout most of this period, The Oregonian, with its usual progressive insight, opposed statehood. It was assumed that because of the recent election of President Buchanan, Oregon would be forced to be a slave state. Buchanan was a Democrat who believed in "popular sovereignty," i.e., that each state should decide the slavery question for itself. President Buchanan was also thought to be working with former Governor Joseph Lane, who was then the Oregon Territory's delegate to Congress. In addition, two days after Buchanan's inauguration in March 1857, the United States Supreme Court handed down the infamous Dred Scott[7] decision and invalidated the Missouri Compromise of 1820. The "Compromise" had prohibited slavery in new states, including Oregon, north of 36 degree, 30 minutes. With the Dred Scott decision, the door was opened for these new states to be slave.

14

In retrospect, one could argue that the majority of early Oregonians were not pro-slave, but good old-fashioned bigots. When the convention met in the Marion County Court House, in Salem, on August 17, 1857, there were 60 delegates, including 39 Democrats, who elected pro-slave Matthew P. Deady president of the convention. Ironically, slavery was not discussed at any length at this gathering. Although pro-slavery Democrats were in control, it was viewed as better politics to leave the slavery question up to the people themselves.[8]

The convention adjourned a month later, on September 18, after producing a document modeled to a certain extent on the Ohio Constitution. The tone of the Convention seemed to anticipate the style of government in Oregon in the future. Among other things, the delegates voted to hire neither an official reporter (to keep a record of the debates) nor a chaplain. These were cheap, not-too pious men. Unfortunately, as a result of their miserliness, the only comprehensive accounts of the meetings are newspaper stories.

Three questions were presented to the voters on November 9, 1857. These were the adoption of the constitution, permitting slaves to be held in the state, and whether or not "free Negroes" should be allowed residence. The verdict was a typically contradictory Oregon election result. The constitution was adopted on a vote of 7,195 to 3,215 and slave owning was rejected 7,727 to 2,645, but the residence of "free Negroes" was turned down by 8,640 to 1,081. Thus our forefathers, and these were "fore*fathers,*" proved themselves more cantankerous than enlightened. They did not want their new land sullied either by slaves or by freed slaves. Oregon finally become a state on February 14, 1859. When the Civil War started, even with its strong Southern sympathies, Oregon cast its lot with the Union.

Civil Liberties and State Constitutions -- A "Stricter State Standard"

Both the Oregon and the U.S. Constitution have a "Bill of Rights." The federal Bill of Rights was originally only a series of limitations on the power of the federal government, but with the post-Civil War passage of the 14th Amendment and its "due process" clause, most of the federal Bill of Rights was made applicable to the states. For instance, states (as well as the federal government) are prohibited from interfering with speech or religion. Certain other rights, such as that of a jury trial and against self-incrimination, were also imposed upon the states. In the late 1970s, state courts started to look to their own constitutions to give their citizens' rights beyond the minimums granted by the federal Bill of Rights. This phenomenon, known as the "stricter state standard," will be discussed more fully in Chapter 6. The term "stricter" is a bit ironic in the sense that it means a "stricter" limit on what a state can do to its citizens. Other states such as New York and California have adopted stricter state standards for their bills of rights.

Oregon's Bill of Rights -- Natural Law and Switchblades

The document produced in 1857 went into effect in 1859 and remains Oregon's basic constitution to this day. Unlike the United States Constitution, the Bill of Rights was incorporated in the original as Article I, with 35 sections. Section 1 is a unilateral declaration of "Natural Law," with the title "Natural Rights Inherent in People." It unequivocally states that the people have the right to "reform or abolish the government in such manner as they think proper."[9] The next five articles have to do with religion:

freedom of worship, freedom of religious opinion, no religious qualification for office, no money appropriated for religion (no chaplains in the Legislature) and no religious test for jurors. Had these gentlemen not been pro-slavery they would have made marvelous members of the American Civil Liberties Union.

Section 9 prohibits unreasonable searches or seizures. While it is one of the shortest sections, Section 9 probably has more case law interpreting it than any other section. Here, the Oregon Supreme Court has particularly exerted itself under the "stricter state standard" doctrine.

Section 15 states that all punishment must be founded on the "principles of reformation and not vindictive justice."[10] In spite of the clear wording of this section, Oregon courts have put little or no stock in it -- the state has had the death penalty on and off through-out its history. How one can be reformed by being put to death is the stuff of theology, not government.

Other provisions of the Oregon Bill of Rights prohibit imprisonment for debt[11] and protect the freedom to bear arms. The latter section says that the people have the right to bear arms to defend themselves and the state.[12] This goes significantly beyond the Second Amendment to the U. S. Constitution. For example, Oregon courts have held that the state cannot prohibit the ownership of switchblades on the grounds that the citizens have the right to own weapons to protect themselves; this includes the right to own just about any weapon.

There are also sections prohibiting corruption of blood,[13] whatever that is, and the granting of titles of nobility.[14]

Government Structure -- The Basics

Article II, relating to suffrage and elections, has some unusual provisions, such as a prohibition against the holding of two "lucrative offices" offices which both pay. There was once a court case that addressed the question of whether one could be both a legislator and a notary public who charges a fee. It was decided that being a notary was not a lucrative office. Regardless, legislators who happen to be notaries still file a statement that they won't charge for notarizing documents. The article also prohibits anyone who has been involved in a duel from holding office. More importantly, it prohibits the use of a secret ballot in the Legislature itself.[15] All votes must be public.

Article III is entitled "Distribution of Powers" and contains a very strong "Separation of Powers," provision.[16] Not only are there to be three separate branches of government, but a person in one branch cannot exercise the duties of a person in another branch. This has been interpreted to mean that a judge may not teach at a state college, regardless of whether or not he or she is paid.[17] It is not the remuneration that violates the separation of powers clause, but the performance of duties.

One exception to this article is the provision that teachers are allowed to serve in the Legislature.[18] This provision was passed after having been put on the ballot by the Oregon Education Association. It covers teachers in kindergarten through twelfth grade, as well as state or community colleges.

Section 3 of Article III, adopted in 1952, authorizes the Legislature's Joint Ways and Means Committee and Emergency Board.[19] These two bodies function respectively during the legislative session and the interim as Oregon's appropriations committee.

In 1978, another section was added to Article III, providing for Senate confirmation of certain gubernatorial appointments, not including judges.[20] The Legislature determines which appointments are subject to confirmation. Senate President Jason Boe pushed the provision through the 1977 Legislature.[21]

Article IV relates to the Legislative Department. Among other things, it limits the number[22] and sets the terms of representatives and senators,[23] i.e., sixty representatives who serve two-year terms and thirty senators who serve four-year terms. There are some very quaint provisions in this article. For example, legislators are free from arrest (not including felonies and disturbing the peace) during legislative sessions.[24] They are also immune from "civil process," that is, they cannot be sued. One Oregon legislator, Bill Markham, a Republican from Southern Oregon, made a career of trying to get this particular section repealed. Every session, some legislator gets picked up for drunk driving and claims immunity. The press is inevitably informed of the shenanigan and reports the incident to the public. The same article also gives legislators immunity for anything they say on the floor of either body.

Sessions of the Legislature are biennial, or once every two years. Section 10a, adopted in 1976, gives the legislature the power to call itself into special session by written request of a majority of the members.

The respective houses are authorized to select their own leaders, adopt their own rules, and judge their own members. In 1993, the Oregon Senate was faced with the dilemma of what to do with State Senator Peg Jolin, convicted in 1992 of "theft by deception" after sending a fundraising letter to lobbyists stating that she had a deficit from her last campaign when, in fact, she had over $20,000 in the bank. The Senate seated Jolin, and Senate President Bill Bradbury appointed her Chairperson of the Business and Consumer Affairs Committee. After two months of public protest, Jolin resigned her seat and was replaced by Eugene Attorney Karsten Rassmusen.

Another section of Article IV has to do with the selection of leadership. If either a speaker of the House or a president of the Senate is not selected within five days of the start of the session, pay stops until the decision is made.[25] The Article also requires that a journal of yeas and nays be kept and deliberations are open to the public. Bills may originate in either house, but revenue bills have to originate in the House of Representatives.[26] This is a typical provision going back to the British Parliament. Before final passage, a bill must be read in its entirety unless the requirement is suspended by a two-thirds vote. For several days in 1993 the minority Senate Republicans (they held fourteen out of thirty seats) refused to suspend the requirement, to protest the Democratic majority not paying them enough respect.

Bills theoretically can address only one subject[27] and must be plainly worded.[28] There can be no "special laws," such as bills to grant divorces (a common practice in the 19th century before divorce was available) or which apply only to one city.[29]

One of the later provisions of Article IV has tremendous impact on how the Legislature does its business. It takes a majority of the elected members to pass a bill in either house, 31 votes in the House and 16 votes in the Senate.[30] Thus being absent is a "no" vote for all intents and purposes.

Finally, one of the most interesting minor provisions is Section 26, which gives each member the constitutional right to "protest, with his (sic) reasons for dissent entered into the journal."[31] One of the orders of business, each day, in both the House and Senate is, "remonstrances," where such protests are heard. These two minute speeches can go from congratulating a championship high school basketball team to an impassioned plea for major legislative action.

Article V outlines the various aspects of the governor's office. The term is four years, and if a vacancy occurs, the secretary of state becomes governor. Next in succession is the state treasurer, the president of the state senate, and the speaker of the house. This Section (8a) was adopted as an amendment in 1972. Before that time, the president of the senate was next in succession. Oregon does not have a lieutenant governor. Although a measure to create the post has been on the ballot several times, the people seem satisfied with the current system.

The governor may make recommendations to the Legislature, call special sessions and grant reprieves, pardons, and commutations.[32] A reprieve is a delay in the execution of a sentence, a pardon is a release from the sentence and a commutation is a change in the sentence. These become controversial when the death penalty is involved. No death sentence has been commuted since 1964, when Governor Hatfield granted clemency to child-killer Jennace Freeman after voters abolished the death penalty in November of that year.[33] At the time of this writing, it is likely that an Oregon governor will soon confront the question.[34]

The governor has the usual veto power over measures passed by the Legislature and has a "line item veto" on appropriations bills.[35] One odd provision says that a governor must give a five day notice of possible intent to veto a bill.[36]

Article VI is the "Administrative Department" provision, establishing the office of secretary of state and state treasurer. Both of these offices will be discussed extensively in the Chapter 4 on the executive branch. The article also authorizes any Oregon county to have a "home rule" charter.[37] This will be discussed later.

Article VII establishes the Supreme Court and authorizes the creation of inferior courts. Judges are elected for six-year terms. One of the more interesting sections of Article VII is Section 3 which states that "no fact tried by a jury shall be otherwise re-examined in any court unless the court can affirmatively say there is no evidence to support the verdict." This provision effectively limits a trial judge's or appellate court's ability to question a factual finding by a jury. In federal court, a judge may reduce the amount of a jury award on the grounds that it is excessive. Because of Section 3, state courts do not have this power.

Other minor provisions include a prohibition against one legislature binding another, i.e., what one legislature can do, another legislature can undo. A "state bank" is prohibited[38] and the state cannot own shares in any public corporation.[39] Article XI-D was put on the ballot and passed by the people in 1932. It allows the state to sell bonds for hydro-electric power development and to essentially establish its own public utilities. The amendment mandates that the Legislature shall put the article into effect. Regardless, the Assembly has ignored this supposed duty for more than sixty years! Cynical observers of government claim that this is a demonstration of the lobbying power of privately-owned utilities; others know that the Legislature just had better things to do.

People versus Taxes

Notwithstanding the above discussion, the most significant provisions of the Oregon Constitution affecting the way in which the state is governed have to do with financial matters. Taxes and spending are the life blood of any government and Oregon is no exception, but the underlying theme of Oregon's Constitution is to limit both. We will return to this topic again in Chapter 11 on school finance, but certain things must be kept in mind during any discussion of government finances in Oregon. First, Oregon has no sales tax. We will shortly discuss why this is the case. Second, until 1990 almost all local government activity, especially schools, were financed mostly by property tax.

Spending is limited by Article IX Section 2. State government cannot spend in the deficit. This is not an unusual provision; many of the fifty states have such prohibitions against deficit spending. State government constantly avoids this provision by selling bonds. Each type --veterans home loan bonds,[40] reforestation bonds,[41] higher education bonds,[42] pollution control, bonds,[43] --housing[44] and small scale local energy loans bonds[45] are authorized by separate amendments to the Oregon Constitution. These bonds are paid back by either the general fund or proceeds of the projects themselves. Regardless, they are all secured by the state's credit; that is, a small property tax could be levied to pay the bonds back.

Except for the issuing of authorized bonds, Oregon government must operate in the black. This has proven to be a very effective measure in keeping the state out of significant debt. Revenue must match or exceed projected expenditures in both budget and practice. If, during a ongoing budget period, it appears that there will be a shortfall, the executive branch will first attempt to meet the shortage by slight administrative changes. If this is insufficient, a special session of the Legislature will be called to raise taxes, cut budgets, or both. The significance of this will be expanded upon later, but basically the prohibition against deficit spending limits the government's options to available revenue.

Until the passage of Ballot Measure 5 in 1990, the most important tax provisions of the Oregon Constitution were found in Article XI Section 11. First, this provision held that no property tax could be levied without a tax base, i.e., a vote by the people authorizing the assessment of a certain amount of tax in one jurisdiction. Until 1990, these local property taxes were the main source of revenue for local government, including schools. More importantly, Section 11 limited the growth of a tax base to six percent a year, the "six percent limitation." This limit was originally adopted in 1916 as a property tax limit.[46] Unfortunately over the years, two things happened to local governments. Fast growing districts, usually school districts, were never able to keep up with the need for revenue because of the six percent limit. Districts with "current" or adequate tax bases found the six percent limit, if fully used, allowed significant annual growth. Voters in many school districts were reluctant to approve new tax bases, but they would approve temporary "serial operating levies" which did not become a permanent part of the tax base. The overall effect of this was that some districts were adequately financed and some were not -- a combination of inequity and instability.

To complicate things further, the most significant tax provision of the Oregon Constitution is actually the effect of several provisions read together. The initiative and referendum will be discussed in Chapter 3, but for our purpose here, one needs to understand that the initiative allows voters to place statutes and constitutional amendments on the ballot by gathering a certain numbers of signatures. The referendum is a similar process, whereby voters may gather a minimum number of signatures to prevent a newly passed law from taking effect until voted on by the people at the next general election. The Legislature can avoid the referendum by placing an "emergency clause" on the bill creating the new law, thus implementing the measure immediately. However, the Constitution prohibits the use of an emergency clause on a revenue bill,[47] so every tax bill passed by the Legislature is the potential subject of a referendum.

The cumulative effect of these provisions is that no major tax reform can be passed in Oregon without a vote of the people. While minor changes such as increases in the cigarette tax or slight changes in the income tax rates are possible, an outright sales tax would certainly be referred. This was and is part of the great dilemma of Oregon politics --the people control the tax system, and if the people don't like the tax system they will cut taxes, but still demand services.

A summary is in order:
- Oregon has no sales tax.
- Until 1990 most local government activities were financed by property tax.
- The state may not spend in the deficit.
- Property taxes may not be levied without a vote of the people.
- Local tax bases cannot grow more than 6% a year.
- No major tax legislation may be passed without a vote of the people.

Clean Government Oregon style -- Caesar's Wife

There is an old cliché that Caesar's wife must not only be virtuous, but beyond suspicion -- without even the appearance of impropriety. If there were a patron saint of government in Oregon it would be Caesar's wife. Government here is notoriously clean. Things which wouldn't merit a mention in Chicago are major scandals here. Politicians have been taken to task for such minor things as writing a personal letter on official stationary, making a political phone call on a state phone and sending shirts out to be laundered while on a state trip.

The Ethics Commission

The Oregon Government Ethics Commission was established in November, 1974, by a vote of the people in reaction to the Watergate scandal. The original measure was submitted to the electorate by the Legislature. In 1993, the name of the Commission was changed to the "Oregon Government Standards and Practices Commission.[48] It has seven members with three appointed by the governor. The remaining four names come from the majority and minority offices, one apiece, in both the House and the Senate.[49] The Commission has a small staff, including investigators.

The Commission oversees a huge list of both elected and appointed officials,[50] including judges, although ethics violations by judges are reported to the Judicial Fitness Commission. All these individuals are required to file yearly Statements of Economic Interest.[51] Candidates for elected state office are required to file, as well as local elected officials. The statute contains an extensive list of the appointed officials who are required to file. These Statements of Economic Interest cover sources of income, property, shared business with lobbyists, honoraria and financial affairs of spouses. Officials must report any directorships and any food or lodging received valued over one hundred dollars.

Elected officials are prohibited from using their office for private gain accepting gifts over one hundred dollars. In 1981, several legislators we staying at a lobbyist's condominium in Hawaii when the value was over 1992, State Senator Paul Phillips ran afoul of the statute prohibiting use of c He was fined $10,000 for sending a letter to a possible employer saying tha a tax break for the business. In the same year, Representative Tom Brian was trying to use his office for personal gain by writing to some Japanese investors on his official stationary. Brian's case was dismissed by a circuit court, but reinstated by the Court of Appeals. It is still pending at this writing.

Legislators are prohibited from soliciting or accepting campaign contributions from January 1 of an odd numbered year (Oregon only has legislative sessions in the odd numbered year) until the end of the legislative session.[53] This avoids "blackmail" -- where there is a fundraising breakfast for the legislator with the crucial vote on the day a bill is up. The governor is also prohibited from soliciting or receiving campaign contributions from January 1 until thirty days after the close of the session.[54] Legislators can receive honoraria for speeches, but they may not request a fee or negotiate. Legislators must also declare any conflict of interest that they might have on a bill they are voting on.[55] Oregon legislators are not allowed to abstain from voting on a measure because of the Constitutional requirement that a bill receive a majority vote of those elected to the body and not a majority of the quorum, to pass. A conflict of interest is hard to define, but if a legislator or a legislator's spouse is a member of a general class which will be affected by a bill, then it is not a conflict of interest.[56] On the other hand, if there are only three people who are affected by a bill and one is your wife, that is a conflict of interest. State Senator Keith Burbidge found himself in this situation in 1981. His wife worked for the state and was one of only a few people affected by a retirement bill. Burbidge did not declare a conflict of interest and was fined by the Ethics Commission for not doing so.

Most legislators play it safe when the question arises. For example, traditionally all the college teachers who serve in the Legislature announce a conflict of interest before the Higher Education budget is voted on. They do this even though there is no real conflict -- college teachers are members of a large class and the law specifically exempts them.

The Government Standards and Practices Commission also regulates legislative lobbying. Anyone who spends more than twenty four hours during a quarter trying to influence the Legislature must register as a lobbyist and file reports with the Commission.[57] Lobbyists, or the lobby as an institution will be discussed extensively in Chapter 7.

Open Government -- What's a Quorum?

Open government in Oregon means open meetings and open records. These "Sunshine" laws were passed in 1973, again, in response to the Watergate scandal. No meeting of a public body may be held without at least a twenty-four hour notice. The notice must include the agenda of the meeting and what the proposed action is.[58] In addition, decisions must be reached in the open. This prohibits bodies from meeting in private. The gathering becomes a "meeting" when there is a quorum. For instance, if there is a legislative committee with seven members, four of them cannot meet alone and discuss official business. This situation can quickly verge on the absurd, if four of the ven members go to lunch or dinner, they are limited as to what they can discuss. Obviously there are frequent, but inadvertent, violations of the law. There are several exceptions to the open meeting law. The major one involves personnel matters. The law does not apply when a body is discussing hiring, firing or other personnel matters.[59]

The "Open Records" law states that all government records are open to the public.[60] There are numerous exceptions to this, including information relating to litigation, test questions, circulation records of public libraries and others.[61] The "Open Records" law does apply to the Legislature. State Senator Wayne Fawbush once received a request from followers of the Bawghwan Shree Rajneesh to inspect his records. The story of the Bawghwan, his Rolls Royces, his commune and his takeover of the small Eastern Oregon town of Antelope has been well documented. Fawbush was the local state senator who opposed the Bawghwan (not a politically unpopular position). A member of the commune showed up at his legislative office and demanded to go through his files as public records. Fawbush had no choice but to allow the action. Nothing of worth was found, but the incident illustrated how far the open records laws can be taken.

Both the Open Meetings Law and the Open Records Law are favorites of the Oregon press. They have used them in numerous lawsuits and always support legislation to limit exceptions to both laws.

---

[1] Carl Sandburg once said that the Civil War was "fought over a verb" whether the United States "is" or the United States "are."

[2] The 21st Amendment to United States Constitution leaves the regulation of alcohol almost entirely up to the states. It is the only area where the states can interfere with interstate commence.

[3] Brown v. Board of Education of Topeka, 347 U.S. 483 (1954).

[4] That is approximately $300 billion per year. See The Economist Diary 1993, (London: The Economist Newspapers Ltd, 1993) 85, 97.

[5] Dick Pintarich and J. Kingston Pierce, "The Achievement of Oregon's Statehood," in Great Moments in Oregon History, Win McCormack and Dick Pintarich Ed. (Portland: New Oregon Publishers, 1987), 48.

[6] Oregon, Secretary of State, Oregon Blue Book 1991-1992 (Salem: Secretary of State, 1991), 416.

[7] Dred Scott v. Sandford, 60 U.S. 383 (1857).

[8] Charles H. Carey, A General History of Oregon (Portland: Metropolitan Press, 1935), vol. 1, 590.

[9] Or. Const. art. I, sec. 1.

[10] Or. Const. art. I, sec. 15.

[11] Or. Const. art. I, sec. 19.

[12] Or. Const. art. I, sec. 27.

[13] Or. Const. art. I, sec. 25.

[14] Or. Const. art. I, sec. 29.

[15] Or. Const. art. IV, sec. 19.

[16] Or. Const. art. III, sec. 1.

[17] In the Matter of Sawyer, 286 OR 594 (1979).

[18] Or. Const. art. XV, sec. 8.

[19] Or. Const. art. III, sec. 3.

[20] Or. Const. art. III, sec. 4.

21 SJR 20, 1977 Legislature.
22 Or. Const. art. IV, sec. 2.
23 Or. Const. art. IV, sec. 4.
24 Or. Const. art IV, sec. 9.
25 Or. Const. art IV, sec. 12.
26 Or. Const. art IV, sec. 18.
27 Or. Const. art IV, sec. 20.
28 Or. Const. art IV, sec. 21.
29 Or. Const. art IV, sec. 23.
30 Or. Const. art IV, sec. 25.
31 Or. Const. art IV, sec. 26.
32 Or. Const. art V, sec. 14.
33 The Freeman incident will be discussed in Chapter 4.
34 The death penalty was reinstituted by initiative in 1978, declared unconstitutional in 1981 and repassed by the voters in 1984. The history of the death penalty will be discussed in Chapter 11.
35 Or. Const. art V, sec. 15a.
36 Or. Const. art V, sec. 15b, (4).
37 Or. Const. art. VI, sec. 10.
38 Or. Const. art. XI, sec. 1.
39 Or. Const. art. XI, sec. 6.
40 Or. Const. art. XI-A.
41 Or. Const. art. XI-E.
42 Or. Const. art. XI-F(1).
43 Or. Const. art. XI-H.
44 Or. Const. art. XI-I(2).
45 Or. Const. art. XI-J.
46 See Carl Hosticka, "Financial Provisions of the Oregon Constitution," Oregon Law Review, 67 (1988), 116.
47 Or. Const. art. IX, sec. 1a.
48 ORS 244.020 (4).
49 ORS 244.250.
50 ORS 244.050.
51 ORS 244.060.
52 ORS 244.040 (1)(a).
53 ORS 260.725 (1).
54 ORS 260.725 (2).
55 ORS 244.120 (1) (a).
56 ORS 244.020 (7).
57 ORS 171.735 (4).
58 ORS 192.640.
59 ORS 192.660.
60 ORS 192.420.
61 ORS 192.510.

CHAPTER 3

DIRECT DEMOCRACY-- FROM POPULISM TO THE CULTURE WARS

> Democracy...is a charming form of government,
> full of variety and disorder, and dispensing a
> sort of equality to equals and unequals alike.
>
> Plato
> The Republic

Introduction

Chapter 3 examines an institution of governance that has controlled Oregon's destiny for almost one hundred years -- direct democracy in the form of the initiative, referendum and the recall. Topics include:

- A discussion of the overriding importance of the initiative, referendum and recall in Oregon politics.
- The history of the adoption of the "Oregon System."
- A record and discussion of the various ballot measures voted on since the adoption of the initiative and the referendum.
- The mechanics of getting a proposal on the ballot.
- Oregon law as it affects where and how signatures can be gathered.

- Ballot measure politics.

- The recall.

- The emergence of the Oregon Citizens' Alliance.

- A brief discussion how the current use of direct democracy relates to the intentions of its originators.

The 800-Pound Gorilla

Oregon's significant role in American political history is exemplified by the fact that the hallmark political mechanisms of direct democracy --the initiative, the referendum and the recall --are known as the "Oregon System."[1] While the third element of this "Populist Trinity" is little used, it is undeniable that the initiative and referendum dominate politics in Oregon.[2] Someone once observed that every major political issue ends up before the United States Supreme Court. Likewise, in this state every major issue ends up before the voters as an initiative or a referendum. There have been over 700 measures on the ballot since the initiative and referendum were instituted in 1902. At last count, Oregon holds the record for the most statewide initiatives.[3]

The initiative and referendum are not confined to Oregon; 28 other American states, mostly in the West, have some version of these mechanisms.[4] The advent of this form of democracy has been called "...one of the most important landmarks in the history of

American political institutions within the twentieth century."[5] Indeed, the initiative and referendum are our political inheritance of the Populist era. They are the embodiment of the phenomenon whereby history determines today's events. In this chapter, we will closely examine both that history and the contemporary use of these procedures. Recent application of the initiative and the referendum compels a re-evaluation of their original purpose and current efficacy.

As you will recall, the "initiative" is a means whereby citizens can collect a certain number of valid signatures and place either a proposed statute or constitutional amendment on the ballot at the next primary or general election.

The "referendum" is really two procedures. A law, newly passed by the Assembly, usually goes into effect 90 days after adjournment, unless it has an "emergency clause." If endowed with an "emergency clause," the proposed statute becomes effective when signed by the governor.[6] Most statutes are passed without an emergency clause. Moreover, as mentioned, the Oregon Constitution does not allow emergency clauses on revenue bills.[7] If a bill is without an emergency clause, and enough signatures are obtained on a referendum petition, the bill will not go into effect until it has been voted on at the next general election. More frequently, the Legislature itself places a referendum on the ballot. This can be either a statute or a constitutional amendment. By definition, there is no need for a referendum petition on a constitutional amendment proposed by the Legislature --changes in the Constitution must always be approved by the people.[8]

Oregon uses initiatives and referenda in phenomenal high numbers, but it is not volume that makes the process so significant. Rather, they make policy outside the usual interaction of the Legislature and the governor. Not only is the initiative an alternative to the normal method of law-making, but once a statute is passed by initiative it is considered almost sacrosanct. The Legislature has the theoretical power to overturn a statutory measure placed into effect by initiative. Significantly, this authority is never exercised because of self-righteous pandering by Oregon politicians to the idea that the "people have spoken." Furthermore, even though the Legislature would be loath to amend or repeal a statute made by "the People," there is a paranoid lack of trust on the part of initiative proponents. More often than not, measures are proposed as constitutional amendments rather than statutes, to foreclose any "tinkering" by the Legislature.

The Legislature and the governor are not only subject to initiatives which have passed, they are under a constant psychological threat of future initiatives or referenda to either reverse their decisions or, more importantly, to limit what authority they do have. Nothing of any consequence is immune from the process, whether it be the death penalty, suffrage, marijuana or taxes. Limited only by the federal Constitution, the initiative and the referendum are the political embodiment of the old joke about where an 800-hundred-pound gorilla sleeps --anywhere he wants!

Before returning to the politics of how the initiative and referendum currently work, it is appropriate to look at the even more fascinating history of how the "Oregon System" came into being.

The "I&R" -- Silver, Gold and the Holdup Session

To understand the present you must know the past -- you need to go up river in the stream of history until you have a sense of the flow of events and personalities. The story of how the initiative and the referendum came to Oregon is as dramatic as any novel -- full of ambition, betrayal, intrigue and the sweep of historical forces. Like so much of history, it is also the poignant story of individuals, in this case, William U'Ren, John Mitchell, and Jonathan Bourne.

The only memorial left today to William S. U'Ren is a small brass statue in front of the Clackamas County Courthouse, south of Portland. As the father of the initiative and referendum, it could argued that he is the single most important figure in the state's political history; but however except for this one display, there is no other monument to U'Ren. Streets, fountains, schools, and lakes are named after lesser lights, but he remains almost forgotten.

U'Ren was born in Wisconsin in 1859 and worked as both a blacksmith and a lawyer.[9] He came to Oregon in 1889, and in 1892[10] he became associated with the Seth Luelling family in Milwaukie, a farming town south of Portland. The Luellings were pioneers in the nursery business and a curious combination of political involvement and spiritualism. Eventually they formed a Farmer's Alliance Lodge which met in Seth Luelling's large house. U'Ren was introduced to the Luellings as a "medium" and he soon became involved in both their spiritual and political activities.[11] Seth's brother, Alfred Luelling, gave U'Ren a copy of James W. Sullivan's book, Direct Legislation by the Citizenship through the Initiative and Referendum, which described the process of direct democracy in Switzerland.[12] The book was an epiphany for William U'Ren and in 1892, with the support of the Grange, several labor unions and the Farmer's Alliance, he helped found the Direct Legislation League which elected him its first secretary.[13] In 1894, the Populist Party of Oregon also elected U'Ren its Chairman, and what was then called the "I&R" became one of the party's planks. That one book would inspire a man to such a significant historical achievement is a tribute to the power of ideas.

The first battle for the initiative and the referendum occurred in the Assembly, but the 1895 Session of the Oregon Legislature proved to be a frustrating experience for U'Ren. He lobbied vigorously for the I&R, but a proposal for a constitutional convention failed. This was, to a great extent, due to the reactionary opposition of The Oregonian. There was great public discontent with the Assembly. Railroads, banks, and corporations controlled what was said to be one of the most corrupt legislatures in the country. It was made up of "briefless lawyers, farmless farmers, business failures, bar-room loafers, Fourth of July orators and political thugs."[14] The opposition of most of the Legislature, and of the state's largest newspaper, seemed to foreclose the adoption of the initiative and referendum by normal means, but U'Ren would try again in 1897.

The second individual involved in this drama was John Hipple Mitchell, truly one of the most incredible characters in Oregon history. Mitchell was born in Pennsylvania, married, deserted his wife, went to California, then moved to Oregon and remarried without getting a divorce. Between 1866 and 1901 he was elected to the United States Senate as a Republican four times. This occurred at a time when state legislatures elected United States Senators; it was Mitchell's 1897 re-election attempt that precipitated the decisive confrontation over the initiative and the referendum.

The final player was Jonathan Bourne, Jr. Bourne was born in New Bedford, Massachusetts in 1855 and came to Oregon in 1878. He was a lawyer, a silver mine owner and a Republican member of the Legislature in 1885, 1886 and 1897.[15] More importantly, Bourne was Mitchell's protégé and chief lieutenant in Multnomah County. He was also Secretary of the State Republican Party. Bourne was elected in the 1896 primary as a Mitchell-Republican and he supposedly assisted other pro-Mitchell legislative candidates by distributing several hundred thousand dollars from the Southern Pacific Railroad.[16] In exchange, Bourne was promised the speakership of the Oregon House. Bourne's activities on behalf of Mitchell occurred in the spring of 1896, before either party had nominated a candidate for president.

The presidential election of 1896 presented America with a stark contrast of economic philosophy and political style. The issue was gold versus silver or, more specifically, the "gold standard." These terms sound archaic to our ears, but they were emblematic of the basic orientations of the various proponents. The Republican Party generally favored the gold standard, which translated into an economic policy of limited credit, support for big business and the East Coast establishment view of how America should be governed. The Democrats and the Populists were for silver, or the free coinage of silver, which meant easy credit. The 1896 contest became gold versus silver, Republican versus Populist and Democrat, big business versus small business and the farmer and, finally, East versus West and South.

Oregon was an anomaly; many of the most important Republicans, including Mitchell and Bourne, favored silver. The Republican Convention of 1896 adopted a strong pro-gold plank and then nominated William McKinley from Ohio as its presidential candidate. Twenty Republican silver supporters from the West walked out of the Convention in protest.[17] For Oregon, the question was whether or not Mitchell would support the nominee or stay with silver.

In the meantime, the Democrats in St. Louis adopted a plank calling for the free coinage of silver at a rate of 16 to 1, then selected William Jennings Bryan as their standard bearer. Bryan, the youngest man ever to be nominated for president, was a fervently pro-silver, thirty-six-year-old former Congressman from Nebraska. In one immortal speech he set the tone for the convention, the election and an era of American politics. Close to 100 years after its delivery, the "Cross of Gold" remains the most famous campaign speech ever given. Bryan mixed religious imagery, economic theory and politics in a transcendent masterpiece of oratory which still affects our lives today:

> Having behind us the producing masses of this nation...we will answer
> their demands for a gold standard by saying to them: You shall not
> press down upon the brow of labor this crown of thorns, you shall not
> crucify mankind on a cross of gold![18]

The Populist Party also nominated Bryan and endorsed free silver. The stage was set for what was probably the most significant ideological clash in the history of American politics.[19] The English economist. Henry George outlined the real issues:

In form, the struggle is on the currency question (gold and silver). But these are only symbols, and behind them are gathered the world opposing forces of aristocratic privilege and democratic freedom.[20]

People embraced Bryan with almost a religious fever.[21] He became known as the "Great Commoner" and the "Silver Knight of the West." While Bryan made 600 speeches, McKinley stayed in Ohio with a "front porch" campaign run by Mark Hanna, the legendary Ohio political boss.

Mitchell visited McKinley and Hanna several times in Ohio[22] and finally made his decision: he would go with the Republican nominee and gold. Senator Mitchell returned to Oregon and was confronted by Bourne, who had heard rumors that he had changed his position. The Senator told Bourne that indeed he supported gold and Bourne responded by saying Mitchell would not be re-elected by the Legislature.[23] Mitchell in return called off the deal to make Bourne speaker. Mitchell not only alienated the "Silver Republicans," but he also had made enemies of the regular Republicans representing Portland's banking and industrial interests. Bryan lost the presidential election to McKinley, but that hardly settled the issue in Oregon.[24]

The Legislature met on January 11, 1897, and the Senate promptly organized by electing Republican Joseph Simon President. U'Ren, Bourne, and the anti-Mitchell regular Republicans knew that they didn't have the votes to stop the election of Mitchell. They did, however, have enough votes to stop the House from organizing and electing a speaker -- and without organization, there could be no election of a senator. The Constitution requires a quorum of 40 members and the 29 dissidents could prohibit a quorum by refusing to take the oath of office. Among these were five silver Republicans, three Democrats, nine anti-Mitchell regular Republicans and thirteen Populists including U'Ren.[25]

The group had three demands: that Mitchell not to be elected U.S. Senator, that Bourne be elected Speaker and that the Legislature pass the initiative and referendum.[26]

The House did meet temporarily to appoint a Credentials Committee, but the Committee refused to report back to the body and a quorum was never achieved. As mentioned, the Oregon Constitution says that if one of the two houses fails to organize after the fifth day the members "shall be entitled to no compensation."[27] Since the Legislature had not met its constitutional duty, no one was paid. Bourne knew what was important; he hired a chef, rented hotel rooms and essentially made it possible for his supporters to live without their regular legislative compensation. This reportedly cost Bourne $80,000![28] Being in a political battle is more enjoyable in some epochs than others.

On February 25, 1897, the Legislature adjourned without organizing, passing a single bill or electing a United States Senator. Bourne and U'Ren were successful due to Bourne's resources and U'Ren's willingness to make the necessary political compromises to achieve his ends. Ambition, principle, and silver money had carried the day.

The Session became known as the "Holdup Session," and many of the Populist legislators who refused to appear were defeated in the next election. Regardless, a consensus developed before the 1899 Session that the I&R would be adopted. Mitchell himself came out in support of the proposal, and the measures were passed in the 1899 and 1901 Sessions. At that time, two legislative sessions had to approve an amendment before it went to the people. The actual proposal for initiative and referendum was sent out to a vote in the General Election of 1902, where it passed by an incredible vote of 62,024 to 5,668!

U'Ren continued to be active during the early part of the Twentieth Century, getting involved in dozens of ballot measures mostly involving the "single tax," a concept he had learned from Henry George. According to George, the only real value was in property, and therefore only property should be taxed. Try as he might, U'Ren never could get this particular form of taxation adopted in Oregon. He died at the age of 90 in 1949.[29]

Jonathan Bourne went on to be elected United States Senator in 1907. Mitchell was returned to the US Senate in 1901, but was convicted by federal jury of land fraud in 1904 and died in 1905.[30]

From '02 to '92 -- Suffrage, Taxes, Fish, Taxes, the Death Penalty, and Taxes

There have been 704 measures on the ballot since the initiative and referendum passed in 1902. Of these, 244 were initiated by the people through petition drives, 50 were referendums and the remainder were placed upon the ballot by the Legislature.[31] A listing of all ballot measures can be found in the Appendix. The high-water mark for ballot measures was in 1912 when there were 44 measures in the General Election!

The list of measures from 1902 to 1992 is a recapitulation of the issues that have confronted and still confront the State of Oregon -- this is the politics and history of the state in this century. Patterns emerge and one develops a sense of what did and does concern the citizens. Our greatest bias is that of short-sightedness; we view political events from a perspective of two or four years at best. If you look closely at the list, you will be amazed to find that many of the same issues are still being debated.

In addition, we have a tendency to assume that the initiative and the referendum are, by their nature, "progressive" instruments that are a means to advance what we contemporaries would consider "liberal causes." Bryan may have lost the 1896 election, but the spirit of Populism seems to live. The initiative and the referendum are the great political legacy of Populism. We feel comfortable with the idea that in Oregon, common men and women do have the power to protect their interests from today's version of Mark Hanna, but, tragically, this has not necessarily been the case. As we examine the initiative and the referendum, past and present, let us keep in mind the original motivation of the proponents, the politics and economics of the Populist Era. Populism was an effort to obtain political power for the economic benefit of common men and women -- the farmer and the laborer. The advent of the railroad, farm mechanization and emerging American world economic power had not resulted in prosperity for the people who settled the West.[32] Oregon's direct democracy was the result of Henry George's battle between "aristocratic privilege and democratic freedom," but does it still function in the role intended by the original proponents? What has the record been?

In Oregon, as in most states, women's suffrage was one of the most controversial issues of the early Twentieth Century. It took four attempts for supporters to achieve success. The proposal was defeated in 1906, 1908, 1910 and finally passed narrowly in 1912 -- 61,265 to 57,104. It is noteworthy that Oregon was one of only two states, the other being Arizona, in which women obtained the right to vote through the initiative process.[33] The local fight for suffrage was led by the elderly, but indefatigable Abigail

Scott Duniway. It was opposed by tavern and saloon owners, who feared that women would support Prohibition.[34] They weren't wrong. In the 1914 General Election, with women voting for the first time, an initiative for Prohibition passed.[35] Similarly, an effort to repeal the constitutional provision which prohibited people of color ("Negroes, Chinamen and mulattos...")[36] from voting was on the ballot two times before finally passing in 1927.[37]

Taxes have been on the ballot 150 times, as proposals ranging from sales tax measures to limitation of property taxes. Seventy-two tax measures were placed on the ballot by the Legislature, 49 by petition and 18 by referendum. Only 10 tax measures proposed by petition have passed in 90 years.

Questions involving fish, a rather unique issue, have been voted on 14 times since 1902. ("Fish," of course, are salmon and "steelhead," an ocean-going trout that returns to freshwater streams to reproduce.) In the early years, political activity on this issue was spawned by the conflict between "fish wheelers" and "gill netters." A "fish wheel" is a contraption resembling a mill wheel which dips into the water taking the fish out. A "gill net" is exactly that, a net strung across a river or stream to catch fish by the gills. In 1908, both groups put measures on the ballot to limit the other's activities and both passed! Most other "fish" confrontations involved efforts to close various rivers and bays to commercial fishing.[38] Fish politics remains much the same in this century. Sport fishers look upon commercial operators as rapacious abusers of a grand resource, and the commercial license holders look upon sports people as do-gooders trying to destroy a "way of life."

The very structures and procedures of government have also inspired numerous measures. In 1908, the recall was passed; in the same year a measure instructing the Legislature to vote for the people's choice for United States Senator was adopted. In 1910 a direct presidential primary was approved by the voters. Additionally in 1910, there were seven measures on the ballot changing county boundaries, such as adding part of Multnomah County to neighboring Washington County. All of these failed, and voters seemed to lose interest in such county issues after the middle of the century.

The Legislature itself has not fared well as the subject of ballot measures. In 1906, public officials were prohibited from receiving free railroad passes. Legislative pay was frozen at $3 a day in the original 1859 Constitution, and it was only after nine attempts, from 1908 to 1942, that the amount was increased.[39]

Other ballot measures go from the dramatic, such as the death penalty, to the almost absurd. In 1912, there was an unsuccessful attempt to create the office of "Hotel Inspector." An "Anti-Compulsory vaccination " measure was put on the ballot in 1916 only to fail, as did a measure to establish the "Roosevelt Bird refuge" in 1920.

Time itself was once the subject of a protracted battle. In 1952, a "standard time" initiative passed, making Oregon one of the few states without daylight savings time. A 1954 daylight savings time initiative failed, as did a referendum placed on the ballot by the Legislature in 1960. One would not think that anyone would care that much about the subject. Daylight savings time was an issue which pitted farmers against business. Farmers were opposed to the concept because cows are milked on their own time and not clock time. Under daylight savings time, farmers had to get up earlier to milk their cows. On the other hand, timber brokers and stock brokers, who both worked with East Coast institutions, wanted daylight savings time because the rest of the country had it. If

Oregon had the same time system as the East coast five hours of the common work day would coincide, but if Oregon did not have daylight savings time then only four hours would coincide. In 1962, when the proponents ran a campaign emphasizing the economic benefits, a measure finally passed to allow daylight savings time.[40]

The measure to "Prohibit Adding Fluoride to Water Systems" failed in 1976, but in 1978 the voters approved an initiative measure to allow the practice of denturism, which is the manufacture and retailing of false teeth by non-dentists. Teeth have not been on the ballot since. In November, of 1980, Ballot Measure 5 was sponsored by the environmentalists to prohibit "...leghold traps..." Although the measure failed, the proponents and opponents engaged in a protracted legal battle over whether or not the opponents used unfair campaign tactics, such as saying that the proposal would have banned mousetraps. In 1982, for the first time, the initiative process was used in foreign affairs; a non-binding measure was placed on the ballot saying that the "People of Oregon Urge Mutual Freeze on Nuclear Weapons." It passed and both super-powers eventually acquiesced.

Nuclear power and radioactive waste have been the subject of several initiatives since 1980. In 1980, a measure passed requiring voter approval of any future nuclear power plant in Oregon.[41] Trojan, the state's only nuclear power plant, located north of Portland on the Columbia River, is owned by Portland General Electric. It has been the target of the anti-nuclear movement since its construction in 1976. There have been three unsuccessful measures to close it --1986, 1990 and 1992. All of these were sponsored by anti-nuclear activist Lloyd Marbet, who heads an organization with the obscure name of "Forelaws Onboard." In 1992, Portland General Electric finally announced that it would close the plant of its own accord.

Marbet and his group have also focused on the radioactive waste issue. In 1984, they successfully placed on the ballot and passed a measure increasing the requirements for "...Disposing Wastes Containing Naturally Occurring Radioactive Isotopes." The measure was aimed at a low level waste disposal site maintained by the Wah Chang company, a manufacturer of exotic metals located in the mid-Willamette valley at Albany. The site is basically a mud lake of "tailings" beside the Willamette River. Wah Chang resisted with a lawsuit and the lake remains untouched today.

Anti-abortion ballot measures appeared in 1986 and 1990. Ballot Measure 6, a 1986 constitutional amendment, would have prohibited state funded abortions. It failed 477,920 to 580,163. The measure was sponsored by Oregon Right to Life and in the 1990 campaign the same group put a proposal on the ballot requiring that a "Doctor Must Give Parent Notice Before Minor's Abortion." The Oregon Citizens' Alliance (OCA) put an abortion ban, Ballot Measure 8, up for a vote at the same general election. Both measures were defeated by a campaign run by the National Abortion Rights Action League, whose heavy handed theme was "no return to back alley abortions!" The Pro-Life people correctly blamed the defeat of their notification measure on its being identified with the more radical OCA abortion ban.

Other interesting recent ballot measures include a legislative-introduced referendum for a statute to require motorcycle riders to wear helmets. This passed in 1988 by a vote of 486,401 to 224,655. Another unsuccessful 1986 initiative effort was to legalize marijuana for personal use, which failed 279,479 to 781,922.

Getting on the Ballot -- Going to Court, Going to the Timber Carnival

The actual process of law making through the initiative and the referendum can be divided into two stages: getting on the ballot, and getting the measure passed. Placing a proposal on the ballot in no way guarantees its passage. We will first examine the mechanics and politics of qualifying an initiative for a public vote.

Two initial points should be made. First, many more initiatives are proposed than ever qualify for the ballot. Secondly, the initiative process is best viewed as a long term effort. Successful proponents of measures do not give up after one or two elections. Some issues, whether they be suffrage, nuclear power or abortion, do not go away.

All laws start with an idea and the initiative is no exception. Citizens, interest groups or even elected officials use the initiative to avoid the traditional legislative process, but there is no requirement that the proposed constitutional amendment or statute be drafted in any particular way by any particular individual. The Oregon Constitution requires that an initiative "... shall embrace one subject only and matters properly connected therewith."[42] The "one subject" rule has been the object of numerous law suits, usually on behalf of parties wishing to keep a particular measure off the ballot.[43] It is easier to win a court case than an election contest. The initial determination is made by the secretary of state, who may ask for the opinion of the attorney general as to whether or not the proposal violates the "one subject" rule.[44] The determination may be challenged in the Oregon Supreme Court, but the attitude of the Court has been very tolerant. Proposals are liberally construed to meet the requirement.[45]

Measures themselves may be drafted by lay persons, lawyers or by the Legislature's own Legislative Counsel Office at the request of a legislator. The actual writing is not technically hard. The form is that of a regular bill that starts with the classic phrase, "Be it enacted by the People of the State of Oregon..." The hard part is anticipating the political effects of specific provisions in the bill. Initiatives are not drafted in a vacuum, but they do not go through the vetting process of hearing after hearing where details are examined and discussed by the proponents as well as opponents. What seems like an innocent provision at an early stage may turn out to be the major issue of the campaign. For instance, in 1990 Ballot Measure 11 allowed a tax credit to people who sent their children to private schools. Unfortunately, the measure also allowed for "home schooling" and would have given parents a $2000 a year payment for every child that they attempted to educate by themselves. It didn't take long before the proponents were having to explain why particularly greedy or irresponsible parents would not merely keep their children at home under the pretense of "home schooling" and collect the money. The measure failed 351,977 to 741,863.

Once a measure has been drafted, it is filed with the secretary of state in the form of a "prospective petition" and must be signed by three chief petitioners and accompanied by a statement of sponsorship signed by 25 registered voters. It also must be accompanied by a statement that petition circulators will or will not be paid. The filing deadline for prospective petitions is not less than four months before the next general election. If the proponents are raising or spending money, they must also file the appropriate papers as a political action committee. The secretary of state immediately sends the prospective petition to the attorney general for the preparation of a draft "ballot title." This ballot title contains a caption of not more than ten words that "identifies the subject of the measure" and a question of not more than 20 words that "phrases the chief purpose of the measure so that an affirmative response to the question corresponds to an affirmative vote on the measure." Finally there is a summary of the measure of not more then 85 words.[46] The attorney general must return the draft ballot title to the secretary of state within five days and the ballot title must pass a readability test established by the secretary of state.[47] This test makes sure that people with only an eighth grade education can read the ballot title. At the same time the attorney general is working on the ballot title, the secretary of state is accepting public comments on whether or not the prospective measure contains more than one subject. The ballot title is returned to the secretary of state and comments on the title are accepted for ten days. Within the next five days, the attorney general reviews all the public comments, revises the title, (if he or she determines it needs to be revised), and certifies the ballot title back to the secretary of state. Within ten days after the title is certified back, any registered voter who has filed a previous written comment, may file a petition with the Oregon Supreme Court for a different ballot title.

The Supreme Court plays a crucial role in the initiative process, not only in regard to the "one subject" issue, but in the reviewing and rewriting of ballot titles. A good ballot title, whether it is the caption, the question or the summary, is absolutely crucial to the passage or failure of a measure. Very few voters have the time or wherewithal to inform themselves about the textual details of ballot measures.[48] A substantial number of voters will vote for or against a proposal based simply on what they read in the voting booth in the ballot title. The words in ballot titles are crucial and both opponents and proponents know this.

This situation places the Supreme Court in a very political position. Its initial decision may have a tremendous impact on whether or not the state adopts a certain policy on abortion, nuclear power or the death penalty. These are not ordinary litigants, but major business, unions or political groups protecting or pursuing their vital interests. Lawsuits involving ballot titles are hard fought and involve the best legal talent in the state. The role of the court is theoretically to decide if the ballot title meets the requirements of ORS 250.035, as outlined earlier, and not whether they can write a better ballot title. To put it another way, is the attorney general's title "insufficient" or "unfair?"

A typical case occurred in 1980, when Pacific Power and Light (PP&L) sued Secretary of State Norma Paulus over the ballot title of an initiative involving energy development.[49] The measure would have created an "Energy Development Commission" to sell bonds for hydroelectric power under Articles XI-D and XI-J of the Oregon Constitution. As mentioned, the older Article XI-D was a successful Depression era "public power" initiative to move Oregon away from investor-owned utilities. Although that initiative passed, the Legislature never put the measure into effect, thus allowing Oregon to remain a private power state.[50] Article XI-J was a legislatively-referred measure for small energy projects originally passed in 1980. PP&L objected to the initial title because it was not clear that the proposed Commission could buy the facilities of private utilities. The opponents of the measure wanted it to look like an unreasonable government takeover that would eventually cost the taxpayers money. The Court modified the title making it clear that the proposed Commission was only prohibited from buying generating plants themselves. (It should be understood that in this situation such a Commission would have the power of eminent domain, and thus could "buy" transmission facilities regardless of whether or not the utility wanted to sell.)

The measure did not make it to the ballot, but it is an excellent example of how the legal challenge to the title relates to the eventual political battle over passage. In this particular case, hundreds of millions of dollars worth of private business assets were threatened by the passage of the measure.

Once the Supreme Court has approved a ballot title, the petitioners must submit the actual form of the petition to the secretary of state for approval. The "petition" is composed of a "cover sheet," which has the actual measure, other information, and a signature sheet for voters to sign.

The petitions are printed by and at the expense of the proponents. It takes 66,771 signatures to put a statute on the ballot and 89,028 signatures for a constitutional amendment. These figures are determined by a formula found in the Constitution, respectively six and eight percent of the "total number of votes cast for all candidates for governor at the election for which a governor was elected for a term of four years next preceding the filing of the petition."[51] To get a sufficient number of valid signatures a significantly higher total number must be submitted to the secretary of state. It usually takes 85,000 signatures being submitted to get the requisite signatures necessary for a statutory proposal to be placed in the ballot.

Gathering these signatures is an immense amount of work. The average petition circulators can get 10 to 15 signatures an hour. The nature of signers dictates the venue for signature collection. Proponents of liberal measures gather signatures in front of the Multnomah County Library or at the doors of Powell's Books in Portland, (the largest bookstore in the world). Portland's Annual Rose Festival Parade in June is a favorite event for both sides of the political spectrum, as hundreds of people stand on the street waiting for the parade with nothing to do. Bus stops and neighborhood events are also popular. According to Bob Kouns, one of the chief petitioners of a successful "Victims' Rights" measure[52] which passed in 1986, the best place for conservative measures is the Albany Timber Carnival in the mid-Willamette Valley. That some locations have a certain ideological ambiance is a commentary on the lifestyles of the left and the right. Without too much imagination, one can picture carriers of pro-environment petitions lurking outside Volvo dealerships, while proponents of tax limitations haunt the parking lots at monster truck shows.

According to Kouns, it takes 12,000 to 14,000 hours of signature gathering to place a measure on the ballot. Cost can run as much as $40,000 or $50,000 for printing, postage, telephone and staff. All of this expense and effort occurs before any campaign for or against the measure happens.

Paying for Signatures -- What is a Public Place?

Until 1982, Oregon had a statute prohibiting the paying of people to gather signatures. The early proponents of the Oregon System looked upon paid circulators as a type of political corruption.[53] Champions of the initiative and the referendum were opposed to corporate economic power, and the idea of buying a place on the ballot was an anathema to them. In 1982, however, the Libertarian Party of Oregon brought suit in U.S. District Court to have the statute declared unconstitutional based on the proposition that a limitation on the ability to spend money was a limitation on free speech. Judge Helen Frye cited both Oregon and United States Supreme Court decisions and ruled the statute unconstitutional on the grounds that "... all means of political expression cost money, and restricting the amount of money that can be spent restricts (the) freedom of speech."[54]

With all due respect, Frye's opinion was to Oregon's direct democracy what the Dred Scott was to the issue of slavery -- an unmitigated disaster. The first unfortunate result of the decision was that in 1984, Scientific Games of America organized and paid for an initiative to establish a lottery in Oregon. The measure passed by a vote of 794,441 to 412,341, but was drafted so that only Scientific Games could supply the lottery tickets for the first few years! Now companies gather signatures for a fee regardless of the measure itself.[55]

Another major question is whether petitioners have the right to gather signatures in shopping centers and supermarket parking lots. Fred Meyer, Inc., has been the major advocate for the position that private property remains private and they have the right to decide who may gather signatures. In 1990, the Court of Appeals ruled that shopping centers have replaced the traditional forums for the collections of signatures.[56] At this writing, the Oregon Supreme Court had not yet ruled on the matter involving individual stores such as Fred Meyer, but it did rule that petitioners must have reasonable access to the common areas of regional shopping centers.[57]

Ballot Measure Politics-- The Devil and Tricks in Six

Ballot measure campaigning is a political art form in Oregon which differs greatly from campaigns for political office. In contrast to regular campaigns, there is no candidate and no record to run for or against. However, not all measures involve campaigns. Some are so uncontroversial that there are no participants on either side. In the 1986 general election, a proposal was on the ballot to amend the constitution to allow the secretary of state to live in a county other than Marion County (where the Capitol is located). No one cared, (except for the secretary of state), there was no campaign, and the measure passed. Other measures fail, even though the supporting campaign efforts far outweigh those of the opposition; the numerous unsuccessful attempts at a sales tax are examples.

More ballot measures fail than pass. Herein is probably the most important aspect of ballot measure politics -- it is much easier to defeat a measure than pass it. As facetious as it sounds, most measures fail on their content and not their personalities. The Devil is in the details and it is usually the details that defeat ballot measures. Earlier, we mentioned the proposal to allow home schooling and its defeat because of a provision that would have made it profitable to keep children away from school. When we say "details" we do not necessarily mean the "objective" details of a measure. Opponents interpret the language of a proposal to their advantage and are under no duty to be "fair." There is a basic psychology to this type of negative campaigning; people are always more comfortable with "the devil they know." It is fairly easy to plant doubts, and once planted it is hard for the proponents to educate the public about their interpretation of the measure.

There have been some legendary ballot measure campaigns in Oregon involving the details of a particular proposal. The master craftsman of this technique was former lobbyist Ken Rinke. Rinke, who is now retired, was involved with dozens of measures in his career, and political aficionados still talk about his 1968 General Election campaign

35

against Ballot Measure 6. This proposal would have allowed the issuance of state bonds to acquire beaches, the bonds were to be paid for with a gas tax on automobiles. Rinke framed the issue in what has become a classic of political sloganeering in Oregon -- "Beware of tricks in six!" He pointed out that trucks did not have to pay the same tax that autos had to pay -- this was one of the "tricks" and it was enough to defeat the measure. He still makes the point, however, that no matter how clever the slogan it has to be supported by fact. "A slogan can be wonderful, but it is no dammed good if you can't back it up."[58]

In a bizarre way, ballot measure campaigns are more honest then those involving candidates. The issues are confronted, albeit in a simplistic manner. When you vote for a candidate, you might get a particular policy, but when you vote for a ballot measure, you have no excuse, the exact wording is in front of you.

Recall -- Sex, Lies and Endorsements

Getting recalled in Oregon is no simple matter. Although the process has been successful against county commissioners and school board members, it remains relatively unusual for a state officials to be removed from office. That doesn't mean that it is not attempted. At last count Governor Barbara Roberts was the subject of three unsuccessful recall attempts because of her stand on timber issues.[59]

Two successful recalls of legislators occurred in 1985 and 1988. Pat Gillis was 24 years old when he defeated Democratic incumbent Annette Farmer for the District 20 House seat in East Multnomah County in 1984. Gillis had worked for Representative Larry Campbell in the 1983 Session when Campbell was House Minority Leader, and Campbell encouraged Gillis to run against Farmer.[60] Annette, who was from Romania, sometimes had trouble with the English language and was considered too liberal for her district. The young Gillis beat Farmer by more than 2,500 votes in an intense and controversial campaign. The son of a high school football coach, he liked to quote Vince Lombardi: "...winning isn't everything, it's the only thing."[61]

Unfortunately, Gillis took Lombardi's advice literally and made two mistakes in his effort to win. He claimed, in his Voters' Pamphlet statement, that he had a master's degree, which he did not, and he pasted together and mailed a phony campaign endorsement letter from the American Association of Retired Persons. The letterhead and the signature of the Chairman of the AARP Legislative Committee had been taken from an earlier letter asking Gillis to fill out a questionnaire. The House didn't seat Gillis the first day of the Session, but later voted to be admit him, with a censure, after extensive hearings on the matter.[62] On February 21, 1985, a Marion County grand jury indicted Gillis for lying in the Voters' Pamphlet. In response, Thomas P. Dennehy, a perennial East Multnomah County activist, filed a recall petition. On March 5 sufficient signatures were turned in to cause an election.[63] On March 26, the voters recalled Gillis by a vote of 4,110 to 3,111[64] and ended his short political career. Gillis was later found not guilty of lying in the Voters' Pamphlet.[65]

Controversy continued to plague House District 20. In the process to replace Gillis, Republican precinct committee persons only nominated one individual to the Multnomah County Commission, instead of the five required by law. The Commission had no choice but to select Portland policeman John Minnis as the new representative. Minnis had lost to Gillis in the 1984 Primary. He later became part of the Republican leadership of the House.

William Alfred Olson was another young Republican who got into trouble with the voters three years after the Gillis affair. Olson was 32 years old when he defeated veteran Democratic State Senator E. D. (Debbs) Potts "Debbs" as he was known, was a conservative Democrat named after the Socialist Eugene Debbs, and had represented the Grants Pass area in the Senate since 1961. He had been Senate President and refused to either campaign or take campaign contributions. Olson presented himself as a hardworking, conservative, evangelical Christian. He sponsored legislation against child pornography and to require people applying for marriage licenses to undergo HIV tests.

On October 12, 1987, without warning and much to the chagrin of his constituents and fellow legislators, Senator Olson suddenly pleaded guilty to a charge of sexual abuse in the second degree. The plea was for an incident involving a thirteen-year-old female in Clackamas County in 1986.[66] Olson apologized and said he had made a mistake, but refused to resign.[67] He was recalled on March 22, 1988, by a vote of 14,822 to 9,667.[68]

Other recalls have been filed, but it generally takes some overt act of dishonesty or hypocrisy to motivate a successful effort. Olson's use of religion, his peccadilloes and his rapid rise and fall were precursors of the politics of direct democracy to come in Oregon.

Culture Wars -- The Emergence of the Oregon Citizens' Alliance

No discussion of the initiative, referendum and recall would be complete without an examination of the Oregon Citizens' Alliance, the OCA. These tools of direct democracy have been the OCA's weapons of choice for its seven tumultuous years in Oregon politics, or what some writers and commentators have called the "culture wars."[69]

How does one explain a movement such as the OCA? The Oregon Citizens' Alliance is part of a national phenomenon of increasing effective political participation by Americans who identify themselves as both religious[70] and politically conservative. The mixing of religion and politics is nothing new in American politics, but it is far beyond this book to thoroughly analyze the genesis of the current conservative movement. Even the terms themselves are inadequate. We use words like "conservative," "right wing" and "religious," and attempt to pigeonhole the latest election results in our comfortable categories. The question of the political parentage of the OCA probably has as much to do with the psychology of Populism, i.e., economic and social discontent, as it does with traditional Barry Goldwater conservatism. Nevertheless, religious conservatives are having an increasing impact on American politics, whether with the presidential campaign of Pat Robertson[71] or anti-gay ballot measures in states such as Oregon and Colorado. Numerous other states and jurisdictions are now confronting similar proposals.[72]

One would not think that this particular state would be fertile ground for a movement with a strong religious component. As mentioned in Chapter 1, Oregon has more people who do not believe in God than any other state in the Union. Seventeen percent of Oregonians are atheists and the rest take their religion in moderate doses. It was Methodist missionaries who first brought the Gospel to the region.

In spite of the state's reputation for "progressive" policies, however, there has always be a dark side to Oregon politics. As previously mentioned, Governor Walter Pierce had his association with the Ku Klux Klan in the 1920s. The state was one of the last in the country to adopt a public accommodations law. We tend to be overly sanguine about mechanisms of direct democracy; we assume that the people, if left to their own devices, will make "right" decisions. Whether or not a decision is "right," of course, is in the eye of the beholder.

The Oregon Citizens' Alliance emerged out of the unsuccessful primary campaign of Joe Lutz against Bob Packwood for the United States Senate in 1986.[73] Lutz, a Baptist minister, got 42% against the incumbent Senator, a phenomenal showing.[74] The group's founders were Lutz, T. J. Bailey, Dick Younts and Lon Mabon.[75] Lutz tried to stay politically active, but ran into hard times with his supporters when he left his wife to have an affair with a woman in California.[76] T.J. Bailey became the Chairman of the Oregon Republican Party, from 1988 to 1990, and was notorious for referring to gays as "fairies."[77] There were objections on the part of some party members to his use of the term. Lon Thurston Mabon, the driving force behind the OCA, is a self-described former dope-using Vietnam veteran and Republican Party activist. Mabon is the current Chairman of the OCA, which claims chapters in 33 of Oregon's 36 counties and is supported by 17,000 donors.[78]

The group's first victory came in 1986 with Ballot Measure 8, a proposal to repeal an executive order prohibiting discrimination in state employment based on sexual orientation which had been promulgated by Governor Neil Goldschmidt . The measure passed 626,751 to 561,355 and was a blow to supporters of equal rights. The opposition to Ballot Measure 8 was spearheaded by the Right to Privacy PAC (RTP), the largest gay political group in the state, and was just the first of ongoing battles between the OCA and RTP.[79]

In 1990, the OCA put a measure, again Ballot Measure 8, on the ballot to ban abortion. As mentioned, this was a total abortion ban and was on the same ballot as Ballot Measure 10, sponsored by Oregon Right to Life, which only required parental notification. Both measures lost, with Ballot Measure 8 failing 355,963 to 747,599 and Ballot Measure 10 going down 530,851 to 577,806.

The real impact of the OCA in the 1990 election was felt in the governor's race. The organization promoted an independent candidate, Al Mobley, who got 13% of the vote. Republican Dave Frohnmayer got 40% and Democrat Barbara Roberts won with 46%. Frohnmayer was later quoted as saying, "They clearly elected Barbara Roberts, that is the OCA's biggest accomplishment."[80]

In 1992 the OCA gathered enough signatures to present the now infamous Ballot Measure 9 to the voters. The initiative classified homosexuality with pedophlia, sadism and masochism and declared them to be "abnormal, wrong, unnatural and perverse." It prohibited the state or any local government from enacting anti-discrimination legislation based on sexual orientation or expending funds to "promote, encourage, or facilitate homosexuality, pedophlia, sadism or masochism."[81]

The Ballot Measure 9 contest was one of the most intensely fought measures in the 90 year history of direct democracy in Oregon. The media, elected officials, business groups and the liberal clergy lined up against the measure. The opposition was again led by Save Our Communities, which was an extension of the Right to Privacy PAC. Both sides received nationwide funding and support. The national media focused on Oregon and Colorado as the two main battlegrounds for this new issue. Further, the controversy over gay rights was exacerbated by Patrick Buchanan's speech to the Republican National Convention, where he attacked homosexuality and inspired the GOP faithful with talk of a cultural and religious war.

One of the most unusual aspects of the Ballot Measure 9 battle was that not one well known politician, of either party, would admit to supporting the measure. In fact, the Democratic Party Chair Jane Doer and her Republican counterpart Craig Berkman appeared together in an anti-Ballot Measure 9 television ad. The OCA's campaign themes varied from homosexuality as a source of damnation to preventing homosexuals from obtaining "special rights." The opponents argued that the proposal was nothing more than bigotry and that "hate was not a family value." The Oregonian took an extremely strong stand against Ballot Measure 9, running not just one, but a series of editorials attacking the proposal.

Ballot Measure 9 lost 638,527 to 828,290, but its companion measure, which did not contain the reference to "pedophlia, sadism or masochism," passed in Colorado.[82] In May of 1993, the OCA filed another anti-gay rights proposal based on the Colorado amendment. Mabon named the new initiative "The Minority Status and Child Protection Act,"[83] and modeled it on the successful Colorado proposition.[84] Measure 9 had passed in most rural areas, and in May, 1992 the voters in the city of Springfield adopted an anti-gay rights initiative. In response to these two circumstances the OCA filed local initiatives prohibiting city and county governments from granting minority status based on sexual orientation. These measures were immediately granted the dubious appellation of "Sons of 9." On May 18, 1993, voters in the Washington County town of Cornelius passed the first "Son of 9" 956 to 595.[85] Approximately 30 other measures were filed in cities and counties and nine qualified for the ballot on the regular June 29, 1993 election date.

Simultaneous with the OCA campaign, the 1993 Legislature was going through its own gay rights battle. The two, almost parallel, processes presented a fascinating example of the interaction between initiative and legislative law making. In addition, the legislative battle became one of intense partisan infighting. The Oregon Senate was controlled by Democrats and the House was controlled by Republicans. The initial gay rights bill was Senate Bill 34 (SB-34), which prohibited discrimination based on sexual orientation, in housing and jobs. Similar measures had been introduced in both houses for the past 20 years without success. SB-34 was the top legislative priority of Labor Commissioner Mary Wendy Roberts, and passed the Senate on April 23 by a vote of 18 to 12.[86] The voting was almost totally along party lines with only one Democrat, Senator Mae Yih of Albany, saying no.

The bill was then sent to the House, and referred to the Judiciary Committee by Speaker Campbell where it languished for weeks. Commissioner Roberts brought intense pressure against both Speaker Campbell and Judiciary Chairman Del Parks, R-Klamath Falls, to hear the bill. Campbell and Parks first told Roberts that the bill would not get a hearing until 31 representatives had committed to vote for the measure on the floor. Roberts got the necessary pledges, but Parks still refused to schedule the bill. Privately, Republicans said the bill was dead because it was being pushed by Commissioner Roberts, who was disliked by them because of her stands on labor issues.

According to the Republicans they were not anti-gay rights, but only anti-Roberts. Democrats replied by attacking Campbell, saying that he was blocking the bill because of OCA support for Republican candidates. Mabon complemented the Speaker in a press interview, saying that the OCA would support candidates "who stand for family values," and that "I have every reason to believe Larry Campbell is a pro-family Speaker of the House."[87]

During the week of June 14, Cathy Kiyomura, a reporter for The Oregonian, took a survey of House members to see whether or not they supported SB-34. Twenty-three members, including Campbell, refused to tell her their positions on the bill; thus on Sunday, June 20, The Oregonian launched what was tantamount to a nuclear strike against the offending members with an editorial entitled, "Cowardice in the House." The piece not only listed the names of the representatives who wouldn't answer but made this observation, "Their refusal to wrestle publicly with this divisive issue gives comfort to bigotry. They are worse than the opponents of SB-34. They are cowards."[88]

They were not amused. Monday morning, on the House floor during Remonstrances, members complained that the paper had gone over the line from journalism to lobbying.[89] Representative Margaret Carter, D-Portland, was one of the few Democrats named. "I told you guys (the media) the other day I needed attention. I got it this weekend. I got all the attention I wanted. I was labeled a coward." John Watt, R-Medford, announced that "There will be a meeting of cowards unanimous at 12:15 p.m. today."[90]

The situation with The Oregonian editorial was exacerbated by a front page story in the same issue, on prayer meetings being held every Monday morning in Speaker Campbell's office.[91] The combination of the two presented a picture of the House as being controlled by the religious right.

On June 23, the issue of a hearing on SB-34 was finally decided. A morning news conference had been organized by an organization called "Parents and Friends of Lesbians and Gays." After the presentation in the news room, most of the parents went to Campbell's office and demanded to see him. TV cameras followed the people into the waiting room, but the Speaker wouldn't meet with them. One of the parents yelled at his chief aide, Dan Jarman, "You take time for prayer meetings here at the Capitol, won't you take time to listen to us?"[92]

At the news conference, Democratic legislators did their best to associate the Speaker and the Republicans with the OCA, saying, among other things, "You scratch Larry Campbell and you'll find Lon Mabon." Representative Gail Shibley, D-Portland, the only open lesbian in the House, related a conversation she had with Campbell in attempt to get SB-34 heard. She had gone to the Speaker and said that the House Democrats were going to bring a motion to discharge[93] the bill from the Judiciary Committee. Would he allow the bill to be heard? "He said he did not want to be pinned down on whether he would allow a vote on the measure, (but) if he had to give an answer, 'the answer is hell no.'"[94] Campbell had finally run out of room to maneuver on the issue.[95]

That afternoon the Republican caucus met without the Speaker and decided they had enough and that the bill should be heard. Campbell left the building and issued a statement saying that he had asked the Republican members to make the decision. Chairman Parks said that all of the gay rights bills would be heard.

The two hearings were held on June 25th and 26th. Over 100 people testified in what was one the most emotional gatherings of the session. Most of the testimony was in favor of SB-34. Some of the most moving testimony came from a member of the House itself. George Eighmey, D-Portland, had only recently been appointed to fill the seat left vacant by Beverly Stein, who resigned to run for the Multnomah County Commission Chairmanship.[96] Eighmey, the first openly gay man to serve in the Legislature, related how he had been removed from his Illinois law firm 12 years before when his partners heard a rumor that he was gay. He had moved to Portland and established a successful practice of his own, but only after having a job offer withdrawn by a Portland firm when they learned of his sexual orientation.[97]

Most of the witnesses opposed to SB-34 based their objection on the theory that homosexuality was a chosen lifestyle and not an inherited trait. There were eight hours of testimony on Friday and six and one half on Saturday. At the end of the testimony, Representative Parks announced that he would schedule a work session to vote on the bills on June 30.[98]

Parks' timing was prophetic. June 29 was the day on which six versions of "Sons of 9" were to be voted on in various local jurisdictions. All six measures passed, including Canby, Douglas County, Josephine County, Junction City, Klamath County and Linn County. Measure 9 had previously passed in all of these localities. The OCA was ecstatic and The Oregonian ran a front page color photo of a beaming Lon Mabon. "This is merely a skirmish," he was quoted as saying, "The battle is going to go on until it comes to another statewide initiative."[99] Mabon also told The New York Times that he had given out 6000 videotapes entitled "The Gay Agenda," with scenes of men and women feigning sex acts during a 1987 gay rights rally in Washington, DC. He said the OCA had also benefited from a backlash against President Clinton's move to allow gays in the military.[100]

The OCA victories presented the legislative players with several dilemmas. Republicans saw the passage of the measures as a sign of OCA strength and, although they would not admit it, most of the same citizens who voted for the initiatives more often than not voted for Republican candidates. In addition, the OCA had managed to turn around most of the opposition to it within the state's Republican Party. As mentioned earlier, Republican State Chairman Craig Berkman had publicly opposed Ballot Measure 9 during the fall campaign and thereby had earned the enmity of the OCA party activists. It was obvious that he would be challenged if he ran for re-election in January of 1993, and Berkman decided not to run. The OCA's own candidate for chairman, Bill Witt, lost by seven votes to former Republican legislator Randy Miller of Lake Oswego.[101] Miller had been the Republican nominee for secretary of state in the fall of 1992. In that role, he had opposed Ballot Measure 9, but after his election to the chairmanship, Mabon announced that he could work with him because of his pro-life position.[102] In May, Miller announced that he wouldn't take a position on the OCA's next anti-gay statewide initiative.[103] Notwithstanding this accommodation, the Republicans in the Legislature were suffering by their association with the OCA. It was obvious that most of the state's media, especially The Oregonian, would continue to pound away at the issue. The OCA was literally a sexier topic than taxes and the Democrats were more than willing to imply that Republicans were bigots because of their association with Mabon.

Democratic legislators had their own agendas and their own problems with the situation. They may have bludgeoned Campbell and Parks into a hearing on SB-34 and they probably had the 31 votes on the House floor necessary to pass the bill. What they didn't have were the five votes in the Judiciary Committee to get SB-34 to the floor. Of the nine members on the committee, only four supported the bill, and these were all Democrats. Parks was the swing vote to get a bill out, and he had the power to call for a vote on the bill in committee. Some Democrats decided that there had to be some kind of victory as a political reply to the OCA measures passed the day before. Other more hawkish members demanded SB-34 or nothing. They wanted to put the Republicans on record as being opposed to "human rights."[104]

One of the more dicey problems for the Democrats was who should get the credit for leading the fight on such a dramatic issue. Representative Gail Shibley had assumed the role as the champion of gay rights ever since her appointment[105] to the House in 1991, when she announced on her first day that she was a Lesbian. Not only was she personally vested in the issue because of her own sexual orientation, but she had become the political Joan of Arc of the gay community. Shibley was not especially interested in pushing SB-34, a measure that Labor Commissioner Mary Wendy Roberts was identified with. Roberts had been supporting gay rights since she was elected to the House in 1972, and was also a favorite of activists in the gay community. Shibley wanted a win and, even though she was not a member of the Judiciary Committee, she began negotiating with Chairman Parks and two other Republican members of the Committee, Rep. Tom Brain, R-Tigard and Rep. Ken Baker, R-West Linn. The Republicans told her they would not vote for SB-34, but they would vote for a "compromise."[106]

When Parks called the Wednesday meeting to order, the initial skirmish was over whether or not SB-34 itself would be called up for a vote. The Chairman ruled a motion to send SB-34 to the floor of the House out of order and threatened to have the offending member removed.[107] He then called HB-3500, a completely different bill, up for a vote. This was the vehicle for Shibley's "compromise;" it had been on the agenda during the two days of hearings on SB-34, but had received no comments and no testimony. In its original form, it prohibited local jurisdictions from enacting ordinances which discriminated against people for matters which had no underlying criminal or civil liability. The language had been drafted by Representative Jim Edmunson, D-Eugene, as a means to stop the OCA initiatives, but unlike the infamous SB-34 there were no anti-discrimination provisions in the bill.

The first committee vote was on a motion to amend out the original language of HB-3500 and insert the anti-discrimination language of SB-34. The motion lost four to five on a straight party line vote. After more maneuvering, the new language that Shibley, Parks and the Republicans had written was introduced. As a nod to the right, the first section of the bill prohibited any political subdivision of the state from granting any group "special rights." The OCA had always used the theme that homosexuals wanted "special rights," although no one was ever quite sure what that meant. The next operative part of the amendment said that the same jurisdictions could not "single out citizens...on account of sexual orientation."[108]

The bill finally passed out of the Committee on a vote of nine to zero. The Republicans were off the hook; they had avoided a vote on gay rights and at the same time couldn't be tagged with the OCA label. Mabon, who watched the proceeding, said, "This is representative lunacy."[109] Nobody seemed to be able to state what the bill actually did, but Shibley maintained it was the best that could be done;

> Is HB-3500 the perfect bill? A technically good bill? No. Is it the bill I would have liked if I were Speaker of the House? No. Is it the best that the House of Representatives is going to come out with in 1993?...Probably yes.[110]

Others were not so kind. "(This is) a classic legislative fudge. There will never be a time when this (civil rights for sexual minorities) won't be controversial," said Jerry Keene.[111] Others were concerned that the bill would invalidate anti-discrimination and gay rights ordinances that had already been enacted in Portland, Corvallis and Ashland. The Deputy City Attorney for Portland, Madelyn Wessel, told The Oregonian, "I can't believe that if the language of the House measure is ambiguous, and it is somewhat ambiguous, that there won't be open season on ordinances like Portland's."[112]

Sid Galton, an attorney and the gay representative on the Portland Police Chief's Forum, was even more critical:

> It's awful! It's worse than nothing. It would be like me, a Jew, endorsing codification of Nazi language in statutes...Who knows what 'special rights' means? In the first place the bill is ambiguous and in the second place it may well overturn Portland and Corvallis ordinances and do nothing in Marion County and other places that have just passed the OCA initiatives. It's confusing. It doesn't say what supporters say it does. It was done badly. One person shepherded it, and *she* didn't do it very well. This is badly flawed, sloppy and inexcusably so. Why are we doing this? Spare us from our friends.[113]

Six days later on July 6, 1993, the House passed HB-3500 by a vote of 38 to 21. Most of the members speaking in support of the bill called it a "truce" in the local battles over gay rights. Mabon charged that the "imperial legislature" was trying to take away the rights of the people to vote on issues.[114] The Senate passed the bill unamended on July 28 and the Governor signed it into law on August 2, 1993.

The OCA and Mabon struck back on July 8, when they announced the formation of a political action committee, the Oregon Citizen's Rights PAC for the purpose or recalling 14 of the House members who had voted for HB-3500. Mabon's stated reason for the recall efforts was that the representatives had violated Article IV, Section 1 of the Oregon Constitution which grants the people the right of initiative and referendum. Half of the recall targets were Republicans and half Democrats.[115] Ironically several of the Republicans were among the most conservative members of the House and had voted for the bill just to avoid voting for a real gay rights measure. The OCA later dropped these efforts, but the culture wars continues on at this very moment in the courts[116] and at the ballot box.

Conclusion -- What would U'Ren think?

This chapter can only be concluded with some rhetorical questions. What would William S. U'Ren's reaction be to Ballot Measure 9? What would his reaction be to Ballot Measure 5 in 1990? Was this the type of direct democracy he had in mind?

As was stated earlier, "populism was an effort to obtain political power for the economic benefit of common men and women..." There is no conceivable way to interpret the likes of Ballot Measure 9 as conferring economic benefit on anyone. We will discuss this further in the concluding chapter "Who Governs."

1   Allan H. Eaton, The Oregon System - -The Story of Direct Legislation in Oregon, (Chicago: A.C. McClurg & Co., 1912), 1.

2   Or. Const. art. V, sec. 1.

3   David D. Schimdt, Citizen Lawmakers, (Philadelphia: Temple University Press, 1989), 261.

4   Thomas E. Cronin, Direct Democracy, (Boston: Harvard University Press, 1989) 51.

5   Joseph G. LaPalombara, The Initiative and Referendum in Oregon: 1938-1948, (Corvallis: Oregon State College Monograph, 1950), 2.

6   An example of the use of the emergency clause would be its recent attachment to a bill changing the date of the meeting of the State Board of Education at which a chairman of the board is selected; "This act being necessary for the immediate preservation of the public peace, health and safety, an emergency is declared to exist, and this act takes effect June 30, 1993." Oregon, Oregon Legislative Assembly, Oregon Laws 1993, Chapter 15.

7   Or. Const. art. IX, sec. 1a.

8   Or. Const. art. XVII.

9   Cecil T. Thompson, The Origin of Direct Legislation in Oregon, (Master's thesis, University of Oregon 1929), 21.

10   David D. Schimdt, Citizen Lawmakers, 262.

11   Cecil T. Thompson, The Origin of Direct Legislation in Oregon, 13.

12   Ibid., 25.

13   Ibid.

14   Kendrick, "The Initiative and Referendum and How Oregon Got Them," McClures, July 1911, 234-48; in Cecil T. Thompson, The Origin of Direct Legislation in Oregon, 16.

15   Harvey W. Scott, History of the Oregon Country, vol. 5 (Cambridge; Riverside press, 1924), 54.

16   Walter M. Pierce, Oregon Cattleman/Governor, Congressman, edited and expanded by Arthur H. Bone (Portland: Oregon Historical Society, 1981), 40.

17   Paul F. Boller, Presidential Campaigns, (New York: Oxford, 1984), 168.

18   Louis Koenig, Bryan - A Political biography of William Jennings Bryan, (New York: G.P. Putnam Son, 1971), 197. Koenig gives a moving description of the speech itself: "As he uttered the words 'crown of thorns,' Bryan raised his hands to the sides of his head; his fingers, spread inward, moved slowly down close to his temples, translating his audience into imagining the thorns piercing his brow and the trickling blood. Upon proclaiming the 'cross of gold,' he held out his arms in crosslike fashion. For almost five seconds, he assumed the posture of one crucified in the flesh. Then he lowered his arms to the side and took one step backward. He started toward his seat in a silence he found 'really painful.' He had almost reached the floor when the mighty volcano of human emotion erupted." Ibid., 197-198.

19   See, Lawrence Goodwin, The Populist Moment, (New York: Oxford University press, 1978).

[20] Robert F. Durden, <u>The Climax of Populism: the Election of 1896</u>, (Louisville, 1966) p.136: quoted in <u>Paul Boller, Presidential Campaigns</u>,(Oxford, New York 1984) p. 167.

[21] Bryan was immortalized by Vachel Lindsay:

> The bard and prophet of them all.
> Prairie avenger, mountain lion,
> Bryan, Bryan, Bryan, Bryan,
> Gigantic troubadour, speaking like a siege gun,
> Smashing Plymouth Rock with his boulders from the West.

Vachel Lindsay, <u>Collected Poems</u>, (New York: Macmillan, ___), 99.

[22] Oswald West, "Reminiscences and Anecdotes," <u>Oregon Historical Quarterly</u>, LI, Number 1 (March 1950), 96.

[23] Walter M. Pierce, <u>Oregon Cattleman/Governor, Congressman</u>, 40.

[24] McKinley's campaign against Bryan had some strikingly familiar Republican elements: "While William Jennings Bryan talked with passion and imprecision about the free coinage of silver, American flags -- literally millions of them became symbols of the struggle to preserve the gold standard. McKinley himself became the nation's patriotic leader. The Republican campaign committee purchased and distributed carloads of flags throughout the country and Hanna conceived of the idea of a public 'flag day" in the nation's leading cities -- a day specifically in honor of William McKinley." Lawrence Goodwin, <u>Democratic Promise - The Populist Moment in America</u>, (New York: Oxford University Press, 1976), 528.

[25] Cecil T. Thompson, <u>The Origin of Direct Legislation in Oregon</u>, 63.

[26] Ibid., 64.

[27] Or. Const. art. IV, sec. 12.

[28] Walter M. Pierce, <u>Oregon Cattleman/Governor, Congressman</u>, 40.

[29] David D. Schimdt, <u>Citizen Lawmakers</u>, 263.

[30] See Jerry A. O'Callaghan, "Senator Mitchell and the Oregon Land Frauds, 1905," <u>Pacific Historical Review</u>, (August, 1952); There is also some fascinating conjecture about Mitchell, President Roosevelt and the Panama Canal. Mitchell was chairman of the Interoceanic Committee and seemed to oppose the President on the Canal. It is maintained that Roosevelt had Mitchell indicted and tried to get him out of the way. The land fraud case against Mitchell, which merits it's own complete work, was unusual. A special US. Attorney was appointed for the case and two different judges were brought in from out of state to hear the matter. Regardless, Mitchell died before the appeal could be completed. William H. Galvani, "Reflections of J.F. Stevens and J.H. Mitchell," <u>Oregon Historical Quarterly</u>, LVII, no. 3 (September, 1943), 320-321. See also Todd A. Peterson and Jack A. Collins, "Years of Growth," in <u>The First Duty - A History of the US. District Court in Oregon</u>, ed. Carolyn M. Buam (Portland: US. District Court Historical Society, 1993), 133-138.

[31] Oregon, Secretary of State, <u>Oregon Blue Book 1993-1994</u>, Salem: Secretary of State, 1993), 327-342.

[32] Lawrence Goodwin, <u>Democratic Promise - The Populist Moment in America</u>, 114.

[33] David D. Schimdt, <u>Citizen Lawmakers</u>, 264.

[34] Ibid.

[35] An earlier Prohibition measure had failed in 1910.

36   Or. Const. art. II, sec. 6.

37   The repeal failed in 1916 by a vote of 100,027 to 100,701.

38   The 1910, 1918, 1927, 1928, 1932 and 1948 elections all had measures closing various rivers and bays to commercial fishing.

39   1908, 1917, 1920, 1921, 1927, 1930, 1938, 1940 and 1942. Further attempts at change occurred in 1950, 1956, 1958 and 1962. The 1950 measure passed and increased compensation to $600 per year, the 1962 amendment finally allowed the Legislature to set its own salary. This has not solved the problem of low pay for elected officials. Although the Legislature can set compensation, members seem to be unable to resist the opportunity to wear political sack cloth and ashes by voting against bills to increase pay.

40   Ken Rinke, telephone interview by author, written notes, Palm Desert California, 8 October 1993.

41   ORS 469.597, Ballot Measure 7, 1980.

42   Or. Const. art. IV, sec. 1, (2) (d).

43   Fidanque v. Paulus, 297 OR 711, 688 P 2d 1303 (1984), OEA v. Roberts, 301 OR 228, 721 P 2d 837 (1986).

44   OAR 165-14-028.

45   OEA v. Philips, 302 OR 87, 727 P 2d 602 (1986).

46   ORS 235.035.

47   ORS 250.039.

48   This is certainly not to say that voters are better informed when it comes to voting for candidates.

49   Pacific Power and Light v. Paulus, 289 OR 31, 609 P 2d 813 (1980); The Secretary of State is always the named defendant in these suits.

50   The story of "private power" versus "public power" in Oregon and the Northwest is an intriguing story that remains to be written.

51   Or. Const. art. IV, sec. 1, (b) & (c).

52   Ballot Measure 10, 1986, passed 774,766 to 251,509.

53   Allan H. Eaton, The Oregon System - The Story of Direct Legislation in Oregon, 149.

54   The Libertarian Party of Oregon et al v. Norma Paulus, et al, No. 82-521FR United States District Court of Oregon, 1982.

55   "Petition hucksterism," The Register-Guard, 10 October 1993, 2B.

56   State v. Cargill, 100 Or App 336, 786 P 2d 208 (1990), Sup Ct review allowed; State v. Dameron, 101 Or App 237, 789 P 2d 707 (1990).

57   Sura Rubenstein, "High court backs political petitioners," The Oregonian, 24 March 1993, B1, B4.

58   Rinke interview.

59   "Initiative Primer," The Oregonian, 2 October 1993, A11.

60   Mark Zusman, "Manchild in the Promised Land," Willamette Week, 11 April 1985, 9.

61   Jeff Mapes, "Turns, twists of Gillis story enliven Oregon politics," The Oregonian, 24 March 1985, B4.

62   Jeff Mapes, "House seats Gillis, approves censure," The Oregonian, 19 January 1988, C1.

63   Jeff Mapes, "Signatures filed seeking recall of Gillis," The Oregonian, 5 March 1985, A1.

64   Jeff Mapes, "East County voters recall Rep. Gillis," The Oregonian, 27 March 1985, B1.

65   Jeff Mapes, "Jury Clears Gillis of Lying in Voters' Pamphlet," The Oregonian, 30 May 1985, A1.

66 "Legislator Pleads Guilty in Sex Abuse," The Oregonian, 13 October 1987, B2.

67 "Olson Refuses to Resign," The Oregonian, 23 October 1987, C4.

68 Oregon, Oregon State Senate, Senate Journal 1987-1988, SE-29.

69 Thomas Edsall, "Buchanan Warns GOP Of Schism on Abortion -- Christians Told Not to Abandon 'Culture War,'" The Washington Post, 12 September 1993, A8.

70 I have tried not to use the term "fundamentalist Christian" in describing the OCA and its activities unless necessary. Religious bigotry comes in some very subtle forms. This term, or for that matter "fundamentalist Muslim" has become an acceptable yet derogatory label used too freely in the popular media. An individual's religious orientation should be irrelevant to the debate on public policy. My fellow liberals are particularly guilty of this sin; men and women who would never mention that a person was Jewish or Methodist, feel all too comfortable whispering that so and so is a "fundamentalist" or even worse a "Mormon." See Stephen Bates, "Fundamentally Out of Fashion," The Washington Post, 7 September 1993, A17.

71 See, "A modern crusade," City and State 19 July 1993; A more interesting discussion of this new religious politics is found in a recent article in The New York Times Magazine. The cover story describes an Oregon family involved with both the Republican Party and the group, "Christian Coalition." The message presented by the story is almost subliminal, a cover photo has Mr. and Mrs. Adkisson and their two daughters glowering, stern faced, directly into the camera in a threatening manner. Robert Sullivan, "Meet the Adkissons," The New York Times Magazine, 25 April 1993.

72 Terry Kinney, "Gay-rights issues hot across U.S.," The Oregonian, 15 October 1993, A20.

73 Sura Rubenstein, "OCA's rise meteoric since start-up in 1986," The Oregonian, 21 June 1993, B1, B4.

74 Foster Church, "Lutz may have lost, but he is still primary's big story," The Oregonian, 25 May 1986, B3.

75 Sura Rubenstein, "Mabon, OCA wield political power," The Oregonian, 28 July 1991, A1.

76 David Sarasohn, "Joe Lutz running for nabob of normal," The Oregonian, 15 December 1991, C8.

77 Jill Smith, "Devil's Dictionary - The Oregon Citizens' Alliance from A to Z," Willamette Week, 8 August 1991, 1,11-14.

78 Sura Rubenstein, "OCA's rise meteoric since start-up in 1986," B4.

79 This measure was later declared unconstitutional by the Oregon Court of Appeals: Merrick v. Board of Education, 116 Or. App. 293 (1993).

80 Jeff Mapes, "OCA creates activists," The Oregonian, 22 June 1993, B12.

81 Oregon, Secretary of State, 1992 General Voters' Pamphlet, 93.

82 Amendment 2 to the Colorado Constitution was eventually declared unconstitutional by the Colorado Supreme Court; Dirk Johnson, "Colorado's Anti-Gay Measure Set Back," The New York Times, 20 July 1993, A6.

83 Sura Rubenstein, "New anti-gay rights measure filed," The Oregonian, 7 May 1993, A1, A18.

84 Other measures were filed in Florida, Idaho, Maine and Michigan; Dirk Johnson, "Colorado's Anti-Gay Measure Set Back," A6.

85 Sura Rubenstein, "Cornelius seen as a 'turning point,'" The Oregonian, 20 May 1993, A1, A20; Dana Haynes, "Cornelius: newest name in gay-rights battle," The Oregonian, 20 May 1993, A20.

[86] Oregon, Sixty-Seventh Oregon Legislative Assembly, <u>Senate Legislative Calendar</u> , 5 August 1993, S-6.

[87] Brad Cain, "Campbell blocking rights measure," <u>The Oregonian</u>, 15 June 1993, B4.

[88] "Cowardice in the House," <u>The Oregonian</u>, 20 June 1993, J2.

[89] Kiyomura is still very uncomfortable with the incident, "Personally I believe public officials are obligated to make their opinions known to their constituents," she said," I had concerns that we were effecting the process (of negotiations) with the survey;" Cathy Kiyomura, interview by author, written notes, Portland, Oregon, 15 September 1993.

[90] "Up Front - Call to Order," <u>The Oregonian</u>, 22 June 1993, B1.

[91] Sura Rubenstein, "Increasingly, Christian right becomes a power in politics," <u>The Sunday Oregonian</u>, 20 June 1993, A1, A22.

[92] Cathy Kiyomura, "House will hold hearings on gay-rights bill," <u>The Oregonian</u>, 24 June 1993, A1, A20.

[93] This motion, under Rule 21 of the House Rules, will be discussed in Chapter 5 on the Legislature. It is an extremely rare parliamentary move.

[94] Cathy Kiyomura, "House will hold hearings on gay-rights bill," A20.

[95] Shibley had related her Campbell conversation to the Democratic caucus earlier that day, but had not yet told the press. She didn't volunteer the statement, but when a reporter, (who had been tipped off), asked her she went public.

[96] The executive slot on the Commission had become vacant due to the death of Gladys McCoy. Stein handily won the position in a run off against former State Senator Vern Cook.

[97] Eighmey also proved to be a very effective and popular legislator known for his intelligence and sense of humor. Toward the end of the Session, Rep. John Minnis, R-Wood Village, appeared late one afternoon on the floor in shorts and a tee-shirt. Minnis, a Portland Police Detective, is one of the most conservative members of the House (see Chapter 5). Representative Margaret Carter took advantage of a break in the proceeding to publicly tease Minnis that his legs were "cute." Eighmey, not too be outdone, grabbed his microphone and replied, "I just want to say that I think Representatives Minnis legs are cute too!" Minnis could have filed a sexual harassment complaint, but he wasn't sure against whom.

[98] Dan Hortsch, "Del Parks to plan gay-rights session," <u>The Oregonian</u>, 27 June 1993, D4.

[99] Sura Rubenstein, "All anti-gay-rights measures pass," <u>The Oregonian</u>, 30 June 1993, A1, A18;

[100] Timothy Egan, "Voters in Oregon Back Local Anti-Gay Rules," <u>The New York Times</u>, 1 July 1993, A6.

[101] Robert Sullivan, "Meet the Adkissons," 44.

[102] Ibid.

[103] Jeff Mapes, "GOP chief won't lead OCA fight," <u>The Oregonian</u>, 7 May 1993, C6.

[104] It would also be less than candid not to explain some of the circumstances surrounding the author's own position and involvement. In the 1992 General election, the author's Republican opponent was one of the few openly gay Republicans ever to run for office, Jerry Keene. Keene was a more than formidable candidate and received substantial support from the national gay community. On a local level however, both the author and Keene were endorsed by the Right to Privacy PAC. In the legislative battle over SB34 they found themselves on the same side of the issue, the author as the member of the Judiciary Committee and Keene as a witness in favor of he bill. In a bizarre way, the earlier election had been a not too subtle contest over who could be the strongest on the issue of gay rights, the liberal Democrat or the

gay Republican -- this could only happen in Oregon; Dan Hortsch, "Emotions run high in race for District 11 House seat, " The Oregonian, 21 October 1992, B4; Dan Hortsch, "Gay-rights hearing passionate but civil," The Oregonian, 30 June 1993, B9.

[105] Shibley was appointed to replace State Representative Phil Kiesling who had been appointed Secretary of State by Barbara Roberts upon her election as Governor.

[106] Ariel Waterwoman, "Stuck between a rock and a hard place - Rep. Gail Shibley takes us on a guided tour of the death of SB-34 and the birth of HB 3500," Just Out, (Portland), 15 July 1993, 9.

[107] The author.

[108] The relevant text of HB-3500 A is: "Section 1. (A) A political subdivision of the state may not enact or enforce any charter provision, ordinance, resolution or policy granting special rights, privileges or treatment to any citizen or group of citizens on account of sexual orientation, or enact or enforce any charter provision, ordinance, resolution or policy that singles out citizens or groups of citizens on account of sexual orientation.." Chapter 556, 1993 Oregon Laws.

[109] Cathy Kiyomura and Dan Hortsch, "Legislators tackle gay rights, sales tax," The Oregonian, 1 July 1993, A1, A15.

[110] Ariel Waterwoman, "Struck between a rock and a hard place --Rep. Gail Shibley takes us on a guided tour of the death of SB 34 and the birth of HB 3500," 9.

[111] Ariel Waterwoman, "Waiting for the dust to settle on HB 3500," Just Out, (Portland), 15 July 1993, 8; Jeff Mapes, "Compromise bill on gays may bring confusion," The Oregonian, 8 July 1993, B1.

[112] Cathy Kiyomura, "House bill to protect gays may do opposite," The Oregonian, 4 July 1993, E6.

[113] Ariel Waterwoman, "Waiting for the dust to settle on HB 3500," 8.

[114] Dan Hortsch, "House Approves truce on gay rights," The Oregonian, 7 July 1993, A1, A11.

[115] Republicans included Ken Baker, Dennis Luke, John Meek, Chuck Norris, Del Parks, Bob Tiernan, and John Watt. Democrats included Lee Beyer, Peter Courtney, Sam Dominy, Jim Edmunson, Kevin Mannix, Michael Payne and Bob Shiprack.

[116] Numerous suits have already been filed involving HB-3500. Supporters of gay rights have been more inclined to use the courts than the OCA. "Not only are we right, but we have better attorneys. We are going to slow, stymie and someday stop this religious tyranny," said Katherine A. McDowell, a member of the ACLU/Lawyers Guild that helped prepare a legal challenge to Ballot Measure 9. Katherine A. McDowell, "Acceptance Speech -- Award of Appreciation," Speech at the Third Annual Oregon Gay & Lesbian Law Association Dinner, Portland Oregon, 18 September 1993.

CHAPTER 4

THE EXECUTIVE BRANCH

I would rather be abused than ignored.

Sylvester Pennoyer
Governor of Oregon

Introduction

This section outlines Oregon's complex executive branch which has six statewide elected officials. The chapter concentrates on the governor and the budgeting process, but also discusses the secretary of state, the treasurer, the attorney general, the superintendent of public instruction and the commissioner of labor and industries. These subjects are presented as follows:

- A description of the six elected executives who govern Oregon.
- The basic role of the executive department.
- The politics of being governor.
- Budgeting and policy.
- Interactions with the Legislature on budgets.
- Other aspects of budgeting.

- Secretary of state.

- State treasurer.

- Superintendent of public instruction.
- Commissioner of labor and industries.
- Constitutional officials versus statutory officials.

Six Executives Over Oregon

Political scientists like to classify governors as being "weak" or "strong" depending how much formal power they have. Oregon's governor would be placed in the "weak" category for several reasons, not the least of which is that he or she shares executive power with five other statewide elected officials. As mentioned in Chapter 2, Oregon has a governor, a secretary of state, a state treasurer, an attorney general, a superintendent of public instruction and a commissioner of labor and industries. All of these individuals are elected independently; three of them are "constitutional" officers, e.g., their offices are authorized by the constitution and not by statute. These are the secretary of state, the state treasurer and the superintendent of public instruction. The attorney general and the commissioner of labor and industries are statutory officers. The significance of this will be discussed later.

In addition to these other statewide elected officials, the governor shares power with 191 appointed boards and commissions. These bodies make policy on matters ranging from apprenticeship (Apprenticeship & Training Council) to water (Watershed Enhancement Board). Most of these boards and commissions are appointed by the governor and most of their members must undergo State Senate confirmation.

The governor plays numerous administrative and political roles: being chief administrator, presenting a program and a budget to the Legislature, and fulfilling other duties such as granting pardons or making judicial appointments, to name a few. Which role is the most important is an academic question because it is an artificiality to separate theses various functions; while they can be discussed separately, they remain interrelated. A governor does not sit at his or her desk and say, "Now I am going to fulfill my role as chief administrator," any more than any other elected official.

The various roles are played simultaneously and with little consideration for any theoretical significance. In other words, officials make so many decisions so quickly that one must approach them as the expressions of a spontaneous art form and not a series of well thought-out chess moves.

The author's 1973 master's thesis was entitled <u>Partisan Voting in the Oregon Legislature</u>, and covered the 1969, 1971 and 1973 Legislative sessions.[1] The work examined how and why certain votes were cast by members of the Legislature and proved, among other profound things, that Republicans tend to vote more conservatively than Democrats! Six years later the author was lucky enough to participate in the very process that he had written about. He found his observations were correct, but he also discovered the time frame in which events such as floor votes, committee votes, and caucuses occurred was much more compressed than he had imagined. Because an official's actions are often analyzed over a long period of time, we tend not to appreciate the hectic pace of the original events. Governors, legislators, and other officials are not plodding master builders erecting a cathedral --they are usually policy gun fighters shooting from the hip.

The Executive Department

The State of Oregon has approximately 20,000 employees, almost all of whom answer to the governor. Among these agencies are the Departments of Human Resources, Corrections, Environment Quality, Parks and Recreation, Higher Education, and dozens of others. These agencies do most of the work of state government. In terms of budgets, the judicial and the legislative branches pale in comparison to the executive. The Assembly has a budget of approximately $38 million and the Judiciary has a budget of approximately $265 million. These amounts are minor when compared with the executive's $6.3 billion.[2] Notwithstanding the fact that there are six statewide elected officials, almost all executive department activities come under control of the governor.

Governors are rarely elected for their administrative abilities and it's obvious that they seldom have anything to do with the mundane operations of agencies. Governors do, however, appoint the heads of the agencies, control basic policies, and, most importantly, exercise budgetary control over agencies' activities.

Another basic duty is just being "The Governor," with the attendant ceremonies and the public appearances. Conventions, visiting foreign delegations, county fairs, parades --all these groups love to have the governor's presence.

Pardons, commutations, and reprieves are little noticed as gubernatorial duties except with respect to the death penalty. A pardon relieves the recipient of the offense, as if it had not happened. A reprieve is a temporary postponement of the execution of the sentence, (only applicable to the death penalty), and a commutation changes the sentence from death to some prison term. At this writing, the current governor, Barbara Roberts, has not had to face the commutation question; Oregon has not had an execution since 1962 when L.S. McGahuey was gassed,[3] although death-penalty cases are slowly winding through the court system.

Over the past several years the governor has taken on a very significant role in the area of economic development. Governor Neil Goldschmidt was particularly good at making deals and wooing industries to the state, such as Wacker Chemical.

The governor has a staff of approximately 30 people, the most important of whom is the chief of staff. The group includes special assistants for education, environmental, and human resources. She also has three press aides, a special projects coordinator, and an executive appointments director. One of the more important positions in the governor's office is that of legal counsel. This person handles general legal questions, extraditions, and judicial appointments. Legal counsel also acts as coordinator for pardons, commutations, and reprieves.

The governor is paid $80,000 a year, lives in a mansion known as Mahonia Hall in Salem, and has a permanent state police bodyguard. She is theoretically commander in chief of the Oregon Air and National Guard and appoints the adjacent general.

If the governor is disabled or dies, she is succeeded by the secretary of state. Next in succession are the state treasurer, the president of the Senate and the speaker of the House.[4] In 1947, the line of succession started with the president of the Senate, then went to the speaker of the House and the secretary of state.[5] As mentioned above, on October 28 of that year, Governor Earl Snell, Secretary of State Robert Farrell and Senate President Marshall Cornett were killed in a plane crash, along with their pilot Cliff Hogue. John Hall, speaker of the House, became governor and was then defeated in the Republican primary in 1948 by Douglas McKay. The chances of this triple disaster happening again are probably beyond comprehension.

Politics and the Governor -- Be Decisive, Don't Close Deer Season

If there were a typical Oregon governor, *he* would be a Republican businessman. Of the 25 chief executives in this century, 16 have been Republicans, eight have been Democrats and one was an Independent. In the nineteenth century half the ten governors were Democrats. Governors, like other politicians, reflect the demographics of their constituencies, but they also reflect their expectations. People generally elect a governor on what they hope he or she will do, but when it comes to re-election, there is an evaluation of what the governor has done. The press, the electorate, and history will judge a governor on the high-profile tasks described above --running agencies, cutting ribbons, and appointing judges are not what one is remembered for. The "politics" of being governor is really the politics of perception, of what people think you are doing. It could be called the politics of leadership, and there could be limited comparison to presidential leadership. Like a president, a governor has the "bully pulpit" of being head of a state, and must propose his or her program to the legislative branch. Unlike a president, a governor has no foreign-relations responsibilities. For a state like Oregon, however, a governor must also be the leading spokesperson to the federal government itself.

It is almost impossible to talk about gubernatorial leadership without talking about personalities. In the author's "political" lifetime he has had first hand knowledge of seven of the state's 35 governors: Robert Holmes, D --1957 to 1959, Mark Hatfield, R -- 1959 to 1967, Tom McCall, R --1967 to 1975, Robert Straub, D --1975 to 1979, Victor Atiyeh, R --1979 to 1987, Neil Goldschmidt, D --1987 to 1991 and Barbara Roberts, D -- 1991 to present. For each of these individuals, there were defining moments, incidents that created their political personas, the "stuff" of their gubernatorial style.

Robert Holmes was a Democratic State Senator, and the owner of several coastal radio stations, when he was elected Governor in 1956 by defeating Elmo Smith for a short two-year term.[6] Holmes was sometimes know as "Ho-hum Holmes," and in the 1958 election, his opponent was the dynamic young Republican secretary of state, Mark O. Hatfield. Close to the general election Holmes ordered deer hunting season closed because of fire danger. Hunters were irate and he was subsequently defeated. There is probably more to the story, but Holmes was defined by the closure of the hunting season.

To this day, Mark Hatfield presents himself as one of the most religious men in American politics. Hatfield has always been opposed to the death penalty; in 1964 he commuted the sentence of Jeannace June Freeman. The death penalty had been repealed by the voters in 1964, but the measure was not retroactive and Freeman was scheduled to be executed in the gas chamber. Her crime remains infamous in Oregon. On May 11, 1961, Freeman and her female lover Gertrude Nunez, threw Nunez's two children off a highway bridge into the 27-story-deep Crooked River Gorge.[7] Regardless, once the death penalty was repealed Hatfield commuted her sentence to life.[8] Although the public most likely disagreed with Hatfield's decision, the decision added to his reputation as a religious man not afraid to stand by his beliefs.

Tom McCall succeeded Hatfield in 1966 when he defeated Democrat Bob Straub. McCall, then secretary of state, was a former radio and TV personality. The press loved him and he is remembered by a whole series of incidents. Among them was famous line in 1971 when he told outsiders to visit, "But don't move here to live."[9] He was a fervent defender of Oregon's environment and remains the state's most popular Governor in memory.

McCall defeated Democrat Robert Straub twice for the governorship, in 1966 and 1970. Straub, a former state treasurer was finally elected in 1974, when he beat Republican State Senator Victor Atiyeh. Straub's style suffered in comparison to McCall. For example, when the energy crises struck, Straub responded by urging the public to put bricks in their toilets to save water. Before his defeat in 1978, bumper stickers appeared saying "NO MORE B.S."

Straub was defeated by the same man he had beat in 1974, Victor Atiyeh In addition to being a state senator, Atiyeh was a partner in one of Portland's oldest family businesses, Atiyeh Brothers' Carpets. Of Syrian descent, the family had come to Oregon at the turn of the century and thrived. During his first term, Atiyeh appeared dull and lackluster, his ratings dropped until he was considered easy prey for his 1982 opponent Democratic State Senator Ted Kulongoski. In the summer of 1982, Atiyeh called a Special Session of the Legislature to deal with a budget shortfall by expropriating approximately $81 million from the State Accident Insurance Fund, the state-owned workers' compensation company. In the opening address to the Special Session of the Legislature,

Atiyeh looked down at his state senator opponent and delivered a stern lecture about saving the state budget -- "You know it is the right thing to do," he said pointing his finger at Kulongoski.[10] Atiyeh never stopped being on the attack during the ensuing campaign and won handily.

Neil Goldschmidt came to the governorship in 1986 with the reputation of having been a dynamic mayor of Portland and a U.S. secretary of transportation under Jimmy Carter. To the astonishment of everyone, Goldschmidt only served one term. His two priorities were economic development and corrections, but it was the corrections issue that furnished his defining moment. Governor Goldschmidt oversaw the largest prison construction program in Oregon's history and appointed a new director of corrections from New Mexico Michael Francke. In the early morning of January 17, 1989, Francke was stabbed to death outside his office. Goldschmidt visited the crime scene and appeared at a news conference the same day. He was visibly shaken, and afterwards seemed to lose his enthusiasm for the office. Later that year, he announced that he was not running for re-election.

Barbara Roberts was the Democratic secretary of state when she defeated Republican Attorney General David Frohnmayer in the 1990 governor's race. Roberts ran a brilliant campaign against Frohnmayer and was lucky enough to have a conservative third party candidate in the race, Al Mobley, to divide the Republican vote. She was also unlucky enough to be elected at the same time that Oregon voters passed Ballot Measure 5 which drastically cut property taxes over a six-year period and mandated that the state general fund make up the lost school revenue. Ballot Measure 5 was mentioned in Chapter 3 and will be discussed extensively in later chapters.

Roberts knew Oregon was going to have to find a new source of revenue, i.e., a sales tax, but she chose to defer the question in the 1991 Session of the Legislature and then engage the voters in a "Conversation with Oregon." This was a comprehensive series of electronic town hall meetings designed to convince the public of the need for new taxes. Roberts didn't include the legislators in the "Conversation" then asked them to approve a sales taxes proposal without any input or changes during the three-day special session which occurred July 1 through July 3 of 1992. The measure failed in the Republican-controlled House, mainly due to the opposition of Speaker Larry Campbell. Roberts reacted bitterly saying that it was because she was a woman that the bill failed. The public was not happy and her ratings dropped to a point in the 1993 Legislative session where only 16 percent of the people approved of her performance. Roberts declined to run for re-election in 1994.

There are certain distinctive features of a successful gubernatorial style. First, decisiveness is rewarded. Voters like politicians who take stands. The first incident related, Governor Holmes canceling the deer hunting season, seems to belie this point, but the decision was a decision *not to do something*. Hunting, by its very nature, is decisive. Not allowing hunting presents an image of indecisiveness.

Second, it seems that a governor's style should be consistent with his or her politics. Hatfield was a moralist and made moralistic decisions. McCall was innovative and his politics were innovative. He was an iconoclast who loved a new idea, such as public access to beaches, or a bill requiring deposits on soft drink bottles. Atiyeh had his own kind of consistency. He was a Republican, businessman and as Governor he projected a stern but effective business attitude. Straub Goldschmidt and Roberts on the other hand, could never seem to make their styles and policies mesh.

The most important arena in which the governor must perform to gain approval is the legislative. "The governor proposes and the Legislature disposes" is a classic description of the relationship. If a governor is going to be a success, he or she must present a program to the Legislature and the Legislature must pass it. Governors are always in a quandary --should they propose a limited agenda or a comprehensive laundry list.

One of the problems with a long list of priorities is that it takes an immense amount of energy on the governor's part to lobby a lot of bills. Even though the governor has his or her own staff, legislators like direct contact. Gubernatorial duties don't stop during a legislative session, but the legislators expect to be courted and paid attention to. Most governors, in fact most chief executives, don't like dealing with the legislative branch; they would rather do the "fun" things such as being briefed by deferential agency heads, meeting with trade delegations, speaking to conventions, and enjoying the public's reverence. Most legislators don't have much respect for the governor, because they know they could do a better job if given the opportunity. Legislators love to tell governors what to do and always have a list of favors they want granted --appointments for friends, support of bills, or even a judgeship. Very few executives have the patience or wherewithal to effectively interact with all the lawmakers necessary to get a program adopted. President Lyndon Johnson was the exception. He had been a majority leader in the United States Senate, and was a master at counting votes, cajoling, and granting favors in exchange for votes.

"Exec" -- Writing Budget, Making Policy

The governor administers state agencies through the Department of Administrative Services, DAS. Until 1993, this agency was known as the "Executive Department." It was merged with the Department of General Services in the 1993 session, but it is still know as "Exec." This organization is the governor's "general staff" -- they give the orders and are the first links in the chain of command; most importantly they control the budget process. DAS has approximately 671 people working for it, a budget of $312 million, and several buildings, including one next to the state Capitol. It controls all agency budgets and personnel: it authorizes how much an agency may spend and how many people it may have on staff.

Government budgeting is an art form in itself, a world where things never are what they seem to be and truth is a precious commodity sparingly used. Oregon uses biennial budgets, e.g., two-year budgets that start on July 1 of the odd-numbered year and go to June 30 of the next odd-numbered year. Budget cycles are known by the numbers of the two years. For instance, at the moment of this writing the state is in the 1993 --1995 budget cycle. The next cycle will be the 1995 --1997 cycle which will start on July 1, 1995, and end June 30, 1997. This is different from the federal "fiscal year" budget cycle which starts on October 1 of each year.

Whether or not two-year budgets work is the subject of intense discussion in "reinventing government" circles. Budget grass always seems to be greener on the other side of the cycle. Those governments with annual budgets look to biennial budgets and vice versa. The biennial budget, starting July 1 of the odd-numbered year, meshes with Oregon's biennial Legislature which starts in January of the odd-numbered year and usually ends in June. The budget is actually "budgets," as there are 96 separate agency budget bills which are adopted by the end of the session just in time for the July 1 starting date. As mentioned earlier, Oregon cannot spend in the deficit, so the total budget must be a balanced budget. Indeed, the budget that is *submitted* to the Legislature by the governor must be a balanced budget. This latter requirement was the result of Republican Governor Atiyeh submitting budgets to the Legislature that assumed revenue increases without actually requesting taxes. The Democratic response, in 1985, was to pass a statute requiring a balanced budget.[11]

Budgets have four types of funds, or sources of money, to spend: general funds, other funds, federal funds, and lottery funds. Lottery funds will be discussed separately. The state's total budget for the 1993 --1995 fiscal year is approximately $20 billion. Of that amount approximately $6.3 billion is the general fund. The key to the budget is the general fund, 84 percent of it comes from the state income tax, other major sources include corporate taxes (6.2 percent), insurance taxes (2.1 percent), cigarette taxes (2.3 percent) and liquor taxes (1.4 percent).[12] General funds can be spent on any program, so this is where the governor and the Legislature can take the initiative. Ninety-nine percent of all budget battles involve questions of how to spend general funds. It is with general funds that the state pays for colleges, prisons, K --12 education and its share of human-resource programs.

"Other funds," are usually fees or dedicated funds such as the gas tax. These moneys can only be used for specific purposes. For example, fishing license fees can only be used for the Fish and Game Department and gas tax money can only be used for roads. Likewise, federal dollars can only be used for their assigned purposes. Most federal money comes into federal programs which the state administers, such as Medicaid.

One of the interesting aspects of budgeting in Oregon is when an agency is receiving "other funds" or federal funds it cannot spend without authorization.[13] Before any money can be expended by a state agency it must be appropriated, even if the agency has received the money from an outside source. Budgets which appropriate money in this manner are called "limitation" budgets or "spending limits" budgets. The limitation theoretically "limits" the amount of "other funds" or federal funds that they can spend. Agencies in other states do not use this system. They can receive federal money and spend it on their own initiative. This requirement is for all non-general-fund money, except grants received by the Department of Higher Education. If any agency receives a federal grant, a private gift, or a court settlement, it must go to the Legislature for a spending limit. The requirement for spending limits is a means to control policy, the size of state government, and the proliferation of programs. Once a program starts with federal money it has a tendency to develop a life of its own. If the federal money ends, the supporters of a program will ask the Legislature to fund it with general-fund money. This takes away the legislative option of funding their programs. Programs never die easily.

Agency budgets can be wholly general funds, other funds, federal funds, lottery funds, or a combination of funds. Each program in an agency will have its own funding source or sources. A budget always starts with a "reversion," the money that is left over from the last cycle. On the other end is the planned "ending balance" which turns into the next cycle's reversion. For instance, consider a small agency with a total biennial budget of approximately $200,000. If the agency ended that last budget cycle with an "ending balance" of $10,000, this is where it would start its new cycle. It would literally have $10,000 "in the bank" as it were. The budgeted ending balance usually resembles the last budget cycle's reversion.

The overall state budget has its own reversion and its own version of an ending balance, sometimes called a "prudent person" reserve. Traditional budgeting says that the overall state budget should have a 2.4 percent-prudent person reserve. It should be noted that when we are talking about these budgets, we are not talking about money that is already in the bank. Our $200,000 agency does not start out the budget cycle with $200,000 on hand. Its budget, indeed the whole state's general fund budget, is a budget based upon anticipated income, not immediately available money.

The theoretical agency will request a new budget from both the governor and the Legislature. Depending on its size, an agency will submit its initial request to the governor in the fall of the even-numbered year.[14] The governor, through DAS, will approve, reduce or perhaps increase the agency's requested budget. Most of the these budget decisions are made by executive-department personnel. If an agency disagrees with the judgment of "Exec" it can appeal to the governor.

It should be remembered that the department is carrying out the overall budget guidelines established by the governor. These guidelines are themselves established by the revenue available and the governor's agenda for the state. Does he or she want to start or eliminate programs? What does a governor want to do, to emphasize -- prisons, schools, welfare, healthcare? These are the political aspects of the budgeting process. The amount of revenue available is determined by the quarterly revenue projections from the Department of Administrative Services and the Department of Revenue.[15]

Once the governor has a final budget, it is submitted to the Legislature by December 1 of the even-numbered year.[16] This gives the Legislative Fiscal Office (LFO) time for their analysis of the budget. The LFO evaluates the budget and assists the members of the Ways and Means Committee in making appropriation decisions. When the legislators work on the budget they will be given a series of figures starting with the total budget amount of two biennia ago, the actual amount spent in the last biennium, the agency's requested amount and, finally, the governor's recommended amount. Our hypothetical agency would submit the following figures:

1989 --91 Actual	1991 --93 Actual	Agency Req.	Gov. Rec.
$180,000	$190,000	$210,000	$200,000

The Legislature theoretically works off the governor's recommended budget. Agency personnel are not supposed to request anything other than the governor's amount and they don't -- in public. In truth, agencies frequently go around the governor's back by contacting legislators informally. This is especially effective where a legislator has served on the Ways and Means Committee for several sessions and has developed a proprietary interest in the agency. They will have the feeling that they know the agency better than the governor or DAS. A smart agency head will have cultivated the relationship over several sessions and will be rewarded for his or her efforts.

Budgets are further broken down into specific categories; each category will have a series of "line items." Most budgets are referred to as "line-item budgets." Thus in our theoretical small agency there would be several "line items" personnel, travel, service and supplies, and so on. As mentioned, each line item would contain an amount for the last budget cycle, the current cycle, the agency's request and finally the governor's recommend amount.

Oregon theoretically uses a "zero base" budget system, whereby an agency has to fully justify every dollar requested. The key term here is "base." A "base," for a single line item or a total budget, is the amount that the agency was authorized in the last budget cycle plus inflation, plus money authorized by the Emergency Board (the Emergency Board will be discussed in the next chapter). The theory behind "zero base" budgeting was that an agency could not assume that it would get the same amount, or "base," in the new budget cycle that it got in the old cycle. Every budget cycle would start with a "zero base." This was supposed to make government more accountable and efficient. In reality, "zero base" budgeting has proven to be very impractical. There just is not enough time for legislative committees to examine every program every session -- to reinvent the wheel, so to speak.

Thus although we say Oregon uses "zero base" budgeting the base budget is usually a "given." It is only in extreme budget situations that agencies are forced to "go into the base" to cut existing programs. Agencies usually only have to justify additions to their base budget. These additions are set forth in a series of "decision packages" within the budget document. The agencies are also required to submit decision packages for reductions in program, but smart agencies always put the most popular programs on the block for reduction.

A lay person reading the preceding discussion will probably react incredulously. The description only confirms the feeling that government is inefficient, that politicians waste money, and that bureaucrats do nothing more than protect their own fiefdoms. This observation would only be partially true. In Oregon, as in other jurisdictions, there is an extremely limited amount of time for legislators to examine budgets, some agency budgets are given an hour or less for a hearing. In a six-month biennial legislative session, there are only so many hours to examine the 96 budgets which are presented. An agency official is no different from any other person with a job to do --he or she knows that the job is important, that no one really understands the importance or complexity of the work. You need to protect the few resources that you have.

Not only does the Legislature approve budgets, it also approves "position authority." It authorizes an agency to hire a certain number of people. This number is an agency's authorized "FTE." "FTE" is an acronym for the term Full Time Equivalent, that is one person working full time. Two people working half time would equal one FTE. Each agency has its total FTE and this cannot be changed without legislative authorization. FTEs are given just like budget amounts: last biennium's FTE, this biennium's FTE, agency request and so forth.

State agency personnel and the various FTEs are kept track of using a special computer system --Automatic Budget Information System or "ABIS" as it is usually known

To reiterate, budgets are put together by agencies, they are modified or approved by the governor through DAS, and then are sent to the Legislative Fiscal Office where they are further analyzed and presented to the Joint Ways and Means Committee.[17]

The governor's budget reflects the governor's policies and the changes made in the governor's budget by legislators reflect their own policy preferences. Again, a tremendous amount of policy is simply how much and where you spend money. But to spend money, you have to have money, and unless there is new or additional revenue, any money for new or enhanced programs must come from existing budgets. The governor has already worked his or her will on the existing budget, gathering and reassigning resources to reflect his or her policies. The same thing happens on a smaller scale in the Ways and Means process. This is where budgeting becomes an art form, an esoteric form of "Dungeon and Dragons," where the players' moves and countermoves are translated into real dollars and effects upon real lives.

Taking the Money

Indeed, the process resembles a game in which an agency presents its budget to legislators, who have their own agendas, and want part of the agency's money to pay for those agendas. There are a very few legislators who want to cut programs in order to cut taxes. It is much easier to point to a specific program, as a political accomplishment, than to a tax cut. Most programs have an identifiable impact on one district. Even the most conservative lawmakers eventually want to increase programs. In the 1993 Session, the House Ways and Means Co-Chair was John Minnis, R-Gresham. Minnis was notoriously anti-tax and anti-government except when it came to *his* programs. He led the fight to cut education budgets and at the same time insisted on increasing money for prisons. Minnis was a Portland Police Detective and believed he knew what was really important for the state. Before you can take the money, as it were, you have to have some credible reasoning process. You have to have some rationale for your actions. A Ways and Means Committee cannot just tell an agency to cut current programs by 10 percent and then turn over the money. Legislators want to appear reasonable. Chapter 5 will discuss some of the institutional aspects of the Ways and Means process, but here we will examine some of the moves and counter-moves in this game. Where and how does a legislator get money out of the governor's budget?

You always start with new programs. If an agency's new program has been funded, you can reject the program and take the money. The next thing that you look at is the agency's services and supplies account. How much money did they spend last time and how much do they want to spend this time? Did they purchase equipment last cycle that they won't need to purchase this next cycle, but still have the money in the budget?

From service and supplies you go to vacancies, unfilled FTE. Even though a position may be vacant, no one is actually in the job, the agency will still be getting funds to pay for the position. Agencies use these moneys to pay for increased salaries for other employees. A person may be hired for a job at one civil service level, but within that level there are certain "merit pay" steps which involve increased pay. If the money for the higher pay is not in the agency's budget, it has to be paid out of salary amounts received for the vacant positions. If the Ways and Means Committee eliminates the vacancy, it can transfer the money to other projects or budgets.

Oregon law requires that all agencies use the attorney general's office for all of their legal matters. The AG's office charges agencies on a per hour basis and this expense is an item in each agency's budget. Since almost all legal expenses are unanticipated, i.e., there is no need for the money until an actual case arises, the Legislature can argue that the agency won't get into trouble and doesn't really need all the money that it has budgeted. Attorney general charges will be discussed later.

Another way to save general fund money is to pay for some salary or expense with federal money or other fund money. For example, an administrator in an agency may be being paid by general fund dollars to oversee federal fund or other fund programs. The Ways and Means Committee can allocate federal dollars, or other fund dollars, to pay the administrator's salary on the grounds that what he or she is doing is a federal or other fund program function. The usual term for this maneuver is "backing out general fund dollars." This is one case where the agency will not object too vigorously to the Legislature's action. There is, however, the threat of federal legal action to recover the misspent dollars.

There are several other ways to turn federal dollars or other fund dollars into general funds. One is building depreciation. Federal law allows the state to charge federal programs for the depreciation of the building which the federal programs use. The same applies to other fund use of buildings. Inevitably, these moneys accumulate and can be used to build new facilities. This relieves the state of the necessity of using general funds for construction.

Finally, there is a Governmental Services Expenses[18] charge that is levied against all programs by the DAS and the Legislature for their "service" in administering all programs. This is an interesting concept, that one part of a government would charge another part for governing. It reminds one of a Medieval execution where the man or woman about to die must pay his or her own executioner. But then again, death and taxes...

These above examples are just the tip of the iceberg as far as budgeting is concerned. Human ingenuity knows no bounds where money is concerned, especially with it large amounts of other people's money.

More Budgeting

The major exception to the usual line-item budget process is the Oregon State System of Higher Education. "Higher Ed," as it is called, does not present a line item budget to either DAS or the Legislature. It requests a lump sum amount with only general descriptions of enhanced or reduced programs at the various colleges and universities. Oregon has eight institutions of higher learning that are supposed to be governed by the 11-member State Board of Higher Education.[19] The theory is that individual schools should not come before the Legislature and ask for increased programs at the expense of other schools. Budget allocations between the schools should be made by the board and not by legislative pork-barrel politics. This is a perfect example of a theory that has no relationship to reality. Each college does have a presence at the Legislature and individual programs are funded.

Over the years, the attitude of the Legislature toward higher education has not been good. Lawmakers have traditionally been under the impression that Higher Ed is "fat" and that colleges do nothing more than waste tax payers' dollars. Much of this attitude is a result of the very fact that the Legislature doesn't look at actual budgets in Higher Ed. When they don't see the detail of line-item budgets, they assume the worse. In addition, there is the impression that Higher Education administrators are overpaid. Whether they are overpaid is questionable, but regardless, they are the best paid of any group of state employees. The highest compensated individual in state government is the Chancellor of the State System who receives approximately $133,000 per year. The President of the Health Sciences Center, who is a physician, would argue that he is underpaid at only $131,000 per year in the medical profession where the average American doctor makes $205,000 a year.[20] Needless to say, such considerations do not go over well with legislators whose salaries are the lowest in state government.[21]

Other salary matters are handled by the Salary Sub-Committee of the Ways and Means Committee. Salaries come in three categories: classified or union employees, unclassified executives, and elected officials. The latter are set by statute and are a perennial source of controversy. Ironically, elected official salaries, including judges, account for less than one-half of one percent of the general fund budget. The lion's share of salary expenditure is consumed by classified or union employees. Almost all salaries in state government are set by negotiations between the unions and the DAS. Once these salaries are established, there is little the Legislature can do but fund them. The assembly has almost no desire to get involved with salary questions. They don't need the political pressure from the unions to grant salary increases or the political heat for giving them.

Capital construction is always an interesting aspect of state government budgeting. Buildings are never cheap, and as we will see, they can become a political liability if the public perceives them to be too expensive. The actual decision to build is made by the Capital Construction Sub-Committee of Ways and Means.

The Secretary of State -- "Phillip" has two "l's."

As mentioned, the secretary of state is Oregon's lieutenant governor and is first in line of succession;[22] traditionally the secretary of state's post has been the stepping stone for future governors. Three of Oregon's last six governors held the secretary of state's office.[23] In many ways, the position is an anomaly. It is a partisan office, but has few if any policy functions and most of its duties are ministerial.[24] For example, the secretary of state is the official keeper of the state seal and can authorize who may use it.[25, 26] The secretary of state is paid $61,500 per year[27] and has a staff of 233 people.[28]

However, the secretary of state is the chief elections officer for Oregon and is responsible for the regulation of campaigns and the holding of elections. Candidates file for office with the secretary of state and are also required to periodically turn in "Contributions and Expenditure" reports.[29] The Secretary has jurisdiction over election law violations and can recommend criminal prosecution to the attorney general. Violations can go from minor infraction such as not putting a "disclaimer" on a letter,[30] to major offenses such as using the term "re-elect," when one is not actually running for re-election.[31]

A major election task for the secretary of state is the preparation and publication of the Oregon Voters' Pamphlet before each primary and general election. The pamphlet is printed as a series of pamphlets for the different jurisdictions. It contains ballot measures, arguments for and against ballot measures, and candidates' statements. The Voters' Pamphlet is an integral part of the Oregon election process and a candidate's

Voters' Pamphlet statement is considered to be *the* most important piece of literature he or she puts out. Legislative candidates are allowed one page and pay a fee of $300, other candidates, for United States senator as an example, are allowed two pages and pay a higher fee. These fees don't cover even a fraction of the actual cost of the pamphlet, so it becomes a form of publicly financed campaigning.

Anyone can buy a page and enter an argument for or against a ballot measure. In addition, each ballot measure has official arguments for and against.

In 1992 anti-gay Ballot Measure 9 elicited ten arguments for and 57 arguments against! One statement has become a tongue-in-cheek classic. It pointed out that eating oysters was prohibited by the Old Testament Book of Leviticus, just as homosexuality was! The Special Righteousness Committee argued that all "immoral" behavior like oyster-eating, beard-shaving and the cross-breading of cattle should also be banned. The argument ended with the unique political slogan -- "AGREE WITH US OR BURN IN HELL." Interestingly enough, the courts sometimes use ballot measure statements to divine the intent of the authors of the measures themselves.

Another very technical duty of the secretary of state is to oversee the filing of "security interests" under the Uniform Commercial Code (UCC). These UCC filings are the means by which businesses know which bank, lending institution, or other business, has a lien on business property such as inventory or equipment.[32] UCC filings work in the same manner as mortgages only on personal as opposed to real property. Thousands of these filing are made each month and the secretary of state has developed an extensive computer system to handle the process of filing and inquiry.

The secretary of state also has the "Audit" function for all state agencies.[33] They essentially check how well financial and other records are being kept. At times these audits can be very political. After the murder of Michael Francke in 1989, the Corrections Division was subjected to a vigorous audit. Now, the secretary of state also has the authority to do "program audits" which go beyond financial matters. The right to do program audits was obtained after a long political battle. A typical governor does not want to be second guessed by the secretary of state on how he or she runs a state agency. This is especially true if the governor and the secretary of state are from different parties.

Being the official custodian of the state archives is another duty of the secretary of state. All state records are eventually turned over to the office and housed in the new archives building. The "Cecil Edward's Archives Building," was completed in 1992 and immediately became controversial. Carpet and light fixtures were expensive, but they were meant to be. The building was supposed to have a monument-like quality. This was the very intent of the original members of the Ways and Means sub-committee that approved the initial plans in the late 1980s.[34]

Regardless, the building was an issue in 1992. Secretary of State Phil Keisling was appointed in 1991 by Barbara Roberts as her replacement after she was elected governor. In Keisling's 1992 campaign to keep the office, his Republican opponent Randy Miller spent most of his time attacking him for the archives building. Keisling won easily in spite of the building.[35]

The Secretary of State was not so lucky when it came to the publication of the 1993-94 Oregon Blue Book.[36] These biennial almanacs have been the source of much of the information in this book and have been published by the secretary of state's office since 1911. The latest edition was 441 pages and is a compendium of every imaginable fact about Oregon including names, photos, and addresses of all elected officials, descriptive listings of agencies, commissions, boards, cities, counties and public institutions, and various financial and budget statistics. It also includes a history of the state, a listing of the state animal,[37] bird,[38] dance,[39] nut,[40] fish,[41] flower,[42] gemstone,[43] insect,[44] rock,[45] and tree.[46] Finally, it contains the Oregon Constitution and a comprehensive list of all print and electronic media.

Along with all the usual information, the 1993-94 Oregon Blue Book also contained 73 very noticeable errors. An embarrassed secretary of state's office had to publish a four- page errata sheet. The book gave incorrect dates, left out biographical information on several officials, (not a great loss in some cases), and even failed to mention one major agency. The unkindest cut of all was the misspelling of Secretary of State Keisling's first name, i.e., "Philip" instead of the correct "Phillip." One observer noted that the book had set a new standard, "Not even close enough for government work."

The State Treasurer -- On-the-Job Training for Wall Street

The current State Treasurer is Democrat Jim A. Hill Jr., the first African-American to be elected to statewide office in Oregon. Hill served as a state representative and state senator before being elected in 1992. The office is partisan and the treasurer is second in line of succession to the governor after the secretary of state.[47] The treasurer is paid $61,500 per year[48] and has a staff of 70 people.[49]

The primary responsibility for the treasurer is being the state's chief investment officer. Investment funds total over $14 billion. The largest of these funds is that for the Public Employee Retirement System.

There is also the Local Government Investment Fund which invests money from cities and counties. This is a large fund and generated $274.5 million in interest in 1990. The state treasurer also plays a crucial role in seeing that the state's bond rating is kept at a high level. Both the state and the local governments sell bonds for roads, construction and other capital projects. These bonds are rated by such organizations as Standards and Poors. The higher the rating ("AAA"), the lower interest has to be paid. Investments are controlled by a "prudent person rule."

The treasurer also processes all state checks and warrants. Because of the interest generated by the state treasurer's handling of various funds, the office uses no general-fund money. One of the more interesting programs is the loaning of bonds and securities to other institutions for a fee. A brokerage will sell stock or bonds that it does not have in its possession. To fulfill the requirements of the law, the brokerage needs to physically have control of the paper, so Oregon bonds or stocks are moved from one side of a safe to another, and Oregon receives a small fee for the temporary use of its property.

The immense size of Oregon's investment portfolio makes it a major player on Wall Street. When the Oregon treasurer talks, money people listen. The treasurer makes frequent trips to New York to negotiate with underwriters and other financial institutions and this has made for a somewhat "close" relationship between the office and Wall Street. Two of Oregon's last three treasurers have resigned to work for Wall Street investment firms, Clay Myers in 1984 and Bill Rutherford in 1987. This prompted the Legislature to pass a revolving-door law which prohibited such employment.[50] Myers and Rutherford were Republicans with a natural affinity to Wall Street and were both successful and respected in their new occupations. Notwithstanding the revolving-door law, it will be interesting to see if a Democrat can get a comparable job in the financial world -- the ultimate in affirmative action.

The Attorney General -- Not So Free Legal Advice

The attorney general (AG) of the State of Oregon runs the largest "law office" in the state with 180 attorneys. The Department of Justice docs all (emphasize *all*) the legal work for the state. This is a partisan office like the governor, secretary of state and treasurer. The attorney general is paid $66,000 per year[51] and has a total staff of 705 people.[52]

The most important aspect of the office is that it has almost total control of all legal matters in which the state becomes involved.[53] State agencies do not have their own legal counsel to handle court cases, instead they use deputy AG's assigned to them by the Department of Justice. As mentioned, the agencies are charged on a per-hour basis by the AG.[54] The current hourly charge is $73 per hour and again, is a line item found in every agency budget. This system was established in 1971 by Attorney General Lee Johnson.

The system has advantages and disadvantages. It does make for an overall coordinated legal strategy for the state: the state speaks with one voice. There is one major problem with the system, however. In a regular attorney-client relationship, the client can fire the attorney. The attorney has to do what the client says unless it is unethical. Here the situation is different. The client cannot fire the attorney and the attorney doesn't really work for the client, but for the AG. A deputy AG is not answerable to the head of the agency, but to the attorney general himself or herself. If policy and legal questions could always be separated this would not be a problem, but there are numerous occasions where this hasn't been the case. There has been a great deal of tension between the AG and the Bureau of Labor and Industries over what the state's position should be in employment discrimination cases.

There are several other functions of the AG's office which are not directly connected to agencies, such as the collection of child support and consumer protection. The attorney general also oversees charitable organizations in the state.

A quasi-judicial service of the AG office is to write official "attorney general opinions." The "opinions" are binding on state agencies and are published like court opinions. Opinions can be requested by any official or agency and the AG charges his or her usual per-hour fee. Some of these opinions can be extremely important in the making of public policy, but unfortunately, they are sometimes wrong.

When officials request an AG opinion they almost always know what the answer is going to be before they formally make the request. Informal contacts and discussions are not unusual. One pays a lawyer to hear what one wants to hear.

Superintendent of Public Instruction -- Leading the Unleadable

Oregon has 295 school districts, a seven-member State Board of Education appointed by the governor, and a nonpartisan elected superintendent of public instruction. Theoretically the superintendent and the board provide leadership and coordination for all of the school districts and Oregon's 16 community colleges. In reality, neither the superintendent nor the board has a great deal of authority over Oregon schools. Most substantive educational policy, for example how many days children are to be in school, is set by the Legislature. Details of administration are handled by the locally elected boards. More importantly, the superintendent and the board have no authority over school finance. (See Chapter 11 on perennial issues.) Thus where there is a superintendent, a board and a bureaucracy known as the Education Department, there really is no "state" system per se. The superintendent is paid $61,500 per year[55] and has a staff of 643 people.[56]

The current superintendent of public instruction, Norma Paulus, has tried to go beyond the traditional limits of the office. She has been a strong advocate of the Oregon Education Act for the 21st Century, a bill passed in the 1991 Legislative Session.[57] The measure was part of the nation wide education reform movement which started in 1983 with the publication of A Nation at Risk, by the National Commission on Excellence in Education.[58]

The original act was sponsored by Rep. Vera Katz, D-Portland. In a rush to look as if it was doing something about education, the Legislature passed the bill but gave it no significant funding. Unfortunately, this has been a pattern in most American jurisdictions. Education reform is easy to talk about, but in the final analysis it takes increased resources. Regardless of educational fashion, excellence takes more teachers who are themselves better educated and better motivated. There is no substitute for good teachers and reasonable class size, but both of these things inevitably cost money. The Katz bill did little for actual teaching conditions. It set higher standards for students, lengthened the school year and funneled high school kids into vocational and college prep programs after the tenth grade.

Commissioner of Labor and Industries --The Other Roberts

In Chapter 1, the peculiar phenomenon of Oregon political nepotism was discussed. As mentioned, the commissioner of labor and industries is Mary Wendy Roberts, the step-daughter of the current governor, Barbara Roberts. Commissioner Roberts is a Democrat and the office, which is partisan, has been held by Democrats since 1955. It was established in 1903 and was originally called the "labor commissioner." The commissioner is paid $61,500 per year[59] and has a staff of 168 people.[60]

The Bureau of Labor and Industries oversees the state's apprenticeship training program, handles wage claims under the Wage and Hour Division and enforces employment laws relating to working conditions.

A more contemporary duty is to enforce laws regarding discrimination in employment, housing, and public accommodations. The bureau maintains a staff of civil rights investigators and processes thousands of claims a year. Commissioner Roberts has been one of the state's strongest advocates for civil rights.

Constitutional and Statutory Officials --Back to the Budgets

As mentioned earlier, there are two types of statewide elected executives in Oregon, constitutional and statutory. The governor, secretary of state, treasurer, and superintendent of public instruction are constitutional officers. The attorney general and the commissioner of labor and industries are statutory officers.

The major consequence of this difference is in budgeting. All budgets go to DAS for evaluation, but the budgets of the three constitutional officers, other than the governor, are not subject to reduction by the governor. This means that even though the attorney general and commissioner of labor and industries are independently elected, there is some control by the governor.

An interesting question is who makes policy for the state? The governor's role is obvious, but policy-making authority for other statewide elected officials doesn't follow constitutional lines. Oregon's secretary of state is a constitutional officer and next in line of succession to the governor, however he or she has little ability to affect the actual policies of the state. The attorney general, on the other hand, has immense power due to his or her control of the state's litigation and the ability to render attorney general opinions.

The obvious question to ask is how much cooperation is there among these six elected officials? The answer is, as much as necessary to make them look good. People do not end up elected to statewide office because they lack ambition. Much of the interaction between these players is political, e.g., they want to be perceived as leaders. All, other than the governor, want to be perceived as future governors. So much of what they say and do is designed to present themselves in the best light. Whether this system of six elected executives is an effective means of government remains to be decided by history.

---

1   Thomas L. Mason, "Partisan Voting in the Oregon Legislature" (M.S. thesis, Portland State University, 1973).

2   Oregon, Legislative Fiscal Office, <u>Budget Highlights, Legislatively Approved 1993-95 Budget</u>, (Salem: Legislative Fiscal Office, 1993) D-12, D-13.

3   The State of Oregon has executed 58 men since 1903. Prior to that executions were carried out by the county sheriffs.

4   Or. Const. art. V, sec. 8a.

5   Or. Const. art. V, sec. 8 (1946).

6   As mentioned earlier, when an Oregon official is replaced, the replacement only serves until the next general election when he or she must run for the office. Holmes defeated Republican Elmo Smith who had replaced the late Governor Paul Patterson who died in office on January 31, 1956. Patterson had been elected in 1954 and would not have had to run for re-election until 1958. Elmo Smith's son, Denny, was elected to Congress in 1980, defeated in 1990 and ran for governor in 1994.

7   Donald P. Myers, "Parole Board to Review Freeman Case," <u>The Oregon Journal</u>, 5 March 1979, 1, 10.

8   Freeman was paroled in 1983.

9   Tom McCall and Steve Neal, <u>Tom McCall: Maverick</u>, (Portland: Binford & Mort, 1977), 190.

10   The man that Governor Atiyeh lectured is now Oregon's Attorney General. Although Republican Attorney General Dave Frohnmayer told the Legislature that the proposed action would be legal, the courts were not impressed and eventually ordered the money given back. <u>Eckles v. Oregon</u>, 306 OR 380, 760 P 2d 846 (1988).

11   ORS 291.216 (7).

12   Oregon, Secretary of State, <u>Oregon Blue Book 1993-1994</u>, Salem: Secretary of State, 1993), 371.168-169.

[13] See ORS 293.550 (5).

[14] Large agencies have a deadline of September 1, while small agencies have a cut off date of August 1. See ORS 291.288.

[15] ORS 291.342.

[16] ORS 291.223.

[17] At least this was the structure until 1993 when House Speaker Larry Campbell changed the system by House Rule and established separate Appropriations Committees.

[18] ORS 291.272 --291.290

[19] ORS Chapter 351.

[20] Statistical Abstract of the United States 112th Ed, 104.

[21] ORS 171.072.

[22] Or. Const. art. V, sec. 8a.

[23] Governors Hatfield, McCall and Roberts.

[24] ORS Chapter 177.

[25] ORS 186.023 (1).

[26] When Governor Victor Atiyeh left office in 1987, he established an international consulting business and listed himself, on his letterhead, as the former Governor of Oregon. He was not allowed to use the state seal and instead used the old seal of the Oregon Territory.

[27] As of July 1st, 1992.

[28] Legislative Fiscal Office, Budget Highlights, Legislatively Approved 1993-95 Budget, C-2.

[29] ORS Chapter 260.

[30] A "disclaimer" is a statement on any piece of campaign material which states who authorized and paid for the piece. ORS 260.522.

[31] This particular offense will cost you your office should you win the election. ORS 260.355.

[32] ORS 79.4025.

[33] Or. Const. art. VI, sec. 2; ORS 293.505, 293.590.

[34] The author chaired the sub-committee.

[35] Other candidates also tried to make the building an issue. One Republican state representative, Jerry Barnes of Ashland, toured his district waving a ragged piece of the carpet and said how proud he was to have voted against such extravagance ($120 per yard). His voters thanked him and promptly retired him for other sins.

[36] ORS 177.120.

[37] Beaver.

[38] Western Meadowlark.

[39] Square Dance.

[40] Hazelnut.

[41] Chinook Salmon.

[42] Oregon Grape.

[43] Oregon Sunstone.

[44] Oregon Swallowtail Butterfly.

[45] Thunderegg.

[46] Douglas Fir.

[47] Or. Const. art. V, sec. 8a.

[48] As of July 1st, 1992.

[49] Legislative Fiscal Office, Budget Highlights, Legislatively Approved 1993-95 Budget, C-2.

[50] ORS 244.045 (3).

[51] As of July 1st, 1992.

[52] Legislative Fiscal Office, <u>Budget Highlights, Legislatively Approved 1993-95 Budget</u>, C-1.

[53] ORS 180.060.

[54] ORS 180.170.

[55] As of July 1st, 1992.

[56] Legislative Fiscal Office, <u>Budget Highlights, Legislatively Approved 1993-95 Budget</u>, C-1.

[57] Oregon, Sixty-Sixth Oregon Legislative Assembly, House Bill 3565.

[58] Kantrowitz, Barbara, et al, "A Nation Still at Risk," <u>Newsweek,</u> 19 April 1993, 46-49.

[59] As of July 1st, 1992.

[60] Legislative Fiscal Office, <u>Budget Highlights, Legislatively Approved 1993-95 Budget</u>, C-2.

CHAPTER 5

THE LEGISLATURE

One should never see either sausage or laws being made.

Attributed to
Otto von Bismarck

Introduction -

This chapter is intended to comprehensively depict the legislative process in Oregon. It covers these topics:

- Legislative lawmaking and its relationship to the initiative and the referendum.
- The constitutional and theoretical nature of legislative power.
- Length and frequency of legislative sessions.
- The effect of small legislative districts on membership.
- Leadership selection.
- Basic rules and procedures.
- Committees.
- Bills.
- Bill referral.
- Committee work.
- Ways and Means.
- Revenue.
- Judiciary.
- Other Committees

- Floor procedures.
- Third readings.
- Legislative maneuvering.
- Keeping track of legislation.
- Socialization of legislators.
- Legislative language.
- Reasons for voting.
- Partisan aspects of voting.
- Control of the legislature.
- Unanticipated events.
- Dynamics of the session.
- Ending sessions.
- The longest session.

From Fish to Nuts

The Legislative Assembly is Oregon's basic lawmaking institution. It considers everything from taxes to crime, from traffic laws to college tuition, from fish hatcheries to the Oregon Filbert Commission. Besides the initiative and referendum, the actions of the Assembly affect the lives of ordinary Oregonians more than any other civic decision-making process. Although the Oregon Legislature is similar to those in other states, it has some unique aspects which give the Assembly its institutional character. This chapter will examine both the typical lawmaking process and these interesting local variations. It will conclude with a description of the most recent session.

Legislative Power --"Be It Enacted..."

As discussed in Chapter 3, "Legislative" authority, in Oregon, is not held solely by the Assembly. The initiative and referendum are the real source of political power in the state when it comes to major issues. Article IV, Section 1 of the Oregon Constitution provides:

> The Legislative Power of the state, except for the initiative and referendum powers reserved to the people, is vested in a Legislative Assembly, consisting of a Senate and a House of Representatives...[1]

Thus, the constitution merely vests power to make laws in the Assembly to the extent it is not reserved to the people by the initiative and referendum. In Oregon, the people temporarily relinquish their legislative power during legislative sessions, when it is "vested" in the Assembly. As the speaker of the House and Senate president bang their gavels to start each legislative session, the Legislature is gingerly given authority to enact laws on *behalf* of the people. This relationship demonstrates an interesting historical "evolution" of the concept of sovereignty. A bill in the British Parliament starts with the phrase, "Be it enacted by her Royal Majesty with the advise and consent of Lords...and Commons." Similarly, a bill introduced in the United States Congress begins, "Be it enacted by the Congress of the United States." But, bills introduced in the Oregon Legislature start with the words, "Be it enacted by the *people* of the state of Oregon," (Emphasis added). All three bodies are democratic, but the "sovereignty" is found in different places. As representative democracy moved to the New World and the American West, it became more "democratic." Politics changed, perhaps even to the extent that it is not "representative" democracy anymore. The great historian Frederick Jackson Turner considered the frontier essential to the continued development of democracy. Turner equated the availability of free land on the frontier with economic power and he observed that "....economic power secures political power."[2]

Legislative Sessions --Beginnings, Endings, Frequency and Length

Each Legislative Assembly formally begins with the governor giving a speech to a joint session of the House and Senate. The end is marked, six or more months later, by the simultaneous declaration of the two presiding officers that the session is adjourned "*sine die*" or "without date."

Only seven states -- Oregon, Arkansas, Kentucky, Montana, Nevada, North Dakota, and Texas -- still have biennial legislatures. In Oregon, the regular legislative session starts on the second Monday in January of the odd-numbered year. Sessions used to last approximately six months, but they are becoming longer. At the turn of the century they were approximately two months in duration. Some increase in the length occurred during the Depression, but it was not until the fifties and sixties that meetings got appreciably longer. The 1981 session was the longest, until 1993, running from January 13 to August 1, a total of 202 days -- due to a budget shortfall and the need to reapportion both legislative and congressional districts. The 1993 session was the Sixty-Seventh Legislative Assembly and lasted 207 days. Special sessions of the Assembly can be called by the governor[3] or the Legislature itself.[4] There have been 28 special sessions and they have varied in length from one to 37 days.[5]

Membership -- The Politics of Small Districts

The Oregon Legislature is a relatively small body, with 60 members in the House and 30 members in the Senate. Two house districts make up each senate district, and after the 1991 census, each of these house districts had a population of 47,372 people -- consequently each senate district had a constituency of 94,744. Approximately 25 percent of the members of the House are new each session; the turnover is less in the State Senate.[6] Representatives serve two-year terms and senators serve for four-year terms, thus half of the Senate is elected every two years.

At the present time, all House and Senate districts are "single-member districts." Before 1971, some legislative districts in urban areas, such as Portland and Eugene, were "multi-member districts." That is, several legislators were elected from one large district, rather than one member from one district. Single-member districts are the result of the efforts of Secretary of State Clay Myers. Myers drew the final legislative lines in the 1971 reapportionment process[7] and eliminated the multi-member districts.

These single member districts have had a significant impact on legislative politics. It was initially assumed that single member districts would favor Republican candidates who could focus their greater financial resources on smaller areas. The opposite has proven to be true. House districts are now small enough that any candidate can literally knock on every door. Although money plays an increasingly important role in legislative races, individual effort continues to be the most important factor in getting elected.

Selecting The Leadership --"What Have You Done for Me Lately?"

Oregon's biennial legislative process really begins immediately after the general election with the selection of legislative leadership for the next session. Leadership includes the speaker of the House, the president of the Senate, the speaker *pro tempore*, the president *pro tempore*, house and senate majority and minority leaders and assistant majority and minority leaders, sometimes known as "whips." The speaker, the president, the speaker *pro tempore* and president *pro tempore* are constitutional officers formally elected by the bodies on the first day of the session. The majority and minority leaders, in both the House and the Senate, are leaders of their parties in the two houses and are elected by the caucuses themselves, ie.g., House Democrats, House Republicans, Senate Democrats, and Senate Republicans meeting as separate groups.

When the majority parties in the House and Senate meet immediately after the November election they select the speaker, the president, and their caucus leaders. Minority parties select caucus leaders only. These post-election caucuses are attended by members who have been re-elected, mid-term senators in the Senate, as well as newly elected members who have not yet been sworn in. Caucuses traditionally take place on either the Thursday or Sunday evening following the Tuesday general election.

Becoming a legislative leader is much more than something accomplished in one meeting. The speakership or the Senate presidency can be the culmination of an entire political career. In the long, ongoing process of leadership selection, friendships are made, reputations are guarded, favors are performed, and grudges are remembered. An individual running for a leadership position starts to garner support months before the actual election in a long and arduous effort. This is an intensely human endeavor and must be seen from the inside to be appreciated in its complex subtlety.

There are four basic reasons why one member will vote for a particular legislator for speaker or president. The first is purely political -- what did you do for me in the last election? Traditionally, leadership hopefuls make substantial contributions to other candidates, essentially using their own campaign treasuries as a political action committee. This is understood by contributors, especially the lobby which is interested in the selection of speaker or president. Thus, speaker candidate "X" goes to interest group "Y" and asks for a contribution, not only to fund his or her campaign, but to finance his or her efforts for speakership. Leadership aspirants will also tour the state recruiting candidates, supplying campaign help and advice, as well as giving financial support. Some of this assistance can be as mundane as taking photos or even going door to door for the prospective legislators. The psychology is simple --a legislator will feel indebted to someone who helped him or her get elected.

The second reason why legislators will vote for someone for speaker or president is their perception of how well the individual will do the job. Competence does play a role; most lawmakers want the legislative session to go well.

A third related factor is ideology. Conservatives do not want a speaker or president who will embarrass them by constantly putting liberal items on the agenda. Portland legislators are considered suspect by rural members and *vice versa*. Where does the leadership candidate stand on the "gut" issues -- sales tax, abortion, gun control, land use, gay rights?

In the last analysis, however, the final reason is the most important. What can the speaker or the president do for you? What committee assignment or chairmanship will they give you? Thus the most political of all phrases -- What's in it for me? In essence, committee slots are used to purchase the speakership or the presidency. Under the rules of both houses, the presiding officers officially appoint the committees at the beginning of the legislative session, but in reality this is the culmination the earlier political process. Bargaining for committee assignments goes on from the moment an individual becomes a candidate for leadership. It becomes an elaborate dance, an extended mating game.

All committees are not equal. Ways and Means (the appropriation committee), Revenue and Judiciary are the most desirable committees. There is almost a pecking order of assignments, starting with the co-chair slot of the Ways and Means Committee at the top, to the chair of Revenue, membership on Ways and Means, chair of Judiciary, then on down to the rest of the committee chairs. Freshman legislators traditionally do not chair committees in the House, so their main concern is committee membership.

Over the years, there has been a proliferation of committees, so virtually everyone gets some desirable committee assignment. There were 17 "standing committees" in the House and 16 standing committees in the Senate in 1991. A "standing committee" is a committee that meets regularly during the session. The math is simple. It takes 31 votes out of 60 to elect a speaker and 16 out of 30 to elect the Senate president. Let's look at the House:

Chairs	17
Ways and Means	8
Majority Leader	1
Speaker Pro Tem.	1
Whip	1
Total	28

These are the positions that people vie for there are not quite 31 plums to hand out, but there are generally enough. Given that there will be a certain number of freshman legislators who cannot expect a chairmanship, everybody will receive some position. Other factors also come into play. There is no formal seniority system in Oregon for either house, but it is a consideration. Legislators let it be known that they consider themselves to have waited in line and to have "paid their dues." This is especially true for the coveted positions on the Ways and Means Committee. The House has several other rules which tend to spread the wealth, as it were (i.e., members of Ways and Means cannot serve on other committees and the speaker, speaker *pro tempore* and Whip cannot chair regular committees, although the majority leader usually does chair the Rules Committee). The Senate does not have these rules and members are allowed more than one major assignment.

Again, the bargaining process is subtle, complex and extended. Overtures are always phrased in tentative terms:

> Speaker candidate --"What committee are you interested in?" (What do you want?)
> Representative --"I like Revenue, it needs strong leadership next session..." (I want to chair Revenue.)
> Speaker candidate --"I can't make any promises, but if I'm speaker I think you would do a great job." (OK, but I need your vote.)
> Representative --"I'll support you." (It's a deal.)

Deals are made, but they are always put in ambiguous language to give the players flexibility, if not deniability. No one wants to admit to ever actually promising something.

To start the initial post-election caucus, where leaders are selected, the most senior member takes the gavel and calls the meeting to order. The first agenda item is the adoption of the rules for the caucus itself. These are crucial, because within the rules are the requirements and procedures for the subsequent leadership elections. From 1979 to 1989, the House Democratic Caucus rules required the winning candidate for speaker to have 31 votes in caucus. Once the rules are adopted, the leadership elections take place, candidates nominate themselves and there are no seconding speeches. In the House, voting is by secret ballot, in the Senate voting is oral.

The position of speaker or president is usually filled first, and it is during this final process that the last political bargaining takes place. It is not unusual for there to be multiple ballots over an extended period of time. There are frequent recesses for small groups of legislators to leave the room to try to "cut a deal." During the pre-caucus negotiations some members will have pledged themselves to vote for a certain candidate until that person releases them. These are the members who want to be rewarded for being early and loyal supporters. Others hold out to the very last to see what they will be offered for their vote. These caucus elections can be relatively quick or they can go on into the session itself. In 1979, it was not until the fifth day of the session that Hardy

Myers, D --Portland, was elected speaker. In 1984, it took Vera Katz, D --Portland, seventeen hours and 100 ballots to be elected speaker. Extended fights over leadership are not uncommon and the Oregon Constitution says that compensation stops after the fifth day of the session if a body fails to organize or select a presiding officer.[8]

Once a caucus meets and selects it leaders, the results are announced to the press. The new majority or minority leaders are considered to have taken office immediately because they are elected by the caucuses and not the bodies themselves. The speaker, president, speaker *pro tempore* and president *pro tempore* become the "speaker-elect," "president-elect" and so on.

At 9:00am on the morning of the first day of the session, the most senior member of the body takes the gavel and calls the House or Senate to order; roll is taken and the credentials committee reports on who has been elected. The members are sworn in. The next item of business is the election of the speaker or president. The majority party nominates the speaker-elect or president-elect, who was actually chosen two months earlier. The minority party traditionally submits the minority leader. The initial vote is cast along party lines, then the minority leader moves that the election be made unanimous. All of these actions are done off scripts that are prepared by the clerk of the House or secretary of the Senate. The speaker *pro tempore* and president *pro tempore* are selected in a manner similar to speaker and president. The clerk of the House,.secretary of the Senate, and sergeant at arms positions are filled on a *pro forma* vote[9] and then rules are adopted. The Legislature is ready for business as the Senate adjourns to the House chamber for a joint session to hear the governor.

The Basic Process -- the Rules and the Power

The legislative process in Oregon resembles an elaborate game in which the "rules" are ultimately important. Power to affect the process is diffuse and circumstantial. It moves from place to place and individual to individual, with no one person having control at all times. Given the right circumstances, the lowliest member can decide the fate of the most important piece of legislation of the session.

The process proceeds along the normal course of legislation through a state assembly or congress. Simply stated, a bill is introduced in one chamber and sent to a committee. The committee may amend the bill and, if it sees fit, send the bill to the floor for passage. If the bill passes, it is sent to the second chamber and referred to a second committee; that committee may also amend the bill and send it to the floor of the second house for passage. If the bill passes and has been amended, it is returned to the original house where the new amendments are then voted on. If the original house does not agree with the amendments, a conference committee is appointed with members from both houses. The differences are ironed out and a final version of the bill is sent from the conference committee to both floors. Once the bill passes both houses, it is sent to the governor for his or her signature or veto.

In Oregon, five major rules shape the process and diffuse power throughout the institution. First, the speaker and the president appoint the committees.[10] The make-up of a particular committee will determine, to a great extent, how any particular bill will fare. Different committees have different ideological predispositions, agendas and differences in their willingness to respond to the presiding officer's wishes. Given the diverse character of the committees, the fate of a bill can easily be determined by what committee it is sent to. Members, lobbyists and other interested parties know this, and thus we come to the second important rule.

The speaker and the president decide which bills go to which committees.[11] Intense efforts are made by the "players" to see that their particular bills go to the right committees. Needless to say, the reverse also occurs: to kill a bill, get it sent to a hostile committee.

There is a temptation to say that Oregon has a strong committee system, but that would not be totally correct. Before a bill is referred, the power resides with the speaker or president. As the bill is sent to the committee, the committee acquires the power over the bill. Bills become the vehicles or the ammunition by which committees and members fight political battles. This ammunition is not unlimited, bill introduction is curtailed by introduction deadlines and committees are only assigned so many bills.

The third rule is that once a committee has jurisdiction over a bill, that jurisdiction is exclusive. Nothing in either the House or Senate rules allows the presiding officer to withdraw a bill from the committee or order the committee to take action on a bill. There are rules, in both the House and the Senate, which allow bills to be withdrawn from hostile committees by a majority of the members on the floor.[12] Attempts at withdrawing bills from committees are almost always unsuccessful. Even though other members may want a bill out of committee and on the floor for a vote, they will not vote for withdrawal for the simple reason that the power of their own committees would be threatened by the next withdrawal vote. Committee members realize that their exclusive jurisdiction over certain bills is their power, their ability to affect the process. In addition, there are provisions in both houses whereby the majority of members of a committee can force a vote on a bill in committee.[13] It might be added that jurisdiction over a bill follows the physical bill; each bill has an original folder and jurisdiction follows the folder. For example, as the a member of the clerk's staff turns a bill over to committee staff, the jurisdiction is transferred.

The fourth rule is related to committee jurisdiction. It states that a committee can only amend a bill within what is known as the "relating clause" of the bill. The constitution requires that bills only address one subject and that subject be expressed in the title of the bill.[14] In the heading of each bill is the phrase "Relating to..." which describes the subject matter of the bill. A committee cannot go beyond the relating clause. A land-use amendment could not be put into a bill with a relating clause saying, "Relating to criminal law..." These rules are known as the "germaneness," rules.[15] Thus, even though a committee has almost absolute power over the fate of a bill, that power is circumscribed.

As mentioned earlier, certain committees have their own agendas and their own goals. If the presiding officer does not send them the bills which have the appropriate relating clauses they can't pursue their agenda. For instance, suppose the Agriculture Committee wants to limit land-use planning; the members and the chairman are rural legislators who feel that zoning and land-use laws are interfering with agricultural operations. Before they can change the land-use laws, they have to have a bill with the proper relating clause, one mentioning "land use." Needless to say, this becomes a very subtle, complex game. Committee power is both limited and enhanced by the relating-clauses rule. The power is limited because the committee cannot go outside the clause, but the power is enhanced when the committee has the right relating clause. It becomes almost a territorial battle between committees, and it goes without saying that the presiding officers are extremely aware of the relating-clause rule.

There is also the situation in which some members may introduce bills solely for their relating clauses. These lawmakers may hide their real intentions while trying to get a good relating clause into a friendly committee. For example, a member might want to limit Oregon's death penalty, but he knows that if he introduces a bill with the clause, "Relating to the death penalty..." the presiding officer, who likes the death penalty, will send it to a hostile committee. Instead, the members introduces a bill with the clause, "Relating to criminal law..." and amending some minor statute. He knows that the death penalty is within the relating clause and he will try to get this supposedly minor bill sent to a friendly committee. Once the committee has the bill the member can amend his anti-death penalty language. Variations on this theme are endless.

The final rule reinforces all the previous rules regarding committees, committee jurisdiction and relating clauses. Neither the House nor the Senate rules allow amendments to bills on the floor.[16] This is unusual for a legislative body. Floor amendments are allowed in numerous state assemblies and in the United States Congress. Again, this rule buttresses committee power. Once a bill is sent to the floor, a committee can be assured that it will be acted on in the form in which it was sent there.

As mentioned earlier, the makeup of a committee will determine the fate of any particular bill referred to it. The speaker's and the president's initial series of committee appointments will help set the political tone of the legislative session. If the leadership wants land use legislation he or she will try to appoint a land-use committee that will be friendly to that type of legislation. At the same time, this has to be placed in the context of the earlier discussion of how leadership is selected. Members have their agendas, as do the presiding officers. There is also the situation, in the initial leadership-bargaining process, when a member will extract a promise from the future leader that he or she will refer a certain bill to a certain committee. This could be either to pass a measure or to kill it.

Speakers and presidents have frequently found that the particular committees they have established won't cooperate with their own agenda. In the 1973 session Speaker Richard Eymann removed Dick MacGruder, D --Clatskinie, and Jeff Gilmour D -- Jefferson, as chair and vice-chair of the Business and Consumer Affairs Committee for failing to act on a consumer-protection bill. Vern Cook D --Gresham, was removed as chair of the Senate Revenue Committee, by Senate President Jason Boe, that same session, for failing to move on Governor Tom McCall's tax-reform plan. Whether or not a presiding officer can change committees, once the session starts, depends on the rules of the body. These rules themselves are subject to negotiations prior to the selection of the speaker or president.

There are other numerous powers that the speaker and the president hold besides the authority to appoint committees and to refer bills. As mentioned earlier, the two houses may disagree on the wording of a bill and a conference committee will be appointed to resolve these differences. These committees are appointed by the respective presiding officers,[17] i.e., on a four-person conference committee the Senate president will appoint two senators and the speaker will appoint two representatives. The conference committee is chaired by the member from the body which originally passed the bill, thus a conference committee on a House bill would have a House chair. Traditionally, the presiding officers will ask the respective committee chair who heard the bill for their recommendations as to who should serve on the conference committee.

Both officers are the administrative heads of their respective bodies and theoretically they appoint all committee staff. In actuality, committee administrators are hired by the various chairs. There is a Joint Legislative Administration Committee[18] which acts as a kind of board of directors for the running of the Legislature, but the body serves more as an official extension of the presiding officers. The Legislature is one of the few remaining places in state government where old fashioned patronage is alive and well. During a legislative session, over three hundred people are given temporary jobs. Both bodies use floor staffs of pages, door keepers, reading clerks and desk personnel. Most of these individuals are hired on a political basis.

Another informal, but extremely important aspect of the presiding officer's role is that of setting general tone for the session. Again, the initial make-up of the committees will have a tremendous impact on what the final product of the legislative session is. If the speaker wants tax reform to be the session's focus, he or she will want a strong Revenue Committee able and ideologically willing to produce a tax-reform package. At the start of some sessions, new or special committees are appointed for specific tasks. In 1989, Senate President John Kitzhaber, D --Roseburg, appointed a new committee on "Health and Bio-Ethics" to handle his health care rationing proposal, Senate Bill-27. In 1991, the new Speaker Larry Campbell, R --Eugene appointed a special Committee on Agency Reform as a follow-up to what had been a GOP campaign theme in the prior election.

Timing is another crucial aspect of the leadership function. This topic will be discussed in detail later, but it needs to be understood that certain things only happen at certain times in the legislative process.

Committees -- Proportionality and Character

The number and composition of the committees in both the House and Senate are controlled by the rules of the respective bodies. The composition and number of members on joint committees, such as Ways and Means[19] and Trade and Economic Development,[20] is controlled by statute. It should be reiterated how much a part of the leadership selection process the committees are. Again, every non-freshman member of the majority party wants to be in a leadership position, to chair a committee or be on Ways and Means (in the Senate, members want dual roles much of the time).

Some committees, such as Judiciary, Revenue and Education continue from session to session and are themselves almost permanent institutions that have continuing existence during the interims as interim committees. However, the roster of committees found in the House and Senate Rules frequently expands or contracts according to the desires of the presiding officer who is simultaneously trying to perform the previously mentioned tasks of getting elected and setting the tone of the session. Traditionally, the speaker-elect and president-elect announce the chairs of the various committees shortly after their own informal caucus elections. This enables the designated chairs to begin the staffing process. As mentioned, the actual committee structure is found in the rules which are adopted during the first day, although the rules themselves are discussed and sometimes fought over in the pre-session caucuses of the majority parties. The actual committee appointments are usually announced the first day of the session after the election of the leadership and adoption of the rules. Interestingly enough, there is always a tension between the members and the person to be elected speaker or president as to whether or not the officers will deliver on all the promises that had to be made to get elected. On several occasions, new speakers and Senate presidents have been embarrassed because they bargained away more desirable committee slots than they had.

The 1991 committee roster looked like this:

House--

Agency Reorganization & Reform	7 members
Agriculture Forestry & Natural Resources	7 members
Business & Consumer Affairs	7 members
Education	7 members
Environment & Energy	9 members
Housing & Urban Development	7 members
Human Resources	7 members
Intergovernmental Affairs	7 members
Judiciary	12 members
Labor	7 members
Legislative Rules & Reapportionment	11 members
Revenue & School Finance	9 members
State & Federal Affairs	7 members
Trade & Economic Development (joint committee)	7 members
Transportation	7 members
Ways & Means (joint committee)	8 members

Senate --

Agriculture & Natural Resources	7 members
Business Housing & Finance	5 members
Education	7 members
Government Operations	7 members
Health Insurance & Bio-Ethics	5 members
Human Resources	5 members
Judiciary	7 members
Labor	4 members
Redistricting	7 members
Revenue & School Finance	7 members
Rules	7 members
Telecommunications & Consumer Affairs	5 members
Trade & Economic Development (joint committee)	6 members
Transportation	7 members
Ways & Means (joint committee)	8 members

"Proportionality" involves the question of how many Democrats and how many Republicans will be on each particular committee. If a party has a majority in the House or the Senate they will naturally want to have majorities on each of the committees. The question then becomes how big a majority on each committee? Under the concept of "proportionality" the committee majorities should reflect the controlling party's majority in the body and not more. This rule was originally introduced in the House in 1979, but has never been in effect in the Senate. For instance, in the 1991 Session in the House, the Republicans had a majority of 32 to 28. Mathematically this means they have 53 percent of the body and likewise should receive 53 percent of the membership of each committee. Members only come in whole numbers: on a seven-person committee the Republicans would have four seats, on a nine-person committee, five. During the past several sessions the controversy over proportionality has involved appointments to the Ways and Means Committee. On the 16-member Joint Ways and Means Committee, the House is allowed eight appointments. Theoretically, this should mean five Republicans and three Democrats, but in the 1991 Session only two Democrats were appointed.

Committees quickly develop their own personalities and reputations. As mentioned, the make up of a committee will have an impact on the legislation that is sent to it. There is the phenomenon of a committee that is hostile to certain legislation. There is also the reverse where the committee becomes ideologically imbalanced and sends legislation to the floor that does not have broad support. For instance, an Environment and Energy Committee made up solely of pro-environment legislators would probably not be as successful at passing legislation as a committee that had members on both ends of the ideological spectrum. The internal committee process and dialogue serve as a check on the committee's actions, if the committee is balanced. Thus, while a speaker or president wants committees that will carry out the agenda of the legislature or the governor, they do not want committees that are so unbalanced that they lose battles on the floor.

Bills, Bills, Bills

Legislatures do their business with bills. "A Bill for an Act," is literally a request for a law, but other measures are used in the legislative process such as "Resolutions" and "Memorials." Memorials are expressions of legislative opinion such as asking the United States Congress to pass a particular piece of federal legislation. "Joint Resolutions" are the vehicles by which questions are sent to the people for a vote -- they may be either statutes or amendments to the constitution. A "Concurrent Resolution" can express legislative congratulations or sympathy.[21] Only bills may be vetoed by the governor and at times measures are referred to the people to avoid vetoes. Almost all measures filed are bills and, unless otherwise noted, this discussion will be about bills.

Bills are drafted by Legislative Counsel, which is the attorney's office for the Legislature.[22] The office is a permanent body and employs an average of 12 attorneys during both the interim and the session. Legislative drafting is a specialized branch of law and the office is noted for its efficiency. Members, agencies and legislative committees can request bills to be drafted. Newly elected members are also given this privilege and there is no limit as to the number of bills that any one member can have drafted. Requests to Legislative Counsel by legislators are confidential.[23]

There are introduction deadlines for both agencies and members. All House members must file their bills by the 36th calendar day (this includes Saturdays and Sundays) of the session and all Senators by the 50th calendar day of the session.[24] Each house member is also given two "priorities," which are bills that may be filed after the deadline. Agencies have a drafting deadline of December 15 of the even numbered year.[25] Committees may also request the drafting of bills. There is also a statutory Joint Legislative Counsel Committee that oversees the work of the Counsel itself. This committee and Legislative Counsel are also responsible for publishing the Oregon Revised Statutes (ORS) and the Session Laws which are the newly revised statutes at the end of each session. In addition, the Committee reviews administrative regulations during the interim for compliance with statutory intent.

House bills are numbered 2000 and up and Senate bills are numbered from 1 and up, thus if a bill is number 2345 one would know that it is a House bill. Budget bills are always 5000 and up numbers and can be either House or Senate bills. There are about 3000 bills filed each session, which is a comparatively high number of measures for a legislative body. Other legislatures limit the actual number of bills that members can file, but in Oregon only the time to file is limited. Of the 3000 bills which are filed, 800 or so will become law; of these 150 will be budget bills to appropriate money to run the various agencies. As mentioned, the Oregon Constitution says that each bill may only contain one subject, which has a tendency to increase the number of bills.

Bills may be filed in several ways. They may be pre-session filed by an agency, a member or an interim committee. They may also be filed during the session by a member or a committee. Every bill (until the 1993 Session in the House) has a "bill backer" attached to it which contains the relating clause, the signature of the person filing it and a list of all ninety members with spaces for their initials should they wish to co-sponsor the bill. The mere act of a member placing his or her initials by their name is all it takes to be listed as a sponsor. Bills are circulated by the members themselves, by their staff and sometimes by interested third parties such as lobbyists.

Numerous bills are also drafted and filed at the request of third parties, and this will appear on the backer and on the face of the bill once it is printed. Most legislators try to accommodate both constituents and interest groups by drafting and filing bills for them. A bill filed at the request of a third party is considered to be the responsibility of that third party as far as lobbying it through the process.

Having many signers on a bill, as co-sponsors, does not guarantee its passage, although it does help. Some particularly respected or influential members are especially sought out as co-sponsors, and other unpopular members are avoided. Getting sponsors for a bill can become an art form, especially when two members approach each other wanting a signature, "'You sign my bill, I'll sign yours." Bill sponsorship is very political. Legislators want credit for successful legislation and want to avoid sponsoring the silly bills which are known as "Turkeys." Some particularly popular bills are even opened up for further sponsorship as they pass so that members can claim credit. In the Legislature, victory does have a hundred fathers and mothers.

Bill Referral -- Getting the Right Bill to the Right Committee
The speaker and the Senate president refer bills to the appropriate committees under their respective rules. However, the speaker is somewhat limited in the House by the jurisdiction rules.[26] The various committees have their jurisdictions described in the rules themselves, and bills are hypothetically supposed to go to committees that have jurisdiction of the particular subject matter. For example, the Judiciary Committee description reads, "Relating generally to the civil and criminal law and the administration of justice."

All bills which spend money or have a fiscal impact in causing an agency or local government to spend money, are sent to the Ways and Means Committee. The speaker and the president also have the ability to give bills "subsequent referrals" to second committees. Most referrals are to the Ways and Means Committee. For instance, a bill which raises court filing fees would first go to House Judiciary then would be given a subsequent referral to Ways and Means. There is no Senate rule on jurisdiction and this gives the senate president somewhat more latitude on what may be done with legislation.

Committees at Work -- The All Powerful Chair

Most legislative activity is committee activity and it is here that the real work of the legislature gets done. As mentioned earlier, not all committees are equal and indeed not all committees are given their proportional share of the bills. While there are 17 committees in the House, more than half of the bills will go to Judiciary, Revenue or Ways and Means.

Each committee has its own set of committee rules (more later), but most of the committees' activities are controlled by the committee provisions of the House and Senate rules. One factor dominates the committee process, that is that the chair of the committee sets the agenda and runs the meetings. Where all members may vote on a bill, only the chair places the bill on the agenda for either a "hearing" or a "work session." A hearing is exactly that, a public hearing at which testimony is taken on the bill, a work session is a meeting at which the bill is amended, voted out or otherwise disposed of. Because of the open-meetings law, all hearing and/or work sessions must be announced with a public notice 24 hours in advance of the actual meeting.[27] Thus, if a bill is never scheduled, it can't be heard or worked on; even if scheduled, if it isn't called up on the agenda by the chair of the committee, it can't pass.

Getting a hearing and/or a work session on a bill is at the very heart of the process. Whether bills are heard or not heard can be an intensely political question. Committee chairs jealously guard their power and are assiduously courted by citizens, lobbyists, interest groups and agencies. At times, the process of influencing a chair can become pure pressure politics. Telephone calls are made, letters are written, friendly legislators are asked to contact the chairman, key constituents or campaign contributors may be asked to bring their influence to bear. Some groups have even gone as far as to demonstrate in front of a chair's home or on the Capitol steps to get a hearing. The politics of this goes deeper than just the preferences of the chair. There are numerous bills filed which the members simply don't want to vote on even though they might have taken formal positions on the bills. Highly charged emotional issues, such as gun control, gay rights, the death penalty and abortion are looked upon as "no win" votes. It is one thing to take a position in a campaign, but it is another to actually go on record with a vote.

A second situation is the "turf battle," where two powerful interest groups are in conflict. If a legislator has the support of both groups, and has no particular interest in the bill, the last thing he or she wants to do is to have to make the hard choice between the two groups if the bill gets out of committee. There are times when a member may publicly support or even sponsor a bill, but then privately go to the chair of the committee and beg him or her to bury the measure. Another variation on this is where the committee chair may oppose a bill, but set it for a hearing or work session as a favor to an interest group. Such favors are not forgotten.

Committee rules are usually adopted at the first meeting of the committee and most of the provisions are non-controversial. However, several rules do play a role in the politics of how the committee actually works. When a committee sends a bill to the floor, those members opposing the bill have the option of filing a "minority report," essentially their own version of the bill. The minority report has to be within the relating clause, so not just any proposal can be sent out. Although minority reports rarely pass on the floor, they can become a means around the usual legislative process. For instance, a Revenue Committee controlled by conservative Republicans would never send out a bill to increase income taxes. But, if a measure was sent out "Relating to taxation...," the liberal Democrats could propose a tax increase as a minority report. The committee rules become relevant *vis a vis* the requirements for minority reports, how many members must sign the report and when notice must be given prior to a member or members filing a minority report. Needless to say, committee chairs dislike minority reports and try to get the committees to adopt rules which discourage minority reports.

There are also questions of what constitutes a quorum and how many votes does it takes to send a bill to the floor or to amend a bill. Usually, a majority of the members of the committee constitute a quorum, but it also takes a majority of the committee to send a bill to the floor.[28] On the other hand, it normally only takes a majority of those present to amend a bill. For instance, it takes five members of a nine-member committee to constitute a quorum or send a bill to the floor, but three out of five members present can amend a bill. How many people are actually present becomes crucial. You might have enough votes to amend the bill, three out of five, but it takes all five votes to send it to the floor. All members are not always present during all committee hearings and this has a tremendous impact on the dynamics of the committee.

In committee, and on the floor, votes may be reconsidered,[29] but before a member can make a motion to reconsider a vote, such as sending a bill to the floor, the member must have been on what is called the "prevailing side." This is a deceptive term unless you place it in the context of the voting requirements just discussed. If a motion is made in a nine-person committee to send a bill to the floor for passage when only the five members quorum are present, then the motion will fail with one negative vote. In other words, a four to one favorable vote will not send it to the floor if five votes are required. Because the motion is considered to have failed, the one negative vote is considered to be the "prevailing" side! Since a member has to be on the "prevailing" side to make a reconsideration motion, the member casting the sole negative vote has a veto power over the future of the bill. Two other aspects should be mentioned. First, as a committee is actually voting on a bill or an amendment, any member can change his or her vote before the chair raps the gavel to the end the vote. Second, the chair always votes last.

A Committee Votes -- Learn to Count -- Don't Go to the Bathroom

The above discussion should give an idea of how subtle and complex the actual voting can be. All these rules work together to create a bizarre, political poker game. In the legislative sub-culture, playing the game well comes under the euphemistic heading of "learning to count."

Most of the action is keyed off the chair of the committee, who has immense control if he will "count." One must always know who supports the bill and who opposes the bill, how many votes are present and what does thier presence add up to. Are there enough members in the committee room to get the bill out? Or better yet, does the chair even want the bill out? A bill can be publicly supported yet killed at the same time. A committee chair may have promised someone that he would call a bill up for a vote, and he might even have promised to vote for the bill. But, if the chair has kept count of how many positive votes are in the committee room at any moment, he can call the bill up for a vote at that exact time when it will fail even if the chair votes for it! Who has made the mistake of going to the bathroom! For example, let's say that six of nine members on a committee support a bill and three oppose it. One the six supporters is the chair who really doesn't like the bill, but for some political reason he or she must vote for it. Now suppose there are only six members in the room and the chairs knows that two of the six oppose the bill, it still takes five votes to get the bill out. If he calls for a vote at the crucial moment when three of the supporters are out of the room the bill will fail on a four to two vote. The chair will have had it both ways and no one will ever be the wiser; he will have voted for the bill and killed it at the same time. Again, because the chair votes last he is in a particularly advantageous position to change his vote so as to always be on the prevailing side and thus have the option to move reconsideration. There are dozens of ways these interactions can take place, and these skirmishes happen with lightening speed during committee hearings.

Hearings and work sessions are run by the chair who brings the gavel down to start the meeting and call witnesses. Members who wish to ask questions must be recognized by the chair and during work sessions all motions must be accepted by the chair. Voting is done orally, the committee clerk calls the roll after the chair places the question before the committee. Actions are finalized by the chair rapping the gavel after a vote. The chair of the committee must know the issue and the players if the process is to work with any dispatch. Particularly adept committee chairs will frequently ask opposing parties to go into the hall to work out compromises. If compromises are reached in committee, floor fights can be avoided.

Ways and Means -- "Powerful Ways and Means"

The Joint Ways and Means Committee[30] is one of the few truly unique institutions in the Oregon Legislature. The Committee was part of our discussion of the budget process in Chapter 4 where we examined how the Ways and Means members can find dollars in the Governor's budget. Here, we are going to be more concerned about the committee itself and its internal operations. Ways and Means started in 1917 and is almost always referred to as "The Powerful Ways and Means Committee." It also should be noted that the name is somewhat of a misnomer. The term "ways and means" usually refers to a taxation committee, such as in the United States Congress, but this "Ways and Means" is really an appropriations committee. In fact, it is the sole appropriations committee. It is where the money is.

The committee has 16 members --eight senators and eight representatives. The respective appointments are made by the two presiding officers and, as mentioned earlier, the positions are coveted political plums. The two co-chairs are also appointed by the presiding officers and considered to be the second-most powerful individuals in the two houses. During the leadership selection process, it is not unusual for the final bargaining to come down to the question of, "Who will get Ways and Means?" Before looking at the co-chairs, let's consider why Ways and Means is so powerful.

First, bills only go to Ways and Means once. Appropriations bills do not have to go through both a house committee and a senate committee. Once a bill passes out of Ways and Means, it goes directly to both floors. Secondly, all bills which spend money, or have any significant fiscal impact, are sent to Ways and Means. As mentioned earlier, numerous bills are sent to the Ways and Means Committee after action by substantive committees. In government, money is power. There is no such thing as a program that doesn't cost money. The new boat ramp, the new college building and the new home for battered women all cost money and they all must go through Ways and Means. These appropriation bills are more than just general fund allocations. As mentioned, all money which is spent by the state, whether it be fees, federal dollars or private grants, must be approved by the Ways and Means Committee.[31] In addition, any significant changes in the number of authorized state employees (FTE) must also be approved by the committee.

Further, one must realize that the Ways and Means Committee is more than just that. In the interim, virtually the same members (seven senators and eight representatives), with the addition of the speaker and the president, become the Emergency Board,[32] which meets every six weeks to handle the state's fiscal matters. This includes moving budgeted money from different categories, approving the acceptance of outside money such as grants and federal allocations, changing authorized staff patterns and, most importantly, allocating money from the "Emergency Fund." This is an approximately $50 million fund which Ways and Means appropriates to itself in its Emergency Board incarnation for use during the interim. Agency budgets frequently contain allocations which can only be released to them by Emergency Board action. The 1991 session approved what was known as the 1991-1993 Budget. Given the budgetary power both in the session and in the interim, Ways and Means deserves the title "Powerful."

The co-chairs of Ways and Means, like the chairs of all committees, control the committee's agenda, but here the situation is little different. *Both* co-chairs must approve action on any bill, not just hearings and work sessions, but also the assignment of a bill to a sub-committee where the actual work is done. Since these are vital money bills, agencies live or die on whether or not their budgets are heard. The co-chairs' power is further enhanced by their relationship to the staff of the committee. The Legislative Fiscal Office[33] is the permanent staff of both the Ways and Means Committee and the Emergency Board. If there was a "general staff" or Praetorian Guard of the Oregon Legislature, these Legislative Fiscal Officers (LFOs) would be it. They are extremely knowledgeable about state budgets, and LFOs frequently go on to head state agencies. The LFO's work directly for the co-chairs and not for the sub-committee chairs, a fact which is learned very quickly by the members of the sub-committees.

Again, the actual work of Ways and Means is done in the six regular sub-committees: Human Resources, General Government, Education, Public Safety, Natural Resources and Economic Development. These sub-committees serve all session and the sub-committee chairs rotate from House to Senate every other session. (At the end of the session, two special sub-committees are appointed to handle salary and capitol construction matters.) Each member of Ways and Means serves on two sub-committees.

Sub-committee chairperson-ships of Human Resources and Education are considered major positions and the very best places to influence both budgets and substantive programs in those areas. Human Resources and Education both have six members, where the remaining sub-committees have four members.

There is another unusual aspect of Ways and Means which adds significantly to the power of the co-chairs. Even though the co-chairs do not serve on the sub-committees, they can, on their own volition, sit in on any meeting and vote. This very rarely happens, but the "threat" is always there. This power, combined with scheduling and staff control, makes the co-chairs very powerful, but there is more.

Each sub-committee is given a certain number of budgets to hear. As mentioned, these budgets contain a series of line items such as salary, equipment, attorney general charges, travel, *et cetera*. The sub-committee starts with the "governor's recommended" dollar amounts. At the end of the process, an allocation is made for each of these items and is called "sub-committee action." This figure can be more or less than the governor's recommended amount, but it is usually less. Sub-committees not only determine the total dollar amount for each budget, but they set the specific amounts for each line item as mentioned above. Again, some budgets can be heard and acted on in one hour, others, such as Human Resources, take months of hearings and work sessions.

The actions of the sub-committees are controlled by a set of informal, but binding rules. Sub-committees may only address matters in the budgets before them. They can cut budgets or move money between budgets within their control. Sub-committees are also frequently given "cut targets" to work with. If a sub-committee has a total of $800 million worth of the governor's recommended budgets before it, it might be told by the co-chairs that it has to cut $50 million from that total amount. The usual informal arrangement is that if they cut beyond the goal, the committee is given 50¢ on the dollar to spend on their own programs! Guess who gets the other 50¢? This is the real source of the power of the co-chairs; they are accumulating money from six sub-committees with which they can fund their own programs.

The sub-committees are usually motivated by these arrangements and an ongoing series of subtle negotiations takes place between the sub-committee members and the sub-committee chairs. Ways and Means operates on a consensus basis with few formal votes ever being taken in the sub-committee. Running tallies are kept by the staff of how much money has been saved and spent. The process is very closed and numerous decisions are made outside of the public view.

The Ways and Means Committee meets as a whole only once a week on Friday mornings to approve the sub-committee actions. Very few sub-committee recommendations are ever rejected and minority reports are not allowed out of Ways and Means. Tradition also says that members must announce to the committee if they intend to oppose a budget on the floor.

As a group, the Ways and Means Committee epitomizes speaker of the United States House Sam Rayburn's famous rubric -- "In this House, the people who get along the best, go along the most."[34] It perceives itself as an elite, powerful body and jealously guards its role. New members of Ways and Means are subtly, but inevitably, socialized into being team players. The ability to bring millions of dollars to bear on one's own agenda is seductive. Conservative Republicans start out swearing they will cut budget after budget and end up cooperating to beef up their own programs. Liberal Democrats, who pledge to increase Human Resource efforts, find themselves carrying bills to cut welfare in order to pay for some nobler endeavor.

General budget decisions for the state are not made by the Ways and Means Committee *per se*. Budget policy for Oregon always starts with the governor's recommended budget. This is where most initiatives and innovations are found. However, the final shape of the budget involves negotiations between the governor, the speaker, the president, the co-chairs and sometimes the chairs of the two revenue committees. General feelings of the House and Senate are relevant, but they are not controlling. Other than the co-chairs, members of Ways and Means have very little influence on the major fiscal decisions such as whether prison will be built or whether college faculties will receive raises.

There is always tension between the Ways and Means Committee and the two houses themselves. Ordinary members are not given actual agency budgets unless they request them and few have the expertise to interpret budgets without LFO assistance. Interesting enough, the greatest budget detail isn't even found in the actual line-item budgets, but in what is known as the "support document." One or two budgets are usually returned to the Ways and Means Committee from the floor of each House out of frustration, but they are only sent back for passage toward to end of the session when the fight has gone out of most members.

Theoretically, the Ways and Means Committee does not handle substantive or non-money legislation. This is not always the case. As mentioned earlier, substantive bills with fiscal impact are sent to Ways and Means as part of the normal process. Also, bills are sent to Ways and Means from the floor, as a method of killing them. Ways and Means is considered the "graveyard committee" of the Legislature. Much to the chagrin of the two houses, substantive bills do frequently come out of Ways and Means. Because of the closed and insider nature of the process it is a favorite place for hidden agendas to be pursued by lobbyists and members who can get the ear of the co-chairs or a subcommittee chair.

Finally, there are what are known as "budget notes." These are short directives addressed to agencies and made part of the budget reports. They are not considered to be law, but for all intents and purposes they have the force of law. Agencies ignore budget notes at their peril, as their response to a budget note written in one session is reviewed by the same sub-committee the next session.

The Revenue Committees -- Oregon's Ireland

There has probably never been a session of the Legislature where taxes weren't a major issue. Generally, school finance is at the heart of any tax question in Oregon. Indeed, school finance has been called "The Ireland of Oregon politics." Governor after governor and session after session of the Legislature confront the same issue year after year. Like Ireland, you can't seem to get out of the morass. It is the rock upon which political careers are shattered.

There are two other factors, beside school finance, which cause revenue questions to be so important. First, there is the basic politics of taxes or, to put it in more fundamental terms, who is going to pay what? This question is as old as government itself. Republicans and their establishment ancestors on the right have always opposed taxes in general -- "Leave the money with us and we'll invest it to create jobs...everybody will benefit in the long run." Democrats and their Populist predecessors look upon taxes as a means to an end --"With taxes we'll build roads and educate children...everybody will benefit in the long run." Under a Republican approach the well-off do not pay any more than the not-so-well off. Under the Democrats the poor pay less and the rich pay more.

Secondly, there are very few significant initiatives that do not take additional revenue. If any particular governor wants to do something, it usually takes more money. More money usually means more taxes. Thus, if the state is going to reform education, fight crime, or help the disadvantaged, the issue becomes a tax issue.

Incidentally, this relationship between the executive and legislative branch has been the same throughout history. The king-queen-president-governor always wants the parliament-congress-legislature to do the dirty work of raising taxes so that he or she can fight a war, build schools, or take care of the poor and thus be accorded the glory he or she deserves. Unfortunately for the king-queen-president-governor, the members of the legislative branch sometimes have their own ideas.[35]

Consequently, the revenue committees are always in the political spotlight in Oregon and their actions are among the most significant of any legislative session. However, the two revenue committees are not equal. All bills increasing taxes must start in the House.[36] This is a legislative norm from the United States Congress to the British House of Commons. Because of this, all major tax legislation, whether it be a new sales tax or a rehash of school finance, is always heard in the house committee first. Inevitably, the legislation stays in the House Revenue Committee until almost the end of the session. It takes time for a committee to work its will on a major bill and time is always on the side of the House Committee.

The two revenue committees, like Ways and Means, are staffed by a permanent office known as the Legislative Revenue Office.[37] It has six full-time employees, which include five economists known as "Revenue Officers." The office staffs both the House and Senate Revenue Committees. The House Revenue Committee has nine members where the Senate Committee has seven members. Among their more important jobs is evaluating the revenue projections made by the state Executive Department.

The Judiciary Committees -- They Love Their Judges

A third of all the bills in the House and the Senate will go to the respective Judiciary Committees. These committees, made up mostly of lawyers, handle all bills having to do with criminal law, tort law, the Uniform Commercial Code, trademarks, corporate law, domestic relations, landlord-tenant law, probate, mental commitments, juvenile law and anything having to do with the judicial branch and the Oregon State Bar. Many of the most controversial and emotional bills end up before the House and Senate Judiciary Committees. Given the sheer volume and importance of the bills, the judiciary committees are perhaps the most important committees in the assembly for non-money matters.

The Senate Judiciary Committee has seven members and the House Judiciary Committee has twelve members and is the largest non-joint committee in the Legislature. The committees have a permanent staff of two attorneys who act as counsel during the session and the interim. Several other attorneys, usually on leave from law firms or other institutions, are hired during the session.

The House Judiciary Committee sits in three sub-committees similar to Ways and Means. The chair of the full committee will usually chair the sub-committee of his or her choice, with senior members chairing the other two sub-committees. Traditionally, the three sub-committees are known as the "Criminal Law," Civil Law," and "Family Law."

One of the most interesting relationships in government is that between the Judiciary Committees and the judiciary itself. The two committees are notorious for endorsing new judgeships and judicial salary increases. The fact that numerous former committee members are on the bench is coincidental.

The Judiciary Committees, like the Ways and Means Committee, frequently run into a type of institutional hostility on the floors of the respective houses. Members will start their speeches with the phrase, "I'm not a lawyer, but..." This usually means that the body has had heard too much technical language and is fed up with "lawyer bills."

Other Committees -- Substance, Money, and Turf

As mentioned earlier, there are 17 session committees in the House and 16 in the Senate. Other committees don't handle near the volumes of bills that Ways and Means, Revenue and Judiciary do. However, many major issues are decided by these committees. This is particularly true in the environmental area. Over the past several sessions, the environment committees have had to confront such subjects as toxic wastes, field burning and forest practices. These are politically charged topics with very strong interest-group participation.

The Human Resources and Education Committees in both the House and the Senate do not play the roles that one would expect them to play. The major issues, in both areas, almost always have to do with money and the money decisions are made by the Ways and Means sub-committees. To make it even more confusing, the Ways and Means sub-committees have the same names as the regular committees, i.e., there is a House and a Senate Education Committee and an Education Sub-committee of Ways and Means. Theoretically, the regular or "substantive" committees handle the policy questions and the sub-committees handle money questions. This does not usually prove to be the case. If a member really wants to have an impact, the member aspires to Ways and Means.

There is one area that Ways and Means is more than willing to leave to the regular Human Resources Committees --the "turf battle" or "scope of practice" issues. These controversies are usually between health-care-provider groups; nurses versus doctors, optometrists versus ophthalmologists (doctors), osteopaths versus doctors, pharmacists versus doctors, dentists versus denturists, chiropractors versus everybody --the list goes on. The "turf" in these "turf battles" is nothing more than professional fees and is taken very seriously by the players.[38]

Floor Action -- More Rules

When a committee sends a bill to the floor of a house for passage, it officially sends a "committee report" that recommends passage of the measure. As mentioned, there are also times when "minority reports" are sent to the floor. In this situation, the committee report is known as the "majority report." Acting on bills is the main activity of the two houses as they meet in what are known as "floor sessions." Both chambers meet daily from ten or eleven in the morning until noon. As the legislative session itself draws to an end, in early or mid-summer, these floor meetings will increase in length until they take up most of the day.

Again, there are some crucial rules, statutes and constitutional provisions that control what exactly happens on the floor of the Oregon House and Senate.

The prohibition against floor amendments was mentioned earlier and should always be kept in mind. A second immensely important provision is the constitutional requirement that bills may only be passed by a majority of the elected members, not just a majority those present on the floor.[39] In other words, it takes 31 out of 60 votes in the House and 16 out of 30 votes in the Senate to pass a bill! In effect, if a member is not present he or she becomes a "no" vote. Other legislative bodies, such as Congress, do not use this absolute majority approach. In addition, all final votes must be record votes. Although there are voice votes, "All those in favor say aye...," these are only on motions and not on the final passage of a bill. To make things even more interesting, the rules require that if a member is present he or she must vote! To the best of anyone's knowledge, there has never been a situation where this particular rule has been tested; members traditionally vote, if present.[40]

The question then becomes how to avoid the situation where members will absent themselves to avoid hard votes --to vote "no" with their feet as it were. Both the House and Senate have unique and no-nonsense provisions known as a "call of the House," or a "call of the Senate." Any six members in the House and two members in the Senate can demand that doors be barred and that no further business be transacted until the absent members are returned to the floor.[41] The "call," as it is known, can be imposed at any time before a vote starts. The sergeant at arms and floor staff stand in front of the exits and politely, but firmly do not allow members to leave. The state police may seize and return those members subject to the call. Any member who is excused from the day's business is not subject to the call. The practical effect of this is that it is hard to avoid voting.

The earlier discussion about being able to count is just as applicable to what happens on the floor as in committee. Calls will almost always occur on controversial bills for two reasons. First, the proponents need an absolute majority of votes for passage and placing a call is the best way to get the members onto the floor. The second reason is more political. Both Democrats and Republicans like to put their opponents on record with politically unpopular votes as ammunition for the next election cycle. Democrats like to make Republicans vote against children's programs (even though they might be too expensive) and Republicans like to make Democrats vote for increased taxes (even though they might be needed). "Put them on record," is a phrase that you will hear frequently.

A call of the House or Senate can also be part of legislative infighting at its zenith. In May of 1977, a coalition of conservative Democrats and regular Republicans stripped Speaker Phil Lang, D --Portland, of all of his powers by amending the house rules in an unprecedented legislative *coup d'etat*. Constant calls were imposed on the House in order to avoid the speaker and his supporters from leaving and breaking the quorum and thus stopping the coalition from amending the rules and taking power.

Aside from constitutional requirements, most other procedures on the floor are controlled by the rules of the body. If the rules do not speak to a particular question, then Mason's Manual of Legislative Procedure[42] (no relation to the author) controls. Mason's is a common manual of procedure and is used throughout the United States. It is updated and maintained by the American Society of Legislative Clerks and Secretaries of the National Association of State Legislatures.

Access to the floor is limited to members, member's assistants, floor staff and accredited reporters. The press is traditionally confined to the back and sides of the chamber and may not go out among the desks. The two side aisles in each chamber are reserved for guests of the members and legislative staff. Lobbyists are not allowed on the side isles.

Members of both houses have floor desks. Before the expansion of the Capitol, these desks alsoserved as their offices when the bodies were not in session. Senators and representatives traditionally hired their spouses as secretaries and they were given a second chair at their desks on the floor. This is a unique tradition and attempts to get them off the floor have always failed. Most of these staff are now considered to be "legislative assistants." They enjoy being on the floor during the sessions and look upon the second chair as being their own kind of "seat" in the legislature. Truth be known, they serve a very useful purpose in keeping track of what is going on. Although the assistants do not actually vote, there are many times when a tardy member rushes back onto the floor and hurriedly asks "What is this...How am I supposed to vote?" The assistant then quietly tells the member how to vote. The quality of legislation has not noticeably suffered.

The floor sessions of the House and Senate are presided over by the speaker and the president in their role as "Presiding Officers." From the moment of the first gavel to call the body to order, to the eventual adjournment, the presiding officer controls the ebb and flow of the business. He or she calls the items on the agenda, or "Order of Business," recognizes members to speak, places motions before the body and rules on questions of parliamentary procedure. The speaker and the president do not preside at all times, however. Other members take the rostrum, or the "chair," during the more mundane periods of legislative business, and the person in the chair is constantly assisted by the chief clerk in the House or the secretary of the Senate.[43] On each rostrum, there is a well-indexed binder containing the appropriate parliamentary phrases to be used as business progresses. The presiding officers also have direct telephone lines to the desks of the majority and minority leaders on the floor to coordinate floor debate.

After the initial roll call, there is an "Opening Ceremony" usually consisting of a prayer given by a member of the clergy invited in by one of the legislators. More often than not, these prayers are too long and all sound the same. Most ministers cannot resist the temptation to ask members to rise above petty politics, to put the interest of the state first and to be inspired by divine Providence. During one prayer in 1963, when Clarence Barton, D --Coquille, was speaker, the minister actually read a list of what bills should be passed--especially a controversial "milk bill." Members were relieved when they found out that he wasn't a real clergyman, but a ringer arranged by Representative Sid Bazett, R -Grants Pass.

"Remonstrances" are the next order. These are short speeches on any topic the members want to speak on, many of them are comments on news items, some are complaints and some are apologies for a prior day's indiscretions. There is a three-minute limit on remonstrances in the House.[44]

Third Readings --Carriers and Motions

Bills are actually passed under the "third reading" portion of the daily calendar. This is a parliamentary term that used to mean that the bill was read a third time. With modern printing there is no need to "read" bills aloud, but the term remains. In the Oregon House, the title of a bill is read the first time when it is introduced and the same title is read a second time on the day before the bill comes up for third reading. The list of bills that will be voted during one particular day is known as the "Third Reading Calendar."

As a bill is voted out of a committee to the floor, the chair of the committee assigns a member, usually of the committee, to "carry" the bill on the floor. This means that the member will be called on by the speaker or the president to present the bill and start the debate on the measure. In the House, a member is given ten minutes for his or her opening speech, then other members are given the opportunity to make five-minute comments for or against the bill. At the end of debate, the carrier is allowed another ten minutes for his or her "closing speech."[45]

The length of time it takes to debate a bill varies with the gravity of the issue. Most bills only have perfunctory debate, if at all, and little time is used by the carrier or the other members. On important bills, the reverse is true. Other than the carrier, each member may speak once, but members may yield time to each other. After all members have had an opportunity to debate the question, members who have spoken before may speak again. While there is no time limit in the Senate, there is also no tradition of trying to filibuster bills.

Decorum during debate is tightly controlled and members must confine their remarks to the question before them. Unlike some other legislative bodies, members of the House are allowed to refer to each other as "Representative So-and-So..." Personal attacks or the questioning of a member's motives are not allowed,[46] but emotions can run extremely high.

During the 1923 selection of Senate President Jay Upton, R --Prineville, Senator George Joseph R-Portland, let it be known that he was armed and that he *would* have his say. "...I'm going to make that speech and if anyone moves, we open fire." Joseph held the floor for an hour and viciously attacked Upton for being a crook and a scoundrel. There had been a feud between the two men over a proposal to have a World's Fair in Portland, (it was eventually held in 1925), and over Upton's alleged anti-Semitism.[47]

Debate on either passage of a bill or a motion may be ended by any member "moving the previous question." Once this motion is made, in either the House or Senate, an immediate vote is taken on whether or not to cut off debate.[48] If the "previous question motion" passes, the carrier, the maker of the main motion, is allowed to give closing remarks.

Games Legislators Play

Although most bills pass with little controversy, there are occasions when opposition develops. It is at those times that motions are made on a bill. The surest way to kill a bill in the Oregon Legislature, is not to defeat it outright, but to dispose of it by a motion. Typically this would be a motion to refer the bill to a hostile committee or to Ways and Means. Motions are also made to refer bills back to the committees which sent them to the floor. Any member may make a motion, but the motion must be made before he or she actually speaks to the bill. Once a motion is made, the motion becomes the question before the body. For instance, a bill may be carried out of the House Judiciary Committee and the carrier may have made an opening speech of ten minutes. The speaker will then ask for further debate and he or she will recognize a member who is standing at their desk in order to be recognized. Before a motion, the member may ask the carrier a question or a series of questions about the bill. The carrier must "yield" to the question, which means he or she agrees to answer. Some questions are purely informational, but many are asked as part of a strategy to defeat the bill. Once the member makes a motion, such as to refer the bill to Ways and Means, the speaker places the motion by repeating it for the record and then he or she calls on the "maker" of the motion to present the motion itself. The member is then given five minutes to "open" or present the motion. At the conclusion of the maker's opening remarks, the speaker will then ask for debate on the motion. The same rules apply in the Senate except for time limits.

Here the process can start all over as the next member may then move to amend the original motion. For instance, if the original motion was to refer the bill to Ways and Means, the amended motion could be to refer the bill to a friendlier committee or back to the original committee. The maker of the second motion is allowed his or her five minutes to open and then debate is opened on the second motion. At the conclusion of the debate, the maker of the second motion is given five minutes to close. If the amendment passes, then the amended motion becomes the original motion and will be finally voted on in that form. If the amendment fails, debate then returns to the original motion. Motions are laid upon motions and are taken in the reverse order that they are made. Remember these are not motions to amend bills, they are procedural motions. There are other motions besides referring bills to committees. These include motions to table and to postpone indefinitely. The motion to table is non-debatable[49] and the vote occurs immediately after the motion is made. Motions only take a simple majority to pass and it is crucial to know who is on the floor at any one time -- again, learn to count! It is during these intense debates and motions that the use of the call is common. If you are supporting a bill and a hostile motion is made you will immediately ask for a call.

How a presiding officer handles these intense debates can be crucial. A speaker or president may support or oppose a bill, but they are usually expected to support the recommendations of the committee chairs. This is not unusual, as the presiding officer and the committee chair are from the same party. A presiding officer can control debate by knowing who is going to make what motion or who will be moving the previous question to cut off debate. When a vote it taken on a motion it may be an oral vote or a record vote. In the House, record voting is done electronically with buttons at the members desks. In the Senate, the roll is actually called. If the presiding officer asks for an oral vote, two members, in either the House or Senate, may demand a record vote by immediately yelling "division!" or "roll call" before the vote is taken or the gavel comes down.[50] If the chair is in doubt as to the "yeas" and "nays," a "division" or a record vote will be held.

Members are also obliged, by the ethics laws, to announce a conflict of interest before they actually vote.[51] A conflict is defined as any vote where a legislator or a family member will directly profit from the vote. This conflict of interest provision does not apply if the member or a relative is part of a general class. For instance, a member would have to announce a conflict of interest if he or she were the only person affected by a change in the state's retirement law. A member would not have to announce a conflict if the bill were to increase retirement for all former state employees. To be on the safe side most members announce potential conflicts of interest in all possible situations. The point is to avoid the possibility of even being accused of a conflict.

Again, voting in the House is electronic. Each member has a green and a red button at his or her desk. Large panels with digital clocks, lights to indicate how members have voted, and vote totals are located on both sides of the chamber. The clocks count down the 30 seconds the representatives are given to vote, and they are also used to time floor speeches. Members must be "within the bar," or actually on the floor of the House during the 30-second time period for their votes to count. If a member has not used the button at his or her respective desk, the chair will eventually ask for their vote from the rostrum. Senators will sometimes not answer as their names are called the first time through the roll. In both cases, their votes will count as long as they were "within the bar." Frequently, members will vote with a thumbs up or down signs to the chief clerk who registers their votes electronically. On very important votes in the House, and all record votes in the Senate, a roll is called.

Voting is the ultimate political act and the hard votes are not taken lightly. A vote is the moment when a promise may be kept or broken, when a political career may be made or destroyed. It can be the only thing in the legislative session that the member will have to explain to his or her constituents. Why did you raise my taxes? Why did you cut the budget for that seniors' program? Why did you make it easier (or harder) to develop farm land? It is on these "hard" votes, the ones that can and will be misinterpreted, that the games are played. Most members do not want to waste politically unpopular votes on bills that are going to fail. Even a Democrat will not vote to raise taxes unless the bill is going to pass. As mentioned, members in both houses will not vote during the initial voting period. At the end of the 30_second voting period in the House, vote totals for and against are flashed on the side panels. In the Senate, members will have kept running tallies of the yeas and nays. Thus, in both bodies, legislators will have a good idea of whether or not a bill is going to pass or fail. As names are called of the members who have held back their votes, each will have to make a political decision. It's common for members to tell proponents of controversial bills that they will be the "thirty-first vote" in the House or the "sixteenth vote" in the Senate. There are some other variations to this mating dance. At times, the two parties will count each other's votes to make sure that the other side has a majority supporting the bill. In the 1991 session, the Democrats in the House had what they called the "rule of sixteen." The Democrats, who were in the minority, would not support any budget unless a majority of the controlling Republicans also supported the budget. This was a way to avoid the politically stinging label of "tax-and-spend Democrats...."

In addition to calling the names of the members who have not voted, the speaker and the president will also accept vote changes before rapping the gavel and announcing the vote. Here is where an even more duplicitous game can be played. A legislator who has casted the politically hard "yes" vote may change to "no" once he or she sees that the bill doesn't need his or her vote to pass. The reverse can also occur; a member may initially vote against a politically popular bill that they personally oppose, only to vote yes when they see it is going to pass anyway. Finally, there are the vote changes which occur merely to be on the prevailing side in order to be able to move for reconsideration. This will typically be done by the carrier of a bill if he or she sees it is going to fail. All of these machinations must occur before the gavel comes down. If the presiding officer wants to foreclose the game playing and finalize the issue it will be a "fast gavel." On the other hand, the gavel may be "slow" as the speaker or president wait for the final card to be played.

Keeping Track of What is Going On --Notices and Notices

As the assembly processes its 3000-plus bills, it becomes crucial for all interested parties to be able to keep track of specific bills. A daily calendar is published which gives the status of every bill and its legislative history. This history includes who sponsored the bill, the dates of introduction, referral to committee, committee hearings and work sessions, and the results of any floor action on the bill. At the end of the legislative session, a Final Legislative Calendar will be published by the clerk of the House and the secretary of the Senate. If a bill has successfully made it through the whole process, the final calendar will also give the date the bill was signed by the governor, the chapter number in the Session Laws (a compilation of all the new statutes before they are integrated into the Oregon Revised Statutes), and the effective date of the new law. The clerk and secretary will also publish a House and Senate Journal which will contain summarized accounts of all floor actions. All committee hearings and floor sessions are taped and part of the public record.

In addition to the calendar, which is published daily, there is an on-line computer system know as OLIS , an acronym for Oregon Legislative Information Service. OLIS will instantly give the status of any bill and will also serve as a computerized legal research tool, able to search for key words and phrases. Terminals are located throughout the capitol and the system can be accessed with a modem. Numerous lobbyists and interest groups employ assistants just to keep track of legislation.

As mentioned earlier, there is a t 24 hour public-notice rule for committee meetings. The actual hearing notices are posted on large bulletin boards outside the House and Senate chambers. However, this rule allows special one-hour notices as the session approaches *sine die* . It is during these last few days, under the special one-hour notice provisions, that the legislature is at its worst. So many committees and conference committees are meeting on such short notice that it is almost impossible to know what is actually happening. Again, committees may only act within the relating clauses of the bills that are before them, but if a relating clause is broad enough, a totally new matter may be introduced and acted on with little notice to interested parties. Giving notice of committee meetings becomes an art in itself. Chairs have been know to have notices posted during long floor sessions when both lobbyists and members are preoccupied with debate on the floor. Once the notice has been up an hour, the members are asked to be excused from the floor for a quick meeting. No one is the wiser. Other committee chairs have been known to post a notice of one meeting, start the meeting, then have a second meeting notice with a controversial agenda item posted as the first meeting is going on. At the end of the magic hour, the original meeting is adjourned and a second meeting is convened. This usually happens with two quick raps of the gavel and members of the public don't know that the agenda has changed!

School for Legislators

There is no school for legislators. Before the session, there is only a short orientation for new members explaining the logistics of how to file a bill and run a legislative office. The real art of legislating, of being an effective member, is learned by watching, listening and doing --"Monkey see, monkey do," as one cynic called the process. Although freshman legislators are expected to be somewhat deferential during the first part of the legislative session, there is no "legislative apprenticeship" such as in the United States Senate. At one time there, new members did not speak on the floor during their first session. Except for chairing committees, and there have been exceptions to this rule, freshmen are full participants in the legislative process.

Over the years, certain norms have developed as to how to become an effective lawmaker:

--Don't make enemies. Always remember that today's enemy may be tomorrow's friend. Good legislators know that alliances and positions shift as the issues change. One should never personalize a conflict, question another person's motives or insult a fellow legislator. Cynicism and ridicule may make for wonderful press, but the object of the attack will never forget it. Even the brightest lawmakers forget this rule at times.

--Learn to count. Not only is there the tactical aspect of this, as discussed earlier, i.e., knowing how many votes you have at any one time in committee or on the floor, but one needs to develop a sense of whether or not a bill will pass. In most cases, having an issue fail on the floor is to the discredit of the chief sponsor and/or the carrier. Controversial questions not only put members on the record, but they use up immense amounts of legislative time.

--Make yourself an expert on one or two issues. People come to respect members who have spent the time and effort to learn the intricacies of particular issues. Hearings, debates, and the constant flow of information can be the equivalent of an ongoing graduate level seminar on a question of public policy.

--Don't speak too much. There seems to be an inverse relationship between the length of legislative tenure and the number of times a member speaks on the floor. The opinions of those who speak infrequently are inevitably given more deference.

--Be decisive. Nothing will get a legislator into more trouble than being on all sides of an issue. Voters may disagree with a member's position, but they will respect decisiveness. On the hard issues such as abortion, gun control, and gay rights, the best thing is to state your position and walk away from the matter.

--Keep your word. If a member tells another member or a lobbyist that he or she is going to vote a particular way, they are expected to keep that promise. This is usually called a "pledge." If you have pledged your vote, you can change your mind;

traditionally however, one must go to the person you pledged your vote to and tell them personally that you have changed your mind. Pledging one's vote is very closely related to "vote trading." Neither one of these processes are as overt as an outsider might expect. Senator Smith asks Senator Jones --"Can you support me on SB-101, the AIDS Commission?" Jones replies, "I think so, but can you help me on SB-201, my milk bill?" "Of course," Smith says. Was a vote traded? Was a pledge made? Absolutely, and both members know it.

--Pride of authorship. This is really an inadequate term, but basically it means that people become emotionally vested in what they consider to be their bills. Bills become like children, sheltered and protected through a dangerous journey. Legislators, lobbyists and other players will compromise, scheme, vote trade, reason and cajole to have their idea become law. This phenomenon goes far beyond reason into almost irrationality. Everybody wants their moment in the political sun.

Legislative Language -- "Turkeys," "Camels," and "Heroes"

There is an amazing amount of legislative jargon that goes far beyond the usual terms of art, such as "third reading," or "call of the House." These are the code words and phrases of a political sub-culture. They not only communicate, but they also convey the norms and mores of that sub-culture.

"Bill has a c problem" --This is shorthand for the bill is short of votes.

"Blind siding" --This term denotes the situation where one member attacks a bill or makes a parliamentary motion without warning his opponent. "Blind siding" is particularly frowned upon between members of the same party.

"Broken his pick" --When someone has "broken his pick" with a legislator the offending individual has so alienated the member that he can never be trusted again.

"Can we help each other out?" --Let's trade votes.

"Carrying water" --When a member is "carrying water "for someone this means he or she is helping out an interest group or a political friend. When you have been "carrying water" for a group all session you might complain by saying that "my arms are getting long."

"Camel's nose under the tent..." --Here a member attacks a bill on the grounds that, while the particular bill may be acceptable, it will set a bad precedent. For instance, a measure may give nurses limited authority to write prescriptions. The opponent will make the point that while the bill is OK, in the next session the same people will want something unacceptable.

"A counter" --A bill is "a counter" if some interest group will be using it to evaluate how well it did in the legislative session. Many groups publish the voting records of the members on their set of issues.

"Don't shoot a man's dog in front of him" -- When a legislator presents a bill to a committee, tradition has it that the committee will not table or otherwise kill the bill while the member is still in the room.

"Do you have 31/16" --Do you have the votes to pass the bill on the floor? Thirty-one votes for the House and 16 votes for the Senate, as mentioned earlier. When a member asks this question about a controversial bill, he or she really wants to know if the proponent has evaluated whether the bill is worth the political price.

"End run" --When a member cannot get a bill out of one committee he may try to get a friendlier committee to adopt his bill by amendment. (See "Gut and stuff.")

"Friendly amendment" --The situation where one member tries to attach his pet bill to another bill in the form of an amendment if the relating clause allows it.

"Get back to me" --This is a not-too-subtle way of saying "no, you can't have my vote." Legislators don't like to give direct negative answers when being lobbied.

"Going up the hill" --Legislators use this metaphor when they describe their particular caucus having to furnish most of the votes necessary to pass a politically unpopular bill, such as a new tax.

"Gut and stuff" --In this instance, a bill with an appropriate relating clause is stripped of all of it original language and a totally new bill is placed into it. This occurs constantly at the end of the legislative session.

"Hero bill" --Some measures are so attractive that every legislator wants to be on record as supporting them.

"Housekeeping bill" --On its face, this means that a bill is totally uncontroversial and has been introduced to correct a technicality. At other times, the carrier of a bill may use the term to downplay the real significance of a bill.

"Holding a bill hostage" --The situation where the chair of a committee lets it be known that he or she will not act on a bill until another bill in another committee is favorably acted on.

"IOUs" --Investor Owned Utilities, has nothing to do with political debt (sort of)

"The KISS principle" --This is an acronym for Keep It Simple Stupid. It is usually applied to tax bills ---the more complex the bill the less the chance of passage.

"Meltdown" --This is where a member loses his or her temper and harangues in committee or on the floor.

"Not in love with the bill" --If a member is carrying a measure that he or she is not really that enthusiastic about, they may casually use this phrase in debate to express their displeasure at the chair who gave them the assignment. Basically, it means "I don't care if you vote against this bill."

"Put them on record" --Discussed earlier, this is the situation where a vote is held to establish a record for the next election.

"Signed off" --If someone has "signed off" on a bill they have approved it.

"Touch bases with" --To seek someone's approval of a bill.

"Turkey" --A ridiculous bill. Unfortunately, it is hard to tell what is or is not a turkey until the bill has been heard.

Reasons for Voting --"Who knows what lurks in men's hearts?"

A member can be motivated to vote for or against a bill by a thousand different reasons. There always is the substance of the bill, is it a good idea, but there is also the politics --who supports it, who does the member feel beholden to? A legislator may cast up to 2,000 votes on the floor and in committee during a legislative session. Quantity is not the only factor. These decisions sometimes have to be made rapidly with little or no time for reflection. There are innumerable instances where he or she has no opinion on a question. Some legislators vote yes as a matter of course; the roll has been called and they have no reason to oppose someone else's issue.

At other times, a lobbyist may come to a legislator and ask for their support, and the member will simply not know the issue or have no particular opinion. If a lobbyist has helped a member in the past, why not vote for their bill? It is in this situation where the regular lobby has very significant impact. Information, as well as influence, is power in the legislative process; if the only information a legislator has is the positive comment of one person asking for his or her vote then that is probably how they will vote. Other bills have so much ideological and political content that the lobby is irrelevant. Oregon legislators will not send a sales tax out for a vote because some lobbyist has asked them to do it.

Motivation for voting one way or another may be ultimately mundane. One member may watch how another member he or she trusts is voting and then vote that way. There is a dark side to this also, as members do "break their picks" with other members, and voting against someone can be a small pay-back for the original wrong.

Voting with Your Caucus --"I belong to no organized political party..."

Will Rogers made one of the classic statements of American politics when he said, "I belong to no organized political party, I'm a Democrat." Today, the same thing can probably be said about both parties in the Oregon Legislature. There is little if any actual party discipline in the sense that a caucus can tell a particular member how to vote on a particular issue. It must be remembered that each Oregon legislator is independently nominated in a primary and elected in a general election. As will be discussed later, the parties in Oregon are very weak and have little or no influence on who their respective standard bearers will be.

The speaker and the president do have their usual powers to appoint committees and refer bills. As mentioned, there have been times when the presiding officers have changed committee membership during sessions. However, there is always a political price to be paid for such an act. The rebellion against Speaker Phil Lang, D --Portland, in the 1977 session was the result of tensions which had been accumulating for years. Inevitably, there seem to be more tensions in the majority caucus than in the minority caucus. Conflicts between the various chairs and the speaker or president seem to be inevitable.

Theoretically, the caucuses are supposed to vote with their leadership on procedural issues. For example, if the speaker rules that a member is out of order in making some comment, the member can appeal the ruling of the chair and a vote would be held on whether or not to uphold the chair. The members of the majority party would be expected to vote with the majority caucus and uphold the speaker's ruling.

The parties frequently caucus off the floor and bills are hotly debated in these private meetings. There are always discussions of the political ramifications of the issues. Although caucuses will develop consensus positions, there is little that can be done to hold dissent members to these positions. Each caucus will have its more conservative and liberal members, and each caucus will have its ideological tension. Although it is rare, a few members have actually changed parties. This happened in the fall of 1991 when Representative Tom Brian, from Tigard, switched from Democrat to Republican and Republican Representative Bob Pickard, of Bend, changed to Democrat. Brian was always considered to be a "conservative Democrat" and explained that he felt more comfortable with the Republican Party's positions. Pickard had numerous battles with Republican Speaker Campbell during the 1991 session over his management style. He charged Campbell with being overly authoritarian, and the speaker responded by allowing few if any bills to the Special Committee on Children's Issues which Pickard chaired.

Control --Parties and Coalitions

Until the 1970s, the norm in Oregon was for both houses of the Legislature to be controlled by Republicans or coalitions of Republicans and conservative Democrats. In this century, regular Democrats have only controlled both houses from 1971 to 1989.

As mentioned earlier, throughout the late 1950s through 1971, the Oregon State Senate was under the control of the "coalition," a combination of Republicans and rural conservative Democrats. The first coalition Senate president was Boyd Overhulse, D --Madras, in 1957. In 1959, it was Walter Pearson, D --Portland, and in 1961 it was Harry Boivin, D --Klamath Falls. E.D. "Debbs" Potts, D-Grants Pass, was president in both 1967 and 1969. The last coalition president was John Burns, D-Portland, in 1971.

Harry Boivin has the distinction of being the only person ever to be both speaker of the House and president of the Senate. In his thirty-six year tenure in Oregon politics, serving intermittently from 1935 to 1971, he was known as Harry "the Fox." In 1935, regular Democrats controlled the House and elected John Cooter, D --Toledo, Speaker. Cooter was elected on a straight partisan vote. At the start of the 1937 Session, Boivin put together the first coalition of rural Democrats and Republicans and was elected speaker.

There is more than enough evidence to argue that the real ideological conflict in the legislature is not Democrat versus Republican, but urban versus rural. An in-depth examination of this is beyond this work, but two points should be kept in mind. First, urban-rural conflict is probably endemic to any legislative body in the world; city people never understand country folk and *vice versa*. Second, the threat of coalition politics always lurks beneath the surface in the Oregon Legislature; every member knows that it has happened before and can happen again. The 1977 "coup" with Speaker Lang was pure coalition politics and is still fresh in the political memory.

Finally, it should be noted that this is a particular brand of "coalition" politics. It is dissimilar to the coalition politics in which multiple parties and the groups negotiate as parties *per se*, such as in Israel, to divide up the positions of power. The coalition politics in Oregon has always involved a few of the majority party, Democrats, combining with the minority party, Republicans, to usurp the positions of legislative leadership.

Unanticipated Events --Meltdowns to Murder

Legislative sessions do not occur in vacuums and every meeting of the assembly seems to have some non-legislative event which becomes the subject of both debate and legislative action. For example, in 1979 the Three Mile Island nuclear accident occurred and nuclear power became one of the major topics of the session.

In 1981 a scandal developed when lobbyist Bob Harris was alleged to have given a Cadillac to State Senator Richard Groener, D-Milwaukie. Harris owned a process-serving service (subpoenas and such) and had pushed a bill through the prior session requiring the Department of Motor Vehicles to use process servers to inform people that their licenses had been suspended.[52] The press went into a feeding frenzy and ethics became one of the main issues for the Legislature.

Perhaps the most dramatic instance of an outside event impinging on the Legislature occurred in 1989. Prisons and corrections were the hot topic that year and a major player was Director of Corrections, Michael Francke. Francke appeared before the House Judiciary Committee on January 16 to push his package of corrections legislation. Tragically, he was found stabbed to death outside his office on the morning of January 17. In August of 1991, Frank Gable, an ex-convict, was convicted of killing Francke and given a life sentence. The murder not only epitomized the very issue of prisons, which was before the legislature at the time, but led to lengthy investigations of the Department of Corrections itself. The final chapter has not been written on either Francke or Gable.[53]

Sex was an issue during the 1993 session. It raised its ugly head in the State Senate on March 24, 1993, when Michelle Mitchell a 25-year-old legislative aide, filed a sexual harassment complaint against her former boss, Senator Rod Johnson, R-Roseburg.[54] Mitchell said that on a trip with Johnson, for a district meeting, he had made sexual comments, touched her, and asked her to go to a motel. She told Johnson to stop, but he continued. The next week she asked the advice of the Legislative Counsel Office and they arranged for her to be transferred to a page job in the House.[55] Mitchell went public when people began questioning why she had transferred. Earlier in the session, Senate President Bill Bradbury had appointed a sexual harassment committee[56] in response to concerns that had been raised by the Bob Packwood controversy. The panel had not adopted rules, so it was hard to accuse Johnson of any specific violation. Senator Jeannette Hamby, R-Hillsboro, called it a "lynch mob" [57] In the meantime, on May 8, Johnson formally apologized to Mitchell and she agreed not to file charges.[58],[59]

Finally, nature itself interfered with the 1993 session in the form of an earthquake in March. For several days, both the House and Senate met in a basement hearing room instead of their respective chambers because of damage to the Capitol building.[60]

Dynamics of a Session --Timing is Everything

It has been said that timing is everything in comedy and politics. But, the sequence of events from organizational caucuses to final gavel is more like a long opera than a comedy routine. People in the Capitol are frequently heard to say that, "It's not over until the fat lady sings!"

Timing is crucial in the legislative process because certain important things must occur before other just as important things can happen. The governor and the governor's opening speech set the agenda for the legislative session. As much as legislators dislike the idea, "the governor proposes and the legislator disposes." Law-makers may affect issues on the periphery, but it is the governor that must lead on the big issues. Again, this relationship or tension between the executive and the legislative is historic.

Once the agenda has been set in January, committees get down to the mundane business of hearing bills for about three months. Most of the big issues, school finance, corrections, and health care, are connected with the fundamental question of how much money is available. The amount of money is determined by three things, two of which have been mentioned before, new taxes out of the House Revenue Committee and budget savings out of Ways and Means. The third and final factor is the most important, and that is how much money will be collected in income taxes as people send in their checks after the April 15th deadline. These revenue projections are not usually known until the middle of May, so it is not until then that any fundamental decisions can be made about the state budget.

There are big budgets and little budgets before the Ways and Means Committee. A small board may have a budget of only $100 thousand, and this can be handled early in the session. The big budgets for the Human Resources Department, higher education, state employees salaries, capitol construction, and basic school support must wait for the mid-May revenue projections before any strategic decisions can be made.

Even more important than the revenue figures is the psychology of the members themselves. It is only in hindsight that making the right choices seems easy. Members only make hard decisions when all other options have been foreclosed. The hard decisions to cut a program, to raise a tax, to offend an interest group will only be made when the members have no other choice. This is why the significant votes are never cast at the beginning of a legislative session. The process needs a time period during which the various plans, proposals and schemes can be evaluated and discussed by not just the legislators, but by all the participants. Witnesses need to be heard, constituents need to write letters and editorial positions need to be taken.

It is also during May that committees begin to realize that their work must come to an end. There is a perception that house committees should be working on senate bills and *vice versa*. On a certain day, the speaker and the president will inform their respective committees that they can only work on the other chamber's bills. In the middle of June, committees themselves are shut down and cannot meet without the permission of the presiding officers.

Toward the end of the session, the decision will be made to bring the hard issues to the floor. The governor and the legislative leaders will reach the conclusion that there has been enough talking, that the members want to go home and it is time to make the painful choices.

Death Marching to *Sine Die*

The end of a legislative session has to be seen to be truly appreciated. For a month or so at the end, both bodies work seven days a week. Dozens of conference committees meet at once and Ways and Means, revenue, and judiciary are in session constantly. Toward the end, fatigue becomes the dominant factor. Members' tempers grow short as the last of their good will and energy are used up in twelve hour days. All of this is exacerbated by the fact that no one really knows when the session will actually end. All agency budgets have to be passed, but even after these bills have cleared, the final hurdle issues seem to stand in the way of adjournment.

The last act is the "death march," a final burst of activity that can go on through the night and into the next day. It has been known to last up to 48 hours. Measures are voted on without copies being in front of the members, as even the Xerox machines can't keep up. But in the end, all the bills that can pass will have passed, the hard choices will have been made, promises will have been broken and every dollar will have been spent.

The House and Senate are directly opposite each other across the Capitol rotunda. At the last moment, the doors to the two chambers open and then the speaker and the president watch each other as they drop the final gavel and the assembly adjourns *"sine die."* The session is over, and both floors are symbolically opened to the public as the power to make laws returns to the people.

'93 --The Longest Session

Some people are said to be twice blessed. The 1993 Legislative Session was twice dammed. It not only became the longest session in Oregon's history, 207 days from January 11 to August 5, but it was notorious for partisan infighting and gridlock. Governor Roberts opened the Session with the shortest governor's speech on record, only 12 minutes, and barely mentioned the Ballot Measure 5 situation. Even though she was the governor, she would not offer her own tax plan.[61]

Republicans controlled the House by a 32 to 28 margin. Democrats barely controlled the Senate with only 16 out of 30 votes. The Senate took five days to organize and Democrat Bill Bradbury of Bandon was finally elected as a compromise candidate on Friday, January 15.

The delay and deadlock was mainly due to Senator Mae Yih, D-Albany, who withheld her vote for president and demanded to be Co-Chair of Ways and Means.[62] Yih, 64, is an extremely wealthy, extremely conservative, native of China whose husband helped start Wah Chang Metals. Eventually, Yih was given the supposedly honorary position of president *pro tempore* and a seat on the Ways and Means Committee.

Where the Senate was disorganization, the House was "organization" taken to its extreme. Larry Campbell, R-Eugene, was re-elected Speaker and promptly announced that the Session should only be 100 days. The Speaker reduced the number of committees from the usual seventeen to nine, took members' names off bills,[63] eliminated free coffee during committee hearings and then, as a final measure of efficiency, hired his son Craig. Campbell removed nine term veteran Tony Van Vliet R-Corvallis as Co-Chair of Ways and Means and replaced him with John Minnis, R-Wood Village. Van Vliet had profound differences with Campbell over taxes, support for higher education and welfare programs.[64],[65]

A third of the way into the session, the House and Senate got into a major conflict over the "basic school support" budget which supplies the state portion of local school finance.[66] Cuts in school funding would become an extremely emotional and political issue. Ballot Measure 5 required that Legislature make up the shortfall in revenue to school districts from reduced property tax, but since the state was already supplying approximately 30% of the funding as "basic school support" it was proposed to cut basic school support itself in order to help make the overall shortfall. The actual cut was approximately $206 million. All the House Democrats[67] and one Republican, Van Vliet, voted against the cuts and thus the measure became a partisan issue ---Democrats supporting schools and Republicans against them.[68]

Much to the chagrin of the House Republicans, the full Senate rejected the bill.[69] In response, on March 19, 1993, Speaker Campbell and Co-Chair Minnis amended the house rules to establish a separate House Appropriations Committee.[70] This all occurred in face of a statutory requirement that all budget bills go to the Joint Ways and Means Committee.[71],[72]

The splitting of Ways and Means proved to be a disaster and was probably more responsible than any other factor for the record length of the Session. On Friday, July 30, the Department of Human Resources was supposed to mail monthly welfare checks, but realized that it had no budget and thus no authority to spend money. Because the bill which would authorize the expenditure had not come out of a House-Senate Conference Committee, 120,000 plus checks were delayed. There had not been an instance of the state being late on any kind of payment since the Great Depression.[73]

As if the check fiasco was not enough, the House Appropriations Committee literally ran out of time to hear bills at the end of the session. The Committee approved 19 agency budgets without hearings and sent them to the House floor in one bill. The carrier of the measure, Rep. Mary Alice Ford, R-Beaverton, responded to pointed questions on the floor by saying that the Senate had done a good job and that the House didn't really have to be concerned about the details.[74]

The tenor of the Session was bitter and acrimonious.[75] Most members knew that the Ballot Measure 5 shortfall was the overwhelming task which faced the Legislature from the very beginning, but Campbell adopted the position that no revenue measures would considered until May. Delna Jones, R --Aloha, Chair of the House Revenue Committee, followed the Speaker's orders and helped create even more tension in the body because of her lack of action. Most Revenue Committee hearings were taken up with tax break proposals for business.[76] The Revenue Committee did produce and the Legislature finally passed a sales tax to be voted on by the people.[77]

As the Session went on and on, media criticism became vehement. The Oregonian called Campbell a "loser"[78] and said that "gridlock" was "too nice a word" to describe the session.[79] The Register-Guard ran a headline saying, "Gridlock in Legislature leaves lawmakers glum."[80] Another Oregonian article, which could only be called scathing, was entitled "Partisan politics commands the stage," and contained this quote from former State Senator Wayne Fawbush

> On a relative scale they are atrocious. On an absolute scale they are less than mediocre. The real problem is, usually you hope that elected bodies will rise to meet the issues of the times. This body is sinking into the swamp.[81]

For better or worse, Campbell did dominate the legislative process in 1993, but he never seemed to be able to get beyond either his politics or his personality. Campbell was a good campaigner and a great fund raiser,[82] but he was his own worst enemy. Steve Duin of The Oregonian summed it up:

> In truth Campbell feasts on partisan politics and punishes caucus members who think the state's problems are more important than Republican posturing. The people who get ahead in his world are those who are good at following orders, not building consensus. They offer him only compliance, not ideas.[83]

As for Governor Roberts, she did her best to put distance between herself and the Legislature in a post session interview with the <u>Willamette Week</u>:

> (<u>Willamette Week</u> --on a scale of 1 to 10 how would you rate the legislative session?) I would give it a six on content and a 1 on style. It was the most divisive, combative, partisan, difficult session I've seen in the history of the modern Oregon Legislature. I think it literally damaged the institution. It was longer than needed to be. Decisions that could have been made early were held for political purposes. I think there was a product, but I think it was so overshadowed by the bad process that I think no one could even see the product.[84]

1 Or. Const. art. IV, sec. 1.

2 Frederick Jackson Turner, <u>Frontier and Section - Selected essays of Frederick Jackson Turner</u>, with an Introduction by Ray Allen Billington (Englewood Cliffs, N.J.: Prentice-Hall, 1991) 58.

3 Or. Const. , art. V, sec. 12.

4 Or. Const. , art. IV, sec. 10a.

5 Oregon, Secretary of State, <u>Oregon Blue Book 1993-1994</u> (Salem: Secretary of State, 1993), 146.

6 The passage of Ballot Measure 3, in 1992, terms limits may make this point moot.

7 Under the Oregon Constitution, the secretary of state does reapportionment if the Legislature is not able to accomplish the task. Reapportionment occurs every ten years afser the Census, and the Assembly has until July 1 before the assignment goes to the secretary of state. Reapportionment is an intensely political process and it has ended up with the secretary of state every time it has been attempted.

8 Or. Const. , art. IV, sec. 12.

9 The clerk of the House and the secretary of the Senate, although nominally elected positions, serve at the pleasure of the presiding officers.

10 Oregon, Sixty-Sixth Oregon Legislative Assembly, <u>Rules of the House</u>, (Salem: Committee on Rules and Reapportionment, 1991), Rule 8.05; Oregon, Sixty-Sixth Oregon Legislative Assembly, <u>Rules of the Senate</u>, (Salem: Committee on Rules, 1991), Rule 8.05.

11 <u>Rules of the House</u>, Rule 9.01; <u>Rules of the Senate</u>, Rule 8.40.

12 <u>Rules of the House</u>, Rule 9.30; <u>Rules of the Senate</u>, Rule 8.42.

13 <u>Rules of the House</u>, Rule 8.20; <u>Rules of the Senate</u>, Rule 8.20.

14 Or. Const. , art. IV, sec. 20.

15 <u>Rules of the House</u>, Rule 8.22; <u>Rules of the Senate</u>, Rule 8.75.

16 <u>Rules of the House</u>, Rule 5.40; <u>Rules of the Senate</u>, Rule 5.40.

17 <u>Rules of the House</u>, Rule 11.05; <u>Rules of the Senate</u>, Rule 11.05.

18 ORS 173.710.

19 ORS 171.555.

20 ORS 171.805.

21 Oregon, <u>Form and Style Manual for Legislative Measures - 1992 Edition</u>, (Salem: Legislative Administration Committee, 1992), 28-36.

22 ORS 173.111 - 173.790.

23 ORS 173.230.

24 <u>Rules of the House</u>, Rule 13.05; <u>Rules of the Senate</u>, Rule 13.10.

25 ORS 171.132.

26 <u>Rules of the House</u>, Rule 8.01.

27 <u>Rules of the House</u>, Rule 8.15(5); <u>Rules of the Senate</u>, Rule 8.15(1); ORS 192.610-192.690.

28 <u>Rules of the House</u>, Rule 8.25(1); <u>Rules of the Senate</u>, Rule 8.10(2).

29 <u>Rules of the House</u>, Rule 10.01; <u>Rules of the Senate</u>, Rule 10.01.

30 As will be discussed later, Speaker Campbell abolished the Ways and Means system in 1993. Whether his change will be permanent remains to be seen.

31 The one exception to this rule is the Oregon State System of Higher Education, there, grant money may be accepted and expended without legislative approval.

32 Or. Const. , art. III, sec. 3; ORS 291.324.

33 ORS 173.410 - 173.450.

34 Quoted in D.B. Hardeman and Donald C. Bacon, <u>Rayburn - A Biography</u>, (Austin: Texas Monthly Press, 1987), 428.

35 This is a little explored, but true phenomenon. The first English Parliaments were called because of the King's need for taxation; Kenneth O. Morgan, Ed. <u>The Oxford History of Britain</u>, (New York: Oxford University Press, 1988), 172. Louis XVI started the French Revolution when he summoned the States General because of the need for money; See, Simon Schama, <u>Citizens</u>, (New York: Alfred A. Knopf, 1989). In 1847, the King of Prussia could not get money to build a railroad to connect Berlin and the East Prussia. Frederick William IV convened a Diet to approve floating of a loan, but the members of the assembly pursued their own agendas except for a young man who became the King's most ardent defender. He thus launched his career in politics, his name was Otto von Bismarck; Edward Crankshaw, <u>Bismarck,</u> (New York: The Viking Press, 1981), 34.

36 Or. Const. , art. IV, sec. 18.

37 ORS 173.800 - 173.850.

38 See, Paul Starr, <u>The Social Transformation of American Medicine</u>, (New York: Basic Books, 1982).

39 Or. Const. , art. IV, sec. 25.

40 <u>Rules of the House</u>, Rule 3.20(1); <u>Rules of the Senate</u>, Rule 3.20(1).

41 <u>Rules of the House</u>, Rule 3.55; <u>Rules of the Senate</u>, Rule 3.55.

42 Paul Mason, <u>Mason's Manual of Legislative Procedure</u>, (St. Paul: West Publishing Co. 1989).

43 These two offices are known for the professionalism and courtesy to members. It is no small task handling the requests and tolerating the foibles of 90 individuals who are very impressed with being elected officials.

44 <u>Rules of the House</u>, Rule 4.01(4).

45 <u>Rules of the House</u>, Rule 6.30(1).

46 <u>Rules of the House</u>, Rule 6.10; <u>Rules of the Senate</u>, Rule 6.10.

47 Walter M. Pierce, <u>Oregon Cattleman/Governor, Congressman</u>, Edited and expanded by Arthur H. Bone (Portland; Oregon Historical Society, 1981), 187; The author particularly likes this story, he has been accused of being overly strident on the floor of the House, but he has never held the body at gun point while going on for an hour.

48 <u>Rules of the House</u>, Rule 3.40; <u>Rules of the Senate</u>, Rule 5.17.

49 <u>Rules of the House</u>, Rule 5.15; <u>Rules of the Senate</u>, Rule 5.15.

50 <u>Rules of the House</u>, Rule 3.15(2); <u>Rules of the Senate</u>, Rule 3.15(2).

51 <u>Rules of the House</u>, Rule 3.21; <u>Rules of the Senate</u>, Rule 3.33.

[52] "Ex-lobbyist relates car, home dealings involving Groener," The Oregonian, 29 March 1981, A1.

[53] Phil Stanford, "Michael Francke - -the case that won't go away," The Oregonian, 6 April 1993, C1, C4.

[54] Gail Kinsey Hill, "Lawmaker accused of sexual harassment," The Oregonian, 26 March 1993, C4.

[55] Ironically, this act of demoting her was probably more grounds for a suit than what Johnson had allegedly done.

[56] The committee was chaired by Senator Tricia Smith, D-Salem, who had her own problems with the law -- in 1991 she pled no contest to possession of marijuana.

[57] Gail Kinsey Hill, "Harassment panelist tries to quit," The Oregonian, 10 April 1993, D3.

[58] On June 22 a second aide, Anne Crowell, related to the press how Johnson had talked to her about the size of her breasts and joked about her mother's mastectomy. Crowell didn't file a complaint and the Senate determined it didn't have jurisdiction because the matter had occurred in the House. Gail Kinsey Hill, "Johnson may face reprimand in Senate," The Oregonian, 23 June 1993, C1, C4.

[59] Before the session was over, Rod stories were being told in both houses. The favorite was how Johnson, a veteran skydiver, had bragged to several women what a thrill it was to parachute at night in the nude.

[60] Cathy Kiyomura, "Quake hazards shift legislators," The Oregonian, 31 March 1983, A1, A14.

[61] Gail Kinsey Hill, "Legislature sets out on hard road to accord," The Oregonian, 12 January 1993, A1, A10; Scott McFetridge, "Governor stumps some legislators," Statesman Journal, 12 January 1993, 2C; "1993 Legislature gets off to unfortunate start," Statesman Journal, 12 January 1993, __; "12-minute time-out," The Register-Guard, 12 January 1993, __.

[62] Ron Blankenbaker, "Senate ends stalemate, elects leader," Statesman Journal, 16 January 1993, 1C.

[63] Taking names off bills was supposed to save time and money, but it had the opposite effect. Before each hearing committee staff would have to go back to the original bill file to find out who the sponsor was so they could notify the member of the hearing.

[64] Steve Duin, "Why legislate when you can waste time?" The Oregonian, 14 January 1993, __.

[65] The Speaker also removed Eldon Johnson, R-Medford, from Ways and Means because he also had been too much in favor of human resource programs in 1991. Johnson, took the humiliation in stride and related how Campbell broke the news to him. "He said he would not put me back on the (budget) committee because he thought I would not physically survive the session -- that I would continue to have too big a heart and would not have the guts to do what we had to do. "Peter Wong, "Johnson locks horns with speaker, loses post," Medford Mail Tribune, 31 January 1993, __.

[66] Oregon, Sixty-Seventh Oregon Legislative Assembly, House Bill 5003.

[67] Representative Dominy and Peterson were excused from the vote so the actual measure passed 31 yeas to 27 nays.

[68] Gail Kinsey Hill, "House OKs big school funding cut," The Oregonian, 5 March 1993, A1, A22.

[69] David Steeves, "Senate rejects education cuts," Statesman Journal, 10 March 1993, 1A, 2A.

[70] Oregon, Sixty-Seventh Oregon Legislative Assembly, House Journal, 19 March 1993; Ron Blankenbaker, "Budget process gains new look," Statesman Journal, 17 March 1993, __.

[71] ORS 171.599.

72　The Speaker acted on the advice of Legislative Counsel that Article IV, Section 11, which gives the House the power to make its own rules, allowed him to take the action. The Joint Ways and Means Committee had been a functioning legislative institution since 1917, so this action was historically significant if nothing else. Several members, including the author seriously considered taking the issue to courtt. Steve Duin, "Armageddon and the 'dead sea scrolls,'" The Oregonian, 30 M7 1993, B&; See Zemprelli v. Scranton, 519 A2nd 518 (1986).

73　"Checks go out after day's wait," Statesman Journal, 1 August 1993, D1.

74　Oregon, Sixty-Seventh Oregon Legislative Assembly, House Bill 5549. The bill included the Board of Dentistry, the Board of Clinical Social Workers, the Board of Optometry, the Board of Pharmacy and the Board of Psychologist Examiners. Some of these budgets were more than a million dollars.

75　Cathy Kiyomura, "Long walk on the low road," The Oregonian, 23 July 1993, C8; See also, Cathy Kiyomura, "Session ends: politics linger," The Oregonian, 6 August 1993, A1, A17.

76　Bill Mackenzie, "Lobbyists' cry: 'Give me a (tax) break," The Oregonian, 19 May 1993, B4.

77　Gail Kinsey Hill, "Now its up to you," The Oregonian 4 August 1993, A1, A12. The measure was overwhelmingly defeated at the November Special Election.

78　Gail Kinsey Hill, "It's Salem's lot: THE WINNERS - the losers & the snoozers," The Sunday Oregonian, 16 May 1993, B6.

79　David Sarasohn, "In Salem, 'gridlock' too nice a word," The Oregonian 1 July 1993, J2.

80　Brent Walth, "Gridlock in Legislature leaves lawmakers glum," The Register-Guard (Eugene) 26 April 1993, 1A, 4A.

81　Dan Hortsch, "Partisan politics commands the stage," The Oregonian 25 July 1993, C4; See also, Steven J. Gould, "Leadership vacuum will sink state, The Oregonian, 19 May 1993, B11.

82　When Campbell announced he was not going to run for re-election he had approximately $70,000 in his campaign fund. Oregon politicians are allowed to keep excess funds for their own use -when asked what he was going to do with his surplus Campbell's reply was blunt and to the point, "I can do any damn thing I want with it." Bill MacKenzie, "Campaign funds make nice nest egg," The Oregonian, 4 September 1993, B1, B4.

83　Steve Duin, "A frightenly close call with Dr. Death," The Oregonian , 11 May 1993, B5.

84　"The Race is On and She's off" Willamette Week, 2 September 1993, 14.

CHAPTER 6

THE JUDICIARY

The law, in its majestic equality, forbids the rich
as well as the poor to sleep under bridges, to
beg in the streets and to steal bread.

Anatole France

Of course judges make law, made some myself
yesterday.

Anonymous Judge

Introduction

The judiciary is ordinarily not thought of as "government" in the same sense as the executive or the legislative branches. Somehow, the courts seem more neutral, removed and unsullied by political considerations. Unfortunately, or fortunately,[1] this is not the case. The judiciary is as involved or more involved in the everyday affairs of government as the other two branches. This chapter attempts to portray both the courts as political institutions and working units of government.

Included are:

- Courts and the common law.
- American courts in general.
- Oregon courts.
- The "personalities" of the courts.
- Judicial fitness.
- Selection of judges.
- Popular election of judges.

- The Oregon State bar.
- The courts and financial matters.
- Municipal courts and Justice courts.
- Sentencing politics.
- Indigent defense.
- Federal courts in Oregon.

The Oldest Branch

Before there was an Oregon, a United States or even an English Parliament, there were the courts as we know them. Both America and this state are "common law" countries. Our courts use a body of law known as the "common law" in their decisions which are not controlled by statute. In addition, there is the "common law method of reasoning," a court makes its determinations, on legal matters, by examining precedent, i.e., how prior courts decided questions in similar situations. A series of previous decisions on a particular topic make up one small part of this body of "common law."

For instance, one can sue for damages caused by a trespassing herd of animals --the owner of the animals must pay for whatever harm the animals caused regardless of whether or not he or she was careless in allowing the trespass:

...where my beasts of their own wrong without my will and knowledge break another's close (fence) I shall be punished , for I am the trespasser with my beasts...for I am held by the law to keep my beasts without their doing wrong to anyone.[2]

This decision is a restatement of the law found in earlier cases and itself becomes part of the law. It is an example of the "substantive"[3] common law and it also illustrates the particular method of reasoning.

Common law exists on a myriad of subjects from what constitutes burglary to the right to change one's name. Parliamentary bodies, including the Congress and the state legislatures, have the right to change common law, but courts continue to use the common law method of reasoning to interpret those very statutes. They examine what the previous cases said about the statute in question. Further, law schools use the "case book method" by reading court decisions instead of statutes to teach the law. The other great legal system is the "civil law" found in Europe. Here, the continental courts rely on systematic bodies of statutes known as "codes" instead of case law.[4] Several other important aspects of the English common law system are still with us including trial by jury, the adversarial nature of the system[5] and procedural aspects of typical court processes such as pleading and burden of proof.

The common law is an integral part of this nation's inheritance from our mother country. The Colonies and eventually the states "adopted" the common law as their own,[6] and in a very real sense our court system is a direct extension of that established by King Henry II, circa 1150 AD. Henry, like every head of state, needed money, and the local courts were slow and cumbersome. So, the King sent his royal justices out to the "shires" to make themselves available to hear certain cases. Most of these were land disputes between the gentry that made up the Norman ruling class of feudal England.[7] Getting a case to court is never easy, but Henry's justices offered quick resolution for a price. Henry needed money and the local aristocracy wanted their land disputes settled. As the royal courts heard more cases involving different subjects, decisions began to be "reported" or written down. Gradually the doctrine of *stare decisis* developed --following the previous decisions, i.e., follow the precedent.

The common law and the common law method are found almost every place in the world where the Union Jack flew. When colonial courts became state courts, after the American Revolution, there was little if any institutional break. Thus our courts, as an institution, have a pedigree that exceeds that of either the legislative or executive branch. Interestingly enough in Oregon, statutes that modify the common law are to be strictly construed.[8] The common law is not one coherent, consistent body of law; different jurisdictions interpret and reinterpret the common law in their own manner.[9] To make matters worse, common law courts in one jurisdiction can cite precedents from other jurisdictions. An English Court can rely on American cases and vice versa. With million upon millions of reported cases as precedents, lawyers are never at a loss for a plausible argument.

American Courts --Plentiful and Powerful

American courts differ from their foreign counterparts in several crucial aspects. First, there is the "power of judicial review," or in simpler terms, the power to declare a statute or a governmental action unconstitutional.[10] Americans are not in the least bit uncomfortable with saying that something is "unconstitutional!" American courts, as the holders of the power of judicial review and the arbiters of government action, are among the most powerful in the world. With a few limited exceptions,[11] no other judicial system has such a vast power to declare laws unconstitutional. We accept our courts as one of the three equal branches of government not realizing how unusual this situation is. When we conceive of something being declared unconstitutional, we usually think of the United States Supreme Court voiding an act of Congress or a state law, but all American courts have the power to declare laws within their jurisdictions unconstitutional. A lower court in Oregon may declare a state statute unconstitutional, but the decision is almost certain to be appealed.[12]

Another unique aspect of American courts is their great number. There are 7,623[13] state courts and 820 federal courts of general jurisdiction[14] in America. There are only about 500 similar courts[15] in England and, notwithstanding the disparity in population, there are approximately four times more courts in the United States than in Britain. This large number of courts is partially a function of the fact there are 51 judicial systems in the United States, 50 state and one federal. This means 51 sets of statutes, constitutions and 50 versions of the common law. (The federal courts do not have their own common law, but borrow from various states when deciding matters involving the common law.) This proliferation of courts, jurisdictions and laws makes the America legal system the most complex and extensive in the world.

It also goes without saying that there are more lawyers in America, approximately 741,000[16] in 1990. There are only about 50,000 barristers and solicitors[17] in England.[18] The United States is also the leader in jury trials; 85 percent of the criminal jury trials take place in America![19]

Finally, the majority of state judges, even though initially appointed by governors, must eventually run for election for terms that vary from four to fourteen years. Oregon judges serve six-year terms.[20]

Oregon --The Supremes , AWOPing and Dog Court

At the top of Oregon's judicial pyramid is the Supreme Court made up of one Chief Justice and Six Associate Justices. The current Chief Justice is Wallace P. Carson, a former Republican State Senator from Salem. "Wally," as he is known to his friends, was one of those rare individuals upon whom there was universal agreement that he was the right person for the job. Notwithstanding "political correctness," Carson is considered to be "a prince of a man." Among other things he also serves as a brigadier general in the Air Force Reserve.

The Court sits in the Supreme Court Building next to the State Capitol in Salem. It is not only the final authority on state legal questions, but also is the administrative body that controls all courts and attorneys in the state. The Oregon State Bar has the *de facto* power to admit and remove persons from the practice of law, but the final authority theoretically remains with the Supreme Court.

In most cases, the Supreme Court has discretion as to what it hears; in other words, appeals are not a matter of right. The Court may assume original jurisdiction in three actions; mandamus, quo warranto and habeas corpus.[21] Among Oregon attorneys, the Supreme Court is affectionately know as "The Supremes."[22]

The Chief Justice in also the administrative head of the state court system which is known as the "Oregon Judicial Department." Actual administration is done by the "state court administrator," currently R. William Linden. The system employs 1,494 full time employees and has a total biennial budget of $260 million.[23]

Below the Supreme Court is the Oregon Court of Appeals with a Chief Judge and nine Associate Judges. The Court of Appeals, unlike the Supreme Court, must hear every case appealed to it.[24]

The Court of Appeals was established in 1969, mainly through the efforts of former Circuit Judge Herbert Schwabe who became its first Chief Judge. Schwabe served from 1969 to 1980 and was perfect for the court's high volume case load. Instead of sitting as one group, the Court of Appeals sits in three judge panels. Civil, criminal and administrative matters all end up before the Court of Appeals, although there is a mechanism for the Court to send particularly important cases directly to the Supreme Court.[25] Schwabe instituted a procedure know as "AWOP" or Affirmed Without Opinion. Here, no written opinion was issued by the court, it merely affirmed the lower court's decision. Many prison inmates have nothing better to do and appeal their convictions; almost all of these verdicts are Affirmed Without Opinion. The phrase has become so common in legal circles that it's been turned into a verb. Almost every lawyer in the state has been "AWOPed" by the Court of Appeals.

There is an extreme disparity between the number of cases heard by the Court of Appeals and the Supreme Court. In 1992, the Supreme Court handled 344 cases where the Court of Appeals processed 5,102 filings.[26] The difference in workload has not gone over well with the Court of Appeals. When Chief Judge George M. Joseph retired in 1992, he made some rather pointed remarks:

> I hoped to leave this job a happy person, but, for a lot of reasons, I have
> become very sour the last couple of years, I don't like being sour, but I'm
> sour -- very sour....The Supreme Court continues as if it were 1860. They
> have all the time and leisure and no pressure on them to produce.[27]

There is a third, almost invisible, appellate court -- the Oregon Tax Court. This court only has one judge, currently Carl N. Byers. He hears all matters arising under Oregon tax law and appeals go directly to the Oregon Supreme Court.[28]

The courts below the Court of Appeals are trial courts. They do actual trials, hear witnesses, accept evidence and engage in all the *Sturm und Drang* of day to day legal combat. The Supreme Court and the Court of Appeals make their decisions based upon the "record" of the lower court. This record, plus the attorneys' briefs and oral arguments constitute the rather boring material of appellate law.

There are two kinds of trial courts in Oregon, the circuit court and the district court. Both of these courts are "courts of record." As mentioned, a "record" is kept which becomes the basis for any appeal. Court reporters are used to produce the transcripts as the circuit court record and in the district court tape recordings are used as the record.

The names "circuit" and "district" have little meaning in and of themselves; other state courts with identical functions go by different names such as "superior court," or "court of common pleas." The circuit court is Oregon's court of general jurisdiction. The district court is the court of "limited jurisdiction." It tries misdemeanors, civil cases under $10,000,[29] and other minor matters that include traffic cases and small claims. There are 94 circuit courts located in 22 judicial districts covering the whole state. In addition, there are 62 district courts in 30 of Oregon's 36 counties. Multnomah County has 14 district and 22 circuit courts.

In 1992, 28,832 civil cases were brought in circuit court. In addition, 55,716 domestic relations, 28,562 criminal, 9,630 probate and 28,066 juvenile, mental health and adoption, cases were filed. The district court processed 325,482 traffic infractions,[30] 92,830 misdemeanors and violations, 17,216 felonies, 34,906 civil cases, and 58,066 small claims matters. The 1992 total case load for the circuit court was 150,806, and for the district court 528,500, all for a grand total of 679,306.[31] Given Oregon's population of approximately three million people, this raises the mathematical possibility that one out of very five Oregonians was somehow involved with the state's courts in 1992.

Circuit judges and district judges are paid identical salaries, $69,600 per year, and have the same six-year terms. The district court is considered the "lower" court, although appeals go directly from it to the Court of Appeals and not to the local circuit court. Ironically, in most of the large jurisdictions such as Multnomah Country, these courts function as one. The Chief Justice of the Supreme Court has always had the power to appoint what are known as *pro tempore* judges to both the circuit and the district court. "pro tem's," as they are called, are substitute judges who are usually respected attorneys who sit part-time. The Chief Justice has appointed all district judges as circuit court pro tem's. The means that a district judge will hear misdemeanors one day as a district judge, and felonies the next day as a pro-tem circuit judge. What this also means is that the circuit judges don't hear traffic cases.

Thus, the relationship between circuit and district court becomes purely one of who has the most prestigious title and does not have to get their hands dirty with what are considered minor matters. There is an interesting "sociology" of judges all over the world and throughout history. Judges like important cases; they would rather decide heavy matters such as the ten million dollar civil case or the sensational murder than minor things like traffic cases, small claims and domestic relations.

There have been numerous attempts to consolidate the circuit and district courts, but all have been vigorously opposed by the circuit court judges. Notwithstanding that *de facto* consolidation has already occurred, the courts remain nominally divided.

There are a few other significant procedural differences between the two courts. District courts, in Oregon use six person juries. This is not unusual; three-fourths of states use juries of less than twelve.[32] However, while the United States Constitution has been interpreted to allow juries as small as six persons in state cases,[33] it is also required that verdict be unanimous.[34] In circuit court felony cases, the requirement is ten out of twelve for a guilty verdict.[35] In civil cases, it is nine out of twelve to find a defendant liable[36] and in capital murder cases, where the death penalty is involved, the verdict must be unanimous, twelve out of twelve.[37]

What is an important case is sometimes in the eye of the beholder. Among the district court's more mundane subjects are animal cases, these hearings are known, somewhat facetiously, as "Dog Court." This is where good citizens are forced to appear to answer for allowing Fido to run loose or letting their innocent pet keep half the neighborhood up all night by its barking. As ridiculous as it sounds, these are very emotional confrontations; people love their pets and hate their neighbors who complain. Other animal cases verge on the bizarre. The author, serving a stint as a crusading deputy district attorney, once tried a Doberman for sheep murder.

Judge Don Londer, now the Presiding Judge in Multnomah Country, sat regularly in "Dog Court." At the end of a trial involving a donkey making excessive noise, he was rewarded by being able to tell the defendant to "Get your ass out of town!" Londer claims to have waited years to make the statement.

Like their counterparts at the State Capitol, the leaders of the judiciary and the legal community in Portland like to gather each morning for coffee at the Standard Plaza. The participants in this ritual are usually the more senior judges and partners in the major law firms. This sounds like some "good'ol boy" nightmare of feminist legal scholar Katherine McKinnon and to a certain extent it is. One of the traditions is that attorneys who have just won the "big case" will drop by for a kind laying-on of hands to welcome them to the major leagues.

Being the judge in the "big case" can also make a judicial career. In 1990 Morris Dees (a civil rights attorney from the Southern Poverty Law Center who became famous for suing the Ku Klux Klan), brought a wrongful death suit against California TV repairman Tom Metzger for the 1988 skinhead beating death of Mulugeta Seraw in Portland. Metzger was in California at the time of the killing, but he ran an organization named White Aryan Resistance or "WAR." The theory was that the attackers had been acting as agents of organization and the trial was in front of one of Oregon's few black judges, Ancer Haggerty. Metzger couldn't afford an attorney and tried to defend himself against the civil suit. He was more than unsuccessful losing a $12.5 million verdict.[38] Haggerty received high praise for his handling of the case and in November of 1993 was nominated to the Federal District Court by President Clinton.[39]

"Muni" Courts and Justices Courts

Many Oregon cities still maintain their own municipal courts to try violations of both state traffic laws and city ordinances, but to a great extent these are traffic courts. Most municipal judges are chosen by their city councils. Portland gave up its municipal court system and replaced it with state district courts. Whether a municipal judge is elected or appointed by the city council depends on the city charter. Most, if not all, municipal judges are attorneys. The same can't be said for justices of the peace.

There are 35 justices of the peace in 21 counties, mostly in rural areas.[40] JP's, as they are called, are authorized by state statute[41] and they do not have to be attorneys. JP's have jurisdiction over misdemeanors, traffic, fish and game violations and civil matters up to a value of $2,500. These down-home courts are more popular with the local citizens than they are with the established Bar and the state has tried gradually to replace JP's with district courts. Justice courts are not courts of record, and an appeal gives the appellant a new trial[42] in district court; or, if the jurisdiction does not have a district court, in the circuit court.[43]

The Personalities of the Courts

Courts, like other institutions, have personalities, a rather ongoing culture that is perpetuated by judges, attorneys and professional sociology. The district courts like to consider themselves "the people's court," traffic cases, small claims, animals, land-lord tenant disputes -- the cases that make up a common person's contact with the law. The circuit courts takes themselves seriously; here fortunes and lives are at stake and the demeanor reflects it. The Court of Appeals resembles an over-worked bureaucrat, too much to do, not enough time to do it and no respect. There is some truth to this, as the Court of Appeals processes more cases than any other court of its size in the country.

The Supreme Court takes itself even more seriously. Issues are major policy questions. The highest courts in other states also have their own corporate personalities. Some are "activist" courts willing to plow new ground with their decisions. The two most notorious of these courts have probably been California and New Jersey. Both have been veritable fonts of new legal theories and rights.[44]

The Oregon Supreme Court is not an activist's court when compared with its counterpart in California. It usually defers to legislative judgment. However, the Court has been a pioneer in another area. As mentioned in Chapter 2, the federal Bill of Rights sets certain minimum standards that the states cannot violate, such as the Fourth Amendment prohibition against unreasonable searches and seizures. The states can grant their citizens more rights under their state constitutions with the doctrine of a "stricter state standard." The Oregon Supreme Court pioneered this idea under the leadership of former Supreme Court Justice Hans Linde One would be less than candid not to point out the judicial politics of the doctrine. During the era when the United States Supreme Court was dominated by Earl Warren, American liberals were more than happy to rely on the federal courts. With a more conservative Supreme Court appointed by Nixon, Reagan and Bush,[45] liberals had to turn to the state courts. Most state bills of rights resemble the federal Bill of Rights and this has proven to be fertile ground for the proponents of individual liberties.

Oregon courts, like all American Courts, make law; they are a significant, but unacknowledged partner in the ever and ongoing process of making public policy in this country. How do we reconcile our supposed democratic form of government with such an undemocratic institution? Courts are eventually responsive to the will of the people, but at the same time they do serve as a break upon some of the vagaries of democracy, or as Professor Henry Abraham said, the courts are,"...democracy hedging its bet."

Bad Judges -- Brain Tumors and Bigamy

Some judges receive notoriety and publicity in high profile trials, but most members of the bench labor in comfortable obscurity. As will be discussed later, even though Oregon judges run for re-election it is rare for a sitting judge to be defeated. "Bad" judges (careless, incompetent or corrupt) are hard to remove from office because of the nature of their work and their institutional position.

In November of 1968, the voters overwhelmingly adopted Ballot Measure 2 and established a mechanism for the removal of judges.[46] The measure, referred by the Legislature, added Section 18 to Article VII (Judicial Department) of the Oregon Constitution and allowed the creation of the "Commission on Judicial Fitness & Disability."[47]

The nine member Commission is composed of three judges appointed by the Supreme Court, three lawyers appointed by the Oregon State Bar and three citizens appointed by the governor who are subject to State Senate confirmation. The current chair of the Commission is Robert E. Joseph, a Portland attorney. Recommendations of the Commission go to the Oregon Supreme Court, and judges can be removed from office or suspended without pay for up to a year. In addition to the suspension, a requirement can be imposed that the judge receive professional counseling or medical treatment. These sanctions might result from a conviction of a crime, willful misconduct that effects the performance of judicial duties, incompetence, violation of the rules of judicial conduct, drunkenness, or drug use.[48]

Cases involving Oregon judges have gone from the tragic to the farcical. In 1977, the Commission moved against District Court Judge Shirley Field for eccentric behavior[49] on the bench. Judge Field had been a Republican State Representative before being appointed to the bench by Governor Tom McCall in 1972.[50] Field's acts included trying a defendant in absentia and finding him guilty, and refusing to grant other defendants their obvious constitutional rights. The report recommending removal said she was "...cursory, abrupt, sarcastic, testy, nasty, hostile, and demeaning toward defendants."[51] Her removal was supported by the Oregon Supreme Court and Governor Straub appointed Kimberly Frankel, a Multnomah County Deputy District Attorney, to the position. Frankel won a six-year term in the fall general election.

As it turned out, the Commission had chosen a very sick woman for its first removal. Prior to the action against Field, the strongest sanction, that had been applied, was a two month suspension of Judge Don Piperin 1977.[52] Field was eventually diagnosed with a brain tumor[53] and there was little doubt that the condition was responsible for her bizarre actions. The operation to remove the tumor was a success, but she couldn't be restored to office. The Commission had done its dirty little job, and that was that.

Robert L. Kirkmanwas appointed to the district bench in 1984 by Governor Atiyeh and seemed to be the perfect candidate. He was a Republican, a Marine Corps reserve officer and a strong advocate of law and order. He also had an affinity for women. Kirkman left his first wife then forged a divorce decree by signing the Presiding Judge's signature. He then married a second woman.[54] Even though Kirkman had committed bigamy, he was not prosecuted and resigned in 1991.[55] The Supreme Court later disbarred the former judge.[56] Governor Barbara Roberts got to make her first appointment and selected Janice Wilson[57] who was sworn in as the first openly lesbian judge in Oregon.

Judicial Selection -- Know the Governor

"A judge is a lawyer who knew the governor." As much as the judicial establishment hates to admit it, there is more than a little truth in this aphorism. All judges in Oregon, regardless of what level, are theoretically elected for six-year terms, but this is more theory than reality. Traditionally, most judges retire before their term expires and the governor appoints their replacements. Once appointed, the new judge must run in the next primary or general election, whichever comes first. In effect, this means that the new judge must run within two years of appointment, but judges are allowed to place the word "Incumbent" after their names on the ballot.[58] It is rare for judges to have any competition in their once every six year election efforts.

The appointment process varies depending on the position sought. For circuit and district court judges, there are local "bar polls" in the county for which the judge is being appointed. A lawyer who wants to be a judge must apply with the governor's office and with the Bar that conducts the poll. The governor does not have to appoint the winner of the bar poll; there have been instances where the governor appointed individuals who did not run in the bar poll. There has always been a tension between the Bar and the governor about judicial appointments, because the Bar considers the selection of judges its prerogative and not the governor's.

For better or worse, bar polls are a kind of professional version of the high school popularity contests. In Multnomah County, only a small fraction of the attorneys voting have had any professional interaction with all of the candidates. Candidates are prohibited from campaigning for office, by bar rules, but committees of attorneys supporting one candidate or another spontaneously emerge. [59]

There are no bar polls prior to appointments to the Court of Appeals or the Supreme Court, but a poll is conducted if there is a contested election for one of the statewide positions. The Board of Bar Governors may make recommendations to the governor as to who is qualified for these positions.

The Bar plays another role in the selection of judges. Lawyers who want to be want to go on the bench are typically very active in Bar affairs, serving on committees, writing for Bar publications and attending Bar functions in an effort to get to know as many of their fellow attorneys as possible.

Interest groups other than the Bar do play some role in judicial selection. Recommendations are made by unions as well as more specialized interest groups such as "Justice Endorsed by Women Lawyers," "Oregon Women's Political Caucus," and "Right to Privacy PAC," the gay and Lesbian interest group.

As mentioned, one of the most important figures in judicial selection is the governor's legal counsel who oversees the process. Robert Oliver did the job for Governor Atiyeh and Cory Streisinger did it for Governor Goldschmidt. Kerry Barnett was Barbara Roberts' legal advisor until he was replaced by Danny Santos, former Chairman of the Oregon Parole Board.[60]

There are innumerable reasons why a governor may or may not appoint someone. In the best of circumstances, it has solely to do with merit. The governor will have examined the various résumés, looked at the result of the bar polls, made discrete inquires and may have actually interviewed all of the candidates. In other situations, the appointment is purely political; an interest group may need to be appeased by having one of their own elevated to the bench, a political friend of the governor may be rewarded for past loyalty, a legislator-lawyer may have been particularly helpful in the prior legislative session. Legislators are a particularly thorny problem; if a governor does not appoint them to the desired post the slight will be remembered. Some appointments are not made because of what the person has done for you but because of what they can do to you! One of the most political situations is where the appointment is made to eliminate the appointee from further political involvement. There have been instances where governors have appointed past and perhaps future rivals to the bench to get them out of the way.

There is almost a bizarre economics of who wants to be a judge. More often than not aspirants for state judgeships tend to come from the middle levels of the profession.

Senior partners in major firms cannot give up their $200,000 a year salaries for $69,600 a year as a judge. On the other hand, that $69,600 looks good to the overworked sole practitioner doing wills and divorces. Being a judge has certain amount of prestige and there is no heavy lifting, i.e., the hours are what you make them. Just in case anyone gets too used to the position, Oregon judges must retire at the age of 75.[61] However, a few individuals have found the profession more boring than satisfying. In 1993, Circuit Judge Garry L. Kahnresigned after less than two years on the bench. Kahn had been a very successful personal injury attorney, prior to appointment by Governor Roberts in 1991, but he found himself isolated from both other judges and friends.[62]

Running for Judge --The Bunny Outfit

Eighty percent of all judges are appointed by the governor.[63] Although they must run for election within the next two years, few, if any, receive significant opposition. Unless the sitting judge has a terrible reputation, it is considered unseemly for an attorney to challenge a sitting incumbent even if he or she has just been appointed. The word "incumbent" following the sitting judge's name on the ballot also has a tremendous impact. Many voters do not vote in judge races, they leave that part of the ballot blank, which makes for a large "undervote." In addition, judge races are notoriously hard contests to raise money in. Judges and candidates for judgeship are prohibited from asking for contributions personally. This means that they must rely on a "committee" to raise money for them. Money remains the "mother's milk" of politics even in judicial races. Given that the best fund-raiser is always the candidate himself or herself, judicial aspirants are under a tremendous disadvantage unless they are incumbents. The size of a jurisdiction may also have profound effect on the races; Multnomah County's population exceeds that of a congressional district. To saturate such an area with media takes hundreds of thousands of dollars.

Regardless, there are judicial races where there is no incumbent; either the sitting judge has allowed his or her term to run out or it is a newly created position where the authorizing statute allows it to be filled by election. There is a basic contradiction in the idea of "running" for judge; the very nature of the office calls for dignity, not the thrust and parry of usual political races. Judicial ethics not only prohibit the raising of money by judge candidates, but the expression of any opinion on a public policy question. Pending or possible litigation issues are also off base. There is little a candidate can talk about other than their qualifications and their support of fairness and efficiency. Because of the budget constraints, these can be very low profile campaigns where the major events are appearances at candidates fairs, shopping centers and service group luncheons. Lawn signs are put up on the main streets and the candidate's personal friends are asked to send postcards to their acquaintances and neighbors.

Interest group participation in these races is limited. The Bar tends to divide into four overlapping groups, the plaintiff's bar, i.e., those attorneys who represent injured clients (sometimes called "personal injury' or "P.I." lawyers). Their counterparts who defend the insurance companies make up the second group. The other two groups are the criminal defense bar and district attorneys. These four groups overlap. P.I. lawyers also do criminal defense and are usually Democrats. Insurance lawyers and district attorneys tend to be Republican. Although judge is a non-partisan office, there is a sense that judicial candidates have some party identification.

One of the more interesting aspects of judicial politics is the phenomenon of ads in the <u>Oregon State Bar Association Bulletin</u>, the profession's monthly magazine. Traditionally, a candidate for judge will take out an early ad as part of his or her campaign for office. These ads say nothing about policy or qualifications, but they list the candidates' "supporters." They are usually huge lists and meant to preempt the opposition, a kind of judicial version of leaving your scent to mark your territory. While candidates cannot ask for money, they can ask for endorsements --and they do. Getting a huge endorsement list is a way to show the possible competition that you have a great deal of support in the Bar itself. It should be emphasized that judicial elections are internal Bar contests much of the time. Unless someone with existing name familiarity runs, the public has little knowledge of judge races. The Bar looks upon judicial office as its turf, and at times a consensus develops that a certain individual deserves to be elected or appointed. Typically, a person wanting to be a judge will put his or her name in several times before being appointed. There are exceptions. Edward Fadeley was elected to the Oregon Supreme Court in 1988 after having been Senate President and unsuccessfully running for governor in the 1986 Democratic primary against Neil Goldschmidt.

Most American state judges are selected under a system similar to Oregon's, i.e., appointed by the governor then elected for full terms. There are a few jurisdictions that have the "Missouri Plan." Here judges do not have opponents when they run for re-election; the ballot merely reads "Shall Judge Smith be retained?" A "Missouri Plan" for Oregon was rejected by the voters in the fall of 1978.[64] As mentioned earlier, elected judges are an American exception to the usual common law country pattern. While attending a meeting in Scotland of common law judges and attorneys, the author served as a panel member discussing judicial selection and was faced with this question from a Canadian judge:

> Mr. Mason, while vacationing in California I met a candidate for the district court campaigning in a shopping center in a pink bunny costume. Can you tell the purpose of this display?

> To get votes, your honor. By the way, how long do you think you can campaign in one of those outfits?

The Bar --A Lawyer's Union

For all intents and purposes, the Oregon State Bar Association (OSB) is the "Lawyer's Union," and is also part of state government. The term "bar" is one of those antiquated phrases like "seat in Congress," or "news desk." In each case, the name of a functional, but mundane, physical object is applied to an institution. There are actual seats in Congress and news desks at newspapers just as each courtroom has a "bar," the railing that separates the audience from the judges and attorneys. "Passing the bar" means not only passing the bar examination, but being allowed to beyond the railing into the front of the courtroom.

The Oregon State Bar is technically an "integrated bar," i.e., a private, professional organization that also serves as a public agency. The Bar has been "integrated" since 1935 when it became the "State" Bar. It had its first meeting as the "Oregon Bar

Association" in October of 1891. No other profession has this relationship with government. The Bar is both a professional association, like the Oregon Medical Association (OMA), and the official licensing body for the state. Physicians are not licensed by the OMA, but the State Board of Medical Examiners. One cannot practice law in Oregon without first joining and continuing to belong to the Bar, somewhat of an ultimate "closed shop."[65] Not all state bar associations are integrated, however. In Colorado, the licensing functions are handled totally by the Supreme Court.

The Board of Bar Governors is not appointed by the governor, like most other state boards and commissions, but elected by the membership of the OSB itself. There are 15 members on the Board: 12 attorneys and three public members appointed by the Board. The President of the Bar is selected by the Board from its own membership[66] and serves a one-year term. As mentioned earlier, the Bar's actual authority to discipline its members flows through the Oregon Supreme Court. In reality, the Court almost always approves the decisions of the Bar. The bar exam and the application process are administered by the OSB, but the exam is graded by the 12 member Board of Bar Examiners which is appointed by the Oregon Supreme Court.[67]

Incidentally, there is no federal counterpart to the state bar associations. To practice in a federal court, one must be a member of the local state bar association.[68] Once a person is member of the state bar, he or she applies to the local federal court and is summarily admitted to practice.

At this writing, the Oregon State Bar has 9,970 active members.[69] Annual dues are currently $316 for over two year members and $252 for under two year members. The OSB maintains a staff of over 100. Besides licensing, the Bar has three other major institutional functions: attorney discipline, continuing legal education and insuring lawyers against legal malpractice.

Attorney discipline is a major concern of the Bar. The organization sanctions lawyers for illegal and unethical conduct. Conduct is controlled by statutes[70] and by the "Oregon Code of Professional Responsibility." This is a set of "disciplinary rules," or "DR's," formulated by the Bar and adopted by the Supreme Court. Offenses range all the way from misappropriation of funds to having sex with a client.

The second major function of the Bar is continuing legal education or, as it is know technically, Minimum Continuing Legal Education (CLE). Attorneys are required to attend 45 hours of classes every two years and the Bar runs an extensive education program to help meet these requirements. Classes and activities given by other groups are also accredited by the OSB. A major portion of the yearly Bar Convention is devoted to letting members know about latest development in the law. After each legislative session, the Bar publishes a summary of the recently passed changes in the law.[71]

The third major function of the Bar, as an institution, is to insure its own members against malpractice. Until 1978, most lawyers bought private malpractice insurance, although there was no requirement to do so. The law,[72] passed in 1977, requires all members of the Bar, with a few exceptions, to purchase insurance from the Bar's "Professional Liability Fund" or PLF as it is known. There is no "conspiracy of silence" among lawyers to protect each other as there supposedly is in the medical profession. Lawyers have no compunction whatsoever about suing each other. Typical lawyer malpractice would be failing to file a civil case before the deadline imposed by the statute of limitations.

The Bar represents the profession before the Legislature, runs programs for attorneys with substance-abuse problems and maintains an extensive system of subject area committees that propose changes in substantive law. These committees are known as "sections" and cover various topics including domestic relations, corporations, et cetera.

As mentioned, the Bar is governed by a President and a Board of Bar Governors elected from six regions. Major policy decisions are made by all members of the Bar at a general meeting held during the annual Bar Convention. History was made in 1992 when Julie Frantzbecame the first women President of the Bar. It had been 107 years since the first female, Mary Gysin Leonard was admitted to practice in Oregon in 1885.[73] Frantz started her career as a public defender and worked her way up through various bar committees and the Board of Bar Governors.

Being President of the Bar is a noteworthy achievement and a badge of acceptance by the profession. It can also be a political statement and a sign of changing times. In 1986, Bernie Jolleswas elected President of the Oregon State Bar; 23 years earlier he had to sue to gain admission to the very organization that he would head someday. His initial application was rejected, in most part, because Jolles had been a member of the Communist Party in New York from 1949 to 1957. The Oregon Supreme Court ruled that Jolles had demonstrated good character by being candid in his application and that further he,"...is free of the Communist influences which distorted his moral judgment..."[74] Jolles was admitted to practice and proved to be a superb attorney. Upon becoming President he was interviewed by the Bar Bulletin and said:

> My own experience in life led me to identify with working people and their unions. Therefore, I naturally chose to represent civil plaintiffs, labor unions, and, early on, persons accused of crime. This was my choice, but candor compels me to state I was never deluged with requests for representation by large corporations. They seemed quite content to struggle along without my services...I have come to realize that virtue and sin are not mutually exclusive...I deal in my practice in terms of cases, not causes. As a result, I have represented employers, businesses, and recently (God help us all) even a bank and its president.[75]

The Bar also takes positions of public policy questions. After an extensive floor debate, the bar adopted a resolution against Ballot Measure 9 in the 1992 election.

The Politics of Sentencing

Both the circuit and district court judges share a common problem when it comes to sentencing convicted criminals. That is, they are subject to the mythology of the "lenient" judge. Along with the "welfare queen" and "big labor unions" this is part of the right wing explanation of what is wrong with America -- reality is something else. Objectively, prison sentences in the United States are among the longest in the world, but public perception of what judges do is more important than actual performance. Judges are elected officials, and no one wants to appear soft on crime. Until 1989, an Oregon judge could give a burglar a 20 year sentence,[76] appear tough on crime, and know full well that the defendant would be released in a much shorter, and more reasonable time by the Parole Board.

Sentencing Guidelines changed that in 1989. Instead of imposing sentences that were meaningless, judges were required to give mandatory sentences under sentencing guidelines.[77] These guidelines are set forth in a grid pattern with categories of offenses on the left side in increasing order of severity, minor offenses are on the bottom and murders on the top. Across the top of the grid are categories for a person's criminal history. These range from several prior convictions for violent felonies to no record at all. Where the various categories of crime and criminal history meet, grid blocks are formed and within those blocks are the actual sentence amounts. Sentencing guidelines serve another purpose, they can be changed to avoid prison over crowding.[78]

Making Money with the Courts

As mentioned, the judicial system is not an insignificant part of the state's general fund budget at $260 million a biennium. Prior to 1981, county governments paid all court expenses except judges' salaries. Although they are funded by the state, the courts are still housed in county courthouses. Most of the actual financial matters involving the courts are rather pedestrian. Filing fees go into the state general fund as do most criminal fines. However, most traffic tickets in Oregon are not considered criminal matters and this is important business for both the state and local governments.

Traffic fines are very significant money. Each traffic court, whether it be a state district court or a municipal court, can net the jurisdiction approximately $100,000 a year. Half of each traffic fine collected goes to the arresting jurisdiction and half to the trying jurisdiction.[79] For instance, if a Lake Oswego City officer issues a citation to motorist for speeding and the offender is convicted in Lake Oswego municipal court, the city gets the whole amount. If a City of Portland "patrolperson" issues the same citation and it is tried in the state district court, only half goes to the city with the other half going to the state general fund. This is real money for both state and local governments. Most traffic tickets are paid through the mail by people forfeiting the "bail" that is written on the front of the citation. The dollar amount, or "bail," used to be established by a "uniform bail schedule" that was written by a committee appointed by the Supreme Court. But in 1993, the Legislature raised the bail schedule and placed it as statute.[80] Some of these new fines were relatively heavy ($280 for going 75 miles per hour in a 65 mile per hour zone)[81] and some cynics thought this was just another means for the state to get out of its financial difficulties.

Indigent Defense --The Bill Nobody Wants to Pay

Both the State and Federal Constitutions have been interpreted to require that an attorney be appointed for a person charged with a crime if they cannot afford one. "Indigent defense" is a perennial problem at both the state and federal level. In Oregon, the Judicial Department handles all indigent defense matters.

Until 1981, the counties paid for indigent defense. With the state takeover of the court system in 1981, the state assumed the responsibility. Neither the Legislature nor the Court is comfortable with indigent defense. The Legislature absolutely hates to pay for attorneys for crooks whom they know are guilty and deserve nothing more than "a short rope and a long drop." The Judiciary itself also dislikes indigent defense. Aside from the expenditure aspect, the judges do not like being involved financially with the defense side of the criminal justice process. They are uncomfortable deciding what any attorney's services are worth.

Actual indigent defense is delivered in three ways. Public defenders (PD's) are quasi-public institutions authorized by statute[82] and the governing bodies of counties. They serve as counterparts to the district attorney's offices, only for the defense. Most PD's work on a contractual basis for the Judicial Department and accept a certain number of cases a month. A second component to the indigent defense system is the indigent defense "contract." Here, private law firms agree to handle a certain number of cases for a monthly fee. These contract firms resemble the PD in their style of criminal defense, except most of these practitioners maintain a private practice on the side. Finally, numerous attorneys do indigent defense on an individual case basis. The attorney is "appointed" to defend one client at a time, and is paid at a rate of $30 an hour.

The "Feds"

If there is an aristocracy in America it is surely the federal bench. The federal system starts with the United States Supreme Court, extends to the 13 circuit courts of appeals, and finally down to the eight hundred or more district courts. The Supreme Court is the most famous and powerful of all courts in America. It has nine Justices, appointed by the President and confirmed by the United States Senate, as are all other federal judges. Oregon has never had anyone appointed to the Supreme Court. The closest it came was in 1873 when President Grant nominated his Attorney General George H. Williams, from Oregon. Williams was not considered capable enough for the task and his name was withdrawn in January of 1874.[83]

The district court is the trial court of general jurisdiction for the federal system. Oregon is one single federal district, but other states, such as California, have two districts. As mentioned, Oregon's seven district judges are appointed by the president and confirmed by the United States Senate. They serve for life, receive a salary of $129,000 a year and retire at full pay. They can declare both state and federal laws unconstitutional and are considered to have much more power over how a case is tried than state judges. Most federal civil cases involve substantial amounts of money and attorneys who practice regularly in federal court consider themselves an elite group. Judge James Alger Fee, who sat from 1931 to 1954, and Judge Gus Solomon who served from 1949 to 1987, established the style for federal judges in Oregon. They both were assertive and somewhat authoritarian.

Gus Solomon had been one of the few people to publicly support Harry Truman in 1948 when he beat Republican Tom Dewey for the presidency. Solomon was the first Jewish lawyer in Oregon to be nominated to the federal bench and his selection was opposed by the large WASPish Portland law firms.[84] He never forgot the insult and <u>never</u> missed an opportunity to remind them who was the judge. Solomon ran his courtroom with an iron hand and adopted a set of local court rules that forced attorneys to resolve many of the issues in controversy before trial. Gus was also known for speed in resolving cases and asking his own questions during trial.

The particular way things were done in federal court had an interesting effect on the local bar. In 1981, a new set of state court trial procedures were adopted. These new rules were developed by both the Council on Court Procedures and the Legislature. The debate over the new rules centered on how much they should or should not resemble the federal rules. It was very evident during the process that the local bar did not want state judges assuming the same authority or demeanor as federal judges. For instance, in state court prospective jurors are asked questions by the attorneys during a process known as *voir dire*. The procedure had been changed in federal court and the judge asked the jurors questions to see whether or not they were prejudiced. The Bar resisted attempts to change to the federal system.

The Federal district court in Oregon has offices in Portland and Eugene. The court has an extensive criminal docket, including bank robberies, and drug offenses.

---

[1] The proper role of a judiciary is a vast subject which we will only touch upon. Courts do make policy, whether or not they should is in the eye of the beholder.

[2] 12 Hen. VII, Keilwey 3b, 72 Eng. Rep. 156. Cited in William L. Prosser, Law of Torts, 4th Ed (St. Paul: West Publishing, 1971), 496.

[3] Law is frequently divided into "substantive law" and "procedural law." The above example is substantive, the process by which you would bring the actual law suit is procedural.

[4] The most commonly used of these "codes" is the *Code Napoleon* or the Napoleonic Code. One American state, Louisiana, theoretically uses the Napoleonic Code. Other codes go back thousands of years such as the Justinian Code, 535 A.D., the Code of Hammurabi, circa 1800 B.C. and the Code of Moses, circa 1200 B.C. (also known as the Ten Commandments).

[5] When we say common law courts are "adversarial" we mean that the party seeking a court's decision has the burden of proof and the court itself does not get involved in the process except to rule on legal matters. Common law judges act more as referees than participants. The other great legal system is the "Civil Law," found in continental Europe, is sometimes called the "inquisitorial system." Here, the judge is an active participant the process.

[6] How the common law became part of American law is actually a bit more complicated. Early colonists were so isolated that they didn't have access to most of the English decisions and to a limited extent developed their own codes. Blackstone's Commentaries on the common law was published in America in 1771 and had the effect of reinvigorating the common law. See Lawrence M. Friedman, History of American Law, 2nd Ed. (New York: Touchstone, 1985), 102.

[7] See R.C. Van Caenegem, The Birth of the English Common Law, 2d Ed. (Cambridge: Cambridge University Press, 1988).

[8] United States F. & G. Co. v. Bramwell, 109 Or. 261, 217 Pac. 332 (1923).

[9] The common law and its development are fascinating topics and no more poignant description can be given than that of United States Supreme Court Justice Oliver Wendell Holmes, Jr.; "The life of the law has not been logic: it has been experience. The felt necessities of the time, the prevalent moral and political theories, intuitions of public policy, avowed or unconscious, even the prejudices which judges share with their fellow-men, have had a good deal more to do than the syllogism in determining the rules by which men should be governed." See Oliver Wendell Holmes, Jr., The Common Law, (Boston: Little Brown, 1881), 1.

[10] Marbury v. Madison, 1 Cranch 137, 2 L. Ed. 60 (1803).

[11] An argument can be made that both France and Germany have endowed their courts with a limited power of judicial review. See Henry J. Abraham, The Judicial Process, 5th Ed. (New

York: Oxford University Press, 1986), 309-319. British courts have never been considered to have the power of judicial review, but, much to the chagrin of the author, some significant British jurists disagree. In an interview with the head of British Civil Court system, he was informed that, indeed, British judges did have the power of judicial review. According to Sir John Donaldson, Master of the Rolls, this is power is usually exercised by a court stating that a minister's action could not have possibly meant what it seemed to mean, and that a proper interpretation of the law would produce a different result; Thomas L. Mason, "A Conversation with the Master," Oregon State Bar Bulletin, October 1985,. __.

12 When a court declares a statute unconstitutional, this ruling only applies in the particular court's jurisdiction. If a Multnomah County Circuit Court declared a state statute void, this ruling would apply only to the one county. If the decision were appealed to the Oregon Court of Appeals and upheld, then the decision would apply to the whole state.

13 Daniel Meador, American courts, (St. Paul: West Publishing, 1991), 19.

14 Courts of "general jurisdiction" generally try felonies and larger civil cases. The term "court of general jurisdiction" is a technical term and can be used across the various jurisdictions to describe major trial courts in the different locales.

15 Henry J. Abraham, The Judicial Process, 258.

16 Daniel Meador, American Courts, 73.

17 The English bar is divided into two segments, solicitors who do the more office oriented legal work and barristers who appear in court. Solicitors out number barristers about ten to one.

18 Henry J. Abraham, The Judicial Process, 89-90.

19 Ibid., 112.

20 Daniel Meador, American courts, 92-97; The Book of States 1988-89 Edition, (Lexington, Kentucky: The Council of State Governments, 1988), 160-165.

21 Or. Const. art. VII, sec. 2; Mandamus is an action to compel a public official to do his or her duty and habeas corpus questions the legality of imprisonment. Quo warranto has been abolished and combined with habeas corpus. See ORS 34.105-34.810.

22 Aside from Carson, the other justices are Ed Fadeley, 63, a former Democratic State Senator and Senate president; W. Michael Gillette, 51, who started his career at the Oregon Department of Justice; Susan Graber, 43, who served on the Court of appeals before the Supreme Court; Richard Unis, 65, from the Multnomah County Circuit Court; and George Van Hoomisson, 63, who was once Multnomah County District Attorney. Fadeley and Van Hoomisssen were directly elected to the Court instead of running for the positions after gubernatorial appointment. Susan Graber has the distinction of being the first Justice to give birth to a child (Rachel) while serving on the court; Fred Leeson, "The other Supreme Court," The Oregonian, 27 June 1993, B1, B4.

23 R. William Linden, Jr., Salem, facsimile to author, 18 November 1993.

24 ORS 2.516.

25 ORS 19.210.

26 Oregon, Secretary of State, Oregon Blue Book 1993-1994, (Salem: Secretary of State, 1993), 140.

27 Janet Davis, "Retiring state judge appeals for respect," Statesman-Journal, 31 December 1992, 1C, 2C.

28 ORS 305.405 - 591.

29 ORS 46.060(1)(a).

30 Most traffic matters are processed as civil, not criminal cases to avoid the necessity of jury trails.

31 R. William Linden, Jr., facsimile to author.

32 Henry J. Abraham, The Judicial Process, 115.

33 Williams v. Florida, 399 U.S. 78 (1970).

34 Burch v. Louisiana, 99 S. Ct. 1623 (1979).

35 Apodaca v. Oregon, 406 U.S. 356 (1972).

36 Or. Const. art. VII, sec. 5 (7).

37 Or. Const. art. I, sec. 8; ORS 1.140 - 1.480.

38 Dan Hortsch, "Metzger loses Oregon Appeal," The Oregonian, 18 November 1993, D5; John Schrag, "Postponed Promises," The Willamette Week, 18 November 1993, 9; See Morris Dees and Steve Fiffer, Hate on Trial, (New York: Villard, 1993).

39 Dave Hogan, "Oregonians appointed to top-level legal posts," The Oregonian, 20, November 1993, D1, D8.

40 Oregon, Secretary of State, Oregon Blue Book 1993-1994, (Salem: Secretary of State, 1993), 138.

41 ORS 51.020.

42 ORS 157.060.

43 ORS 157.010.

44 Stephen Wermiel, "State Supreme Courts Are Feeling Their Oats About Civil Liberties," The Wall Street Journal, 16 June 1988, 1,__.

45 President Carter was not fortunate enough to make any appointments to the Supreme Court.

46 Ballot Measure 2 passed 690,989 yes votes to 96,065 no votes.

47 Or. Const. art. VII, sec. 2; ORS 1.410-1.480.

48 Ibid.

49 "Defender says judge prejudiced," The Oregonian, 6 July 1977, A10.

50 "Field becomes district judge," The Oregonian, 15 July 1972, C3.

51 John Painter, Jr., "Removal of Judge Field recommended." The Oregonian, 20 September 1977, A1.

52 John Painter, "News Analysis: Fitness panel comes of age," The Oregonian, 20 September 1977, B1.

53 "Ousted Judge Field has brain tumor surgery," The Oregonian, 26 April 1979, B1.

54 Dave Hogan, "Judge admits forgery, bigamy - Robert L. Kirkman says he should be left on his job because his trouble didn't affect his rulings," The Oregonian, 15 September 1990, A1.

55 Fred Leeson, "Kirkman to resign Multnomah County Judgeship," The Oregonian, 4 January 1991, A1.

56 Charles Beggs, "Oregon Supreme Court disbars former judge," The Oregonian, 2 May 1992, B1.

57 "Roberts' First Judicial Appointment - Janice Wilson sworn in," The Oregonian, 11 April 1991, C4.

58 ORS 254.125(2)(b).

59 Some local bar associations, such as in Multnomah and Lane County, also have committees hat evaluate candidates.

60 Fred Leeson, "Public service takes a new direction," The Oregonian, 30 November 1993, B-5.

61 Or. Const. art. VII sec. 1a.

62 Fred Leeson, "Bored county judge says he's returning to private practice," The Oregonian, 7 July 1993, B-4.

63 Wallace Carson, speech to the House and Senate Judiciary Committees, 1 March 1993.

64 Ballot Measure 1, November 7, 1978.

65 ORS 9.160.

66 ORS 9.025 - .130.

67 ORS 9.210.

68 There is a Washington, D.C. Bar Association that admits people to practice in D.C. Also, there are provisions made for attorneys from other jurisdictions to practice in both federal and state court in Oregon.

69 Robert Oleson, Director of Public Relations - OSB, Facsimile to author, 16 December 1993.

70 ORS 9.460 - .520.

71 Attorneys volunteer to write chapters in the Bar's biennial Legislation book.

72 ORS 9.080(2).

73 Oregon State Bar, "One-half century --An illustrated time-line of significant of the Bar in Oregon" 4.

74 In re Bernard Jolles, 235 OR 262, 277 (1963).

75 Quoted in "An Interview with Bernie Jolles," Oregon State Bar Bulletin, October 1986, 4.

76 ORS 164.255, ORS 161.605.

77 ORS 137.669.

78 ORS 167.655(3).

79 ORS 153.630.

80 ORS 153.623.

81 ORS 153.623(3)(e)(B).

82 ORS 151.010.

83 Henry J. Abraham, Justices & Presidents - A Political History of Appointments to the Supreme Court, 2n Ed. (New York: Oxford University Press, 1985), 129.

84 Steven Lowenstein, The Jews of Oregon 1850 - 1950, (Portland: Jewish Historical Society of Oregon, 1987), 173.

CHAPTER 7

SPECIAL INTERESTS AND THE LOBBY

Politics: Who Gets What, When, How.

Harold D. Lasswell

Follow the money.

"Deepthroat"

Introduction

An examination of politics in any American state would be incomplete without a look at special interests and their institutional link to government: the lobby. Chapter 7 includes:

- The increasing role of special interests.
- Money and politics.
- The business lobby.
- The professional's lobby (lawyers, doctors, etc.).
- Unions.

- Public interest group lobby.
- The religious lobby.
- Governments lobbying governments.
- The Capitol Club.

- Lobbyist involvement in political campaigns and ballot measures.

Special Interests --The New Reality

Politics in Oregon involves "special interests." That should be no surprise. "Special interests," in one form or another, have always been a part of the American political process and will continue to be so as long as people have the constitutional right to petition government.[1] The question is not so much one of the existence of special interests, but of their nature, their increasing influence and their effect upon democracy as we have known it.

"Special interests" is a problemsome term because it has now become a pejorative phrase. It should never be forgotten that one person's "special interest" is almost always another person's legitimate issue. A further clarification of terms is probably in order; "special interest" is a general term referring to any group, formal or informal, which wants to influence a government decision making process. "Lobbyist" refers to an individual who represents a special interest group before the Legislature. In Oregon, lobbyists have to be registered with the Government Standards and Practices Commission.[2] Because of this requirement, it is much easier to identify lobbyists than groups themselves. Earlier, we referred to the lobby as the "institutional link" between special interests and government. In a manner, lobbyists represent special interests to the Legislature the way attorneys represent litigants to the courts.[3] It should be noted that different governments themselves employ lobbyists to influence other governments. The term "lobby" can either be a verb, "to lobby," or a noun referring to lobbyists as a collective group. This will be discussed further.

With a few exceptions,[4] the most powerful special interests are generally concerned with the more "economic" aspects of government. Our chapter's initial epigraph is Harold Laswell's immortal description of politics, "...Who Gets What, When and How." The phrase is about who pays taxes and who get benefits. While this chapter is more about the "who," it is probably relevant to briefly discuss the "what," i.e., the benefits.

The benefits of government can be more than the obvious, such as health care and education. Among other "benefits" can be how a particular economic interest is taxed, regulated, subsidized, franchised or even paid directly. Business interests like to portray themselves as just wanting to be left alone. Notwithstanding the *laissez faire* myth, there never has been a time when government and business were not inextricably involved.[5] Commercial and agricultural interests were active at the very inception of the federal government, lobbying for roads and a national bank.[6] Then, as now, the economic establishment wanted more than low taxes. There is also the most the most obvious aspect economic special interest -- they literally have the money to be influential.

Special interest politics in modern America is not bribing elected officials into doing your bidding. That would be a naive, simplistic and unnecessary. Today, you make elected officials your beholden friends by furnishing the money necessary to run successful campaigns. There are more special interest groups, more lobbyists, more money being spent on campaigns and more intense campaigns than ever before. Which of these increased elements came first is an academic question. In the 1993 Session of the Oregon Legislature, there was an all time high number of registered lobbyists -- 1,430.[7] That was a ratio of almost 16 lobbyists for every one of the ninety legislators. A more relevant question is, why these changes? One answer is simply that we have more government and, therefore, more government decision making to be influenced. It can also be argued that there is an increasing awareness on the part of groups that they can influence government. In the author's view, however, the most important element is that of the role of money in campaigns. Why do so many politicians rely on special interest money? The answer is that they have to.

Money Doesn't Talk --It Swears

Money has always been the "mother's milk of politics," but what was once was a necessary evil has become a dominating obsession. From 1980 to 1990, the average cost of campaigning for the Oregon House of Representative has increased tenfold --from $3,500 to $35,000.[8] These amounts pale in comparison to money spent in larger states such as California or New York where legislative races can cost nearly a million dollars. The author's own experience has been even worse. He spent $2,500 on his first general election campaign for the Legislature in 1974 --in 1992, he spent approximately $70,000. This is close to a three thousand percent increase in almost twenty years. It is essential to understand that there has been a simultaneous increase in the number of special interests.

Most money for campaigns comes from political action committees, or PACs. They are established by special interest groups and run by lobbyists. PACs are the political levers of special interest groups. They are perhaps the most important means of getting people elected to office. It takes a lot less effort for a candidate to raise $500 from PAC than to raise the same amount from personal friends at $25 a donation. A major contribution, especially in today's political atmosphere, is like a life preserver to a drowning man. If a special interest keeps you from drowning, i.e., gets you elected, you are going to return the phone calls, and the group is going to have access. A grateful legislator will give it the benefit of the doubt. In politics, one takes care of one's friends. Being the friend of an office holder is influence, and influence is the most important thing when it comes to getting things done.

There is also the effect that money has had on the very nature of political campaigns. Unrestrained spending has combined with modern media and polling to create a kind of political arms race among politicians. Campaigns have become more sophisticated, more intense and more negative. They have become professionalized contests where both sides use refined techniques to capture a winning number of voters. Issues that concern the candidates themselves are secondary to voters' preferences discovered in surveys, focus groups and tracking polls. In the 1970s, it was considered sophisticated to do a simple poll at the beginning of a campaign; now in-depth surveys are done constantly. Negative campaigning has become an art form.[9] Surveys are used to probe the voter's psyche, to find which issues they will respond to, what their "hot buttons" are. What are the issues that would change a voter's mind -- "If you knew that Candidate X had been convicted of drunken driving, would that change how you would vote?" A laundry list of possible topics is reviewed until the "wedge" issue is found. That's the issue that will "wedge" the voters away from your opponent. Before the advent of these techniques, candidates resembled quaint duelists. One took the measure of his opponent, gauged the wind/issues and fired a shot. Now campaigns resemble two high tech aircraft constantly tracking each other with polls and trying to estimate where the opponent will be before a series of negative hit pieces are fired.

There is an uncomfortable public awareness that politicians have become too responsive to special interests. "Gridlock" has become the all too appropriate descriptive term for government that is unable to act in a decisive manner.

"When you look at the results in terms of legislation, you see the impact of lobbying has grown to the point where we have gridlock," observed Dave Buchanan, the executive director of Oregon Common Cause. "Every potential solution to the problem (Buchanan was talking about tax reform) is blocked because there is enough money to keep it from coming to fruition."[10]

If money is coming to play such detrimental role in politics why not limit the amount that can be spent? Other democracies such as England have imposed campaign spending limitations, why not do the same in the United States? In the landmark case of Buckley v. Valeo,[11] the United States Supreme Court invalidated most campaign spending limits. The Court reasoned that the ability to spend money was tantamount to free speech. Unfortunately, this conclusion was reached by office holders who themselves never have to run for office. The effect of the court's well intentioned decision was to create a political environment dominated not by free speech, but by the ability to spend money. The situation in Oregon is further exacerbated by an even earlier decision of the State Supreme Court, which reached the same conclusion based upon state constitutional grounds.[12] In Deras v. Myers,[13] the Oregon Court found state campaign spending limits unconstitutional.

Who are these guys anyway? Here are just a few of the players.

Business --IOU's to Bubble Gum

The largest business group in Oregon is the Associated Oregon Industries with 2000 members statewide. It has a staff of approximately 30 people, offices in Salem and fields six lobbyists during the Legislative Session.[14] AOI's issues range all the way from the basic tax policy to worker's compensation and collective bargaining matters. As a group, AOI is considered to be very influential. For example, during the 1989 effort to "reform" worker's compensation, AOI was considered to be the voice of Oregon business. They were "at the table," during the negotiations which were held at Governor Goldschmidt's mansion, Mahonia Hall. AOI maintains a modest PAC, it gave out $96,539.73[15] in the 1992 General Election, mostly to Republicans. This is not unusual, AOI's philosophy is almost classically Republican -- low taxes, low wages and not a little anti-union.

The Portland Chamber of Commerce used to be very evident in Salem during the legislative session, but it has been almost totally eclipsed by AOI. The National Federation of Independent Business (NFIB) represents smaller businesses than AOI. They too are interested in workers' compensation and tax issues. The NFIB has opposed the sales tax.

The utilities have always had a major political presence in Oregon. With a few exceptions, such as the Eugene Water and Electric Board (EWEB), utilities in Oregon are private utilities and not public utilities or Public Utility Districts known as "PUD's." As mentioned, the private utilities are known as IOU's or Investor Owned Utilities. While Washington is a public utility state, Oregon is a private utility state. The reasons for this go far beyond this book. Washington also has a tradition of a stronger Democratic Party and stronger labor movement.

The two largest IOU's are Pacific Power and Light (PP&L) and Portland General Electric (PGE). PP&L is a large regional company and PGE is local. From the 1930s and until the 1970s, power issues in the Legislature were those public power verses private power. This same battle was fought at a national level during the New Deal.[16] It was in the '30s that electric power took the Northwest economy beyond timber, fishing and agriculture. This was the era in which Woody Guthrie wrote "Roll on Columbia" as part of a New Deal art project. The federal Bonneville Power Administration made Boeing Aircraft possible when it furnished electricity to the aluminum plants along the Columbia River.

Regardless, Oregon power companies have spent sixty years successfully defending themselves against public power advocates. Oregon statutes have always provided for the formation of PUD districts that can take over the assets of IOU's,[17] but the IOU's have always had the clout to make the process as hard as possible. As mentioned in Chapter 2, although Article XI-D[18] of the Oregon Constitution mandates that the Legislature shall sell bonds for the development of hydro-electric power, the IOU's have been able to block the provision since its adoption.

From the 1930s to the 1960s, the left made the public power the issue, but with the advent of nuclear power the issue became the environment. In 1976, PGE began generating power from the Trojan Nuclear power plant located on the Columbia River approximately thirty miles north of Portland. Nuclear power was the *bête noire* of Oregon liberals until 1992 when PGE announced it was shutting the plant. As mentioned in Chapter 3, Trojan had been the target of numerous ballot measures[19] and innumerable bills in the Legislature.

There are utilities other than electric companies, Northwest Natural Gas has always maintained a substantial political presence, as has U.S. West, the state's largest phone company. They both have a substantial political action committees that contributes to Republicans and Democrats. Tom Berry lobbies for gas company, Gary Wilhelms, a former Republican Representative, and Ginny Lang represent U.S. West. All three are well liked and respected.

All the utilities are also extremely interested in matters involving the Public Utility Commission (PUC). This appointed three member body regulates rates for all public utilities in Oregon.[20] While PUC Commissioners can't be lobbied directly, their controlling statutes can be affected.

Other groups have more defined issues. The Associated General Contractors (AGC), the construction industry, has three primary issues. The first and foremost is the gas tax! AGC's biggest projects are highways and in Oregon the gas tax, which pays for roads, is constitutionally dedicated to highways,[21] ergo the AGC will do just about anything to protect and promote the gas tax. This is an interesting position for a relatively conservative group of rough and tumble builders, but after all, highways are about as American as government can get. The second big issue for AGC is worker's compensation, how much each builder pays in worker's compensation rates is crucial to profitability. Worker's comp will be discussed in Chapter 11 on Perennial Issues. The third issue for AGC is a bit esoteric, construction liens. To simplify it too much -- who is responsible when a supplier delivers materials to a sub-contractor and the "sub" doesn't pay? AGC wants to make sure that when the unpaid bill becomes a lien on the property, the general contractor is not on the hook. AGC is also a bit unusual in that it is an organization with a very masculine image and a female lobbyist, Kim Mingo, who does an excellent job.

Another somewhat masculine industry, timber, has an unusual number of women lobbyists. Carolyn McGreevy represents James River Corporation, Peggy Sato lobbies for Georgia Pacific and Pat Amedeo is C & D Lumber's person in both Salem and Washington, DC. None of the three has ever "worked in the woods," as one of them admits, but they are very respected. Amedeo, a former staff person for Governor Atiyeh is especially knowledgeable on natural resources issues.

Timber is big business in Oregon, and the above companies along with Boise Cascade, Longview Fiber, International Paper, Pope and Talbot, and Willamette Industries make quite a presence in Salem. One of the larger timber companies, Louisiana Pacific, had no need of a lobbyist. It hired the 1991 & 1993 Republican Speaker of the House, Larry Campbell, as a "government relations" person.

Taxes and the environment are the big issues for the forest industry. On the tax side, the question is whether timberland should be taxed for the value of the timber on it or taxed like other agricultural land, i.e., at a much lower rate. The timber companies prefer the latter; they want timber taxed like a crop, that is, they would rather pay a higher one time tax at the point of harvest than constant taxes as the timber stands on the land. On the environmental side, timber companies are very concerned with the Forest Practices Act which controls how they harvest their logs.

Financial institutions also have a strong political presence in Salem. These are the banks, the savings and loans, and the credit unions. The Oregon Bankers Association is represented by long time lobbyist Frank Brawner. Although the banks would seem naturally oriented toward Republicans, Brawner has had good relationships with Democrats. He was an early and strong supporter of Barbara Roberts in her successful bid for the governorship in 1990.

The "Dean" (the individual with the longest tenure) of the Oregon lobby is Dave Barrows who represents the savings and loans. They are officially known as the Oregon League of Financial Institutions. Barrows started in Salem in 1950s as a House staff member and now shares his lobby business with his son Tom. Barrows has an obsessive interest in Portland's National Basketball Association team, the Trailblazers. He has probably been to every home game in twenty years, and is always accompanied by a state legislator. Reporters, who get their own free tickets, love to write stories about the outings.

The financial institution's big issues are usury, credit card rates, and class actions.[22] Some issues they support sound very minor, but are worth income to them. They lobbied vigorously for a statute allowing direct deposit of state worker's pay checks. At first blush, this sounds inconsequential item until one realizes that the pay checks of twenty-thousand plus workers can generate significant interest in the extra two days that direct deposit results in.

Both Brawner and Barrows have significant political action committees. The banks have had more cash in recent years. They are larger by their very size and have not yet gone through the same trauma that the savings and loans have.

The retail food industry also has strong lobby. Oregon's largest food retailer, Fred Meyer, Inc., is represented by Cheryl Perrin. Perrin is probably the most powerful non-elected women in Oregon politics. She has substantial discretion as to whom contributions are made to. She is refreshingly blunt in her lobby style and only asks for a vote when it is really needed. An unusual bill came up in 1981 which had to do with handicap parking spaces. One of the disabled groups wanted a measure that would have allowed disabled people to patrol parking lots in their wheelchairs and issue citations to people who had parked in handicapped spaces without a permit. Wonderful idea, but Fred Meyer, with more parking lots than any business in Oregon, saw the potential for liability. They were afraid that a disgruntled offending driver might send the wheelchair and its occupant careening across the parking lot in response. The bill was sent to House Judiciary and the Chairman could never find time to hear the bill.

Another retailer is Southland Corporation, the people who run the "7-11" convenience stores. They use Mark Nelson, one of the most successful independent lobbyists in Oregon. Their issues range from worker's compensation to how many returnable bottles they have to accept from a customer under Oregon's Bottle Bill. Contributions from Southland are always in amounts of "X hundred and seven dollars and eleven cents," which again reminds one where the money came from.

Insurance companies employ several lobbyists and are concerned with one issue, i.e., making sure they never have to pay off on the policies they sell. They spend half of their time before the judiciary committees trying to limit their liability and the rest in front of the human resources committees making sure that few, if any, medical treatments are required to be covered under insurance polices. Insurance company contributions go overwhelmingly to Republicans.[23]

High tech has become a very significant lobby force in recent year. The American Electronics Association (AEA), Tektronix, and Hewlett-Packard are all active. This has been the one portion of the business community that has been extremely supportive of higher education in Oregon. Jim Craven represents the AEA, Gary Conkling and Dave Fiskum represent Tektronix, and Jerry Fischer represents HP. Conkling has been particularly effective in promoting graduate education to assist Oregon's electronics industry in Washington County. The AEA political action committee is relatively small, it gave out $23,352 in the 1992 General Election.[24]

The individuals and groups discussed above are just a sampling of the businesses active in Oregon politics. There is an amazing diversity. In 1993, State Representative Del Parks, R-Klamath Falls, introduced a bill to ban bubble gum that looked like a tobacco product. To everyone's delight the man that lobbied against the bill was none other then Jim Bouton the author of <u>Ball Four</u>, a best selling inside account of major league baseball. Bouton, it seems, was the inventor of "Big League Chew" a bubble gum made to look like chewing tobacco. He and Jim Markee, a local lobbyist, managed to convince enough legislators that the bill was not worth passing.

Professional Groups --Only Protecting the Public

Among the various professional groups, it is hard to say which is the most powerful. It is easy, however, to say which is the most active, that is, makes the most political contributions to candidates --the Oregon Trial Lawyers. Trial lawyers not only contribute through their political action committee, the Concerned Oregon Lawyers Trust (COLT), but they are also notorious for contributing on their own. By their very nature, they are advocates, and they are more directly affected by legislation. Where most people are impacted in a secondary manner, lawyers must actually work with the statutes. The Trial Lawyers usually support more Democrats than Republicans although there are exceptions. They feel they are protecting the "little guy," the citizen injured by the large corporation, the one who can't get a fair settlement from the large insurance company. The irony is that for the past ten years the Trial Lawyers have been almost totally on the defensive. Public concern about the "litigation explosion" and tort reform has not made for a particularly friendly atmosphere. The trial lawyers were particularly stung in 1987 when the Democratic Speaker of the House, Vera Katz, pushed through a "tort reform" bill over their objections. In 1989, she did the same thing again with 'workers' compensation "reform." Both measures were very fashionable and had the universal support of the business community. Katz was rewarded for her efforts by getting the extensive business support when she successfully ran for mayor of Portland in 1992.

Other issues that concern lawyers are handled by the Oregon State Bar itself which has three lobbyists. Bar issues tend to be little less partisan than Trial Lawyer issues, but some can be controversial in their own way. The Bar always supports measures to increase judge's compensation, which is never a popular issue.

On the other side of the professional arena is the Oregon Medical Association (OMA), the Trial Lawyers' blood enemy. The "Docs" have never had any sense of humor about being sued for malpractice. The Oregon Medical Association Political Action Committee is as large as the Trial Lawyers', but doctors don't give as much individually. Regardless, the MD's had tremendously successful sessions from 1985 through 1991 because the President of the State Senate was a doctor, John Kitzhaber. It always helps to have one of your own running things. The OMA's main lobbyist is C. Scott Gallant, a slight, chain-smoking little man known as the "Prince of Darkness" to his adversaries. Gallant has been criticized for refusing to compromise on some issues.[25]

Other professional groups in the medical field include the nurses represented by Brian DeLashmutt; the hospitals, represented by Ed Patterson; Kaiser, represented by Bruce Bishop; the dentists, represented by Jane Myers; the osteopaths and optometrists, represented by Jack Kane; and the chiropractors, represented by Chuck Bennett. Kane is probably the more effective, and of these smaller groups, the nurses are the best liked.

Both the pharmacists and the drug manufacturers lobby actively. Drug prices are a crucial part of the Oregon's Medicaid program, and affect both the pharmacies and the manufacturers, but their goals tend to differ. Chuck Gress is the lobbyist for the pharmacists. Even though they have an economic interest in the subject, the pharmacists seem try to keep drug prices low instead of high.

The author introduced a bill in 1993 to control drug prices as part of nation-wide effort at health care reform. First Lady Hillary Rodham Clinton's Heath Care Task Force requested a copy of the measure and much to the author's chagrin several drug manufacturer lobbyist came to Oregon to find out about the bill. In a somewhat cute side-bar story The Oregonian ran this quote:

"I feel like some wild animal put on display for the Washington lobbyists. I wish I was a fourth as powerful as these guys think I am."[26]

One of the most respected health care related groups is the Oregon Psychologists Association. Nan Heim and Jody Fischer handle legislative issues for this organization. They arrange weekly brown bag luncheons during the legislative session, where the "Psychologist of the Week" lectures on how to handle stress or some other appropriate topic. The Mental Health Association is represented by Sandy Millius.

Finally, the realtors should be mentioned as a professional group, although they are more of a business organization. They are concerned with both licensing issues and more substantive matter such as land-use planning. The Oregon Association of Realtors' person in the Capitol is Genoa Ingram

Conflicts between these professional groups come under the generalized term of "turf battles:" basically who gets to do what for the public, who gets to put the eye drops in the eyes, who gets to write the will. These conflicts are always fought using the terms of "protecting the public" and never who gets paid. There is never any love lost between the professions. The doctors are on top of the heap and are always defending themselves from the lawyers who themselves want to make sure that the practice of law is limited. Nurses are a threat to the MD's, and the chiropractors are hated by everyone.

Unions --Disorganized Labor

As mentioned, Oregon is not a strong labor state like its neighbor to the north, Washington.[27] Traditional labor groups, such as the AFL-CIO, are not near as strong as the public employees or education unions. The Teamsters and the Longshoremen have always had their own brand of clout, but to a certain extent they are outside the mainstream of the labor movement. Other groups that are particularly active are the Firefighters Union, the Pulp and Paper Workers Union, the United Transportation Union, the Communications Workers, and Food Processors.

The current President of the AFL-CIO is a former machinist, Irv Fletcher. Labor's biggest concerns are collective bargaining, worker's compensation and minimum wage. Working conditions and safety issues are also major labor issues. These would include a "worker right to know" about toxic substances in the workplace.

The AFL-CIO carries on most of it political activity through it Committee on Political Education (COPE) which is their PAC. It contributed $90,812 in the 1992 General Election, mostly to Democrats.[28] Individual unions also make political contributions.

If there was one piece of legislation that strengthened the labor movement in Oregon, it was the Public Employees Bargaining Act. This gave public employees the right to organize and the right to strike (with a few exceptions). In addition to this, there is a "fair share" provision to the act. This means that an election can be held in a bargaining unit, and if it is successful all workers will have to pay union dues regardless of whether or not they belong to the union. These two provisions have been an absolute boon to the public employees unions.

There are two large public employees unions in Oregon: the American Federation of State County and Municipal Employees (AFSCME), and the Oregon Public Employees Union (OPEU). Both these unions are relatively influential and have considerable political action committees. OPEU's political action committee gave out $337,382.34 in the 1992 General Election.[29] OPEU especially has influence over Salem legislators because so many of the state workers are concentrated in the area. During the 1993 Session, there was a Republican bill to freeze state worker's salaries (HB-2640). As attractive as this was, the Republican controlled House could not pass the measure because of the defection of several of the members of the majority such as Gene Derfler, R-Salem. Derfler, a taciturn, conservative business man from Salem, had been a consistent anti-labor vote until he realized how many OPEU members were in his district. He suddenly became very concerned about collective bargaining rights.

By far the biggest and most powerful union in the state is the Oregon Education Association (OEA). The teachers are the political equal of several Panzer divisions. They have thousands of members and their PAC, People for the Improvement of Education (PIE)is the largest in the state. In the 1992 election, they gave out $398,243.55.[30] In addition, they can produce hundreds of volunteers teachers to canvass for candidates of their choosing. Not only will OEA produce dollars and bodies, but they will also do substantial amounts of free printing, no small thing in legislative races where printed media is the norm.

The OEA maintains a staff of four lobbyists, although most of the work is done by Don Satchell and John Danielson. "Big John" is a legend in Oregon politics. Danielson is a good six-foot four inches in height and has the weight to match. He is the institutional memory for the Legislature on education finance issues, and to top it off, he is an astute

135

campaign strategist. Danielson takes frequent polls, and concentrates OEA's vast resources in crucial races. In addition to being politically effective during elections, OEA has an extremely effective lobby style. Not only can they can generate hundreds of letters to legislators, but they focus on just a few issues a session. When they lobby, they mean it. Representative Howard Cherry, MD. D-Portland, used to tell a story about how the OEA once defeated a bill by merely having a single sheet of paper distributed to the House members with the phrase, "OEA does not support this bill." No explanation, no testimony in committee, no personal contact was needed.

OEA usually supports more Democrats than Republicans. Teachers, by their very socio-economic status tend to be Democrats and Democratic lawmakers identify with school and teachers. Republicans, on the other hand, tend to identify with school boards and school boards tend to be Republican. The Oregon School Boards Association (OSBA) has a much smaller PAC than OEA and more often than not supports Republican candidates. The conflict between the two organizations was almost always over the rules of collective bargaining.

Recently however, OEA and OSBA have found themselves on the same side of major educational issues in the school finance crisis created by the Ballot Measure 5, property tax limitation which passed in 1990.

There are two other education-union interest groups, the Oregon School Employees Association, which is a classified employees group, and the Association of Oregon Facilities. The latter group is the state lobby arm of the American Association of University Professors. This faculty group retains Mark .Nelson as its lobbyist. Higher education salary issues are always much harder than K-12 salary issues.

The "PIG's"

The term "PIG" is a complementary acronym and not residual 1960s term. How things change. The "PIGs" are the Public Interest Group lobby. They are groups which do not represent a business interests. Among these groups are the Oregon Environment Council, Oregon Fish Forever, Oregon Student Public Interest Group (Ralph Nader's people), Water Watch, Oregonians in Action (anti-land-use planning), Oregon Gun Owners Association, and Legal Aid. Other groups which might fit into this category are the American Civil Liberties Union, represented by Dave Fidanque; Oregon Right to Life represented by Lynda Harrignton; Planned Parenthood represented by Maura Roche;[31] and the gay rights group, Right to Privacy, represented by Nan Heim and Jody Fischer. Needless to say, several of these groups would not want to be in the same paragraph with each other.

The Religious Lobby --Don't Mention God

As mentioned earlier, Oregon is not a particularly religious state, but there are two religious organizations that lobby, the Ecumenical Ministries of Oregon (EMO) and the Oregon Catholic Conference. EMO uses a liberal version of the "Church Lady" to represent it, Ellen Lowe. An extremely sweet person, Ellen and her organization are opposed to the death penalty, opposed to racism and for health care for all.

The Catholic Conference is represented by Bob Castagna, a Jesuit-trained attorney. It has gotten involved in several weighty issues other than abortion. The Conference was one of the few groups to oppose the Oregon Health Plan in 1989 because it involved rationing.[32] They have also opposed euthanasia, the death penalty, and abortion. The Oregon Catholic Conference is probably the most consistent group in Oregon politics.

One thing you will never hear either of these groups mention is God. The arguments and testimony are almost always phrased in terms of "good public policy," or "morality."

Governments Lobbying Governments

Odd as it seems, governments spend a great deal of time and energy lobbying other governments. This takes place both at the state and the federal level. Cities, counties, school districts and special districts are just a few of the government bodies that lobby the Oregon Legislature. Even more unusual is the fact that the state government lobbies itself; some agencies have their own representatives in Salem.

The League of Oregon Cities is represented by seven registered lobbyists. Philip Fell is a former legislative staffer and the best known of these. Cities are concerned about a variety of issues, but transportation funding and land-use planning are two of the most important. They are also very concerned with cigarette and liquor taxes -- the cities get a small portion of these for their own coffers. Several cities maintain their own lobbyists including Portland, Salem and Eugene. Some smaller cities like Lake Oswego will also assign a staff person the part time duty of monitoring the Legislature.

The Association of Oregon Counties is even bigger, with eight lobbyists. The counties are particularly concerned with criminal justice issues because they maintain most of the jails throughout Oregon. They also are involved with probation and parole legislation and have extensive mental health and vocational rehabilitation programs.

There are also lobbyists for school districts, transportation districts, public ports, judges, district attorneys and water districts.

As mentioned, state agencies also have lobbyists. These include the Department of Transportation, the Department of Human Resources, the Bureau of Labor and Industries, the Judicial Department and the State System of Higher Education. One might ask why doesn't state government speak with one voice? The answer is simply there is too much to do and the necessary working knowledge is only at the agency level. The governor also has her own lobbyist who tries to relay the executive's position on the major issues.

The Third House

The term "lobby" goes back to the pre-Civil War days when favor seekers would wait in the lobby of the Willard Hotel[33] in Washington DC. for newly elected Abe Lincoln to pass through on his way to his rooms. Lincoln stayed at the Willard before moving into the White House only a few blocks down Pennsylvania Avenue.

Again, the term "lobby" can be either a verb or a noun, it is a fascinating topic. The Oregon lobby was the subject of University of Oregon Professor Harmon Zeigler's 1969 book, Lobby Interaction and Influence in State Legislatures.[34] Zeigler's thesis was that the lobby in Oregon was unique in that it was self-regulating, and served a very useful informational function. Most of what Zeigler wrote is still true.

Oregon's lobby is self-regulating. Most lobbyists belong to the Capitol Club, a four hundred plus member organization that has been in existence since 1959. It incorporated, has by-laws, publishes an extensive directory and sponsors several large social functions for legislators such as the biennial "Hello Party." More importantly, the Capitol Club has rules of professional conduct and a Professional Responsibility Committee to enforce the rules. Some of the proscriptions are relatively mundane, such as a prohibition against using state phones for business, but others are more interesting. For instance, if a lobbyist is talking to a legislator, a second lobbyist may not interrupt the conversation -- once you have a lawmaker's ear, it's yours. Another rule prohibits arranging for a bill to be introduced just so that the lobbyist can lobby against it.

There is no one way that individuals get into the lobby business. Many of them are lawyers or public relations people. A goodly number are ex-legislator such as former Senate President John Burns, former State Senator Keith Burns, and former Republican Minority Leader Roger Martin. The two Burns are not related and both are extremely well liked and respected. As mentioned, many are former staff members who now work as lobbyists. One of the best of these is Diana Godwin who was counsel to the Senate Judiciary Committee at one time, she now represents Regional Disposal Inc. on waste (garbage) matters. Others include Allan Tresidder, who now lobbies for the Trial Lawyers and Jennifer Ulum who represents Sacred Heart Health Systems. Tressider's partner, Kristin Granger, has her own rock group entitled "The Bitch Creek Nymphs" named after a dry fly.

The lobby refers to itself as the "Third House," and they are serious. They do play an integral function both in session and out, but it's during elections that they gather the "clout" to be used during the long cold winter of the Legislative session.

The Full Service Lobby

Several of the particularly effective lobbyists not only contribute to campaigns but they act as campaign consultants actually running campaigns. Several of the major lobbyists will run campaigns for and against ballot measures. It is not unusual for a lobbyist to defend his clients both in the Legislature and at the Ballot box. Nan Heim, Mark Nelson and Roger Martinare particularly good at this role.

---

[1] U.S. Const. amend I.

[2] ORS 171.735 (4).

[3] In addition, interest groups do not confine their activities to trying to influence the decisions of elected official alone. Administrative agencies in their rule making capacity are also the focus of their efforts. Finally, there is a somewhat unique aspect to special interests in Oregon, and that is the role they play *vis a vis* the initiative and the referendum. The same groups and individuals that try to influence the Legislature are also players when it comes to ballot measures.

[4] The most obvious exceptions are the groups concerned with the morality issues, such as abortion and homosexuality.

[5] Lawrence M. Friedman, A History of American Law 2nd ed, (New York: Touchstone, 1985) 76-85.

[6] See Frank Bourgin, The Great Challenge -- The Myth of Laissez-Faire in the Early Republic, (New York: George Braziller, Inc., 1989).

[7] "Session yields a bumper crop of lobbyists," Statesman Journal, 29 March 1993, 2C.

[8] Phil Keisling, "Big Bucks for Small Offices," The New York Times, 16 February 1993, __, As mentioned before, Keisling is Oregon's current Secretary of State.

9   A candid *mia culpa* is in order here. The author knows whereof he speaks. He has been known to raise a goodly amount of money and throw some rather hard punches (but only when unjustly provoked). Also, there is little objective about the above discussion of the lobby and lobbyists. Like anyone in politics the author has his favorites and his not-so-favorites, let the reader beware.

10   "Session yields a bumper crop of lobbyists," 2C.

11   Buckley v. Valeo, 424 U.S. 1, 96 S. Ct. 612 (1976).

12   Or. Const. art. I, sec. 8.

13   Deras v. Myers, 272 OR 47, 535 P. 2nd 541 (1975). The plaintiff, Warren Deras, had run against State Representative Vera Katz, as Republican, in northwest Portland in 1974. Deras was better lawyer than candidate. He was defeated by Katz, but won his own suit to declare the state spending limits unconstitutional. Because he had acted as his own attorney he was awarded attorney fees by the Supreme Court. Deras still is the de facto attorney for the Republican party on matters having to do with campaign finance.

14   Telephone interview with Donna Lewis, AOI Director of Communication, written notes, Salem OR, 20 June 1994.

15   Oregon, Secretary of State, Summary of Campaign Contributions and Expenditures - 1992 General Election, (Salem Secretary of State, 1993) 148.

16   D.B. Hardeman and Donald C. Bacon, Rayburn - A Biography, (Austin, TX: Texas Monthly Press, 1987), 167-199.

17   See ORS Chapter 261.

18   Or. Const. art. XI-D.

19   1986, 1990 and 1992.

20   See ORS Chapters 756 - 772.

21   Or. Const. art. IX, sec. 3a.

22   They do not like statutes which penalize usury, i.e., too high interest rates. They also do not like laws that limit the rates they may charge on credit cards. The bank and the other financial institutions are opposed to any measure that make it easier to file class action law suits. Class actions are suits in which numerous plaintiffs may join together and sue the same defendant. Oregon banks have been subject to such suits on behalf of depositors.

23   The astute reader can probably figure out that the author is not in love with insurance companies.

24   Summary of Campaign Contributions and Expenditures - 1992 General Election, 185.

25   Steve Duin, "They're all bozos on the same bus," The Oregonian, 18 May 1993, B9.

26   Mapes, Jeff, "Upfront-Verbatim-Drug Wars," The Oregonian , 22 March 1993, B-1.

27   Oregon has never had large industries like those located in Western Washington. In the early part of the century much of the attempted organizing of timber mills, in Oregon, was done by the International Workers of the World (IWW) or as they were known the "Wobblies." The IWW was never a popular union in Oregon and to a certain extent that is why Oregon lagged behind Washington in labor organizing. Timber was eventually organized, as were other larger industries.

28   Summary of Campaign Contributions and Expenditures - 1992 General Election, 186.

29   Ibid., 155.

30   Ibid., 196.

31   Roche has the distinction of perhaps being the most humorless person in Salem. She once served as an intern in U.S. Senator Bob Packwood's office in Washington, D.C. and when the Packwood sexual harassment controversy erupted in 1992, Roche became one of the accusers. She claimed that the good Senator had once told a dirty joke in front of her and she was offended. The only problem was, she couldn't remember the joke.

32   The Oregon Health Plan has been and will be discussed in numerous other works.

33   The newly restored Willard is very proud of its place in history and will show you a copy of the bill that the President paid with his first paycheck.

34   Harmon Zeigler and Michael Baer, <u>Lobby Interaction and Influence in State Legislatures</u>, (Belmont CA: Wadsworth, 1969).

CHAPTER 8

POLITICAL PARTIES AND ELECTION LAW

I belong to no organized political party, I'm a Democrat.

Will Rogers

Republicans raise dogs, Democrats raise kids and taxes.

Anonymous

If you want a Republican politician to do something
you threaten him, with a Democrat you temp him.

Rep. Jim Edmunsen

Introduction

Political parties don't play a great role in Oregon politics. To an extent, the length of Chapter 8 reflects that. Nevertheless, parties and election law play a part in the governmental process. Topics include:

- A brief history of political parties in Oregon.
- The nature of the parties today.
- Third parties.

- Oregon's role in the presidential nominating process.
- Election law.

History --Southern Democrats, Whigs and Republicans

Political parties, like other institutions, are a product of their history. As mentioned, the first political controversy in Oregon was whether or not the area should become part of Great Britain or the United States. This debate did not involve parties per se. Parties did play a role in the next major issue -- should the territory become a state? In the years prior to statehood, Democrats in Oregon tended to be Southern Democrats with Southern sympathies.[1] At the first meeting of the Democratic Party in 1850, a resolution was adopted supporting statehood. The Whigs, later turned Republican, opposed statehood.[2] The Democrats prevailed, and Oregon became a state in 1859.

The Democrats were fairly successful in the latter 1800s, electing five out of 10 governors. From 1900 to the early 1970s, one could argue that the state was solidly Republican --a one-party state. Of the 18 elected governors in this century, only eight have been Democrats, and three of these were elected during and after the 1970s. The Republicans usually controlled both the Legislature and statewide offices. There have been a few exceptions to this early GOP dominance. Governor George Chamberlain (elected in1902), Governor Oswald West (1910), Governor Walter Pierce elected in 1922 and Governor Charles Martin (1934) were all Democrats. However, Martin was only nominally a Democrat. He was Republican by his orientation, rhetoric and politics. A retired Army Major General, he opposed public power and the New Deal. Martin even supported euthanasia of aged or "feeble-minded wards of the state," to save money.[3] In the 1930s, he was considered ruthless; today he would be considered on the cutting edge of bio-ethics.

Regardless, by the start of the twentieth century, the majority of Oregon voters were Republican. When Democrats, like Chamberlain and others, won, it was because of their individual popularity and not their party.

Regular Democrats did control the Oregon House for one session in 1935 during the Great Depression.[4] There was another bright spot from 1957 to 1963 when the regular Democrats controlled the House. Robert Holmes was elected Governor in 1958. They also elected Richard Neuberger to the United States Senate in 1954.[5]

Democrats had a theoretical registration edge starting in 1956, 451,179 to 404,659, but it was not until the 1970s that Oregon had a true majority of Democrats. Democratic voter turnout is always substantially less than Republican turnout, so raw numbers are deceptive. As of the 1992 General Election, Democrats out number Republicans 792,115 to 641,914. Unfortunately for both parties, the number of "other" registrations (independents, Libertarians, et cetera) has sky rocketed from 13,114 in 1956 to 340,420 in 1992. The cause of these changes, migration, national political trends, and other factors are beyond this work, but Oregon has ceased to be a "one party state" as it was for much of its history. In 1994, it is very much a two party state, with a Democratic Governor, a Republican House, a Democratic Senate, two Republican US Senators, four Democratic and one Republican Congressional delegates and four out of four Democrats in the remaining partisan state-wide offices.[6]

The Parties Today --The Revenge of the Nerds

Oregon's two major political parties are weak institutions at best. Candidates have not relied on them for any significant help in decades. One observer noted that Oregon has a "star system" political process. The politicians are the "stars." They develop their own organizations and support groups almost to the exclusion of the parties. Both the Republican and Democratic party are the bailiwick of the activists, the true believers -- political nerds as it were. The foundation of the parties are the precinct committee persons -- two are elected from each precinct every two years in the Primary Election.[7] The precinct persons, in each county, make up the "central committees." The central committees, in turn, elect delegates to the state central committees. Being a precinct person, for either party, carries little responsibility and even less glory. The duty of a committee person is theoretically to attend monthly central committee meetings and to distribute packets of sample ballots and candidate literature to his or her precinct in the elections. Many precinct committee person slots are vacant. Any person can ask to be appointed by the central committee to a vacancy in his or her precinct or an adjoining precinct.

The people that make the effort to become involved are usually the very committed. For Democrats, this means the "party" is more to the left than Democrats are in general. For Republicans, it means the opposite, a party that is more to the right than most registered Republicans. Each party gathers in convention and adopts a platform. Delegates are selected by the country central committees, but there are so many positions available, that anyone who wants to attend the state convention can.

State party conventions and platforms can be a source of embarrassment for both parties' elected officials and candidates. At the 1972 State Democratic Convention, delegates adopted a plank favoring the abolition of private property.[8] Oregon Republicans refused to be outdone and once elected a genuine Communist-hunting, radio preacher as party chair. Among Walter Huss's other notable accomplishments was the leading of the battle *against* naming a street in Portland after Martin Luther King, Jr..

The only other time when precinct people have power is when a vacancy occurs either in an elected partisan office or in a party nomination.[9] Oregon has a peculiar law that when a vacancy occurs in a partisan office, the replacement must be of the same party as the previous office holder. How the replacement is selected depends on what level the office is. Replacement legislators are selected by the county commissioners of the area which the legislator will represent, but the list that the commissioners must select from is submitted to them by the party precinct persons of the legislative district.

Party nominees for various offices have been known to die or drop out of a races between the primary and general elections. Here, the precinct people have more power, they pick the replacement. The precinct committee people from a legislative district, a congressional district or even the state as a whole would select the replacement nominee. In 1974, the nominee for the United States Senate, Wayne Morse, died and was replaced by Betty Roberts. A similar thing happened in 1986. Congressman Jim Weaver resigned the nomination and it was given to Rick Bauman. Both Roberts and Bauman lost to Bob Packwood in their respective General Elections.

Finally, precinct committee people do have some role in the selection of delegates to the national party conventions every four years. Although most delegates are proportionally allocated to the winners of the presidential primary, a few are selected solely by the party.[10] Oregon does not use a winner-take all presidential primary system; if a candidate gets more than 35% of the vote, he or she is allocated delegates in the same proportion.[11]

Third Parties --Libertarians, the OCA, and Perot People

Third parties have never been very successful in either America or Oregon, but they've had impacts on elections. The Libertarians earned a place on Oregon's ballot in 1980 by meeting the statutory requirements to be recognized as a minor party.[12] As mentioned, the Oregon Citizens' Alliance had a tremendous impact on the 1990 gubernatorial election when they fielded Al Mobley to run against both Democrat Barbara Roberts and Republican Dave Frohnmayer. Mobley got 13% of the vote, insuring Roberts win. Ross Perot's American Party qualified as a major political party in 1992 when it polled more than the required 20% of the vote.[13]

Presidential Primaries --The Glory that Once Was

Time moves on, and it has left Oregon's May presidential primary behind. From the late 1940s to the early 1970s, the Oregon primary was a significant contest and was treated as such by the those seeking the presidency. In 1948, Republican Tom Dewey, an underdog, decisively beat Harold Stassen and became his party's nominee --only to lose to Harry Truman. The Dewey-Stassen fight also had the first live, nation-wide, broadcast debate. In 1948, it was on radio and wasn't until 1960 that the candidates debated on TV with Kennedy and Nixon.

One of the interesting aspects of the Oregon Presidential Primary is that the secretary of state has the power to place a candidate's name on the ballot on the secretary's own volition. The statute allows this if the "candidate's candidacy is generally advocated or is recognized in the national news media..."[14] "Candidates" may avoid this by filing a withdrawal with the secretary of state.

Some presidential primary contests have become local political legends. In 1960, Jack Kennedy charmed the state and spawned a generation of young idealists who hold the reins of power today. In 1964, Nelson Rockerfeller beat Barry Goldwater with the slogan "He cared enough to come!" Oregonians have always loved to be courted by presidential candidates. Eugene McCarthy stunned the country by beating Robert Kennedy in 1968. Winning the Oregon primary was considered to be the ideal kickoff for the primary in California which occurs about three weeks later. In spite of Oregon, Kennedy won California, only to be shot on election night. In 1976, Idaho Senator Frank Church won the primary beating both Jerry Brown and Jimmy Carter. But by the 1980s, more and more states had rescheduled their primaries before Oregon's. In 1984, Walter Mondale conceded the state to Gary Hart without a single appearance.

The public perception is that Oregon's primary is still important. In truth, the national campaigns look upon it as a very late sideshow. While local media and voters expect a week or more of national figures crisscrossing the state, the reality is one or two days of appearances.

All national presidential campaigns have common characteristics. There are usually three groups involved. First there are the enthusiastic true believing workers, second there are the local politicians who have picked their horse in the national race in hopes of a federal appointment, and finally, there is the national staff that is sent in from out-of-state. These young men and women are the same regardless of who the candidate is. They are usually from Ivy League schools, try to give the impression that they have a direct line to the "big guy" and have to beaten about the head and shoulders to learn anything about the local political necessities.

Election Dates --Too Much of Good Thing

Oregon's General Election is on the first Tuesday after the first Monday of November in each even numbered year[15] and the Primary Election is on the third Tuesday of May in even numbered years.[16] There are five possible election dates each year. In the even numbered years, these five would include the regular Primary and General Election.[17] The other dates are for special elections which usually involve local tax matters. Until 1981, there were even more possible election dates. Many voters felt they were being bludgeoned by schools seeking new tax bases or operating levies -- too much of a good thing. The legislative response to this was to reduce the number of possible elections. Passage of Ballot Measure 5 in 1990 has made this almost a moot point.

Election Law --Ice water and "The Best Politician Money can Buy"

In 1904 Oregon adopted the open primary, i.e., where a party's nominee for an office was selected by election and not a convention. Even before the Seventeenth Amendment to the US. Constitution in 1913, Oregon had endorsed the direct election of United States senators in 1908. These early changes in election law were considered significant reforms in their day.

Election law *per se* is usually the sole concern of those involved in politics. Unless you are running for office, you could spend your whole life and not know or care about violations of an election law. But if you are involved, you had better learn the rules and learn them well. Politics is a sport where fouls count.

The most important rules are the deadlines. Campaigns start a long time before the public ever hears about them, and deadlines start to run more than a year before the General Election. In fact, that is the first deadline. A candidate for the legislature must live in his or her district at least one year before the General Election.[18] This means that if one is going to run, one must make sure is on the right side of any line in November of the odd numbered year before the election. A candidate must also be a member of the party for 180 days before the filing deadline.[19]

The next important date occurs 70 days before the Primary Election --the filing deadline.[20] Again, the secretary of state is Oregon's chief election officer and sets up shop in the House chamber of the Capitol. Large boards are placed on the side of the room with slots for the various candidates names. Filings are accepted by clerks sitting at the dais until precisely 5:00pm. As mentioned, "Filing Day" is a gathering for politicians, lobbyists, media and hangers-on. A person may withdraw his or her name as well as file for the office. There are always surprises as names go up and down on the big board. The crowd has no small resemblance to the chorus of race fans from <u>Guys and Dolls</u> singing "I've got the horse (candidate) right here, his name is Paul Revere." Everybody is looking for a winner, everybody loves the race.

The next deadline is at 5:00pm. on Thursday, two days later. The is the cutoff point for a candidate's material to go into the Voters' Pamphlet.[21] Few states have these brochures which allow candidates to make one or two page statements. Some of the information is required by statute, and people have been tried for lying in the voter's pamphlet.[22] But most of what presented is carefully crafted campaign rhetoric. A candidate's picture and statement are among the most important parts of a campaign. A great number of voters religiously read the pamphlet, and it is the ultimate political nightmare for one to miss the pamphlet deadline. Incidentally, pictures must be no more than one year old and meet other requirements such as no lapel pins or uniforms.

There are other unusual election law provisions in Oregon, one of which is that candidates cannot give "anything of value" to voters while campaigning.[23] This means that in Oregon there are none of the pencils, fingernail files or the other political detritus found in other states. Both political parties maintain booths at the State Fair in August, and at the turn of the century, it was determined ice-water, given at the Democratic booth, was <u>not</u> "something of value." To this day, ice water is still given out. The Republicans have never been accused of giving anything away.

Every piece of campaign literature must have the phrase "authorized by 'such and such' campaign."[24] Candidates who forget the "disclaimer" are fined. Editorial endorsements must always have the date upon which they were issued, lest a candidate use an endorsement from one election in another election. One of the greatest taboos is the use of the word "re-Elect." No one may use the term "re-elect" unless he or she is actually running for another term to the same office that they currently hold.[25] People who are appointed to office and then run, such as most judges, are allowed to fudge with the term "re-tain." In 1968, Alice Corbett won a Democratic nomination for State Senator in Multnomah County only to have her opponent, Vern Cook declared the winner because she used the term "re-elect" inappropriately. Corbett had been in the State Senate, but had been out of office for a little over a year when she ran again.[26]

Oregon allowed twelve word slogans to appear on the primary ballot besides candidates' names up to 1982. One populist legislator, Wally Priestly, D -Portland, used to call the slogans the "poor man's billboard." Before they were abolished, the writing of these slogans was an art. A man running for sheriff said "Have gun, will travel." A women dance hall owner touted herself as "The best politician money can buy." Much to the author's chagrin, a political columnist once named his ballot slogan the ultimate say-nothing-sound-good-phrase --"Re-elect Tom Mason, experienced, hardworking, an outstanding record."

At one time, Oregon had a very liberal last minute voter registration law. Citizens could register up to and including election day itself. In 1986, this was repealed and replaced with twenty-day cut off. This was after the Bhagwan Shree Rajneesh started a commune in central Oregon and attempted to bring in homeless people to vote in the local elections to take over the Wasco County government. The Bhagwan was not successful, but his efforts were enough to kill election day registration.

Vote-by-mail was passed in 1981 after an intense fight in the Legislature.[27] Initial opposition came from the Oregon Education Association which thought that the type of person that would send in a mail ballot would also be the same type who would vote against school bond measures. Vote-by-mail has become one of those instances which illustrate the old Chinese aphorism about "Victory has a hundred fathers." Norma Paulus, former Secretary of State, candidate for governor and current Superintendent of Public Instruction likes to take credit for vote-by-mail because it was enacted on "her watch" as Secretary of State.[28]

---

[1]   Supporters of the future Confederacy promoted the idea that Oregon should become part the "Republic of the Pacific." The theory was to surround the North with independent countries sympathetic to the South.

[2]   Terence O'Donnell, "Oregon History;" in Oregon, Secretary of State, Oregon Blue Book 1993-1994, (Salem: Secretary of State, 1991), 3788.

[3]   Robert E. Burton, Democrats Of Oregon: The Pattern of Minority Politics, 1900-1956, (Eugene: University of Oregon Press, 1970) 70.

[4]   John Cooter, D-Toledo, was Democratic Speaker in 1935. As mentioned in Chapter 5, Harry Boivin, D-Klamath Falls, became coalition Speaker in 1937.

[5]   United States Senator Wayne Morse was orginally elected as a republican in 1944, but became a Democrat in 1955. He was re-elected as a Democrat in 1956.

[6]   These include secretars of state, treasurer, comissioner of labor and industries and attorney general. The fifth statewide office, superintendant of public instruction is non-partisan.

7   ORS 248.015 - 248.029.

[8]   The author attended this convention, but neither voted for the plank nor inhaled.

[9]   ORS 249.190 - 249.200.

[10]   Actual delegate selection is controlled by party rule.

[11]   ORS 248.315.

[12]   ORS 248.008.

[13] ORS 248.006(10(a). This requirement is now 15%.

[14] ORS 249.078(1)(a).

[15] ORS 254.056(1).

[16] ORS 254.056(2).

[17] ORS 255.345.

[18] Or. Const. art. I,V sec. 8.

[19] ORS 249.046.

[20] ORS 249.037.

[21] ORS 251.065.

[22] See Chapter 3 on recall -- Pat Gillis.

[23] ORS 260.665.

[24] ORS 260.522.

[25] ORS 260.550.

[26] Cook v. Corbett, 251 OR 263, 446 P.2d 179 (19680).

[27] ORS 254.465 - 470.

[28] In truth she played a minor role. The bill to establish vote-by-mail was introduced by the author and Representative Peter Countney.

CHAPTER 9

LOCAL GOVERNMENT

You ain't quick enough to go up against our Sheriff.

Tilghman, <u>Dugout</u>

Don't fight city hall...

Anonymous

Read my lips, you're fired!

Portland Mayor Bud Clark
to Chief of Police Jim Davis

Introduction

There is an irony in the study of government --the closer government is to the individual the less important it becomes as a subject. Local government, in its various shapes and forms, affects individual lives more than any other political structure in America. Chapter 9 attempts to cover these topics:

- The general nature of local government in Oregon.
- History and evolution of local government.
- Fundamental services performed.
- Home rule.
- Oregon's largest county.
- County issues.
- County politics.
- A typical smaller county.
- Cities and their variation in size.

- Portland.
- Police and the mayor.
- School boards.
- The Port of Portland.
- Metro.
- Mass transit.
- Boundary commissions.
- Special districts.

Street Level Government --"County dog or city dog?"

There are over 1600 local governments in the State of Oregon. These include 36 counties, 240 cities, 340 school districts, 23 port districts, three mass transit districts, two boundary commissions, one regional government and approximately 1,000 special districts. With few exceptions, such as the Port of Portland and the Tri-Met Mass Transit District, most of these local governments are elected.

These jurisdictions are responsible for incredibly diverse activities -- police, fire, roads, jails, schools. and water, to name a few. This is street-level government: sewers, garbage, speed limits, and building permits. Unfortunately, these are not separate entities with well-defined jurisdictions or functions; overlap is more the rule than the exception, cities are located within counties, and districts are located within districts. Some duties, such as law enforcement and animal control, are shared.

When Neil Goldschmidt was a Portland City Commissioner, he was responsible for (among other things), animal control. Neil's office replied to phone complaints with this question," Is that a city dog or a county dog you want picked up?" They would then explain that if the dog was west of 82nd Avenue it was a "city dog" and if it was east it was a "county dog" and they weren't responsible for it. Let's start with the counties.

From "Shires" to Vector Control

Oregon's 36 counties still fulfill a very traditional role. Unlike states, which were modeled after sovereign nations, counties have always been administrative units of higher governments. In England, the county was originally the Anglo-Saxon "shire," the jurisdiction of the King's sheriff. "Sheriff" itself comes from the word "shire." Most sheriffs are still doing what they have always done, enforcing the law, seizing property and running jails. The King's man with a sword turned into the legendary gun toting law-man of the American West and subsequently became the modern deputy with a computer console in her car and a nine millimeter on her hip.

The word "County" is of French derivation from the term "cunté," which means domain of a count or earl.

Counties, both ancient and modern, have always been involved in law enforcement, courts and tax collection. However, Oregon counties furnish numerous other public services including: "public health, mental health, community corrections services, criminal prosecution, hospitals, nursing homes, airports, parks, libraries, land-use planning, building regulation, refuse disposal, elections, air-pollution control, veterans services, economic development, urban renewal, public housing, vector control, county fairs, museums, dog control, civil defense, senior services and many others."[1] "Vector control" for the uninitiated is spraying for mosquitoes and other pests.

The Fundamentals --Life, Death and Taxes

Counties are probably the most fundamental units of government in America. We literally live and die with them; birth and death certificates are issued by county governments all over the United States. Another basic function is the recording of all deeds, mortgages, land plats, conveyances of interest in and liens on real property.[2] The recording system, maintained by each county, is the essential government institution that enables one to own and transfer property and collect debts though the courts. This system is the very base of our economic system. After all, how does one "own" property? You can hardly put it in your pocket and a person can only physically defend so much land. In the last analysis, property ownership is based upon a formalized agreement of society, i.e., government. The government that puts this agreement into effect is county government.

Real property conveyances include deeds, land sale contracts, and trust deeds. Before a deed or other conveyance is truly valid, it must be registered and thus the legal doctrine of "first in time, first in right." A deed that is unrecorded is invalid against a later deed if the later deed was registered first. In other words, someone could sell property twice and the second buyer would have the right to the property if he registered his deed first.

The same priority system also applies to liens on property. In addition to liens, voluntarily registered by the property owners, there are involuntary liens. Any circuit court judgment against an individual automatically becomes a lien against all real property owned by the individual in the county. Liens follow property and the lien holder can eventually collect the lien by "executing" on the property which practically means having the county sheriff sell the property to satisfy the lien. When property is sold in this manner, the lien or mortgage holders are paid off in order of priority, that is, when they registered their interest with the county clerk. This same recording system is an integral part of the means by which most local taxes are collected in Oregon.

Cumulatively, counties are probably the largest tax collectors in the State, other than the federal government. Property taxes are based on assessments established by the various county assessors and then collected by the counties. The total tax levied on any particular piece of land includes the taxes imposed by the county itself, the city, the school district and any other taxing jurisdiction that the property is located in. The tax bill that the owner receives lists what amount of the total tax goes to what jurisdiction. Before property tax can be collected, however, a value has to be placed on the property by the county assessor's office. Oregon law requires that every time an interest in property is transferred, the value has to be included in the document filed in the deed records. The fact that a transfer is not valid until registered compels people to file, and the reported values become part of the assessment process. There is more to the assessment of property values, and the process itself consumes a substantial amount of county revenue.

Another land related function is land-use planning and zoning. The counties are a major part of the process and have the primary responsibility for submitting land-use plans to the State under Oregon's pioneer land-use statute, Senate Bill 100, adopted in 1973.[3,4] In developing counties such as Washington, Clackamas and Deschutes, the politics of the county commission is the politics of development. Real estate and development interests are the major political players with the most to win on lose. They contribute to campaigns and lobby commissions to see that there is enough available land for development.[5]

Another basic function of the counties are elections. They print the ballots, administer the actual elections and report the final vote tallies to the various jurisdictions. All levels of government, Federal, state, city, school board, et cetera, use counties to hold their elections. This is why presidential candidates and the local water board candidates appear on the same ballot. Although election mechanics are controlled by state statute and supervised by the secretary of state, precinct boundaries, staffing of polling places during, counting of votes and voter registration are done by the county clerks or the directors of elections in the larger counties.

Home Rule --Semi-Sovereign

There are two kinds of counties in Oregon: "Home Rule Counties" and regular counties. Article VI Section 10 of the Oregon Constitution, adopted by the people in 1958, allows the various counties to adopt "home rule charters," which basically give them control over their local affairs such as the structure of the county government and the imposition of local taxes.[6] In 1973, all counties were granted this home-rule authority by statute.[7] This gives Oregon counties a kind of semi-sovereignty. Prior to the adoption of these home rule provisions, the counties were mostly extensions of the state government. According to the national Advisory Commission of Intergovernmental Relations, Oregon counties have a high degree of local autonomy.[8] Eight of Oregon's 36 counties are home rule counties. These are Benton, Clatsop, Hood River, Jackson, Josephine, Lane, Multnomah and Washington Counties.

One of the constant debates in Oregon government concerns what is, and is not, within the power of a home-rule county. To use the language of the Oregon Tax Court, "...Whether the matter is one of paramount municipal concern or is of paramount statewide concern."[9] In that particular Tax Court case, the issue was whether or not Multnomah County could levy a property tax for public assistance when a state statute prohibited such a tax for three years. The Court decided that the state statute took precedence because it was passed for the benefit of all state taxpayers. Other cases have involved retirement benefits, judges compensation,[10] and court clerks[11] to name a few.

As mentioned, non-home rule counties now have powers substantially like those of home-rule counties. All of the home rule counties, and sixteen of the non-home rule counties, operate with a board of county commissioners. These boards have from three to five members. Eight of the smaller counties use a "county court" system with a "county judge" and two commissioners. In addition to being the executive of the county, a "county judge" may exercise some judicial functions such as probate and other matters.[12]

There seems to be little relationship between which counties are home-rule counties and which have particularly effect governments. Lane and Washington County are considered to have relatively effective county government, whereas Multnomah and Clatsop County are considered to have less effective governments.

There is extreme disparity in size between Oregon's largest and smallest counties: Multnomah has a population of 605,000,[13] while Wheeler County,[14] in the central part of the State, only has a population of 1,500. Nonetheless, there is community of interest between the large and small counties on issues such as law enforcement and taxation.

Multnomah County --Large but Weak

Multnomah County is the largest county, in population, in the state, but the county government is not a particularly powerful. In fact, the Multnomah County Commission is an anomaly. There are several reasons for this, not the least of which is that most of Multnomah County's population base of 605,000 is composed of the city of Portland, which alone has 458, 275 people.[15] The city government handles most of the municipal functions that a county would normally handle such as law enforcement, roads, sewers and fire protection. In fact, Multnomah County contracts with Portland for police in some areas. The Multnomah County Sheriff's Office had substantial law enforcement duties before the transfer to the city, but now it is responsible for corrections and patrols in the few unincorporated rural areas of the County.

Multnomah County is 465 square miles[16] in area and is the smallest Oregon county. It runs from East to West along the Columbia River and a bit beyond to where the Willamette River joins the Columbia. Portland is the west quarter of the County. The eastern part the County has several modest size towns including Gresham and Troutdale.

The current County Commission has five elected districts members and a presiding officer who is elected at large. The structure of Multnomah County government has been a ongoing source of political controversy. The home rule charter was adopted in 1968 and the elected office of sheriff was abolished. The major proponent of these changes was Don Clark, who became Chair of the County Commission. In 1982, a group of citizens from the "East County" area began successful effort to "reform" Multnomah County government. Two of the proponents, Ray Phillips and Tom Dennehy were angry at Multnomah County for going to the 1981 Legislature and having a statute passed mandating that sewers be installed in East County. Phillips and his cohorts had an ongoing battle with what they considered the liberals running both Portland and Multnomah County. East County has been a veritable font of populist politics for over twenty years, including the successful 1982 effort that rewrote the Charter. Although Phillips died in the mid-1980s, he had tremendous impact on government in Oregon. He was involved with more issues than the Multnomah County charter. Phillips also ran several unsuccessful state-wide property-tax limitation measures starting in 1978 --these measures later led to the successful Ballot Measure 5 in 1990.

Among other things, this charter reform imposes a two term limit on the commissioners and the presiding officer, and prohibited County elected officials from running for other offices in mid-term. This provision has been particularly troublesome because there is no definition of "running for another office."[17] The rewrite reinstated the Sheriff's office as an elected position and prohibited Multnomah County from having a paid lobbyist! In addition, the new charter said that pay could not be raised without a vote of the people. It wasn't until 1988, when another charter was adopted on the recommendations of a commission, that the Commissioners were given the power to raise their pay.

Regardless, Philips's efforts weakened Multnomah County Government and were the precursors of things to come.

County Issues --Money and Mandates

All local governments, regardless of size, have at least two common concerns -- mandates and money. The Association of Oregon Counties represents the general interests of the counties in the Legislature. Generally, the counties oppose any mandates from the state which would cause them to spend money. This is a similar situation to the relationship between the federal and state governments. An example of a mandate might be a hypothetical state law requiring county health officials to inspect any residence found to have had illegal drug manufacturing for toxic chemicals -- sounds wonderful, but who will pay for those health officials. In a few instances, mandates have even been lifted. Until 1982, the counties were responsible for the cost of appointed attorneys for indigent defendants. In 1993, as part of the state's response to Ballot Measure 5, there was an unsuccessful attempt to return indigent defense to the counties.

County governments are constantly in search of new revenues to run programs, especially as the counties become more and more oriented toward human resource. At one time, the counties maintained "poor farms" and county hospitals as part of welfare. Multnomah County gave up its hospital and instituted a program called Project

Health. This was supposed to be a low income health program aimed at the uninsured. In addition to the usual health efforts, Multnomah County runs teen health clinics in Portland High Schools.

Counties have tried to raise money in a variety of ways. Multnomah County tried to establish a utility tax, but it was referred to the voters by referendum. Columbia County imposed a two cent per ton gravel tax, this raises about $300,000 per year. Counties have also been instituting numerous fees for building permits, building inspections, sub-surface sewer permits and zoning variances.

At one time, western Oregon counties received $50 million a year from the Federal government. This is their share of timber revenues off of the "O & C" county forest land. The "O & C Act" is a 1937 Federal law involving railroad land and timber on those lands. "O & C" stands for "Oregon and California."[18] Until recently Lane County received 60% of its budget from the O&C program. Other counties receive less, Multnomah County receives a nominal amount and Columbia County gets $600,000 a year. The Spotted Owl Controversy has resulted in a twenty-five percent reduction in O&C money. Needless to say, the counties have been trying to make up this short fall.

Air quality is an issue in Southern Oregon. It is also an area where the recalling of county commissioners is almost a community sport. Several county commissioners have been involuntarily retired in recent years. This part of the state has a character of its own, not unlike Multnomah County's East Side. The Southern part of the state was populated by Southerners and the politics there still reflects that.

County Politics --Low Profile Government

We have already noted the peculiar status of Multnomah County government, i.e., not very powerful and politically overshadowed by Portland. Other county governments in the metropolitan area play a much more significant role. Washington County and Clackamas County are respectively the second and third largest counties in the state with populations of 340,000 and 294,500.[19] Clackamas is governed by a board of three county commissioners. Washington County is run by a County Commission with five members. Four of them are part time and all non-partisan. The actual administration of the county is done by the chair of the commission. Law enforcement, jails, human resources and land-use planning are the big issues for both of these counties.

Typically, an Oregon county spends the largest share of its budget on law enforcement activities, including a sheriff, a county jail and a county probation department. Counties also pay for most of the cost of each of the thirty-six district attorney offices. Counties do not pay for court room staff, but they do pay for courtrooms themselves. Interestingly enough, if a county increases spending on the sheriff's office there will have to be a commensurate increase in the amount spent on prosecution and jails -- more police mean more arrests which mean more prosecutions which mean more people going to jail.

Other services that counties are involved in are parks, roads, animal control, bridges and libraries. Multnomah County has the largest library system in the state with fourteen branches and over a million volumes.[20]

A Typical County --With a Few Exceptions

Columbia County could described as a typical Oregon County -- although it is mostly rural, it borders on the city of Portland and Multnomah County. It is 687 square miles in area, has a population of 38,8000 and is located on the Columbia River north of Portland.[21] The county seat is St. Helens, named after the volcano, Mount St. Helens, located approximately thirty-five miles northwest across the Columbia. Another unusual thing about the county is that it is also the home of Trojan, Oregon's only (soon to be closed), nuclear power plant. Other than a reactor next to a volcano, Columbia County is typical.

Columbia County's general fund budget is approximately $8.5 million, most of which is raised from the property tax. That amount must be divided between assessment and taxation, law enforcement, the jail, the District Attorney, juvenile services, the County Clerk, economic development, emergency services, the maintenance of County facilities (such as the court house), and road repair. Although most human service activities are funded with State dollars, the county supplements senior transportation and mental health services. Columbia County is governed a three person board of county commissioners chaired by Michael Sykes.[22] Commissioners are paid $43,000 a year and are partisan office holders.

Cities --Portland to Greenhorn

Portland is the largest of Oregon's 240 cities[23] with a population of 458,275. Oregon's smallest city is Greenhorn with a population of three. Greenhorn is located in Baker County off Highway 7 and is also the highest city in the State, its elevation is 6,270 feet. It is the only municipality that exists under Oregon's "Ghost Town" statute. This measure says that a city whose populations falls below the number of people necessary to fill elected city offices can remain incorporated as an "historic ghost town."[24] Greenhorn was created under a United States patent from President Taft in 1912. The City has only three residents, but it has nine officials who are appointed under this statute by the Baker County Commission. While Mayor George Massinger and the other officials do not live in Greenhorn, they do own property there.[25]

Cities are incorporated under a process found in Chapter 221 of the Oregon Revised Statutes. A petition is filed with the county and must be signed by 20% (in a county under 300,000, 10%) of the registered voters in the area that the proposed incorporation is to take place. The area must not be within a presently incorporated city and there must be at least 150 registered voters.

The process is complex and a proposed city must comply with Oregon land-use laws. For example, Sunriver is a resort in Central Oregon, outside of Bend, with a population that varies between three and fifteen thousand people depending on the season. Even though Sunriver maintains roads, sewers and a police force it was deemed ineligible for incorporation because it lacked low-income housing.[26]

Keizer, one of Oregon's newest cities, is an example of a more successful effort. It was formed out of the incorporation of an area north of Salem in 1982. In the same year, the infamous Rajneeeshpuram was incorporated. In 1985, the incorporation was declared illegal by the U.S. District Court as a violation of church and state.

City government means police, fire, sewage, roads, parks, water and other municipal services. Larger cities also have housing, and economic development programs and other human service programs However, the most important of these municipal services is always law enforcement.

Portland --The Biggest City Budget

Portland's annual budget illustrates the variety of tasks just described. All sources of revenue for 1993-94 total $855.9 million, $251.2 million of this amount is the beginning fund balance; $149.4 million (17.5%) are from property taxes, $194 million are from service fees such as water charges, and the rest is from business license fees, franchise fees and other sources such as cigarette and liquor taxes.[27]

Expenditures equal this amount. The largest is for utilities at $318.2 million dollars, again, this is water and sewers expenses. These utilities, police and fire are what people live in cities for. If you live in the country, you have to dig your own well, take care of your own sewage and probably don't get much police protection. Public safety, both police and fire, has an expenditure of $205.4 million dollars. Police use $80.0 million,[28] fire $55.3 million,[29] the Bureau of Emergency Communications $8.5 million[30] and "Fire and Police Disability and Retirement" cost $40.6 million.[31] Portland police and firefighters have never been included in the Public Employee Retirement System (PERS) which covers just about every other state, county and municipal workers. While PERS is fully funded, the Portland system is not. This means that Portland pays retirement out of the general fund, there is no "money in the bank," as is the case with PERS which has close to $30 billion in investments that pay retirement benefits. The distinction is a bit academic. State and other governments contribute to the retirement fund as the workers are paid. The whole situation is a kind of "pay me now or pay me later" quandary.

Other large components of Portland's budget include Parks, Recreation and Culture at $28.5 million ,[32] Transportation at $85.5 million[33] and the Bureau of General Services at $40.6 million.[34]

There are 4,785 City employees, of which 1,171 are Police Bureau and 771 are Fire Bureau employees.

The Police and the Mayor -- The Massacre at Fat City

The political history of Portland is almost the history of the relationship between the mayor of and the Police Department. Police don't like judges, they don't like politicians and they especially don't like any Mayor who interferes with their Department.

The Department is always the largest consumer of city dollars. Police as group have a unique psychology, they perceive themselves as unappreciated outsiders who are constantly under attack from criminals, politicians, judges and liberal do-gooders. They are the thin blue line between order and anarchy. It wasn't until 1970s that police were given the right to bargain. The Portland Police Association was organized as a strong union, and its leadership has never been afraid to get involved in controversial issues.[35]

The tension in this situation is embodied in the relationship between the Mayor, the Chief and the Department itself. That relationship has not always been hospitable. At the turn of the century, Portland's mayor once fired every officer in the Department. The Department wants to be run by one of its own while the mayor wants someone to do his or her bidding. Under the Portland City Charter, the chain of command goes from the mayor, to the city commissioner in charge of the police, the chief, then to the Department itself. However, because the mayor assigns departments to the commissioners, he or she has theoretical control over the Department. Mayors have frequently given the Police Department to themselves, sometimes to their regret.

After he was elected Mayor in 1972, Neil Goldschmidt hired Bruce Baker, from Berkeley, California, as Chief. After Goldschmidt became Secretary of Transportation, the appointed Mayor Connie McCreedy kept Baker even though he had little if any support from the Department. Ron Still was the Chief under Frank Ivancie until Ivancie was defeated by the colorful Portland tavern owner Bud Clark.

Clark wore a beard, rode a bicycle to City Hall and listed his religion as "heathen." He had achieved national notoriety by posing for a poster depicting him standing in front of a bronze statue of women on Portland's Transit mail holding his raincoat open. The caption read "Expose Yourself to Art."

Mayor Clark started his administration by hiring the first female police chief in any major metropolitan area, Penny Harrington. Penny had been in the Department for 20 years and had filed numerous successful suits to obtain promotions. Harrington was in office less than 14 months when accusations surfaced that her husband, another police officer, had leaked information to a restaurant owner friend that he was about to be arrested on drug charges. Mayor Clark, instead of firing or supporting her, proved his political amateurishness by appointing a panel to look into the allegations. The subsequent public investigation turned out to be municipal version of the Chinese "Death of a thousand cuts" to Harrington as hearings went on for two months. Penny eventually resigned and unsuccessfully sued the City on grounds of sexual discrimination.[36]

Clark then appointed one of the police regulars, Jim Davis, as Chief. They clashed over access to certain internal police reports by Portland's version of the a "Citizen's Review Board," the "Police Internal Investigations and Audit Committee."

The Mayor met the Chief for breakfast at the Fat City Cafe in Multnomah Village, a picturesque group of antique stores and small businesses located in Southwest Portland. Fat City is an old style diner now selling high cholesterol breakfasts to slumming yuppies. Appropriately, it is four doors down from "Murder by the Book," a funky little store specializing in crime novels.

The booth, in which they sat, now has a small plaque saying, "Site of the Fat City Massacre" because of the following conversation, which occurred when Clark asked for the records;

> Davis -- "Read my lips you can't have them."
> Clark -- "Read my lips, you're fired."

Davis stayed with the Department and unsuccessfully ran against Clark for mayor in 1988.

Clark's next Chief was Richard Walker. He seemed to have relatively good relations with the Mayor, but he resigned after slapping one of his women officers, Rikki Venemon, in a kind of 90s version the infamous General Patton incident. Venemon sued Walker and the City, but settled out of court before the Chief resigned.

Clark's next chief was Tom Potter, another regular, but to say the least, somewhat of a surprise to the boys in blue. After being in office for a while, Potter announced that his daughter Katie, also a Portland police officer, was a lesbian and he would continue to support her. Potter appeared in uniform in a Gay Rights Parade and became the darling of Portland's liberal community. He seemed to be almost philosophical about the situation. "I have no doubt that I will be known as the 'gay rights chief."[37]

On a more substantive side, the Chief became a major advocate for the concept of "community policing," or bringing the police closer to the neighborhoods. Potter's tenure was plagued by numerous shooting incidents in which officers seemed to overreact by unloading their Glock pistols into local citizens under somewhat questionable circumstances. One women, Maria Sandoz, who was hit 22 times, was found to be holding an air pistol.[38]

When Vera Katz was elected Mayor in 1992, most people expected her to keep Potter. However, they clashed over the police budget and Potter resigned. In June of 1993, Katz appointed the first Afro-American officer to be Chief, Charles Moose.[39]

School Boards --The Most Important Governments

The are 295 elementary and secondary school districts in Oregon, 29 Education Service Districts and 16 community college districts. These school districts serve a population of 498,614 elementary and secondary students.[40] All of these districts are governed by elected boards. The role of the superintendent of public instruction has already been discussed and school finance will be examined in Chapter 10 on Perennial Issues. Regardless, it could be argued that school boards are ultimately the most important of governments. These are the institutions that educate and care for our children.

Education Service Districts were instituted by the Legislature to provide economic support services to smaller school districts.[41] These services includes "central purchasing, library curriculum materials, special teachers and special instruction services."[42]

Other than education service districts, there are three types of school districts: elementary districts which provide education for students kindergarten through sixth or eighth grade, union high school districts which serve students in grades seven or nine through twelve from a number of different elementary school districts, and unified or county school districts which offer programs from kindergarten through twelfth grade.

All of these school board have important functions regarding curriculum and personnel. The most important roles, however, are budgeting and bargaining with teachers about salary. The local school boards establish the budgets for the schools within the parameters set by state statute. This means that some schools districts will have some programs and others will not depending on how the budget is written. Budgets are always a function of revenue. Currently, Oregon education is in a tremendous state of flux because of Ballot Measure 5. Before Ballot Measure 5, Oregon schools were locally funded, but now the state is taking over the main funding role; this situation will inevitably lead to state control.

All local school boards have local budget committees made up of parents and other citizens. These budget committees make the initial decisions; how much money to put in foreign language, talent and gifted programs and physical education. Teachers have had the right to collective bargaining since 1973. Most teachers are represented by the Oregon Education Associations, and a few are represented by the American Federation of Teachers or the Oregon School Employees Associations. Bargaining issues can be more than just wages: they may concern working conditions, class size and vacation.

The Port of Portland --Where the Big Boys Play

There is a joke among Oregon politicians that some day they would like to have real power and serve on the Port of Portland. The "Port" is one of the most important government entities in Oregon. Trade is a major part of Oregon's economy and tremendous amount of it goes through the Port of Portland. The Port (although there are 23 ports in the state, the Port of Portland is the "Port") has an annual budget of $478 million. The Port maintains five marine terminals, Portland International Airport, three general aviation airports, the Portland Ship Repair Yard and six industrial properties.[43] The Port also runs dredging operations on the Columbia River. It is governed by a nine person commission appointed by the governor. The Port of Coos Bay also has appointed commissioners, all other ports elect their commissioners. The Port was established in 1891. In 1901, the original statute was amended to allow Port commissioners to be elected by the Legislature, and in 1911, a provision was made for appointment by the governor, but the measure was ruled unconstitutional. In 1925, the law was again changed back to election by the Legislature, but the 1931 Legislature provided a means of selection by popular election.

It was in 1935 that gubernatorial appointment was finally settled on. However, in 1987 that statute was changed to make it clear they serve at the "pleasure" of the governor.[44] Until then, the commissioners were independent once appointed. This change was the result of a battle between newly elected Governor Goldschmidt and Commissioner Peter Brix who, along with another commissioner, refused to resign at his request. This statute also allows the governor to appoint the president of the Port. Appointment to the Port has always been a major political plum, a kind of ultimate club for the big boys. Attempts to allow for popular election have never been successful in the Legislature.

The current President is Mr. Robert Ames, President of the First Interstate Bank. The Executive Director is Mike Thorne, a former eastern Oregon wheat rancher and veteran State Senator. Thorne served as Co-Chairperson of the powerful Ways and Means Committee for several sessions and was considered one of the most influential legislators ever to serve in Salem. General Counsel is Cory Streisinger, former legal advisor to Governor Goldschmidt.

The Port has always been at the very heart of big business in Oregon and has had more than it share of controversy. In 1932, Governor Julius Meier appointed Frank Akin to audit the Port of Portland. Meier had appointed Akin, a professional auditor, after Meier's former law partner, Bert Haney, had been elected to the Port Commission. Akin concluded, after three months, that James H. Polhemus, the General Manager, had mismanaged the enterprise. In February of 1933, Aikin testified before a State Senate Sub-Committee, but they concluded that there was not sufficient evidence to proceed. In May of that year, the Port Commission started its own investigation lead by Commissioner Bert Haney. Most of the investigation centered on preferential dry-dock rates being given to State Steamship Company and the selling of used equipment below costs. The Oregonian opposed the investigation on the grounds that is was merely political. The still alive Journal [45] supported the investigation.

On November 20, 1933, Frank Akin was found shot dead in his apartment. Even after extensive publicity and a more intensive investigation, the murder remained unsolved. The Commission eventually exonerated itself and business returned to normal.[46]

The role of the Port expanded over the years, but with fewer murders.

Metro--The Government that Garbage Built

Prior to 1978, regional governmental matters in the Tri-County area were handled by the Columbia Region Association of Governments (CRAG). CRAG was not popular, and in 1977 the Legislature put a measure on the ballot, in the Tri-County area, reorganizing it into the Metropolitan Service District (MSD). The Ballot Title read "Abolishes CRAG..." The voters passed the measure and MSD was established. Initially it had thirteen elected councilors from district and an "Executive" elected at large. It is the only elected regional government in the United States.

MSD later changed it name to Metro, but its duties remain the same; operation of the Washington Park Zoo in Portland, solid waste, regional transportation planning, management of the urban growth boundary and management of the Portland Convention Center. At first glance these seem like relative minor matters, but there is nothing minor to the problems of waste in the urban area. One of the biggest issues ever facing Metro was the establishment of the a new land fill for the urban area. Metro selected a site at Arlington in central Oregon. It then entered into a extended lease with Waste Management Systems to run the land fill.

The first executive officer of Metro was Rick Gustafson, a former State Representative. He was defeated in 1986 by the current executive officer Rena Cusma after a controversy involving sloppy bookkeeping and budgeting.

Until 1991, Metro seemed to be government looking for a home; its functions were important, but it was little understood by the public. It had no permanent tax base and was continually returning to the Legislature for funding. In the 1991 Session, the Legislature authorized a Metro Charter Review Committee to write and submit a new charter to the voters of the district. Among other things, the proposed charter reduced the number of councilors from thirteen to seven and made them salaried positions. Prior to that, Councilors only received a daily per diem for attending meetings. The new salary was to be $23,000 a year for a part-time job. The new ballot title started "Should people adopt charter to limit Metro powers..."

The Measure passed and at this writing Metro was in the process of implementing its new charter. It is probably doubtful that Oregon voters even in the metropolitan area intended to establish a whole new form of government in addition to the counties and cities. In 1978 and 1992, the magic words "abolish" and "limit" worked. Whether Metro will continue to grow and evolve remains to be seen.

Mass Transit --Get on the Bus

There are three mass transit districts in Oregon operating under ORS Chapter 267; Eugene's Lane Transit District, the Salem Area Transit District and the Tri-County

Metropolitan Transportation District (Tri-Met). The Salem District is run by an elected board and uses voter approved property taxes to partially pay for the bus system known as the "Cherriots." The Lane and Tri-Met districts are governed by boards appointed by the Governor. Both of these districts rely on a payroll taxes as well as fares.[47]

Tri-Met is a large organization with an operating budget of $100 million. It has 74 bus routes in addition the MAX light-rail system from Gresham to downtown Portland. Tri-Met is now constructing "West Side " light-rail which will extend the system west to Hillsboro. Mass transit has been the darling of Oregon's more progressive, i.e., liberal, politicians, and Tri-Met benefited immensely from Neil Goldschmidt's term as Secretary of Transportation in the Carter Administration. The 1991 Legislature allocated state money for the "West-Side Light Rail" to match federal dollars for the project.

Tri-Met is a municipal corporation, and its employees are government workers. The Transit Workers Union is one of the strongest in the State and has been very successful in its legislative efforts by combining political muscle with the transit good-will. Transit workers are government employees, however; oddly enough, they are not all within PERS. The 1991 Legislature passed a bill phasing the Transit Workers into PERS. This was a major victory for the Union. Another thing that the Union has always wanted is the inability to strike. This sounds contradictory, but if transit employees were not allowed to strike, as police and fire fighter are not allowed to strike, their labor disputes would be settled by binding arbitration. Over the long run, binding arbitration has proven to be much more profitable to the public employee unions than striking.

One thing that neither the Transit Union, Tri-Met itself, liberal politicians nor all the King's horses nor all the King's men have been able to do is open the Constitutionally protected gas tax-highway fund for mass transit.

Boundary Commissions --The Impossible Dream

Oregon has two boundary commissions, the Lane Area Boundary Commission and the Portland Metropolitan Area Boundary Commission. Both of these bodies are authorized by ORS Chapter 199. The Lane Commission had seven members and the Portland Commission has 13 members, both are appointed by the Governor.

The Portland Area Boundary Commission oversees government "structure" in the Tri-County area and is financed by an assessment against the governments within its jurisdiction. The Commission has a budget of approximately $300,000 per year and has a staff of four and a half people. Both the Lane and the Portland boundary commissions were established in 1969 with the intent of reducing fragmented, unequal taxation. Decisions were to be made logically, orderly and efficiently. To say this is an impossible task is an understatement.

Boundary Commission authority covers cities, counties and special districts and no annexation may proceed without the Commissions approval. Indeed annexations are the major task of the Commission. As mentioned earlier, proposed cities must get Boundary Commission approval. The last two applications to the Portland Commission were in 1983 and were unsuccessful. Both Aloha, the area between Beaverton and Hillsboro in Washington County, and the unincorporated area of Multnomah County wished to form cities. The Multnomah County area proposed the name of "Columbia Ridge," the name "Aloha" was already in use for the locale. Both applications were rejected on the grounds that neither area had made provisions for sewers. The individuals behind the

Columbia Ridge effort were the same individuals who successfully sought to amend Multnomah County's charter, i.e., Ray Phillips and Tom Dennehy. They did not wish to become a part of Portland and wished to avoid the effect of the previously mentioned sewer legislation.

Special Districts --The Permanent Temporary Governments

Fire protection districts have existed in the United States since 1759, these were the first special districts. In Oregon, special districts came into being shortly after World War II. Theoretically, these districts were to provide services to localities outside cities on a temporary basis, before the areas were annexed. If anything, special districts stand for the proposition that there is no such things as "temporary" government.

Special districts are authorized under ORS Chapter 198 and the separate chapters for each of the particular types of districts. There are over one thousand special districts in the state and they are represented before the Legislature by the Special Districts Association of Oregon. These districts exist for a myriad of purposes including cemeteries, water, drainage, emergency communications, health, highway lighting, irrigation, library, park, utility, road assessment, rural fire protection, sanitary authority, soil and water conservation, transportation, television translator, vector control and water improvement. The special districts' formation process basically means that the voters and landowners in the affected area file a petition with local county commission or boundary commission. If all requirements are met an election is held, and if successful the district is formed. One of the largest special district is the Unified Sewage District in Washington County.

---

[1] Oregon, Secretary of State, Oregon Blue Book 1993-1994, (Salem: Secretary of State, 1993), 302.

[2] ORS 205.130.

[3] Oregon, Legislative Assembly, Senate, 57th Session, Senate Bill 100.

[4] For an excellent discussion of this subject see Carl Abbott, Deborah Howe and Sy Adler, ed., Planning the Oregon Way -- A Twenty Year Evaluation, (Corvallis: Oregon State University Press, 1994).

[5] Thanks to Professor and State Representative Carl Hostika who has done extensive work in this area and brought this fact to my attention.

[6] Or. Const. art. VI, sec. 10.

[7] ORS 203.035.

[8] Oregon, Secretary of State, Oregon Blue Book 1993-1994, 302.

[9] Dept. of Revenue v. County of Multnomah, 4 OR 133 (1970).

[10] Higgins v. Hood River County, 245 OR 135, 420 P 2d 634 (1966).

[11] Buchanan v. Wood, 79 Or App 722, 720 P 2d 1285 (1986).

[12] Or. Const. art. VI(O), sec. 11 & 12.

[13] Oregon, Secretary of State, Oregon Blue Book 1993-1994, 313.

[14] Ibid., 313.

[15] Ibid., 297.

[16] Ibid., 313.

[17] McCarthy, Nancy, "Charter provision aside, Collier conducts campaign," The Oregonian, May 7, 1993, C-2.

18 The story of the "O&C" counties is a wonderful bit of Northwest History. See <u>The O & C Lands</u>, (Eugene OR: University of Oregon, Bureau of Governmental Research, 1981) or James long, "Of Grants and geed," <u>The Oregonian,</u> 23 may 1993, A1, A16-17.

19 Oregon, Secretary of State, <u>Oregon Blue Book 1993-1994</u>, 301.

20 Woodward, Steve, "Books, Bucks and Ballots," <u>The Oregonian</u>, 2 May 1993, L1, L3.

21 Oregon, Secretary of State, <u>Oregon Blue Book 1993-1994</u>, 304.

22 Commissioner Michael Sykes, interview by author. Written notes, Salem, 11 May 1993.

23 Oregon, Secretary of State, <u>Oregon Blue Book 1993-1994</u>, 275.

24 ORS 221.862-872.

25 City Recorder Brad Poyser, telephone interview by author. Written notes, Portland 13 May 1993.

26 Oregon, Legislative Assembly, House, Judiciary Committee, Hearing on HB-3233, 67th Legislative Assembly, 12 May 1993, testimony of Michael Levin,. Sunriver Owners Association.

27 City of Portland, <u>Mayor's Proposed Budget-City of Portland-Fiscal Year 1993-1994</u>, 14.

28 Ibid., 20.

29 Ibid., 23.

30 Ibid., 29.

31 Ibid., 26

32 Ibid., 33.

33 Ibid., 69.

34 Ibid., 93.

35 Fred Leeson, "Police pressure fails to sway judge's sentence," <u>The Oregonian</u>, 16 June 1993, D2.

36 Tom Hallman, "Harrington: I had to start a new life," <u>The Oregonian</u>, 2 May 1993, D1, D6.

37 Michael Rollins, "Retiring Portland police chief's career hit some highs, and lows," <u>The Oregonian,</u> 27 June 1993, D1, D8.

38 Holly Danks, "Autopsy shows man hit by five shots," <u>The Oregonian</u>, 3 June 1993, C1, C3.

39 Holly Danks, "Moose pins on chief's stars," <u>The Oregonian</u>, 30 June 1993, B1, B5.

40 Oregon, Secretary of State, <u>Oregon Blue Book 1993-1994</u>, 174.

41 ORS Chapter 334.

42 Oregon School Board Association, <u>Covering Education --A Reporters Guide to Education, 1986</u>, Salem, Oregon, 53.

43 Oregon, Port of Portland, <u>1993 --1994 Budget</u>, (Portland: Port of Portland, 1993), 5.

44 Oregon, Oregon Legislative Assembly, <u>Session Laws 1987</u>, Chapter 51.

45 MacColl, E. Kimbark, <u>The Growth of a City - Power and Politics in Portland, Oregon 1915 to 1950</u>., (Portland: Georgian Press, 1979), 442-446.

46 Ibid.

47 Oregon, Secretary of State, <u>Oregon Blue Book 1993-1994</u>, 86.

CHAPTER 10

MEDIA IN OREGON

Hot lead can be almost as effective coming
from a linotype as from a firearm.

John O'Hara

The press is free when you own the press.

Margaret Sanger

Introduction

For the past ten years, Oregon has been a destination resort for the national media. The Rajneesh, Diane Downs, Bob Packwood and Tonya Harding[1] have probably done as much for economic development as any high tech industry. Aside from covering these notorious luminaries, media plays an immensely important role in how Oregon is governed. These topics are covered:

- The dominance of Willamette Valley media.
- Print media in general.
- The phenomenon of a one-newspaper state.

- Other aspects of print journalism.
- Radio and TV.
- Free press in Oregon.

Into the Valley

As mentioned in Chapter 1, Oregon is an isolated state with only one major city, Portland. This municipality and its environs constitute a single metropolitan area with more than a million people, over one-third of the state's total population. The Willamette Valley, which stretches south below Portland, contains a majority of the rest of the state's media and the "Valley" news dominates the state. The only major media market in Oregon, both print and electronic, is the "Valley."

Print Media --From the Spectator to the Tribune

The distinction of being the state's first newspaper belongs to the Oregon Spectator, first published at Oregon City on February 5, 1846.[2] Interestingly enough, California did not have its first paper until seven months later when the Californian was put out August 15.[3]

Oregon currently has 109 newspapers of varying sizes. Five are seven-day-a-week dailies and six are daily except Saturday or Sunday.[4] There are only seven papers with daily circulations above 20,000. Of these seven, four are in the Willamette Valley and have a combined circulation of approximately 475,000 readers. The remaining three newspapers outside the Valley have a total readership of approximately 73,000. The largest newspaper in the state is The Oregonian, which currently has a circulation of

321,000. Eugene's <u>Register-Guard</u> is the next largest with a readership of 74,000. The <u>Statesman-Journal,</u> in Salem, is third in circulation at 59,000. Again, all three of these papers are in the Willamette Valley. <u>The Oregonian</u> is more than four times the size of its nearest rival and is the twenty-eighth largest paper in America.[5] After the <u>Statesman-Journal,</u> the next largest paper in the state is Medford's <u>Mail-Tribune</u> in Jackson County. This is the state's southwestern most county which borders northern California. <u>The Oregonian</u> is the only newspaper with a state-wide circulation, although readership drops off significantly in southern and eastern Oregon. <u>The Christian Science Monitor,</u> <u>The Wall Street Journal</u>, <u>USA Today</u> and <u>The New York Times</u> are available daily in the Willamette Valley. <u>The San Francisco Chronicle</u> can be found in Ashland, the home of Oregon Shakespeare Festival.

Oregon has a statutory definition of what is considered a newspaper for the purpose of publishing official notices.[6] Some extremely small papers meet this criteria. An example is the 451 person circulation <u>Dayton Tribune</u> published in Yamhill County thirty miles south of Portland. At this writing, there were ninety-nine of these smaller papers with circulations under 20,000. These range from the Dayton paper to the Klamath Falls <u>Herald & News</u> which has a circulation of 18,637. In addition, there are three large weeklies with relatively large circulations; <u>The Willamette Week</u>, with a circulation of 60,000 and the <u>Northwest Labor Press</u> with a circulation of 52,000, are both located in Portland. Salem has the <u>Capitol Press</u> with 35,000 readers. None of these three publications meet the statutory requirements for a "newspaper."

In addition to the regular press, there are twenty-eight college papers in the state. Three of these are dailies, the <u>Daily Emerald</u> at the University of Oregon, the <u>Daily Barometer</u> at Oregon State University and the <u>Vanguard</u> at Portland State University. These and the other college papers have served as training grounds for many of Oregon's top journalists. Some of these papers, such as the <u>Vanguard,</u> have been known to endorse candidates and ballots measures in the same manner as the regular papers.

A One-Newspaper-State --<u>The Oregonian</u>

Although <u>The Oregonian</u> was not the state's first newspaper, there is no doubt that it vastly exceeds all competitors in both circulation and political influence. Other smaller states have similar situations where one paper dominates the media, such as the <u>Des Moines Register</u> in Iowa or the infamous <u>Union Leader</u> in New Hampshire. <u>The Oregonian</u> is an extremely profitable paper with extensive advertising and it has always played a pivotal role in Oregon politics. At its founding in 1850, <u>The Oregonian</u> was a "Whig" paper started by a group of established Portland businessmen to promote the interest of the city.[7] The first publisher was Thomas Dryer.[8] Harvey W. Scott owned and ran the paper from 1865 to 1910. The paper developed an intense rivalry with the <u>Statesman</u>, now the <u>Statesman-Journal</u>, in Salem and the two papers were inevitably on opposite sides the issues. The editor of the latter once called the editor of the former a "pimp" in an editorial, proving the free press is most free when you have the press. As mentioned, <u>The Oregonian</u> opposed statehood for the territory on the grounds that Democrats would control the government![9]

Portland had three major newspapers through the 1930s with the others being the Journal and the Telegraph. The latter ceased publication before the 1950s and the Journal "folded" in 1982. At one time, the Journal actually exceeded The Oregonian in circulation. The editor of the Journal was killed in a helicopter crash and circulation started to decline. Portland still had two major papers.

The Oregonian was purchased by Samuel Newhouse in 1950. On November 10, 1959, both daily papers were struck by the stereootypers' union in what proved to be one of the bitterest labor disputes in Oregon history. For a short while the two papers published one edition together, then they separated for the remainder of the strike. Numerous staffers left the papers and attempted to start a third daily called the Reporter. In 1961 Newhouse, now in the form of a newspaper chain, bought the Journal for $8,334,000.[10] The strike continued on until April 24, 1965 when the union finally gave up. Local advertisers refused to support the Reporter and it eventually went bankrupt.

Like so many other afternoon dailies, the Journal became the victim of television and economics. TV took the afternoon audience and it was economically more advantageous for an owner to run one large paper than two smaller papers. With the demise of the Journal, Oregon became essentially a one newspaper state.

As mentioned, The Oregonian was originally a "Whig" paper, but later became staunchly Republican. The Journal was Democratic. Currently, The Oregonian could be described as a moderate to conservative Republican paper. It has taken somewhat inconsistent editorial stances for abortion, against the death penalty, for nuclear power and for gay rights. Although considered Republican, the paper has endorsed candidates of both parties for major office including successful Democrats Neil Goldschmidt and Barbara Roberts for Governor in 1986 and 1990. For the first time in its 152 year history, The Oregonian endorsed a Democrat, Bill Clinton, for President. In March of 1992, The Oregonian made national news when it announced that it would cease to use Indian related names for sports teams such as the Washington Redskins.[11] The Oregonian also had one of the few black editors in America, Bill Hilliard.

Clout, Twits and Sex Ads

The Oregonian and the Statesman-Journal are the only papers in the state with full-time political columnists. The senior and more respected of the two is Ron Blankenbaker of the Statesman-Journal. "RB" is a dapper bear of a man with a talent for walking the journalistic tightrope between being a well informed insider and writing interesting pieces without burning his friends. For twelve years, Blankenbaker has run a Christmas charity drive entitled "Pompous Twits Anonymous." Throughout the year he gives out "Pompous Twit" awards to local pols for various political sins such as a spouse appointed to a state job (the author's ex-wife) or spending a record amount of money to get elected. At Christmas, the twits are invited to assuage their conduct by contributing money, which, among other things, purchases clothes and groceries for needy families. In 1991, five thousand dollars was contributed to a battered women's shelter in Salem. TV stations usually cover the distribution of the needed goods, and needless to say, the opportunity for such public atonement is never turned down by the offending politicians. Since the organization's inception, every Oregon governor and member of Congress has managed to earn a "Pompous Twit."

The Oregonian's political columnist is Steve Duin, a former sportswriter. Duin is not as popular with politicians as Blankenbaker, but he is known for his excellent prose.

In 1974, the Willamette Week was started by Ron Buel, a former staff member and campaign manger of future Governor Neil Goldschmidt. Initially, the paper was considered a liberal Democratic alternative to the establishment Oregonian. Unfortunately, the publication declined into sensationalist tabloid whose most interesting features are the "personal" ads for romances. The Willamette Week also receives a not insignificant portion of its revenue from telephone sex advertisements.[12]

Radio and TV --Commentators and Community Stations

Oregon's first radio station was KGW, in Portland, which went on the air in 1922. Its first TV station, KPTV, started broadcasting in 1952 and is also located in Portland. The state currently has sixteen commercial television stations and three public channels. It has 157 radio stations of which 65 are FM and 92 are AM. Fifty-three of these stations are actually duplicate stations where the same programs are broadcast on both FM and AM.

The major radio stations in Portland are currently KEX, KOIN and KXL. KGW radio was very strong throughout most of its fifty-year tenure until it switched to an all "talk-show" format. The move proved to be disastrous, and in 1991, KGW AM began to only simulcast KINK-FM rock music. KINK had started as KGW's companion FM station. From 1933 to 1945, The Oregonian owned both KEX and KGW. Westinghouse bought KEX in 1945 and Gene Autry, the cowboy singer, owned the station from 1962 to 1984. It is currently the property of Great American broadcasting.

In the 1950s and early 1960s, Portland's radio stations played a significant role in the forming of public opinion by the use of news commentators. Future Governor Tom McCall did political commentary on KGW as did the author's father, Jess Mason. John Salisbury, at KXL, expanded several decades of news commentaries into a book -- Messages for Americans. With the advent of television, political commentary declined and what had been fifteen minute essays on radio evolved into two minute blurbs on TV.

Talk radio is as popular in Oregon as anywhere in the United States. In the metropolitan area, KXL maintains a talk/news format. Oregon Public Broadcasting's KOAP-FM presents the most comprehensive news coverage with "All Things Considered" for an hour each evening preceded by half an hour of local news entitled "Oregon Considered." Oregon State University Professor of Political Science Bill Lunch does political analysis and covers the Legislature for KOAP.

In the 1960s, Robert Bruce started Oregon Audio News as a state news service to feed local stations. Based in Salem, the service continues today and is now run by Bob Valdez.

Oregon's first TV station was KPTV which started broadcasting in 1952. KPTV started as an unaffiliated independent and today remains the largest independent in America. KOIN started in 1953, KGW began broadcasting in 1956 and KATU started in 1962.

The most significant Oregon TV personality was, of course, Tom McCall, who became Governor. McCall successfully made the transition from radio to TV. Again, the media loved McCall, and he was always good copy with pithy outrageous comments for the press. These included a request for Nixon's Vice-President Spiro Agnew to resign, the infamous "don't stay," request and the idea that Oregon should have its own navy.

166

Radio stations in more rural areas, play a unique role in keeping their local communities informed about some very mundane but necessary activities. These range from what high school club is having a bake sale to what highway is closed because of snow. These stations have a different sound and tenor than the Portland broadcasters. A good example of one of these stations is KAJO in Grants Pass. One person will be the whole news department and will cover everything from the county fair to forest fires. Typically, Oregon media personalities start at these smaller stations and move to the larger markets.

Free Press --Oregon Style

The term "Fourth Estate," for the press or media is a common, but little understood phrase -- the aphorism comes from France before the Revolution of 1789. The aristocracy was the first estate, the clergy the second and the bourgeoisie the third. These were the sources of power in society. Eventually, the press assumed the title of the "Fourth Estate," the forth source of power in society -- a source of power other than government, church or business. And so it is in Oregon.

Media in Oregon is not unique; again, there are other "one-newspaper" states.[13] Notwithstanding electronic media or competition from smaller papers, The Oregonian is the "press" in Oregon. But unfortunately, even the press is not immune from the effect of a monopoly of power or self interest. Theoretically, competition should curb self interest, should keep the press "free." In Oregon, there is no major competition for The Oregonian and the state probably suffers for it. Defenders of The Oregonian claim that it is not a monopoly situation because the paper has to compete with television and radio. This is a duplicitous argument at best. For all of its impact, electronic media disappears into thin air once broadcasted. When there is one paper, it becomes the sole source of public fact -- the public record. Competition between print and electronic is competition for advertising and not competition between like products.

The recent scandal, arising from allegations of sexual harassment against United States Senator Robert Packwood, illustrate this point. The Washington Post was doing an extensive investigation of the allegations against Packwood before the November 3, 1992 General Election. The Oregonian was aware of both the allegations and the Post investigation. Regardless, it endorsed Packwood for re-election over Congressman Les Aucoin. Packwood won re-election, and on November 22 the Washington Post printed its story.

Local media reaction, especially on the part of The Oregonian, can only be described as outrage, not just at what Packwood had supposedly done, but at the fact they had been scooped by a paper three thousand miles away. Why the Post didn't run the story before the election is up to conjecture and will most likely be the topic of numerous soul searching articles in the Columbia Journalism Review, the official conscience of media in America. Regardless, why didn't the state's major paper print the story? The point is this; had The Oregonian felt the heat of any competition, it would have probably printed the story, but there was no competition and thus no story.

When it came to a really significant story, however, The Oregonian did not drop the ball. The paper was the first to break the Tonya Harding story; in fact, it broke it and it broke it and it broke it. On January 18, 1994 The Oregonian reached a new high by having the front page of its Sunday edition exclusively stories about the wayward skater and her 'Three Stooges' accomplices. Bosnia, health-care and Clinton notwithstanding, the paper knew what was important.[14]

1 Even the international media has not been immune. The staunchly conservative Britiash magazine The Ecomomist couldn't resist the Harding story: "The top story in America has nothing to do with health-care reform...It is the drama of the country's two top women ice-skaters....The two stars are, of course, portrayed as a complete contrast. Miss Kerrigan...combines grace and beauty with perfect manners....Tonya Harding says all the wrong things....she indulges in drag racing, hunting and pool...Miss Kerrigan is so appealling because she can sell the American dream....Without film-star good looks, from a broken home, driven by ruthless ambition, she (Harding) may be closer to what a lot of America is like.' "America on ice," The Economist, 5 February 1994, 27.

2 Turnbull, George S. History of Oregon Newspapers (Portland: Binfords & Mort, 1939), 24.

3 Ibid.

4 Oregon, 1991-92 Oregon Bluebook, pp. 262-269.

5 Source, Audit Bureau of Circulation- Schaumburg Ill..

6 ORS 193.00.

7 Turnbull, George S. History of Oregon Newspapers , 56.

8 The Oregonian, "Trivia and Visitor's Guide -- Pamphlet," 1993.

9 Turnbull, George S. History of Oregon Newspapers, 70-77

10 John A. Lent, Newhouse, Newspapers, Nuisances, (New York: Exposition Press, 1966), 190-191.

11 "French and Indian Word Wars," New York Times, 15 March 1992, A-16.

12 "Bad, Bad Girls, We Never Sleep," "Gay Action Line," "Cross Dressers," Release Yourself," "Red Hot and Live." Willamette Week, 12 March 1992, 62-63.

13 See Carl Lindstrom, The Fading American Newspaper, (New York: Doubleday, 1960).

14 Interestingly enough, the only people that attempt to defend The Oregonian work for it. Nobody seems to have a good word for the paper. It used to be known as the "Old Gray Lady," now its detractors refer to it as "The Boregonian" or "The "Whoregonian."

CHAPTER 11

SCHOOL FINANCE AND OTHER PERENNIAL ISSUES

> That men do not learn very much from history is the
> most important of all lessons that history has to teach.
>
> Aldous Huxley

> No one is ever a hero on tax reform. These are the hard
> ones to go up the hill on, no medals, just purple hearts.
>
> Representative Peter Courtney

Introduction

Earlier in Chapter 3, we discussed many of the issues which have appeared on the Oregon ballot throughout the years. As important as they are, most of those measures could not be classified as "perennial issues." Chapter 11 examines school finance and the other topics which have dominated Oregon politics for most of its history. These include:

- The nature of perennial political issues.
- School finance at both the local and state level.
- Controversies around natural resource issues.
- Higher education.
- The death penalty.
- Workers' compensation.

Two-Edged Swords and Tiger Riding

Hindus supposedly believe that existence is a series of repeated cycles, constant repetition until perfection is achieved. Politics is similar, certain issues never seem to go away; politicians are constantly trying to get them right, to solve the unsolvable. In Oregon, these issues are not just the concern of one or two elections or legislative sessions, but of decades of political turmoil. The same phenomenon occurs at the national level; slavery, Prohibition and civil rights are examples. None of these issues were resolved quickly, and the effects of some of them are still with us today.

What is a "perennial" state issue is subjective. For our purposes, Oregon's perennial issues include school finance, the death penalty, land and natural resources, higher education, and workers' compensation.

These issues are, by definition, very political. They continue to be the topics of constant debate, political campaigns, initiatives, referendums, courts cases and legislation. This is the raw material of Oregon politics. There has probably never been a candidate for office in Oregon who did not have a position on school finance. It is also important to recognize that these perennial issues are two-edged swords. A candidate can get elected because of his or her stand on an issue and this is especially true in the era of single issue politics -- abortion, guns and gay rights. Unfortunately, much of today's successful campaigning is the crafting of coalitions of special interests. Chapter 7 examined the increasing role of special interest groups in Oregon politics.[1]

On the other hand, once elected, an official is expected to do something about the particular perennial issue that got him or her elected. Here is the problem, perennial issues are "perennial" because they are not simple or easy to solve. To use another metaphor, campaigning on a perennial issue is "Tiger riding." The ride can be spectacular, but one could very well end up inside of the tiger. Voters can be unmerciful, they want solutions, not excuses.

The question remains --why does an issue remain perennial, and why are certain problems so hard to solve? An arbitrary survey of these issues reveals that there are usually two, if not three, elements present. These include the objective conditions driving the issue, the economic aspects of the issue and the ideology of the issue. For example, there are two objective conditions driving the abortion issue. First, not all pregnancies are wanted; and second, depending on your point of view, abortion involves the taking of life. These two conditions have become the basis for the ideological debate that has ensued. The debate is one of the value of life versus the value of personal freedom. This particular issue is interesting because there is little, if any, economic content.[2] Other perennial issues have tremendous economic content, such as school finance and workers' compensation. As we examine each of these perennial issues let us keep these three elements in mind.

School Finance --The Never-Ending Quest

Earlier we described school finance as Oregon's Ireland -- a morass of irreconcilable interests and passions. This is the issue that has dominated the state's politics for most of this century. School finance is not a controversy that is unique to this state. Thousands upon thousands of local school boards exist all over America. Other states, such as Texas,[3] Michigan,[4] and California are on the horns of the school finance dilemma, an issue that involves every child and every taxpayer in this country. It is an especially complex issue in Oregon because of the initiative and the referendum.

At the heart of every state's school finance controversy is the fundamental contradiction of public education, i.e., all of society paying taxes to educate children. This seems like a simple proposition, but inherent within it is an ancient political conflict over the redistribution of societal resources. Those who have money have never been particularly happy about being taxed so that other people's children can be educated. Adlai Stevenson once said that, "The most American thing about America is the common school system." In order to understand school finance, one must appreciate that it is an argument over different philosophies of government. Paying for schools is probably the basic means of redistributing wealth in the American governmental process. Because schools are financed at the state or local level, voters are able to exert a greater influence on these matters. Voters do not have direct control over Medicaid, Social Security, or any of the other federal programs which themselves redistribute wealth.

When we discuss school finance in Oregon, we are really talking about the desirability of three types of taxes: property tax, income tax, and sales tax. These three methods of taxation are the only ones which can possibly furnish adequate revenues to run the schools. Property tax was originally thought to tax wealth, but it has never been popular among the masses. The property tax was Oregon's main source of state revenue before the income tax. It wasn't until 1917 that a state income tax was made possible by a constitutional amendment. An income tax statute was passed by the Legislature and successfully submitted to the people in 1923 for a vote. The tax act passed on a vote of 58,647 to 58,131. The same income tax was repealed by initiative in 1924. The resolution came in 1929 when the Legislature finally passed the Property Tax Relief Act of 1929, which levied a personal income tax and dedicated the revenue to off-setting the then state imposed property tax. Oregon has not had a *state* property tax since 1940.[5] This measure was referred to the people by referendum petition, but it was not repealed.

A property tax limitation measure first appeared on the Oregon ballot in 1934, but was defeated. Subsequent attempts at property tax limitation were made in 1936, when two measures were on the ballot, 1952, 1968, 1978, 1980, 1982, 1984, 1986, and 1990. All were unsuccessful until 1990. After 56 years of controversy, Oregonians finally passed Ballot Measure 5, which made property tax limitation law in Article XI, Section 11b of the Oregon Constitution.

It would be helpful to again review the basic parameters of school finance in Oregon. These are the "objective conditions" driving the controversy:
- Oregon has no sales tax.
- Until 1990, most local government activities (including schools) were financed by property tax.
- The state may not spend in the deficit.
- Property taxes may not be levied without a vote of the people.
- Local tax bases cannot grow more than 6% a year.
- No major tax legislation may be passed without a vote of the people.

Another addition factor should be considered:
- Oregon has a high income tax compared with other states, the fifth highest in the county as a percent of personal income.[6]

As mentioned earlier, until 1992, schools were mainly funded by local property taxes. The voters had to authorize a specific amount of money to be collected or "levied" (this was applicable to all local governments). This amount of money was known as a "tax base." And again, any tax base for any school district or local government could be increased 6% a year. Some school districts had adequate tax bases and others did not. The only way to obtain a new tax base was by a vote of the people, and voters in many districts were reluctant to authorize new tax bases. Districts without an adequate tax base either ran out of money or asked for temporary "excess" levies. Numerous districts were forced to close schools until levies were approved.

The crux of this controversy is that Oregon does not have a balanced tax system; it has a high income tax and <u>had</u> a high property tax. In 1989-90, Oregon had the third highest property tax in the land, only exceeded by Maryland (number two) and New York (number one).[7] As mentioned, there are only three sources of major revenue that are adequate to finance schools -- income tax, property tax and sales tax. The sales tax is sometimes known as a consumption tax and is considered "regressive" by those on the left; the less wealth you have, the greater proportion of your income goes to taxes.

Property tax, as a revenue source, has several disadvantages. First, it penalizes people for investing a larger proportion of their income in their homes. Second, for many individuals, the amount of the tax is a lump sum, compared to the income tax, which for most people, is deducted from one's salary. Property tax is supposed to have some relation to the taxpayers ability to pay; theoretically, the value of your house reflects your income. However, with more and more elderly individuals, this is not the case.

There were other problems with the property tax, not the least of which was that it seemed to continually be raised. There were two reasons for this. The 6% budget increase limit turned out to be no limit at all. If a taxing entity used the 6% provision every year, the tax base will double in under ten years. As mentioned earlier, one's total amount of property tax reflects the cumulative amount of all the property taxes levied. Property taxes are usually expressed in a percentage of the total value of the property or in dollars per thousand. Before the passage of Ballot Measure 5, Oregon counties had an average levy of 2.656% or $26.56 dollars per thousand. The highest rate was in Wasco County at $33.73 per thousand.[8] For a $100,000 house this would mean 3.373% of $100,000 or $33.73 X 100, i.e., $3,373 per year. The property tax bill would show the owner what amount and what percent went to what government. Of the total amount, 52% would go to the local school districts and the rest to other local jurisdictions, i.e., the county, the city, community colleges, ports, et cetera. The problem was that when increases in a levy were proposed to voters they never thought of the matter in cumulative terms. Entities such as the Port of Portland would easily sell their levies to the unwary public as only costing each citizen a few cents per month. Over the years, however, all these levies and the 6% allowed increases raised property taxes substantially.

Individual assessments on property are also a factor. Theoretically, properties are assessed at their "true cash value." We mentioned in Chapter 9 that each property conveyance must have the amount of the transaction on it when it is registered. Property assessment is a major task carried on by the counties. The total value of assessed property in Oregon for 1991-1992 was $112.1 billion! The value of residential property has increased at a greater rate than the value of business property. All property is on the same tax roll. That is, there is no difference between how residential property and business property is taxed. Before 1978, the assessed values of business property exceeded that of residential property; i.e., businesses paid a greater share of property taxes than residences. After 1978, this changed.

Until the passage of Ballot Measure 5, the assessed value of any particular piece of property did not determine its tax per se. Oregon had what is known as a rate based system. The total amount of tax collected was established by the cumulative tax bases. The relative assessments established that portion of the total amount that a particular piece of property would pay. The tax rate is figured by dividing the tax base by the total assessed value. To use an example, if a jurisdiction had an authorized tax base of $100,000 and assessed property worth $5,000,000, the tax rate would be $100,000/$5,000,000= .02¢ or $20 per $1,000 of property value. If that $5,000,000 of total assessed value were made up of two pieces of property of equal value, $2.5 million a piece they would each pay half of the total tax due, i.e., $50,000. However, if the value of one piece of property increased at a greater rate than the value of the other piece, the tax would change. If the value of one piece of property went to $3 million and the other went to $4 million, then the total assessed value would be $7,000,000 and the tax rate would drop to .014¢ or $14 per thousand of assessed value. The more expensive property would pay $57,142.80 in taxes, and the cheaper property would pay $42,857.20. The total tax collected would not have changed, but the person with the more expensive property would be under the impression that all taxes had gone up.

Thus, not only did the tax bases/levies go up in the decades prior to Ballot Measure 5, but the proportion paid by homes also went up. Fortunately, or unfortunately, more people own homes than businesses and people, not businesses, vote.

Prior to 1987, this situation remained totally uncontrolled. assessments changed and taxing districts asked for increases in levies at the same time schools were closing. At the 1987 passage of the "Safety Net," Oregon was notorious for school closures. The "Safety Net," allowed schools without adequate tax bases to operate on the prior years budget regardless and thus avoid closures.

Throughout this decades-long debate, the sales tax has kept returning. A kind of great bastard child of Oregon politics. Every time it comes home, both it and the problem are larger. It has been unsuccessfully on the ballot nine times: 1933, 1934, 1936, 1944, 1947, 1969, 1985, 1986, and 1993. In May of 1990, there was even a series of five "advisory" votes asking the public their preference in tax reform to reduce property taxes. The first question was whether or not the people wanted tax reform to reduce property tax, this measure passed easily. The next two questions had offered income tax increases to finance property tax reduction, these both failed. Two sales tax options also failed, but one received the highest number of yes votes, 222,611 to 374,466 no votes. Oregon is only one of five states without a sales tax. Oddly enough, no state has ever imposed a sales tax by a vote of the people.[9]

The history of property tax relief is long and checkered. As mentioned, the first property tax limitation appeared in 1934. All of these efforts were initiatives, and most were championed by activists like Ray Phillips from East Multnomah County. The real push came in the 1978 General Election. Earlier that year, Proposition 13 had passed in California and the "Tax Revolt" spread across the United States. The 1978 proposal was Ballot Measure 3.

Parallel to these citizen efforts were a series of gubernatorial and legislative responses to the situation. However, the goals of the activists and the goals of those in government were not exactly the same. The activists primarily wanted lower property taxes and less intrusive government. Governors and the legislatures wanted lower property taxes and adequately funded schools; they wanted to stop school closures. Again, schools were closing in some districts, due to lack of money, at the same time that people were complaining because their property taxes were too high. Schools did stop closing after the 1987 Safety Net, but that did nothing to ameliorate the tax situation.[10] The people present an initiative and the Legislature and the governor have responded with either a sales tax or an increase in the income tax. This continues to be the pattern.

In May of 1973, the Legislature submitted the "McCall" tax plan to the people as a means of both reducing property tax and stabilizing school funding. It accomplished this with higher income taxes to increase the state's share of basic school support. Unfortunately the proposal failed. In 1974, a measure to establish new tax bases for all schools failed at the general election. In 1977, the Legislature, under the leadership of Senate President Jason Boe, submitted a "Safety Net" for schools to the voters. This bill would have preserved a portion of all tax bases, but it also failed 252,061 no votes to 112,570 yes votes. The pivotal year was 1978 when Proposition 13 passed in California. Ray Phillips and his people put Ballot Measure 3, which was literally a Xeroxed version of Prop 13, on the ballot. In response, the Legislature met in Special Session and put its own plan, Ballot Measure 6, on the same ballot. Both of the measures failed, but it was evident to the Legislature that the issue was not going to go away.

In the 1979 Session, the Legislature passed a program which would pay 30% of all home owners' property tax up to $500. The program had an immense price tag on it of over $500 million per biennium. This basically was the Legislature using income taxes to reduce property taxes. State revenues were high during the 1979 Session, and the state could afford it. The Legislature even put the program on the ballot as a statute in 1980. With tongue in cheek, they asked the question "should the 30% tax relief program continue?" Needless to say the measure passed overwhelming. There was a 1% property tax limit on the ballot in 1980, but it also failed. The 1.5% limit barely failed in 1982, 504,836 yes votes to 515,626 no votes. The 1984 version of the same measure failed 599,424 yes votes to 616,252 no votes. At the same time these votes were occurring, the 30% property tax relief program was slowly being diminished by lack of revenue; Oregon's economy had taken a downturn, starting in 1980, and the state could not afford the program anymore. In 1985, a 5% sales tax was submitted to the people after a tumultuous legislative session, but the measure was defeated 234,804 yes votes to 816,369 no votes. At the 1986 General Election, two sales tax measures were on the ballot with another 1.5% limit. All three measures failed.

The Safety Net proposal approved by voters in 1987 was the first "positive" vote on the subject since 1929. There was no property tax limit on the 1988 ballot, but Ballot Measure 5 appeared in 1990 and passed. It was a refined version of the earlier measures and said that reduced school moneys would be made up by the state from the general fund. Ballot Measure 5 sequences in over a six year period and reduces property tax from the 1990-1991 level of approximately 2% to 3% ($20 to $30 per thousand dollars of assessed value) to %1.5 ($15 per thousand) in 1995. In the 1991-1993 biennium, the state had to make up a short fall of only $362 million by modest cuts in state budgets. In the 1993-95 cycle, however, the shortfall was 1.6 billion dollars which forced almost 17% cut in all state programs. The amount due in 1995-1997 will be $2.8 billion dollars forcing another cuts of around 20% in state programs.[11]

Ballot Measure 5 literally burned the state's bridges in the tax reform war. As the measure comes into effect, the state will be forced to either adopt a new source of revenue or relegate itself to having the poorest funded prisons, schools, colleges and welfare programs on the West Coast, if not in America.

To say that this is a complex is an understatement, but at the moment this is the situation with school finance in Oregon:

- The State will have to shut down major programs to pay for Ballot Measure 5 in 1995-97.
- There is still public resistance to a sales tax.
- There is resistance to raising the income tax sufficiently to pay for Ballot Measure 5.

The truth is that the people never have been able to tax themselves. The Ballot Measure 5 dilemma is really a dilemma of "democracy." Politicians love to say that the people always make wise decisions, but nothing could be further from the truth. Wisdom has never been cumulative, and the fact that a particular policy has received a majority vote doesn't make it a wise policy. People don't like taxes and will not vote to raise them significantly. However, they do want services. Ironically, this "political gridlock" is not in Congress or the Legislature, but in society itself.

The seeds for this situation were sown eighty years ago. Earlier, we mentioned the constitutional provision which prohibited an emergency clause from being included on a revenue measure. Again, in combination with the referendum, this effectively means that no major tax reform can take place without a vote of the people. This situation is not an accident. In 1910, the people adopted an initiative which became Article IX Section 1a[12] of the Oregon Constitution. It said that no tax bill could be passed without a vote of the people. The measure was part of the effort by William S. U'Ren to have the state adopt a "single tax," the grand idea of British economist Henry George. George maintained that since property was the source of all wealth (Marx thought labor was), that it was the only thing that needed to be taxed. The Legislature had not been interested in the "single tax," so the stated purpose of the proponents was to take the taxing power away from the Legislature.

The next Legislature responded with the current Article IX Section 1a which prohibits an emergency clause on any revenue bill.

U'Ren opposed the change saying:

> The real purpose of these amendments is to take from the people the power to control tax laws, and give that power back to the Legislature. That is what Big Business wants, and what the State tax commission wants.[13]

Regardless, it passed, and even in modified form, the amendment makes it so the Legislature can not solve the tax problem. At this moment, there is no conclusion to this drama, but we will return to the topic in the concluding chapter.

Land and Resources --Fish and Farmers

People didn't come to Oregon because of its world famous-opera. They came because of its land, its water, its fish and the game. Regardless, land, water, fish and game are like everything else that is desirable in nature; there is never enough for everybody. By our natures, we all are greedy, and we all want natural resources for ourselves and not the unworthy interlopers who happened to just arrive off the Oregon Trail, Interstate 5 or at the Portland International Airport. We stole them first and have the right to keep them.

As mentioned in Chapter 3, fish have been on the Oregon Ballot 14 times. The current reason for fish politics has more to do with dams on the rivers than anything else.[14] The advent of extensive hydroelectric power, such as the Bonneville System on the Columbia River, has significantly effected the number of fish. Salmon and steelhead are often able to swim up fish ladders, but not downriver through hydroelectric turbines.

Historically, the state's response to the decrease of fish has been to create more and more fish hatcheries to make up for the lost fish. The problem with this has been that hatcheries are very expensive. This would be acceptable, but most of the fees paid to finance the fish hatcheries are paid out of sport rather than commercial licenses. Sport people are paying more and getting less. The Northwest Steelheaders and Trout Unlimited are groups that would like to ban commercial fishing and gill netting. Again, as mentioned in Chapter 3, this becomes a conflict between life styles. The very water that fish swim in is also a perennial issue.

How can water possibly be a problem in Oregon which is notorious for rain? It especially is an issue in eastern Oregon where water is the key to economic success. Water is also a major concern of the environmental community, and thus there is a continuing conflict between the environmentalist who want to limit the use of water and the ranchers/farmers who want to maximize its use.

Game is another heated issue in Oregon. One of the oddest controversies is between hunters and ranchers over elk. Hunters want elk encouraged and cultivated so they can kill them. Ranchers want them killed earlier because they eat their crops.

The major natural resource controversy in Oregon has to do with land. It is not that there isn't enough land, it's just that there is a limited amount of arable land. As mentioned in Chapter 9 the 1973 Legislature passed Senate Bill 100 that established the Land Conservation and Development Commission (LCDC). This was, and is, the most comprehensive system of land-use planning ever established in the United States. Based upon the premise that farmland should be preserved and that development should be regulated, it aimed at maintaining the state's pristine quality. There have been three unsuccessful attempts to repeal LCDC since it was passed in 1973.[15] The real tension over land-use planning has to do with the concept of limiting what people can do with their land. It is one thing to preserve farmland and another to tell the farmer that he or she cannot sell his or her land for a development. After a lifetime of hard work, people don't take kindly to being told that they can't cash in the family homestead for several million dollars and retire.

Higher Ed --Too Many Colleges for a State that Doesn't Care

Oregon has too many colleges. Most medium states have one liberal arts university, one university for engineering and agriculture and a series of smaller institutions. Alabama, Arizona and Oregon's neighbor to the north, Washington, follow this pattern. Washington has Washington State at Pullman, in eastern Washington, and the University of Washington in Seattle. Most often in these medium size states, the liberal arts university is located in the state's most populous city. The University of Alabama and the University of Arizona are respectively located outside Birmingham and in Phoenix.

The problem in Oregon is that both its liberal arts university, the University of Oregon (U of O), and its engineering and agriculture school, Oregon State University (OSU), are located in the southern part of the Willamette Valley rather than in Portland. The U of O is in Eugene and OSU is in Corvallis. Oregon needed a college in Portland and after World War II and an extension center was established there. After much controversy, Portland State College was established and later became Portland State University (PSU). Oregon has three universities when it only needs two. The U of O is the oldest and claims the title of the state's "flagship" university, OSU has a well defined role as the engineering and agriculture school. PSU has a kind of undeniable geography driving its development. Like Seattle, and other urban areas, Portland and its surrounding high tech industry needs a university. This has created a situation where there is inherent and unavoidable competition for state resources.

This situation would be bad enough were it not exacerbated by the fact that the relations between the Oregon States System of Higher Education and the Legislature have never been good. As mentioned in Chapter 4, the system is the only state agency that does not submit a line item budget to the Legislature. Theoretically, this keeps the individual schools from lobbying the Legislature, but the actual effect is that the Legislature has little understanding of the real financial condition of the schools. Because the Legislature doesn't know the details of the budget, it assumes that colleges are wasting state money. The truth is that the Oregon schools have the second lowest faculty salary level on the West Coast paired with the second highest tuition. Oregon has never seemed to have the same interest in its colleges that either Washington or California have had. "Oregon has never been a state where people say they have made a major commitment to higher ed," observed C. Peter Magrath, the President of the National Associations of State Universities and Land-Grant Colleges.[16]

In addition, Ballot Measure 5 is having a tremendous impact on Oregon's higher education. In the 1993 Session, higher education was asked to take a 20% cut. The proportion of state budget devoted to colleges has dropped over the past twenty years, in 1973 it was approximately 17%, in 1993 it was down to 10%.[17] One commentator observed that in 1985 Oregon spent twice as much on colleges as prisons, but if the present trend continues the situation would be reversed by the year 2000, i.e., Oregon will be spending twice as much on prisons! In the 1993 session of the Washington Legislature, the higher education budget was expanded and it was decided to increase the number of students by 10,000. At the same time, Oregon was attempting to downsize its system by 4,000 students.[18] Smelling blood in the educational waters, Washington has now started to significantly expand its Vancouver campus of Washington State University.

The Death Penalty

One of the most fascinating uses of the Initiative and the Referendum has been in regard to the death penalty. Oregon is probably unique among American jurisdictions in that its homicide law is a layered accumulation of legislative acts, ballot measures and court cases which all are the results of a century old debate over the death penalty. Homicide statutes and the political question of capital punishment are inextricably intertwined. What should be the most understandable portion of Oregon's criminal code, unfortunately, resembles a lawyer's version of an archaeological dig.

Until 1914, Oregon law required the death penalty for any person convicted of murder in the first degree.[19] Two death penalty repeal measures were placed before the voters by petition in 1912 and 1914. These efforts were lead by Governor Oswald West who was opposed to the doctrine of "an eye for an eye."[20] The repeal failed in 1912, and passed in 1914 by 157 votes with a tally of 100,552 to 100,395!

The attitude of both the Legislature and the public changed within a short time and in 1919 Governor James Withycombe complained that there was no punishment for treason. He also expressed his concern about the emergence of the International Workers of the World as a radical force in American politics.[21] More importantly in that year, a brutal murder occurred in which the lack of the death penalty seemed to motivate the defendant to commit the crime.

When Clarence Johnson killed Eunice W. Freeman, The Oregonian ran a front page story entitled "Slayer Says Law Invited Crime." "I can't believe I would have done it if I had thought there was a chance of me hanging for it... I thought about it a good deal, and I don't think I would have done it if there had been any danger of me swinging for it," Johnson is reported to have said.[22]

Withycombe died in 1920 and was succeeded by Secretary of State Ben Olcott who called a special session to place the death penalty on the ballot. The Legislature did as asked and also passed a bill providing the death penalty for first degree murder should the Constitution be amended. Capital punishment was thus restored in 1920 by a vote of 64,956 to 38,774.

Public opinion again changed in the 50s and early 60s. A repeal attempt failed in 1958 by a margin of 264,434 to 276,487. In 1958 and later in 1964, major political figures endorsed the repeal including Governor Mark Hatfield and future Governor Tom McCall.[23] Oregon State Penitentiary Warden Clarence Gladden supported the repeal and made the astute observation that the poor get executed while the rich get off.[24] The 1964 repeal was successful by a vote of 455,654 to 302,105.

Between 1964 and 1978, the mood of the state again reversed. This was a period of national social upheaval, and unfortunately for Oregon, there was also a series of sensational murders. Nineteen sixty-nine was the year Jerome Brudos pled guilty to the killings of three young women whom he had kidnapped, tortured, raped, and mutilated.[25] Brudos received three consecutive life sentences. In 1974, Carl Cletus Bowles was serving life in the Oregon State Penitentiary for a 1965 killing of a Lane County Sheriff's deputy[26] when he was given a temporary leave to visit his girlfriend in a Salem motel.[27] Bowles escaped and subsequently kidnapped and killed an elderly Eugene couple. He pled guilty and received two life terms.[28] Richard Marquette was convicted of the 1961 killing and dismembering of Joan Caudle, but then was paroled in 1973.[29] In 1975, Marquette killed and butchered three Salem women[30] and was returned to prison.

State Representative Cecil Johnson tried to get the 1977 Legislature to reenact the death penalty, but he was unsuccessful.[31] In frustration, he started a successful petition drive to place the question on the ballot in 1978. In addition to the Brudos, Bowles and Marquette, Johnson was concerned about the general increase in murders all over the state.

Ballot Measure 8 was based upon a Texas statute, and in the 1978 General Election, the measure restored the death penalty by a vote of 537,707 to 318,610. The saga continued, and in 1981 the Oregon Supreme Court declared Ballot Measure 8 unconstitutional in State v. Quinn.[32] The court objected to the provision which allowed the death penalty to be imposed by the judge and not the jury. Earlier in 1980, Charmel Ulrich was kidnapped, raped and killed by Anthony Butler, William Jackson and Randy Smith. Upon hearing of the Quinn decision Ulrich's killers immediately changed their pleas from not guilty to guilty and received life sentences. A neighbor of the slain girl, Dedi Streich, was so outraged that she began the long process of collecting signatures to restore the death penalty.

Streich was eventually successful and a statutory death penalty was re-enacted in 1984 by a vote of 893,818 to 295,988. The companion constitutional amendment, to exempt the death penalty from the Oregon Constitution's prohibition against cruel punishment, passed 653,009 to 521,687.

An examination of this history reveals an almost tragic pattern, i.e. liberal sentiment against the death penalty leads to repeal after several attempts, then some heinous crime or crimes[33] brings reenactment.

Workers' Compensation --The Ghost of the "un-holy Trinity"

Workers' compensation has not always been "workers'" compensation, it was once "workman's'" compensation. The issue first appeared on the ballot in 1913. Workers' safety has always been a management and labor issue, but until the advent of the workers' compensation system, laborers had little if any protection from on-the-job injuries. There were three legal doctrines used by companies to defend against suits by injured workers: assumption of risk, contributory negligence and fellow servant. The un-holy Trinity barred recovery if a worker voluntarily took a chance, was negligent himself or herself, or was injured by another worker. The initial system was enacted by the Legislature in 1913 and approved by a referendum in November 4 of that same year. It was known as "Workmen's Compensation" and initially only covered hazardous occupations, such as logging and construction. Employers could reject participating in the program and farming was specifically found to be non-hazardous. The initial program was run by the "State Industrial Accident Commission."[34] The system remained basically the same until the 1968 when it became a "three way system." After extensive lobbying by the insurance companies, a statute was adopted under which compensation insurance was furnished by private insurance companies, businesses insuring themselves as "self insureds" and state insurance. The state company was known as the State Accident Industrial Fund or "SAIF."

As the system evolved, it became one of the most expensive in the country. Every legislative session had its series of "comp" bills; management would try to limit awards to workers while labor would try to increase benefits. Other groups developed a vested interest in the system, i.e., doctors, chiropractors, lawyers, insurance companies and rehabilitation firms. Workers' compensation became an industry in itself, and it became a major political issue in 1980s.

In 1979, SAIF was changed from a state agency to an independent non-profit company. SAIF was relatively successful --in fact it was too successful. In 1982, the Legislature "borrowed" 81 million dollars from SAIF to make up a budget shortfall which occurred after the regular Session. As mentioned previously, this action was taken during the June 14,1982 Special Session of the Legislature. Atiyeh had gotten the informal approval of Attorney General David Frohnmayer who said that the action was legal. Earlier that day, legislators had been privately briefed by Frohnmayer's Chief Deputy Stan Long as to what the real situation was. Long, a former Eugene attorney, was known for his attitude of political expediency and willingness to do the necessary "dirty work." Stan didn't mince words when he said his job was merely, "To take the money." The Oregon Supreme Court later found the action to be illegal.[35]

Long continued his career as a hired gun and was named head of the Department of Commerce in 1987 to oversee its dismantling. In October of 1988, Long was appointed president of SAIF and in February of 1989 he announced that SAIF had a 49 million dollar deficit. SAIF also said it had a 10.3 million dollar loss in 1989. In December of 1989, 7000 businesses had their insurance canceled and in January of 1990 Governor Goldschmidt appointed a special task force known as the Mahonia Hall Group to reform workers' compensation. In May of 1990, the Legislature adopted most of the group's proposals, and in July of that year, SAIF cut it rates by ten percent. However, in May of 1991, SAIF was audited by the secretary of state and it was found that it did not have a loss in 1989, but made a 26.4 million dollar profit. The Ethics Commission investigated Long for lying to the Legislature, but took no action. Long, having demonstrated what a devoted and honest public servant he was, took a job as an insurance company executive at a somewhat higher salary than he was making at the state.

Workers' compensation is still a issue in Oregon. There is too much money to be made by too many people for it not to be.

1   Interest groups that are concerned with perennial issues are subject to a peculiar phenomenon because of the long term nature of the issues. The groups themselves become vested in the controversy -- resolving the issue in not in the "interest" of the special interest.

2   Unless you happen to be part of the industry that provides access to abortion.

3   "Texas Meets School-Financing Deadline," The New York Times, 1 June 1993, A8.

4   Isabel Wilkerson, "Tiring of Cuts, District Plans to Close Schools, The New York Times, 21 March 1993, 12.

5   Oregon, Legislative Revenue Office, Basic Tax Packet -- Research Report , (Salem OR: Legislative Revenue Office, 1993), D1.

6   Ibid., 12

7   Ibid.

8   Ibid., 4

9   City Club of Portland, City Club Bulletin Vol 74 No. 51, Tax reform in Oregon, (Portland: City Club of Portland, 1993) 35.

10   Interestingly enough, it could be argued that the passage of the "Safety Net" led to the passage of Ballot Measure 5. Until the Safety Net, voters had somewhat of a release for their frustrations. With school closures avoided, a tax limit became more palatable and more attractive. Governor Goldschmidt looked upon the Safety Net as just the first step in overall tax reform. The theory was to stop school closures, update tax bases and then reduce property taxes with a sales tax. However, the plan fell apart in May of 1989 when the voters rejected Ballot Measure 1 which would have updated all school tax bases. Goldschmidt chose not to run for re-election, and like so many other things, the job remained unfinished.

11   Oregon, Legislative fiscal Office, Budget Highlights, Legislatively Approved 1993-95 Budget, (Salem: Legislative Fiscal Office, 1993), 3.

12   Or. Const. (1910) art. I,X ,sec. 1a.

13   Quoted in Oregon Legislative Assembly, Legislative Research, "Report 83:026," (Salem: Legislative Research, 1983), 3.

14   Indian treaty rights have not played as large a role in fish questions as they have in Washington for several reasons.

15   1976,1978 and 1982.

16   Brian Beehan, "Future Bleak for higher education," The Oregonian, 30 May 1993, A18.

17   Ibid.

18   David Sarasohn, "On Higher Ed, not quite high enough," The Oregonian, 30 May 1993, B-8.

19   Kantor, "Brief Against Death," 17 Willamette Law Review 629, 631(1981).

20   Robert H. Dann, "Abolition and Restoration of the Death Penalty in Oregon," in The Death Penalty in America, ed. Adam Bedau (Chicago: Aldine, 1964), 344.

21   Ibid., 345.

22   "Slayer Says Law Invited Crime," The Oregonian, 2 October 1919, sec. 1, 1.

23   "Candidates Urge Repeal of Capital Punishment," The Oregonian, 11 October 1964, 33.

24   "State Warden Backs Death Penalty Ban," The Oregonian, 16 October 1964, sec. 1, 33.

25   "Case tests Oregon justice: Brudos belongs in prison," Statesman-Journal, 1 April 1989, Sec. A, 8.

26   "Kidnapping Assault Charged to Bowles," The Oregonian, 18 June 1975, 2.

27   "Warden told to Explain killer's escape," The Oregonian, 22 May 1974, 1.

28   "Bowles admits Hunter murders, get two life terms," The Oregonian, 13 November 1975, Sec A, 1.

29   "Accused convicted in 1961 slaying," Statesman-Journal, 23 April 1975, 34.

30   Janet Davis, "Marquette Admits Slaying third women," Statesman, 4 June 1975, 1.

31   Cecil Johnson, interview by author, written otes, Portland, Oregon, December 14. 1990.

32   State of Oregon v. John Wayne Quinn, 290 Or 383 (1981).

33   Other notorious individuals of this era probably played a role in this psychology; i.e., Randy Woodfield the "I-5 Bandit," and Manuel Cortez who killed two Ashland girls in 1980.

34   Oregon, Secretary of State, Oregon Blue Book 1951-1952, (Salem: Secretary of State, 1991), 44.

35   Eckles v. Oregon, 306 OR 380, 760 P 2d 846 (1988).

CHAPTER 12

WHO GOVERNS ?

Blacksmithing...was my trade...it has always given color to my
view of things...I wanted to fix the evils in the conditions of life. I
couldn't. There were no tools....Why had we no tool makers for
democracy?[1]

William S. U'Ren

The hammer that destroyed the temple was forged in the temple.

Anonymous

Introduction

This concluding chapter attempts to bring together several of the themes examined.
It makes judgments about the fundamental nature of Oregon politics, i.e., who governs,
what has given them power, and whether the current situation constitutes effective
government. The chapter concludes with a discussion of the politics that led to the
current situation and makes somewhat sanguine recommendations for change. Specifics
include:

- The need to reach conclusions in
  political analysis.
- Leadership in a democracy.

- Who governs.

- The four factors that have changed
  Oregon government.
- The end of representative democracy.

- What constitutes effective government.

- The political conditions which have
  produced significant changes.
- The misuse of the initiative and the
  referendum.
- Recommendations for change.

No Abstentions

So, who governs Oregon? Where are the real political decisions made? Better yet,
what has happened to Oregon's democracy? It would be duplicitous for the author to
come to no conclusion -- after twenty years in politics to put on his academician's hat and
give a properly qualified call for more research. In the "real world" of politics, decisions
must be made and conclusions must be reached. There are no abstentions in this state's
assembly and our discussion deserves the same decisiveness.

Political Leadership in a Democracy

The well-known scholar James McGregor Burns did an extensive discussion of "leadership." Like many political scientists, Burns was enamored with the executive, and only briefly related leadership to the law-making process itself. Regardless, his theory was expressed this way:

> Who are the leaders and who are the led? Who is leading whom to where? For what purpose? With what results?....Leadership is the reciprocal process of mobilizing, by persons with certain motives and values, various economic, political and other resources,...in order to realize goals independently or mutually held by both leaders and followers....Much of what commonly passes for leadership -- conspicuous position-taking without followers or follow-through, posturing on various public stages, manipulation without general purpose, authoritarianism --is no more leadership than the behavior of small boys marching in front of a parade, who continue to strut along Main Street and the procession has turned down a side street toward the fairgrounds...The test of...leadership...is [its] contribution to change, measured by purposes drawn from collective motives and values.[2]

Burns' description is a good starting point for an evaluation of how decisions are made in Oregon. Traditional political institutions do exist in this state, but as we have learned, there are more compelling factors. Most major policy questions in Oregon are not resolved by elected leaders acting in traditional roles through traditional institutional means. The initiative and the referendum processes have effectively created a situation where political decision-making is outside the structure of representative democracy.

Meet Your Leaders.

The obvious answer to our first question is this -- Oregon is governed by those who dominate the politics of the state by use of the initiative and referendum. This is not to say that "the people" *per se* govern Oregon. "The people" do not file and promote initiatives or referenda, individuals do. Thomas Cronin discusses this in <u>Direct Democracy</u>:

> Direct democracy processes have not brought about rule by the common people....Direct democracy devices occasionally permit those who are motivated and interested in public policy issues to have a direct personal imput by recording their vote, but this is a long way from claiming that direct democracy gives a significant voice to ordinary citizens on a regular basis. The early claim was considerably overstated.[3]

Individuals now "govern" with the I&R in a fashion similar to what was once done by governors and other elected officials. A person who successfully seizes upon an issue and translates his or her position into a constitutional amendment, or statute, will have a far greater impact on the course of this state than any office holder. This is not to say that ordinary means of political decision-making do not change state policy. Land use planning was a legislative product, but it has been three times subjected to the gauntlet of the initiative and referendum.[4] Notwithstanding the I&R, 98% to 99% of all laws are passed by the Legislatures.[5] The point is that the <u>strategic</u> decisions are not being made by representative democracy. When a proposal like Ballot Measure 5 totally transforms a state's fiscal underpinnings, nothing else really matters. To a great extent, this is a variation on the process that Burns was talking about --"mobilizing...values and other resources," "to realize...goals mutually held..."[6]

We have discussed some of the people that have been able to accomplish this task -- William U'Ren, Ray Phillips and Lon Mabon. Added to that list should be Don McIntire, the leading proponent of Ballot Measure 5. Over a ninety year period, they have controlled the destiny of Oregon. They have, in their own fashion, been our true leaders. These gentlemen embody the founding of direct democracy and its use from 1902 to 1992, but also its contemporary abuse.

They have not only governed, but they have <u>changed the way we are governed</u>. U'Ren harnessed the discontent of the Populist Era and forged the tools which ruled Oregon for most of this century, but now these very tools have further changed the nature of Oregon's democracy. The initiative and referendum, Article IX Section 1a, Ballot Measure 5, and term limits are the four watershed events that have produced a quantum change in Oregon government. It is appropriate to review these four things that have so changed this state's democracy:

- First, of course, is the initiative and the referendum which were adopted in 1902, the "Oregon System."
- Second, withdrawing from the Legislature the power to impose new taxes -- Article IX, Section 1a of the Oregon Constitution, passed in 1912.
- Third, is the 1990 approval of Ballot Measure 5.

This new constitutional amendment removed the property tax as the major source of revenue for schools and put Oregon in a financially untenable situation. Prisons, colleges and human resource programs cannot be maintained at reasonable levels without replacement revenue. Ballot Measure 5 has had a structural impact on state government. Until 1990, the state's fiscal affairs were under the control of the governor and the Legislature. Even after the 1912 Article IX, Section 1a, which rendered the Legislature unable to impose new taxes, the<u> body still had control of existing budgets</u>. Measure 5 changed that, by cutting property taxes and at the same time compelling the state to make up the short fall. Money is power and Ballot Measure 5 took the power away from representative government.

Don McIntire and the proponents of Ballot Measure 5 introduced a kind of "junk bond" theory into Oregon politics. For the uninitiated, the junk bond schemes of the 1980s allowed our latter day robber barons to purchase companies with cash they did not have. The junk bonds were merely promises that once an asset rich enterprise was bought those very assets would be sold to pay off the bond purchasers. The problem with this scam was that it killed the very companies that were the subject of the take-overs. McIntire did the same thing with Ballot Measure 5; the only money available to make up for lost property taxes was the very cash that was already being spent for other state programs. In essence, the "assets" of state government were being sold so that business could have reduced taxes.

The fourth and final event which changed Oregon government was the passage of term limits in 1992. Ballot Measure 3, now Article II, Section 19 of the Oregon Constitution, limits terms for all state elected officials. There is a *life time* limit of six years in the House and eight in the Senate and one may serve no more than a total of twelve years in the Legislature. There are also limits on members of the US Congress and the US Senate elected from Oregon. Term limits will effectively remove institutional memory from the legislative branch of government. Knowledge is power, and institutional memory is vital to effective knowledge. No significant human endeavor is better engaged in when the participant has a reduced amount of experience. One does not select a surgeon or lawyer because of their lack of knowledge. Numerous solutions to ongoing problems have been tried and have failed. Without institutional memory, the Legislature will constantly re-invent the wheel with already failed answers.

During the 1993 Session of the Legislature, one of the advocates for term limits was given a painful object lesson of what their eventual effect would be. State Senator Gene Timms (R-Burns) had supported term limits, but Timms was appointed to the budget-writing Ways and Means Committee. He was amazed to learn that you needed knowledge and experience to deal with complex issues. "I was for term limits when I came here this session, and I campaigned for them last fall. Now they scare me to death."[7]

Term limits were supposed to reduce the power of government, but may well have the opposite effect. Un-elected staff and bureaucrats will become even more powerful because they alone control the information.

Regardless, term limits are a national phenomenon just as the Tax Revolt was. Fourteen other states have also passed term limits and conservative theoreticians such as George Will see them as the final solution to gridlock government.[8] He says term limits themselves have been deemed to be the most "..the most broadly based successful movement in the nation."[9]

The Cumulative Effect - the End of Representative Democracy.

Perspective is an dangerous thing in politics; it lets you see where you have been and the inevitability of where you are going. Taken all together, the events from 1902 to 1992 have irrevocably changed the nature of our government. Oregon has ceased to be a "representative democracy" and is now a "direct democracy." The truly grand decisions will not be made by the governor and Legislature, but by those who are able to sell the public on their latest simple solutions to complex problems. The question is, can Oregon be governed this way? Will it be good government?

Good Government --Knowing It When You See it.

Identifying "good government" is a dubious task: good compared with what? Like obscenity, we know good government when we see it. If anything, good government is *responsive, accountable* and is *protective of individuals' rights*.

Being responsive means that a government is able to react to changing circumstances, to institute or abolish programs in response to needs. This may be the biggest problem with Oregon's new direct democracy. When you modify a decision-making system, you affect the very decisions that are made. Representative democracy decided issues in a certain way, the legislative process involved hearings, testimony, amendments and other mechanisms. There were compromises, the balancing of interests and negotiations -- these factors do not exist with our new status quo.

We know we cannot control what issues will confront Oregon. Prediction is next to impossible; who could have anticipated AIDS, or the depletion of the ozone layer? I would submit that Oregon's new direct democracy will not be adequately able to respond to changing circumstances. Future dilemmas will reflect the increasing complexity of the society and the economy. Complex problems do seem to lend themselves to simple solutions, but unfortunately they are usually wrong.

One factor will particularly impact decision making. Because of Ballot Measure 5 there will be substantially less budget discretion to respond to future needs. Unless another source of revenue is found, the state general fund budget will not, for all intents and purposes, be available to react to future crises. Resources will not be available because they have been committed, not through a flexible legislative appropriation process, but through the initiative process. At this writing, there is a further effort to reduce the budget authority of the governor and the Legislature. The "Kids First" initiative, being proposed by K-12 education advocates, would automatically set aside a large portion of the general fund to pay for local schools and community colleges.

Ironically, Ballot Measure 5 has started to thwart the very purposes of earlier popular ballot measures. Both Measure 10 in 1986, the Victim's Right Bill, and 1988's Ballot Measure 4 which increased criminal sentences resulted in higher prison populations. Regardless of the earlier measures, the state will now have to reduce the number of available prison cells because of Ballot Measure 5.[10]

The second aspect of good government is accountability. It is interesting to compare what happens after a decision is made by a representative democracy with what happens after a policy is established by an initiative or referendum. In both instances, individuals turn their views into law. In a representative democracy, elected officials use the their success to enhance their claim to office. A governor wants the Legislature to adopt his or her program, not just for the content of the program, but to further his or her re-election. The same is true for other elected officials, they have a vested interest in the success of a policy. Along with the power comes the responsibility. If you are wrong, you are penalized, you are held responsible, you are voted out of office.

The initiative and the referendum differs, one is not usually kept in office because of a successful effort. Here, the exercise of the power carries no responsibility with it, because the actors are not usually part of the government.

There is also the question of checks and balances, an aspect of our political system that has served us well at both the state and federal level. The executive, the legislative and the judicial branches all serve to moderate each other's actions through the various mechanism such as the veto, legislative power to override, and judicial review. Although statutory ballot measures are subject to judicial review, they are not subject to the veto. Indeed, if the measure is a constitutional amendment, the only check is to be found in federal court. Others would argue that because this is the people exercising power directly, there is no need for checks, that direct democracy is not suspect like other forms of government. History would present a different view; there is such a thing as the "tyranny of the majority" and perhaps the current situation is a manifestation of that concern.

The final attribute of our hypothetical good government is whether or not it respects the rights of individuals. Ironically, this probably the worst aspect of Oregon's new direct democracy. We discussed Ballot Measure 9 in Chapter 3, but unfortunately, Measure 9 was not the first use of the initiative and referendum to limit to human rights. The infamous anti-Catholic "Compulsory Education Bill" was successfully promoted by the KKK in 1922.[11] The death penalty has passed more times than it has failed; one recent criminal law measure, Ballot Measure 10 in 1986, diminished defendant's rights; and Ballot Measure 8 reversed Governor Goldschmidt's ban on discrimination.

The battle over Ballot Measure 9 has caused former Oregon Supreme Court Justice Han Linde to re-examine the use of direct democracy.[12] On certain questions, Linde argues that the use of the initiative is illegal under the "Guaranty Clause" of the United States Constitution, "[t]he United States shall guarantee to every State in this Union a Republican Form of Government."[13]

The former Justice's exhaustive article is a *tour de force* discussion of what a "Republican Form" government is in America. The essay needs to be read in its entirety to be appreciated, but it powerfully asserts that the guarantee of a republican government means the protection of minorities from what Linde calls "collective passion." Linde says that:

> To its architects, republican government thus depended on deliberation
> by representative institutions not only for rational public policies; it also
> was the essential safeguard of civil and religious rights.[14]

In this analysis, the former Justice points out that it is the very stigmatization and identification of a group for ideological or sectarian reasons that is improper. Allowing ballot measures as a means for one group to attack another for racial, religious or ideological grounds presents a threat to effective government as we know it. Other supporters of direct democracy are also starting to question its use in the area of individual rights.[15] Linde and the other critics have not yet examined the effect of the I&R on Oregon government in general. It has taken the trauma of Ballot Measure 9 to force an examination of the process as it relates to rights, but in the long run, more than individual rights may suffer.

Politics --'02 to '92

That U'Ren and his inheritors have had a tremendous impact on Oregon history is obvious, but how does one explain the public support for such far reaching measures? How did we get to where we are? Before U'Ren, Phillips, Mabon and McIntire could be successful, they had to harness public opinion. There are similarities and dissimilarities between the historical circumstances at the turn of the century and of the 1990s.

In Chapter 5, we mentioned Frederick Jackson Turner and his thesis of how important the frontier was to democracy. Turner also observed that it was society's malcontents went West.[16] He related how the availability of free land led to economic power and economic power led to renewed democracy.[17] Is it no coincidence that the Western Frontier ended about the same time that Populism emerged. Where were the malcontents, or more aptly the dispossessed, to go once the Pacific was reached? What was the political effect on democracy of the demise of the frontier and the availability of free land? According to Turner, the frontier ended in 1880,[18] and at the very same time, there was change in the economy of the United States. Post-Civil war economics seems terribly removed from any present day consideration, but it was those very conditions which precipitated the Populist revolt. Financial institutions had bought $450 million worth of Union bonds to help fight the war, and they paid for with infamous "greenbacks," worth 50¢ on the dollar. Because of the adoption of the Gold Standard the bankers were paid back in gold dollars worth 100¢ on the dollar! Taxpayers made up the difference.[19]

Government policies also reduced the available money supply, thus causing deflation and falling prices. Although population and agricultural production increased, a limited money supply meant that less and less was paid for agricultural produce. Where farmers had been getting a theoretical dollar a bushel, they were now getting ¢50 a bushel. Where their income had decreased, their debt had remained the same. As Lawrence Goodwyn has pointed out, "To the nation's farmers, contraction (deflation) was a mass tragedy which eventually led to the Populist revolt."[20] Populism was the result of millions of American farmers being literally enslaved by debt and was an effort, "...through democratic politics to bring the corporate state under popular control..."[21] This was all happening at a time when there was no social "safety net" to cushion the effects of both ongoing conditions or other disasters such as the "Panic" of 1893. From our vantage point, as the beneficiaries of years of progressive policies, it is hard to appreciate the conditions of the turn of the century. Turner described the situation in his own erudite language:

> In the second place, (the first instance was the end of the frontier) contemporaneously with this there has been a concentration of capitol in the control of the fundamental industries as to make a new epoch in the economic development of the United States....the rise of the Populist Party in the last decade, and the acceptance of so many of its principals under Mr. Bryan, show in striking manner the birth of new political ideas, the reformation of the lines of political conflict....Under the forms of the American democracy is there in reality evolving such a concentration of economic and social power in the hands of a comparatively few men as may make political democracy an appearance rather than a reality? The free lands are gone. The material forces that gave vitality to Western democracy are passing away. It is in the realm of the spirit, to the domain of ideals and legislation that we must look for Western influence on democracy in our own days.[22]

Turner correctly saw that the initiative and the referendum were part of the Populist response to the end of the frontier and the contemporaneous concentration of economic power. He considered Populism and its program "socialist," but acknowledged it importance:

> It is not surprising that socialism shows noteworthy gains as elections continue; that parties are formed on new lines; that the demand for primary elections, for popular choice of senators, initiative, referendum

188

and recall are spreading and the regions once the center of pioneer democracy exhibit these tendencies in the most marked degree. They are the efforts to find substitutes for the former safeguards of democracy, the disappearing free lands. They are the sequence to the extinction of the frontier.[23]

Populism did not cease with no effect.[24] President McKinley died and was replaced by Teddy Roosevelt and he himself won in 1904 to become the most "progressive" Republican President ever elected.[25] Politics has a way of doing that, yesterday's radicalism becomes today's respectability.[26] Regardless, the public psychology of the Populist Era was such that voters felt compelled to change the basic form of Oregon's government. The combination of an unresponsive government and economic conditions was sufficient. One could argue that Populism's most lasting effect was not from electing people to office, but changing policies themselves.

In the 1990s, there was a similar public mood. The Legislature was perceived as having not reduced property taxes; it *seemed* unresponsive. The irony was that it was the people, and not the Legislature, who had constantly rejected tax reform proposals. But politics is perception and not reality. In 1990, when Ballot Measure 5 finally passed, there was the objective fact that property taxes were too high no matter who was to blame. The increase in home values had caused more and more of the tax burden to shift from business to residences. The situation was further exacerbated by deteriorating economies both at the state and national level. During the 1980s, Oregon faced unemployment rates which exceeded the nation's as the timber industry went through major changes discussed earlier. This was also the decade in which money and negative campaigning seemed to play more and more of a role in politics. Special interests seemed to take care of everything but the public interest. Government was not looked upon as the servant of the public, but the tool of economic power.

However, a closer examination of the circumstances reveals some striking dissimilarities. The onerous economic conditions of the 1870s, 80s and 90s were far beyond those of 1990s.

The point to be emphasized is this --both Populism and subsequent progressive policies were meant to rectify economic injustices. Cornel West, in his excellent book Race Matters, correctly identifies what the cumulative purpose had been: "The historic role of American progressives is to promote redistributive measures that enhance the standard of living and quality of life for the have-nots and the have-too-littles."[27] The initiative and the referendum were supposed to be the tools to promote the well being of the common man and women. What has been done?

The New Cross of Gold

U'Ren's tools of Populism are being turned against the very interests they were meant to protect. It is an incredible irony that the very processes which Frederick Jackson Turner criticized as being "socialist" are now being used to the opposite effect. Earlier we mentioned the darker side of the history of the initiative and the referendum in Oregon -- the long time it took to remove racial references, anti-Catholic ballot measures, etc. These instances existed, but it has not been until recently that the far right wing of American politics and especially the Republican Party have gone on the offensive using these techniques of direct democracy. Ballot Measure 10 in 1986 --Victims' Rights, Ballot Measure 4 in 1988 --mandatory sentences, Ballot Measure 8 in 1988 -- negating Governor Goldschmidt's anti-discrimination order, Ballot Measure 5 in 1990, Ballot Measure 7 in 1990 --a successful anti-welfare proposal, Ballot Measure 9 in 1992 and finally Ballot Measure 3 in 1992 --term limits. These have all been exercises in fear-mongering, bigotry, and anti-government bashing on the part of the far right. The same process continues this moment with proposals to reduce public pensions and wages paid on public construction jobs.[28] For some reason, the most reactionary segment of the political spectrum has managed to convince the average Oregonian that the real problems of society are due to government itself or the lack of values. Cornel West again:

> And given the way in which the Republican Party since 1968 has appealed to popular xenophobic images--playing the black, female, and homophobic cards to align the electorate along race, sex, and sexual orientation lines--it is no surprise that the notion that we are all part of one garment of society is discredited.[29]

There is an emerging pattern -- the use of collateral issues as a justification for attacks. What has been accomplished by progressive politics? Diana Gordon comments:

> The link between getting tough on crime and reversing the mildly redistribute policies of the New Deal and the Great Society was the "permissiveness" of modern society, which embraced a wide range of manifestations from vandalism and drug taking to homosexuality and simple laziness. Variously attributed to the decline in the nuclear family, dependence on social welfare programs, and government interference with dynamism of the market, the so-called moral decline of the country was presented to the public by neoconservative intellectuals, conservative legislators, and the Reagan administration as a cancer that would destroy the nation...[30]

Crime, welfare, government, homosexuality have all been the subject of recent Oregon ballot measures as we have seen. The inheritance of the initiative and the referendum is being squandered. Would a Bryan or a U'Ren support a ballot measure which has the effect of taking money away from public schools so that apartment owners could pay less property taxes? Most of the tax relief of Ballot Measure 5 went to business and not homeowners.[31] McIntire was selected "Oregonian of the Year" by the apartment owners for his work in passing Ballot Measure 5.[32]

Let's again return to what would U'Ren think of Ballot Measure 9? There is probably a good answer in the description of one of his first political experiences in Colorado. As a law student in Denver he watched anti-Chinese riots in the 1880s:

> The mob marched through the streets crying, "The Chinese must go," and threatening to kill them. These innocent foreigners were being persecuted. At his [U'Ren's] request he was appointed a deputy to "protect the poor Chinaman," and he kept his badge until one of the men

on the inside informed him that the mobs were not natural, that they were gotten up by the good citizens to go to the polls to vote for "law and order and the Republican party."[33]

The words are worth repeating --"Law and order and the Republican party." Nothing seems to have changed; the right wing and the Republican Party are still appealing to the dark forces of bigotry. What would U'Ren think about Ballot Measure 9? The answer is obvious.

There is a further irony to this situation. The harbingers of the right have not only used the initiative and the referendum in an effort to spread hate, but they have used them to attack what has been the greatest and most noble endeavor undertaken by American government -- education itself. Again, Stevenson's comment, "The most American thing about America is the free common school system." No other institution has touched and improved the lives of virtually every American. Notice that Stevenson said "free" and that is what has always stuck in the craw of the American Tory class.

Public schools have never been popular with right wing elements. As we mentioned, schools cost money and have been a basic means to redistribute income. The new attack on our schools has been two pronged. First were the tax limitation measures themselves, and then these were followed by the "school choice" initiatives. Oregon defeated such a choice measure in 1990, but the right continues to put the such proposals forth such as California's Proposition 174. The schools that are bled to death by tax limitation measures are attacked for their inferior quality. The Wall Street Journal has made school choice its solution to all that ails society.[34] The truth is that the solution to better public education is realistic funding, not pie-in-the-sky schemes of supposed "choice."

In an October debate over the 1993 sales tax, Don McIntire revealed how he, the chief advocate of Ballot Measure 5, really felt about public schools. McIntire said that the public school system was a "...government-run, unionized monopoly...that has grown to be a behemoth."[35] Mr. McIntire then got more specific and called the public schools "socialist mishmash."[36] His solution is, of course, allowing educational choice and having the public schools teach only the "basics," whatever those are?

Articles of faith

There is deep underlying assumption in Oregon that because the people have made a decision, it is a correct decision. As we mentioned in Chapter 5, members of the Legislature are constantly talking about the wisdom of the people. After the passage of Ballot Measure 5 politicians fell all over themselves talking about how right the people were, a kind public confession of political sin.

The I&R are considered sacrosanct in Oregon politics; they are articles of faith, a local political catechism. Someone once observed that institutions destroy themselves by taking their most important principle to an extreme. The initiative and referendum have now taken democracy to an extreme. Aristotle observed, in his Politics, that democracy eventually leads to demagoguery and then to the end of democracy itself.[37] There is something to his observation. At one point, he even discusses direct law making and rejects it:

> Where the offices are filled by vote, without any property qualification, and the whole of the people has the vote, candidates for office begin to play the demagogue, and matters are brought to pass in which *the law itself is included in popular sovereignty*...To prevent this result - or, at any rate to diminish its full effect - the proper course is to give the vote to separate tribes and not to the whole of the people. (Emphasis added)[38]

We mentioned earlier that good government is effective government; it takes care of its people, it adapts, it changes. When a representative democracy does not govern well, officials are turned out of office. What will happen with Oregon's new direct democracy? For Aristotle, the demagogue was successful because he or she was presented simple, appealing solutions. When the solutions didn't work, the people became even more frustrated and turned to dictatorship. At both the national and state level, we are seeing and hearing more and more demagoguery as government becomes less and less effective.

Where will this all lead? As problems remain unsolved, more and more simplistic solutions will be proposed. Good government remains good government and simplistic solutions won't solve society's problems, no matter how many talk show hosts use the latest scheme to sell soap. Representative democracy is an institution whose time has not passed, and those of us who respect it should not be afraid to defend and promote it.

Parting Shots

We have already discussed whether or not Oregon's new direct democracy will be "good" government. Former Justice Hans Lindes analysis of the initiative, as it applies to measures which target groups of citizens for ideological or sectarian reasons, is applicable in a broader sense. It is useful to move our final consideration away from the more salient issues such as Measure 9 and answer a modified version of the second of the two questions with which we started this chapter - not just where is Oregon going, but is our new direct democracy a constitutionally acceptable form of government? Earlier, we mentioned Hans Linde's article on whether or not the "Guaranty Clause" to the United States Constitution would preclude initiatives on certain subjects. His piece was addressed to a relatively narrow question, but his reasoning can answer our broader question. While he did not address the cumulative effects of the four particular factors we have been talking about, Linde did outline what the historical and constitutional requirements of a republican form of government were:

> The court recognized that a state would not be republican if it abolished its legislature and reduced it to a powerless advisory body and required all laws to be made by popular vote. How would lawmaking without the required republican institutions nevertheless be consistent with republican government? Justice Bean did explain, beyond his off-hand comment that the legislature could amend or repeal such a law "at will." But it radically reverses the safeguards of lawmaking to make those injured by a measure obtain repeal from the legislature or the governor. Moreover, the courts comment excludes initiatives like Measure 9 that would place a law directly into the constitution.[39]

Linde was discussing one of the few cases to consider whether or not the initiative was compatible with the republican form of government, <u>Kadderly v. City of Portland</u>, 44 OR. 118, 74 P. 710(1903). The basic reasoning of the decision was that the initiative was compatible because the usual institutions of representative democracy, governor, legislature and courts were still present. Thus we come the ultimate question, does the Legislature still effectively exist as an institution of representative democracy? This author would argue that the legislature has been so stripped of real power that Oregon has violated the requirement for a republican form of government. The most troubling aspect of this conclusion is that it is a question of degree, the cumulative effect of all four measures that we have talked about.

Consider what the effect would be if a future constitutional amendment set judge's terms at two years, limited each person to one term and established the salary of the newly selected magistrates at twice the minimum wage? In essence, our court system would be reduced to a group of temporary, underpaid clerks. The courts would remain courts in name only. If the United States Constitution requires that direct democracy coexist and not supplant representative democracy, then the real effect of such a measure would not be allowed. One could argue that in both this hypothetical and in Oregon's current situation, the initiative has not been used to protect the legitimate political interests of citizens, but to inappropriately diminish the power of branches of government. This is not to say that Ballot Measure 5 could not reduce taxes, but it is to say that it could not remove the spending power from the Legislature.

Term limits are particularly problemsome; we have had limitations on the governor and other officers, but these were reasonable limits, eight years. At what point does a term limit make an office ineffectual? To rephrase our prior hypothetical, what if a constitutional amendment required that Oregon elected a new governor every six months? The result would be absurd; there, in effect, would be a figurehead governor. The new term limits on the legislators, and congressional representatives will have that same effect. Again, this is a question of degree, but such questions must be answered.

Is the recommendation of this work that the courts should limit Oregon's new direct democracy on the grounds that it has ceased to be a republican form of government? Yes, but a very qualified yes. We have talked about the "culture wars," the politics of special interests, the change to a direct democracy and its possible ramifications. As the introduction indicates, the perspective of this book is that of a liberal Democrat. For the past forty years, the political weapon of choice for liberals has been a combination of court and constitution. It would be unwise to further unleash the very institutions which have themselves created a substantial part of the problem. The courts have turned part of the initiative and referendum process into a commercial enterprise by allowing the paying for signatures. They have allowed special interests to dominate the electoral process by rejecting campaign spending limits. Courts are, in the final analysis, elitist institutions. What would the effect be of further judicial intervention in the political process? Much of what has been written here has been critical of the OCA and others on the right. As critical as one might be, it would arrogant to summarily dismiss those views. Perhaps the real problem with representative democracy was that it was not representing the very people it purported to.

Any return to representative democracy in Oregon must be a return to real representative democracy. This return, or "reform," if one might, must not worsen the current situation. It must leave us in a better place than it found us.

1   Cecil T. Thompson, The Origin of Direct Legislation in Oregon, (Master's thesis, University of Oregon, 1929), 21, 22.

2   James MacGregor Burns, Leadership, (New York: Harper and Row, 1978), 425-427.

3   Thomas E. Cronin, Direct Democracy, (Boston: Harvard University Press, 1989), 225.

4   1976,1978 and 1982.

5   Thomas E. Cronin, Direct Democracy, 228.

6   James MacGregor Burns, Leadership, 425.

7   Quoted in, Charles Beggs, "At Capitol, judgment still mixed on term-limits law," The Oregonian, 27 July 1993, B4.

8   See George Will, Restoration, (Freepress: New York 1992).

9   George Will, "Term-limits success vexes politicians vexes politicians," The Oregonian, 24 June 1993, C7.

10   Oregon, Legislative Assembly, House, Judiciary Committee, Hearing on SB-139, 67th Legislative Assembly, 21 June 1993, testimony of Dee Dee Kouns.

11   Again, this was declared unconstitutional by the United States Supreme Court. See, Pierce v. Society of Sisters, 268 U.S. 510 (1925).

12   Hans A. Linde, "When Initiative Lawmaking Is Not 'Republican Government: The Campaign Against Homosexuality," Oregon Law Review, Vol. 72 (1993), 20.

13   United States Constitution, Article IV, section 4.

14   Hans A. Linde, "When Initiative Lawmaking Is Not 'Republican Government: The Campaign Against Homosexuality," 33.

15   "Anti-gay-rights ballots abuse initiative system," Statesman-Journal, 20 June 1993, 10A.

16   Frederick Jackson Turner, The Frontier in American History, (New York: Henry Holt, 1948), 32.

17   Frederick Jackson Turner, Frontier and Section - Selected essays of Frederick Jackson Turner, with a Introduction by Ray Allen Billington (Englewood Cliffs, N.J.: Prentice-Hall, 1991), 58.

18   Ibid., 37.

19   Lawrence Goodwyn, The Populist Moment, (New York: Oxford University Press, 1978), 10-11.

20   Ibid., 12.

21   Ibid., XXII.

22   Frederick Jackson Turner, The Frontier in American History, 245-246.

23   Frederick Jackson Turner, Frontier and Section - Selected essays of Frederick Jackson Turner, 162-163.

24   Bryan continued his fascinating career including being Secretary of State under Woodrow Wilson. In 1925, Bryan served a special prosecutor in the famous "Scopes Monkey Trial" in Dayton Tennessee, where Scopes, a teacher, was tried for teaching Darwin's theory of evolution. The defense attorney was Clarence Darrow and the nation followed the spectacle through the reporting of H.L.Menken. Bryan allowed himself to be placed on the stand as an expert on the Bible and be cross examined by Darrow in one of the most dramatic moments in American legal, political and intellectual history. Although Bryan did not do particularly well under Darrow's assault, Scopes was convicted. Louis W. Koenig, Bryan, (New York: G.P. Putnam's Son, 1971) 632-658. Years later the relationship be Populism and fundamentalism remains as strong. Things seemed to have changed little since the Scopes trial.

25 Frederick Jackson Turner, <u>Frontier and Section - Selected essays of Frederick Jackson Turner</u>, 166.

26 Theodore Roosevelt busted the "trusts" (big business) and protected the environment. Much of what the Populists proposed became policy under TR.

27 Cornel West, <u>Race Matters</u>, (Boston: Beacon Press, 1993), 63.

28 At the time of this writing it is not evident whether either will get on the ballot.

29 Ibid., 6.

30 Diana R. Gordon, <u>The Justice Juggernaut</u>, (New Brunswick: Rutgers University Press, 1990), 237.

31 Jeff Mapes, "Measure 1 is like a crystal ball," <u>The Oregonian</u>, 31 October 1993, E3.

32 "Upfront-McIntire Tapped," <u>The Oregonian</u>, 18 August 1993, B1.

33 Cecil T. Thompson, <u>The Origin of Direct Legislation in Oregon</u>, 22-23.

34 "Choice Reality," <u>The Wall Street Journal</u>, 21 September 1993, A22; 'Choice Politics," <u>The Wall Street Journal</u>, 15 October 1993, A12. Their solution to the crisis in public education is to give parents vouchers so they can bail out of the system. Poor children will supposedly be allowed into the best of schools on vouchers alone.

35 Quoted in Gail Kinsey Hill, "Activist, legislator clash publicly over tax," <u>The Oregonian</u>, 21 October 1993, E1, E9.

36 Ibid., E9.

37 Aristotle, <u>The Politics of Aristotle</u>, trans. Ernest Baker (New York: Oxford University Press, 1958), 215.

38 Ibid., 216-217.

39 Hans A. Linde, "When Initiative Lawmaking Is Not 'Republican Government': The Campaign Against Homosexuality," 26.

APPENDIX

The following material is a comprehensive listing of all state Initiatives and Referendums in Oregon since 1902. Each entry has nine fields relating to the particular ballot measure.

Election Type	Election Date	Ballot Type Num		Title	L/P/R	Yes Vote	No Vote	Passed

The type of election refers to "general," "special," and "primary" elections, and the election dates are given as the year, the month and the day. "Type" refers to whether the measure is a constitutional amendment or a statute. Ballot numbers were not always used, but we have assigned numbers to the various measures to correspond with their listing in the Oregon Bluebook(s). The "Title" is the actual title that appeared on the ballot. The field entitled "L/P/R," is an abbreviation for "Legislature," "Petition" or "Referendum." A measure with the designation "Legislature" was placed on the ballot as a Legislative referral, "Petition" refers to Initiative Petition and "Referendum" refers to a measure placed on the ballot by Referendum petition. "Yes" and "No" votes are self-explanatory and the final field designates whether or not the measure passed, "T" for passage and "F" for failure.

Election Type	Election Date	Ballot Type	Num	Title	L/P/R	Yes Vote	No Vote	Passed
G	02-Jun-02	Am	1	Initiative and referendum	L	62,024	5,668	T
G	06-Jun-04	Am	1	Office of state printer	P	45,334	14,031	T
G	06-Jun-04	St	2	Direct primary nominating election law	P	56,205	16,354	T
G	06-Jun-04	St	3	Local option liquor law	P	43,316	40,198	T
G	04-Jun-06	Am	1	Equal suffrage amendment	P	36,902	47,075	F
G	04-Jun-06	Am	2	Requiring referendum on any act calling a constitutional convention	P	47,661	18,751	T
G	04-Jun-06	Am	3	Giving cities sole power to amend their charters	P	52,567	19,852	T
G	04-Jun-06	Am	4	Authorizing state printer's compensation to be regulated by law at any time	P	63,719	9,571	T
G	04-Jun-06	Am	5	Initiative and referendum to apply to all local, special, and municipal laws	P	47,687	16,735	T
G	04-Jun-06	St	6	General appropriation bill, state institutions	R	43,918	26,758	T
G	04-Jun-06	St	7	Amendment to local option liquor law	P	35,297	45,144	F
G	04-Jun-06	St	8	Purchase of the Barlow toll road by the state	P	31,525	44,527	F
G	04-Jun-06	St	9	Prohibiting free passes on railroads	P	57,281	16,779	T
G	04-Jun-06	St	10	Gross earning tax on sleeping, refrigerator, and oil car companies	P	69,635	6,441	T

G	04-Jun-06	St	11	Gross earnings tax on express, telephone, and telegraph companies	P	70,872	6,360	F
G	01-Jun-08	Am	1	To increase compensation of legislators from $120 to $400 per session	L	19,691	68,892	F
G	01-Jun-08	Am	2	Permitting location of state institutions at other than state capitol	L	41,975	40,868	T
G	01-Jun-08	Am	3	Reorganization system of courts and increasing the number of supreme court justices from three to five	L	30,243	50,591	F
G	01-Jun-08	Am	4	Changing date of general elections from June to November	L	65,728	18,590	T
G	01-Jun-08	Am	5	Equal suffrage	P	36,858	58,670	F
G	01-Jun-08	Am	6	Giving cities control of liquor selling, poolrooms, theaters, etc., subject to local option law	P	39,442	52,346	F
G	01-Jun-08	Am	7	Modified form of the single tax amendment	P	32,066	60,871	F
G	01-Jun-08	Am	8	Recall power on public officials	P	58,381	31,002	T
G	01-Jun-08	Am	9	Authorizing proportional representation law	P	48,868	34,128	T
G	01-Jun-08	Am	10	Requiring indictment to be by grand jury	P	52,214	28,487	T
G	01-Jun-08	St	11	Giving sheriffs control of county prisoners	P	60,443	30,033	T
G	01-Jun-08	St	12	Requiring railroads to give public officials free passes	R	28,856	59,406	F
G	01-Jun-08	St	13	Appropriating $100,000 for building armories	R	33,507	54,848	F
G	01-Jun-08	St	14	Increasing annual appropriation for University of Oregon from $47,500 to $125,000	R	44,115	40,535	T
G	01-Jun-08	St	15	Fishery law proposed by fishwheel operators	P	46,582	40,720	T
G	01-Jun-08	St	16	Fishery law proposed by gillnet operators	P	56,130	30,280	T
G	01-Jun-08	St	17	Instructing legislature to vote for people's choice for United States Senator	P	69,668	21,162	T
G	01-Jun-08	St	18	Corrupt practices act governing elections	P	54,042	31,301	T
G	01-Jun-08	St	19	Creating Hood River county	P	43,948	26,778	T
G	08-Nov-10	Am	1	Permitting female taxpayers to vote	P	35,270	59,065	F
G	08-Nov-10	Am	2	Providing separate district for election of each state senator and representative	L	24,000	54,252	F
G	08-Nov-10	Am	3	Repealing requirements that all taxes shall be equal and uniform	L	37,619	40,172	F
G	08-Nov-10	Am	4	Permitting organized districts to vote bonds for construction of railroads by such districts	L	32,844	46,070	F

G	08-Nov-10	Am	5	Authorizing collection of state and county taxes on separate classes of property	L	31,629	41,692	F
G	08-Nov-10	Am	6	Permitting people of each county to regulate taxation for county purposes and abolishing poll taxes	P	44,171	42,127	T
G	08-Nov-10	Am	7	Giving cities and towns exclusive power to regulate liquor traffic within their limits	P	53,321	50,779	T
G	08-Nov-10	Am	8	Prohibiting liquor traffic	P	43,540	61,221	F
G	08-Nov-10	Am	9	Permitting counties to vote bonds for permanent road improvement	P	51,275	32,906	T
G	08-Nov-10	Am	10	Extending initiative and referendum, making term of members of legislature six years, increasing salaries, requiring proportional representation in legislature, election of president of senate and speaker of house outside of members, etc.	P	37,031	44,366	F
G	08-Nov-10	Am	11	Permitting three-fourths verdict in civil cases	P	44,538	39,399	T
G	08-Nov-10	St	12	Establishing branch insane asylum in eastern Oregon	L	50,134	41,504	T
G	08-Nov-10	St	13	Calling convention to revise state constitution	P	23,143	59,974	F
G	08-Nov-10	St	14	Requiring Baker county to pay $1,000 a year to circuit judge in addition to his state salary	R	13,161	71,503	F
G	08-Nov-10	St	15	Creating Nesmith county from parts of Lane and Douglas	P	22,866	60,951	F
G	08-Nov-10	St	16	To establish a state normal school at Monmouth	P	50,191	40,044	T
G	08-Nov-10	St	17	Creating Otis county from parts of Harney, Malheur, and Grant	P	17,426	62,061	F
G	08-Nov-10	St	18	Annexing part of Clackamas county to Multnomah	P	16,250	69,002	F
G	08-Nov-10	St	19	Creating Williams county from parts of Lane and Douglas	P	14,508	64,090	F
G	08-Nov-10	St	20	For protection of laborers in hazardous employment, fixing employers liability, etc.	P	56,258	33,943	T
G	08-Nov-10	St	21	Creating Orchard county from part of Umatilla	P	15,664	62,712	F
G	08-Nov-10	St	22	Creating Clark county from part of Grant	P	15,613	61,704	F
G	08-Nov-10	St	23	To establish state normal school at Weston	P	40,898	46,201	F
G	08-Nov-10	St	24	To annex part of Washington county to Multnomah	P	14,047	68,221	F
G	08-Nov-10	St	25	To establish a state normal school at Ashland	P	38,473	48,655	T

G	08-Nov-10	St	26	Prohibiting the sale of liquors, and regulating shipments of same, and providing for search for liquor	P	42,651	63,564	F
G	08-Nov-10	St	27	Creating board to draft employers' liability law for submission to legislature	P	32,224	51,719	F
G	08-Nov-10	St	28	Prohibiting taking of fish in Rogue river except with hook and line	P	49,712	33,397	T
G	08-Nov-10	St	29	Creating Deschutes county out of part of Crook	P	17,592	60,486	F
G	08-Nov-10	St	30	Bill for general law under which new counties may be created or boundaries changed	P	37,129	42,327	F
G	08-Nov-10	St	31	Permitting voters in direct primaries to express choice for president and vice president, to select delegates to national convention, and nominate candidates for presidential electors	P	43,353	41,624	T
G	08-Nov-10	St	32	Creating board of people's inspectors of government, providing for reports of board in Official State Gazette to be mailed to all registered voters bimonthly	P	29,955	52,538	F
G	05-Nov-12	Am	1	Woman suffrage	P	61,265	57,104	T
G	05-Nov-12	Am	2	Creating office of lieutenant governor	L	50,562	61,644	F
G	05-Nov-12	Am	3	Divorce of local and state taxation	L	51,582	56,671	F
G	05-Nov-12	Am	4	Permitting different tax rates on classes of property	L	52,045	54,483	F
G	05-Nov-12	Am	5	Repeal of county tax option	L	63,881	47,150	T
G	05-Nov-12	Am	6	Majority rule on constitutional amendments	L	32,934	70,325	F
G	05-Nov-12	Am	7	Double liability on bank stockholders	L	82,981	21,738	T
G	05-Nov-12	Am	8	Majority rule on initiated laws	P	35,721	68,861	F
G	05-Nov-12	Am	9	Limiting state road indebtedness	P	59,452	43,447	T
G	05-Nov-12	Am	10	Limiting county road indebtedness	P	57,258	43,858	T
G	05-Nov-12	Am	11	Income tax amendment	P	52,702	52,948	F
G	05-Nov-12	Am	12	County road bonding act	P	38,568	63,481	F
G	05-Nov-12	Am	13	Abolishing senate; proxy voting; U'Ren constitution	P	31,020	71,183	F
G	05-Nov-12	Am	14	Statewide single tax with graduated tax provision	P	31,534	82,015	F
G	05-Nov-12	St	15	Statewide public utilities regulation	R	65,985	40,956	T
G	05-Nov-12	St	16	Creating Cascade county	P	26,463	71,239	F
G	05-Nov-12	St	17	Millage tax for university and agricultural college	P	48,701	57,279	F
G	05-Nov-12	St	18	County bonding and road construction act-grange bill	P	49,699	56,713	F
G	05-Nov-12	St	19	Creating state highway department-grange bill	P	23,872	83,846	F

G	05-Nov-12	St	20	Changing date state printer bill becomes effective	P	34,793	69,542	F
G	05-Nov-12	St	21	Creating office of hotel inspector	P	16,910	91,995	F
G	05-Nov-12	St	22	Eight-hour day on public works	P	64,508	48,078	T
G	05-Nov-12	St	23.	Blue sky law	P	48,765	57,293	F
G	05-Nov-12	St	24	Prohibiting private employment of convicts	P	73,800	37,492	T
G	05-Nov-12	St	25	Relating to employment of county and city prisoners	P	71,367	37,731	T
G	05-Nov-12	St	26	State road bonding act	P	30,897	75,590	F
G	05-Nov-12	St	27	County bonding act	P	43,611	60,210	F
G	05-Nov-12	St	28	Providing method for consolidating cities and creating new counties	P	40,199	56,992	F
G	05-Nov-12	St	29	Tax exemption on household effects	P	60,357	51,826	T
G	05-Nov-12	St	30	Tax exemption on moneys and credits	P	42,491	66,540	F
G	05-Nov-12	St	31	Revising inheritance tax laws	P	38,609	63,839	F
G	05-Nov-12	St	32	Freight rates act	P	58,306	45,534	T
G	05-Nov-12	St	33	Abolishing capital punishment	P	41,951	64,578	F
G	05-Nov-12	St	34	Prohibiting boycotting	P	49,826	60,560	F
G	05-Nov-12	St	35	Giving mayor authority to control street speaking	P	48,987	62,532	F
G	05-Nov-12	St	36	Appropriation for university	R	29,437	78,985	F
G	05-Nov-12	St	37	Appropriation for university	R	27,310	79,376	F
G	05-Nov-12	St	38	"Single tax, Clackamas county"	P	1,827	3,787	F
G	05-Nov-12	St	39	Single tax, Coos county	P	1,113	1,909	F
G	05-Nov-12	St	40	Prohibiting building of courthouse in Harney county before 1916	P	778	391	T
G	05-Nov-12	St	41	To establish a national bank in Jackson county	P	1,975	2,379	F
G	05-Nov-12	St	42	Making Port of Portland commission elective	P	13,931	18,668	F
G	05-Nov-12	St	43	Single tax, Multnomah county	P	11,146	23,901	F
G	05-Nov-12	St	44	Abolishing Wallowa county high school	P	1,031	655	T
S	04-Nov-13	St	1	State university building repair fund	R	56,659	40,600	T
S	04-Nov-13	St	2	State university new building appropriation	R	53,569	43,014	T
S	04-Nov-13	St	3	Sterilization act	R	41,767	53,319	F
S	04-Nov-13	St	4	County attorney act	R	54,179	38,159	T
S	04-Nov-13	St	5	Workmen's compensation act	R	67,814	28,608	T
G	03-Nov-14	Am	1	Requiring voters to be citizens of the United States	L	164,879	39,847	T
G	03-Nov-14	Am	2	Creating office of lieutenant governor	L	52,040	143,804	F
G	03-Nov-14	Am	3	Permitting certain city and county boundaries to be made identical, and governments consolidated	L	77,392	103,194	F

G	03-Nov-14	Am	4	Permitting state to create an indebtedness not to exceed 2 per cent of assessed valuation for irrigation and power projects and development of untilled lands	L	49,759	135,550	F
G	03-Nov-14	Am	5	Omitting requirement that "all taxation be equal and uniform"	L	59,206	116,490	F
G	03-Nov-14	Am	6	Changing existing rule of uniformity and equality of taxation-authorizing classification of property for taxation purposes	L	52,362	122,704	F
G	03-Nov-14	Am	7	Enabling incorporated municipalities to surrender charters and to be merged in adjoining city or town	L	96,116	77,671	T
G	03-Nov-14	Am	8	Providing compensation for members of legislature at five dollars per day	L	41,087	146,278	F
G	03-Nov-14	Am	9	Universal constitutional eight-hour-day amendment	P	49,360	167,888	F
G	03-Nov-14	Am	10	$1,500 tax exemption amendment	P	65,495	136,193	F
G	03-Nov-14	Am	11	Public docks and water frontage amendment	P	67,128	114,564	F
G	03-Nov-14	Am	12	Prohibition constitutional amendment	P	136,842	100,362	T
G	03-Nov-14	Am	13	Abolishing death penalty	P	100,552	100,395	T
G	03-Nov-14	Am	14	Specific personal graduated extra-tax amendment of article IX, Oregon constitution	P	59,186	124,943	F
G	03-Nov-14	Am	15	County officers term amendment	P	82,841	107,039	F
G	03-Nov-14	Am	16	Proportional representation amendment to Oregon constitution	P	39,740	137,116	F
G	03-Nov-14	Am	17	State senate constitutional amendment	P	62,376	123,429	F
G	03-Nov-14	Am	18	Department of industry and public works amendment	P	57,859	126,201	F
G	03-Nov-14	Am	19	Equal assessment and taxation and $300 exemption	P	43,280	140,507	F
G	03-Nov-14	St	20	To establish state normal school at Ashland	L	84,041	109,643	F
G	03-Nov-14	St	21	To establish state normal school at Weston	L	87,450	105,345	F
G	03-Nov-14	St	22	Eight-hour day and room-ventilation law for women workers	P	88,480	120,296	F
G	03-Nov-14	St	23	Nonpartisan judiciary bill prohibiting party nominations for judicial officers	P	74,323	107,263	F
G	03-Nov-14	St	24	Municipal wharves and docks bill	P	67,110	111,113	F
G	03-Nov-14	St	25	Consolidating corporation and insurance departments	P	55,469	120,154	F
G	03-Nov-14	St	26	Dentistry bill	P	92,722	110,404	F
G	03-Nov-14	St	27	A tax code commission bill	P	34,436	143,468	F
G	03-Nov-14	St	28	Abolishing desert land board and reorganizing certain state offices	P	32,701	143,366	F

G	03-Nov-14	St	29	Primary delegate election bill	P	25,058	153,638	F
G	03-Nov-14	St	30	Harney county jack-rabbit bounty bill	P	1,156	793	T
G	03-Nov-14	St	31	Local measure readjusting salaries of Hood River county officials	P	1,502	678	T
G	07-Nov-16	Am	1	Single item veto amendment	L	141,773	53,207	T
G	07-Nov-16	Am	2	Ship tax exemption amendment	L	119,652	65,410	T
G	07-Nov-16	Am	3	Negro and mulatto suffrage amendment	L	100,027	100,701	F
G	07-Nov-16	Am	4	Full rental value land tax and homemakers' loan fund amendment	P	43,390	154,930	F
G	07-Nov-16	Am	5	For Pendleton normal school and ratifying location institutions	P	96,829	109,523	F
G	07-Nov-16	Am	6	Permitting manufacture and regulating sale 4 percent malt liquors	P	85,973	140,599	F
G	07-Nov-16	Am	7	Prohibition amendment forbidding importation of intoxicating liquors for beverage purposes	P	114,932	109,671	T
G	07-Nov-16	Am	8	Rural credits amendment	P	107,488	83,887	T
G	07-Nov-16	Am	9	Statewide tax and indebtedness limitation amendment	P	99,536	84,031	T
G	07-Nov-16	St	10	Anti-compulsory vaccination bill	P	99,745	100,119	F
G	07-Nov-16	St	11	Bill repealing and abolishing the Sunday closing law	P	125,836	93,076	T
G	07-Nov-16	St	12	Crook County-Crook county rabbit and sage rat bounty bill	P	2,500	1,055	T
G	07-Nov-16	St	13	Crook county - Bend for county seat bill	P	1,126	2,441	F
G	07-Nov-16	St	14	Harney county - Bill abolishing county high school	P	637	1,445	F
G	07-Nov-16	St	14	Harney county - Harney county two mile limit law against sheep	P	723	1,342	F
G	07-Nov-16	St	15	Harney county - Bill abolishing county high school	P	637	1,445	F
G	07-Nov-16	St	16	Jefferson county - Madras for county seat bill	P	839	514	T
G	07-Nov-16	St	17	Jefferson county - Metolius for county seat bill	P	448	1,028	F
G	07-Nov-16	St	18	Klamath county - County maintenance of Klamath Falls, Oregon	P	1,275	1,423	F
G	07-Nov-16	St	18	Lake county - Lake county rabbit bounty bill	P	1,049	589	T
S	04-Jun-17	Am	1	Authorizing ports to create limited indebtedness to encourage water transportation	L	67,445	54,864	T
S	04-Jun-17	Am	2	Limiting number of bills introduced and increasing pay of legislators	L	22,276	103,238	F
S	04-Jun-17	Am	3	Declaration against implied repeal of constitutional provisions by amendments thereto	L	37,187	72,445	F

S	04-Jun-17	Am	4	Uniform tax classification amendment	L	62,118	53,245	T
S	04-Jun-17	Am	5	Requiring election city, town, and state officers at same time	L	83,630	42,296	T
S	04-Jun-17	St	6	Four hundred thousand dollar tax levy for a new penitentiary	L	46,666	86,165	F
S	04-Jun-17	St	7	Six million dollar state road bond issue and highway bill	L	77,316	63,803	T
G	05-Nov-18	Am	1	Establishing and maintaining Southern and Eastern Oregon normal schools	L	49,935	66,070	F
G	05-Nov-18	St	2	Establishing dependent, delinquent and defective children's home, appropriating money therefor	L	43,441	65,299	F
G	05-Nov-18	St	3	Prohibiting seine and setnet fishing in Rogue river and tributaries	R	45,511	50,227	F
G	05-Nov-18	St	4	Closing the Willamette river to commercial fishing south of Oswego	R	55,555	40,908	T
G	05-Nov-18	St	5	Delinquent tax notice bill	P	66,652	41,594	T
G	05-Nov-18	St	6	Fixing compensation for publication of legal notices	P	50,073	41,816	T
G	05-Nov-18	St	7	Authorizing increase in amount of levy of state taxes for year 1919 (submitted by state tax commission under chapter 150, Laws 1917)		41,364	56,974	F
S	03-Jun-19	Am	1	6 percent county indebtedness for permanent roads amendment	L	49,728	33,531	T
S	03-Jun-19	Am	2	Industrial and reconstruction hospital amendment	L	38,204	40,707	F
S	03-Jun-19	Am	3	State bond payment of irrigation and drainage district bond interest	L	43,010	35,948	T
S	03-Jun-19	Am	4	Five million dollar reconstruction bonding amendment	L	39,130	40,580	F
S	03-Jun-19	Am	5	Lieutenant governor constitutional amendment	L	32,653	46,861	F
S	03-Jun-19	St	6	The Roosevelt coast military highway bill	L	56,966	29,159	T
S	03-Jun-19	St	7	Reconstruction bonding bill	L	37,294	42,792	F
S	03-Jun-19	St	8	Soldiers', sailors' and marines' educational financial aid bill	L	49,158	33,513	T
S	03-Jun-19	St	9	Market roads tax bill	L	53,191	28,039	T
S	21-May-20	Am	1	Extending eminent domain over roads and ways	L	100,256	35,655	T
S	21-May-20	Am	2	Limitation of 4 per cent state indebtedness for permanent roads	L	93,392	46,084	T
S	21-May-20	Am	3	Restoring capital punishment	L	81,756	64,589	T
S	21-May-20	Am	4	Crook and Curry counties bonding amendment	L	72,378	36,699	T
S	21-May-20	Am	5	Successor to governor	L	78,241	56,946	T
S	21-May-20	St	6	Higher educational tax act	L	102,722	46,577	T

S	21-May-20	St	7	Soldiers', sailors' and marines' educational aid revenue bill	L	91,294	50,482	T
S	21-May-20	St	8	State elementary school fund tax	L	110,233	39,593	T
S	21-May-20	St	9	Blind school tax measure	L	115,337	30,739	T
G	02-Nov-20	Am	1	Compulsory voting and registration	L	61,258	131,603	F
G	02-Nov-20	Am	2	Regulating legislative sessions and the payment of legislators	L	80,342	85,524	F
G	02-Nov-20	Am	3	Single tax	P	37,283	147,426	F
G	02-Nov-20	Am	4	Fixing term of certain county officers	P	97,854	80,983	T
G	02-Nov-20	Am	5	Anti-compulsory vaccination	P	63,018	127,570	F
G	02-Nov-20	Am	6	Fixing legal rate of interest in Oregon	P	28,976	158,673	F
G	02-Nov-20	Am	7	Divided legislative session	P	57,791	101,179	F
G	02-Nov-20	St	8	Oleomargarine bill	R	67,101	119,126	F
G	02-Nov-20	St	9	Port of Portland dock commission consolidation	P	80,493	84,830	F
G	02-Nov-20	St	10	Roosevelt bird refuge	P	78,961	107,383	F
G	02-Nov-20	St	11	State market commission	P	51,605	119,464	F
G	02-Nov-20	St	12	Umatilla county herd law	P	4,490	2,132	T
S	07-Jun-21	Am	1	Legislative regulation and compensation amendment	L	42,924	72,596	F
S	07-Jun-21	Am	2	World war veterans' state aid fund, constitutional amendment	L	88,219	37,866	T
S	07-Jun-21	Am	3	Emergency clause veto constitutional amendment	L	62,621	45,537	T
S	07-Jun-21	St	4	Hygiene marriage examination and license bill	L	56,858	65,793	F
S	07-Jun-21	St	5	Women jurors and revised jury law	L	59,882	59,265	T
G	07-Nov-22	Am	1	Permitting Linn county tax levy to pay outstanding warrants	L	89,177	57,049	T
G	07-Nov-22	Am	2	Permitting Linn and Benton counties to pay outstanding warrants	L	86,547	53,844	T
G	07-Nov-22	Am	3	Single tax amendment	P	39,231	132,021	F
G	07-Nov-22	Am	4	1925 exposition tax amendment	P	82,837	95,587	F
G	07-Nov-22	Am	5	Income tax amendment	P	54,803	112,197	F
G	07-Nov-22	St	6	Compulsory education bill	P	115,506	103,685	T
S	06-Nov-23	St	1	Income tax act	L	58,647	58,131	F
G	04-Nov-24	Am	1	Voters' literacy amendment	L	184,031	48,645	T
G	04-Nov-24	Am	2	Public use and welfare amendment	L	134,071	65,133	T
G	04-Nov-24	Am	3	Bonus amendment	L	131,199	92,446	T
G	04-Nov-24	Am	4	Workmen's compulsory compensation law for hazardous occupations	P	73,270	151,862	F
G	04-Nov-24	St	5	Oleomargarine condensed milk bill	P	91,597	157,324	F
G	04-Nov-24	St	6	Naturopath bill	P	75,159	122,839	F
G	04-Nov-24	St	7	Income tax repeal	P	123,799	111,055	T
G	02-Nov-26	Am	1	Klamath county bonding amendment	L	81,954	68,128	T

G	02-Nov-26	Am	2	Six per cent limitation amendment	L	54,624	99,125	F
G	02-Nov-26	Am	3	Repeal of free Negro and mulatto section of the constitution	L	108,332	64,954	T
G	02-Nov-26	Am	4	Amendment prohibiting inheritance and income taxes	L	59,442	121,973	F
G	02-Nov-26	Am	5	The recall amendment	L	100,324	61,307	T
G	02-Nov-26	Am	6	Curry county bonding or tax levy amendment	L	78,823	61,472	T
G	02-Nov-26	Am	7	Amendment relating to elections to fill vacancies in public offices	L	100,397	54,474	T
G	02-Nov-26	Am	8	Klamath and Clackamas county bonding amendment	L	75,229	61,718	T
G	02-Nov-26	St	9	The Seaside normal school act	L	47,878	124,811	F
G	02-Nov-26	St	10	The Eastern Oregon state normal school act	L	101,327	80,084	T
G	02-Nov-26	St	11	The Eastern Oregon tuberculosis hospital act	L	131,296	48,490	T
G	02-Nov-26	St	12	Cigarette and tobacco tax bill	R	62,254	123,208	F
G	02-Nov-26	St	13	Motor bus and truck bill	R	99,746	78,685	T
G	02-Nov-26	St	14	Act appropriating 10 per cent of self sustaining boards' receipts	R	46,389	97,460	F
G	02-Nov-26	St	15	Income tax with property tax offset	P	50,199	122,512	F
G	02-Nov-26	St	16	Bus and truck operating license bill	P	76,164	94,533	F
G	02-Nov-26	St	17	Fish wheel, trap, seine, and gillnet bill	P	102,119	73,086	T
G	02-Nov-26	St	18	Income tax bill	P	83,991	93,997	F
G	02-Nov-26	St	19	Oregon water and power board development measure	L	35,313	147,092	F
G	02-Nov-26	St	20	Amendment fixing salaries of county officers of Umatilla county	L	1,988	2,646	F
G	02-Nov-26	St	21	To provide salaries for certain officials of Clackamas county	L	2,826	6,199	F
S	28-Jun-27	Am	1	Repeal of Negro, Chinaman, and mulatto suffrage section of constitution	L	69,373	41,887	T
S	28-Jun-27	Am	2	Portland school district tax levy amendment	L	46,784	55,817	F
S	28-Jun-27	Am	3	Criminal information amendment	L	64,956	38,774	T
S	28-Jun-27	Am	4	Legislators' pay amendment	L	28,380	81,215	F
S	28-Jun-27	Am	5	Voters' registration amendment	L	55,802	49,682	T
S	28-Jun-27	Am	6	State and county officers salary amendment	L	46,999	61,838	F
S	28-Jun-27	Am	7	City and county consolidation amendment	L	41,309	57,613	F
S	28-Jun-27	Am	8	Veterans' memorial and armory amendment	L	25,180	80,476	F
S	28-Jun-27	Am	9	State tax limitation amendment	L	19,393	84,697	F
S	28-Jun-27	St	10	Income tax bill	L	48,745	67,039	F

S	28-Jun-27	St	11	Property assessment and taxation enforcement bill	R	31,957	70,871	F
S	28-Jun-27	St	12	Nestucca bay fish closing bill	R	53,684	47,552	T
G	06-Nov-28	Am	1	Limiting power of legislature over laws approved by the people	P	108,230	124,200	F
G	06-Nov-28	St	2	Five cent gasoline tax bill	P	71,824	198,798	F
G	06-Nov-28	St	3	Bill for reduction of motor vehicle license fees	P	98,248	174,219	F
G	06-Nov-28	St	4	Income tax bill	P	118,696	132,961	F
G	06-Nov-28	St	5	Deschutes river water and fish bill	P	78,317	157,398	F
G	06-Nov-28	St	6	Rogue river water and fish bill	P	79,028	156,009	F
G	06-Nov-28	St	7	Umpqua river water and fish bill	P	76,108	154,345	F
G	06-Nov-28	St	8	McKenzie river water and fish bill	P	77,974	153,418	F
G	04-Nov-30	Am	1	Repeal of state payment of irrigation and drainage district interest	L	96,061	74,892	T
G	04-Nov-30	Am	2	State cabinet form of government constitutional amendment	L	51,248	135,412	F
G	04-Nov-30	Am	3	Bonus loan constitutional amendment	L	92,602	101,785	F
G	04-Nov-30	Am	4	Motor vehicle license tax constitutional amendment	L	71,557	115,480	F
G	04-Nov-30	Am	5	Motor vehicle license tax constitutional amendment	L	63,683	111,441	F
G	04-Nov-30	Am	6	Constitutional amendment for filling vacancies in the legislature	L	85,836	76,455	T
G	04-Nov-30	Am	7	Legislators' compensation constitutional amendment	L	70,937	108,070	F
G	04-Nov-30	Am	8	Anti-cigarette constitutional amendment	P	54,231	156,265	F
G	04-Nov-30	Am	9	Rogue river fishing constitutional amendment	P	96,596	99,490	F
G	04-Nov-30	Am	10	Lieutenant governor constitutional amendment	P	92,707	95,277	F
G	04-Nov-30	Am	11	People's water and power utility districts constitutional amendment	P	117,776	84,778	T
G	04-Nov-30	St	12	Two additional circuit judges bill	R	39,770	137,549	F
G	04-Nov-30	St	13	Income tax bill	R	105,189	95,207	T
G	04-Nov-30	St	14	Amendment fixing salaries of county officers of Umatilla county	R	1,320	2,651	F
G	08-Nov-32	Am	1	Taxpayer voting qualification amendment	L	189,321	124,160	T
G	08-Nov-32	Am	2	Amendment authorizing criminal trials without juries by consent of accused	L	191,042	111,872	T
G	08-Nov-32	Am	3	Six per cent limitation amendment	L	149,833	121,852	T
G	08-Nov-32	Am	4	Tax and debt control constitutional amendment	P	99,171	162,552	F
G	08-Nov-32	Am	5	State water power and hydroelectric constitutional amendment	P	168,937	130,494	T

G	08-Nov-32	St	6	Oleomargarine tax bill	R	131,273	200,496	F
G	08-Nov-32	St	7	A bill prohibiting commercial fishing on the Rogue river	R	127,445	180,527	F
G	08-Nov-32	St	8	Higher education appropriation bill	R	58,076	237,218	F
G	08-Nov-32	St	9	Bill to repeal state prohibition law of Oregon	P	206,619	138,775	T
G	08-Nov-32	St	10	The freight truck and bus bill	P	151,790	180,609	F
G	08-Nov-32	St	11	Bill moving university, normal and law schools, establishing junior colleges	P	47,275	292,486	F
G	08-Nov-32	St	12	Tax supervising and conservation bill	P	117,940	154,206	F
G	08-Nov-32	St	13	Personal income tax law amendment bill	P	144,502	162,468	F
S	21-Jul-33	Am	1	Federal prohibition repeal constitutional amendment	L	136,713	72,854	T
S	21-Jul-33	Am	2	Soldiers and sailors bonus limitation amendment	L	113,267	75,476	T
S	21-Jul-33	Am	3	County manager form of government amendment	L	66,425	117,148	F
S	21-Jul-33	Am	4	Prosecution by information and grand jury modification amendment	L	67,192	110,755	F
S	21-Jul-33	Am	5	Debt and taxation limitation for municipal corporations constitutional amendment	L	82,996	91,671	F
S	21-Jul-33	Am	6	Repeal of Oregon prohibition constitutional amendment	P	143,044	72,745	T
S	21-Jul-33	St	6	State power fund bonds	L	73,756	106,153	F
S	21-Jul-33	St	8	Sales tax bill	L	45,603	167,512	F
S	21-Jul-33	St	9	Oleomargarine tax bill	R	66,880	144,542	F
S	18-May-34	Am	1	County indebtedness and funding bond constitutional amendment	L	83,424	96,629	F
S	18-May-34	Am	2	Criminal trial without jury and non-unanimous verdict constitutional amendment	L	117,446	83,430	T
S	18-May-34	St	3	Bill authorizing a state tuberculosis hospital in Multnomah county	L	104,459	98,315	T
S	18-May-34	St	4	Bill authorizing a state insane hospital in Multnomah county	L	92,575	108,816	F
S	18-May-34	St	5	School relief sales tax bill	R	64,677	156,182	F
G	06-Nov-34	Am	1	Limitations of taxes on taxable property constitutional amendment	P	100,565	161,644	F
G	06-Nov-34	Am	2	Healing arts constitutional amendment	P	70,626	191,836	F
G	06-Nov-34	St	3	Grange power bill	R	124,518	139,283	F
S	31-Jan-36	Am	1	Compensation of members of the legislature constitutional amendment	L	28,661	184,332	F
S	31-Jan-36	St	2	Bill changing primary elections to September with other resulting changes	L	61,270	155,922	F

S	31-Jan-36	St	3	Sales tax bill	L	32,106	187,319	F
S	31-Jan-36	St	4	Bill authorizing student activity fees in state higher educational institutions	R	50,971	163,191	F
G	03-Nov-36	Am	1	Amendment forbidding prevention of regulation of certain advertising if truthful	P	100,141	222,897	F
G	03-Nov-36	Am	2	Tax limitation constitutional amendment for school districts having 100,000 population	P	112,546	203,693	F
G	03-Nov-36	Am	3	Amendment limiting and reducing permissible taxes on tangible property	P	79,604	241,042	F
G	03-Nov-36	Am	4	State hydroelectric temporary administrative board constitutional amendment	P	100,356	208,741	F
G	03-Nov-36	St	5	Bill amending old-age assistance act of 1935	R	174,293	179,236	F
G	03-Nov-36	St	6	Non-compulsory military training bill	P	131,917	214,246	F
G	03-Nov-36	St	7	State power bill	P	131,489	208,179	F
G	03-Nov-36	St	8	State bank bill	P	82,869	250,777	F
G	08-Nov-38	Am	1	Governor's 20-day bill consideration amendment	L	233,384	93,752	T
G	08-Nov-38	Am	2	Amendment repealing the double liability of stockholders in banking corporations	L	133,525	165,797	F
G	08-Nov-38	Am	3	Legislators' compensation constitutional amendment	L	149,356	169,131	F
G	08-Nov-38	Am	4	Constitutional amendment legalizing certain lotteries and other forms of gambling	P	141,792	180,329	F
G	08-Nov-38	St	5	Bill requiring marriage license applicants medically examined, physically and mentally	L	277,099	66,484	T
G	08-Nov-38	St	6	Townsend Plan bill	P	183,781	149,711	T
G	08-Nov-38	St	7	Citizens' retirement annuity bill: levying transactions tax to provide fund	P	112,172	219,557	F
G	08-Nov-38	St	8	Bill regulating picketing and boycotting by labor groups and organizations	P	197,771	148,460	T
G	08-Nov-38	St	9	Water purification and prevention of pollution bill	P	247,685	75,295	T
G	08-Nov-38	St	10	Bill regulating sale of alcoholic liquor for beverage purposes	P	118,282	222,221	F
G	08-Nov-38	St	11	Slot machine seizure by sheriffs and destruction on court order	R	204,561	126,580	T
G	08-Nov-38	St	12	Prohibiting slot machines, pinball, dart, and other similar games	R	197,912	129,043	T
G	05-Nov-40	Am	1	Amendment removing office time limit of state secretary and treasurer	L	163,942	213,797	F

G	05-Nov-40	Am	2	Amendment making three years average people's voted levies, tax base	L	129,699	183,488	F
G	05-Nov-40	Am	3	Amendment repealing the double liability of stockholders of state banks	L	157,891	191,290	F
G	05-Nov-40	Am	4	Legislators' compensation constitutional amendment	L	186,830	188,031	F
G	05-Nov-40	Am	5	Amendment legalizing certain gambling and game devices and certain lotteries	P	150,157	258,010	F
G	05-Nov-40	St	6	Bill changing the primary nominating elections from May to September	R	156,421	221,203	F
G	05-Nov-40	St	7	Bill to further regulate sale and use of alcoholic liquor	R	158,004	235,128	F
G	05-Nov-40	St	8	Bill repealing present liquor law; authorizing private sale, licensed, taxed	P	90,681	309,183	F
G	05-Nov-40	St	9	Bill to repeal the Oregon milk control law	P	201,983	213,838	F
G	03-Nov-42	Am	1	Legislators' compensation constitutional amendment	L	129,318	109,898	T
G	03-Nov-42	Am	2	Rural credit loan fund repeal amendment	L	101,425	88,857	T
G	03-Nov-42	Am	3	Amendment specifying exclusive uses of gasoline and motor vehicle taxes	L	125,990	86,332	T
G	03-Nov-42	Am	4	Amendment authorizing regulation by law of voting privilege forfeiture	L	101,508	103,404	F
G	03-Nov-42	St	5	Cigarette tax bill	R	110,643	127,366	F
G	03-Nov-42	St	6	Bill restricting and prohibiting net fishing coastal streams and bays	R	97,212	137,177	F
G	03-Nov-42	St	7	Bill distributing surplus funds to school districts, reducing taxes therein	P	136,321	92,623	F
G	07-Nov-44	Am	1	Amendment to provide alternative means for securing bank depositors	L	228,744	115,745	T
G	07-Nov-44	Am	2	Amendment authorizing change to managerial form of county government	L	175,716	154,504	T
G	07-Nov-44	Am	3	Amendment authorizing "Oregon War Veterans' Fund", providing tax therefor	L	190,520	178,581	T
G	07-Nov-44	Am	4	Amendment to authorize legislative regulation of voting privilege forfeiture	L	183,855	156,219	T
G	07-Nov-44	Am	5	Constitutional amendment increasing state tax fund for public school support	P	177,153	186,976	F
G	07-Nov-44	Am	6	Constitutional amendment providing monthly annuities from a gross income tax	P	180,691	219,981	F

G	07-Nov-44	St	7	Bill providing educational aid to certain veterans World War II	L	238,350	135,317	T
G	07-Nov-44	St	8	Bill imposing tax on retail sales of tangible personal property	L	98,697	269,276	F
G	07-Nov-44	St	9	Burke Bill; only state selling liquor over 14 hundredths alcohol	R	228,853	180,158	T
S	22-Jun-45	St	1	Bill authorizing tax levy for state building fund	L	78,269	49,565	T
S	22-Jun-45	St	2	Bill authorizing cigarette tax to support public schools	L	60,321	67,542	F
G	05-Nov-46	Am	1	Providing for succession to office of governor	L	221,547	70,322	T
G	05-Nov-46	Am	2	Authorizing Chinamen to hold real estate and claims	L	161,865	133,111	T
G	05-Nov-46	Am	3	Permitting legislative bills to be read by title only	L	145,248	113,279	T
G	05-Nov-46	Am	4	Increasing number of senators to thirty-one	L	88,717	185,247	F
G	05-Nov-46	St	5	Authorizing tax for construction and equipment of state armories	L	75,693	219,006	F
G	05-Nov-46	St	6	Establishing rural school districts and school boards	L	155,733	134,673	T
G	05-Nov-46	St	7	Regulating fishing in coastal streams and island waters	R	196,195	101,398	T
G	05-Nov-46	St	8	To create state old-age and disability pension fund	P	86,374	244,960	F
G	05-Nov-46	St	9	To create basic school support fund by annual tax levy	P	157,904	151,765	T
S	07-Oct-47	St	1	Taxing retail sales for school, welfare, and governmental purposes	L	67,514	180,333	F
S	07-Oct-47	St	2	Cigarette tax bill	R	103,794	140,876	F
G	02-Nov-48	Am	1	Six percent tax limitation	L	150,032	268,155	F
G	02-Nov-48	Am	2	Authorizing indebtedness for state reforestation	L	211,192	209,317	T
G	02-Nov-48	Am	3	Fixing qualifications of voters in school elections	P	284,776	164,025	T
G	02-Nov-48	Am	4	World War II veterans' bonus	P	198,283	265,805	F
G	02-Nov-48	St	5	Authorizing state boys' camp near Timber, Oregon	L	227,638	219,196	T
G	02-Nov-48	St	6	Amending licensing and acquisition provisions of hydroelectric commission act	R	173,004	242,100	F
G	02-Nov-48	St	7	Oregon old age pension act	P	313,212	172,531	T
G	02-Nov-48	St	8	Increasing personal income tax exemptions	P	405,842	63,373	T
G	02-Nov-48	St	9	Oregon liquor dispensing licensing act	P	210,108	273,621	F
G	02-Nov-48	St	10	Prohibiting salmon fishing in Columbia river with fixed appliances	P	273,140	184,834	T

G	02-Nov-48	St	11	Question of authorizing additional state tax, to be offset by income tax funds (statutory referendum)	R	143,856	256,167	F
G	07-Nov-50	Am	1	Fixing legislators' annual compensation	L	243,518	205,361	T
G	07-Nov-50	Am	2	Lending state tax credit for higher education buildings	L	256,895	192,573	T
G	07-Nov-50	Am	3	Augmenting "Oregon War Veterans' fund"	L	268,171	183,724	T
G	07-Nov-50	Am	4	World War II veterans' compensation fund	P	239,553	216,958	T
G	07-Nov-50	Am	5	Legislative representation reapportionment	P	190,992	215,302	F
G	07-Nov-50	St	6	Increasing basic school support fund by annual tax levy	L	234,394	231,856	T
G	07-Nov-50	St	7	Needy aged persons public assistance act	R	310,143	158,939	T
G	07-Nov-50	St	8	Providing uniform standard time in Oregon	R	277,633	195,319	T
G	07-Nov-50	St	9	Making sale of promotively advertised alcoholic beverage unlawful	P	113,524	378,732	F
G	04-Nov-52	Am	1	Appointing superintendent of public instruction	L	282,882	326,199	F
G	04-Nov-52	Am	2	War I veterans' state aid sinking fund repeal	L	454,896	147,128	T
G	04-Nov-52	Am	3	Voters establishing new tax base	L	355,136	210,373	T
G	04-Nov-52	Am	4	Extending loan eligibility to Korean War Veterans	L	465,605	132,363	T
G	04-Nov-52	Am	5	Legalizing state emergency board	L	364,539	194,492	T
G	04-Nov-52	Am	6	Amendatory act titles	L	315,071	191,087	T
G	04-Nov-52	Am	7	Fixing terms of state legislators	L	483,356	103,357	T
G	04-Nov-52	Am	8	Liquor by the drink sales	P	369,127	285,446	T
G	04-Nov-52	Am	9	Pari-mutuel betting prohibition	P	230,097	411,884	F
G	04-Nov-52	Am	10	Motor carrier tax decrease	P	135,468	484,730	F
G	04-Nov-52	Am	11	Legislative reapportionment	P	357,550	194,292	T
G	04-Nov-52	Am	12	Domiciliary hospital for aged mentally ill	L	480,479	153,402	T
G	04-Nov-52	Am	13	Six mill state property tax limitation	L	318,948	272,145	T
G	04-Nov-52	Am	14	Motor carrier tax increase referendum	R	409,588	230,241	T
G	04-Nov-52	Am	15	School district reorganization	R	295,700	301,974	F
G	04-Nov-52	Am	16	Cigarette tax	R	233,226	413,137	F
G	04-Nov-52	Am	17	Standard time initiative	P	399,981	256,981	T
G	04-Nov-52	Am	18	Milk control bill	P	313,629	337,750	F
G	02-Nov-54	Am	1	Salaries of state legislators	L	216,545	296,008	F
G	02-Nov-54	Am	2	Subdividing counties for electing state legislators	L	268,337	208,077	T

G	02-Nov-54	Am	3	Constitutional amendments --How proposed by people	L	251,078	230,770	T
G	02-Nov-54	Am	4	State property tax	L	208,419	264,569	F
G	02-Nov-54	St	5	Mental hospital in or near Portland	L	397,625	128,685	T
G	02-Nov-54	St	6	Establishing daylight saving time	P	252,305	300,007	F
G	02-Nov-54	St	7	Prohibiting certain fishing in coastal streams	P	232,775	278,805	F
G	02-Nov-54	St	8	Repealing milk control law	P	293,745	247,591	T
G	06-Nov-56	Am	1	Authorizing state acceptance of certain gifts	L	498,633	153,033	T
G	06-Nov-56	Am	2	Salaries of certain state officers	L	390,338	263,155	T
G	06-Nov-56	Am	3	Qualifications for county coroner and surveyor	L	455,485	182,550	T
G	06-Nov-56	Am	4	State tax laws --immediate effect authorized	L	175,932	487,550	F
G	06-Nov-56	Am	5	Salaries of state legislators	L	320,741	338,365	F
G	06-Nov-56	St	6	Cigarette tax	R	280,055	414,613	F
G	06-Nov-56	St	7	Prohibiting certain fishing in coastal streams	P	401,882	259,309	T
G	04-Nov-58	Am	1	Fixing state boundaries	L	399,396	114,318	T
G	04-Nov-58	Am	2	Increasing funds for war veterans' loans	L	232,246	318,685	F
G	04-Nov-58	Am	3	Salaries of state legislators	L	236,000	316,437	F
G	04-Nov-58	Am	4	Capital punishment bill	L	264,434	276,487	F
G	04-Nov-58	Am	5	Financing urban redevelopment projects	L	221,330	268,716	F
G	04-Nov-58	Am	6	Modifying county debt limitation	L	252,347	224,426	T
G	04-Nov-58	Am	7	Special grand jury bill	L	357,792	136,745	T
G	04-Nov-58	Am	8	Authorizing different use of state institutions	L	303,282	193,177	T
G	04-Nov-58	Am	9	Temporary appointment and assignment of judges	L	373,466	125,898	T
G	04-Nov-58	Am	10	State power development	L	218,662	291,210	F
G	04-Nov-58	Am	11	County home rule amendment	L	311,516	157,023	T
G	04-Nov-58	Am	12	Authorizing discontinuing certain state tuberculosis hospitals	L	319,790	195,945	T
G	04-Nov-58	St	13	Persons eligible to serve in legislature	P	320,751	201,700	T
P	20-May-60	St	1	Salaries of state legislators	L	250,456	281,542	F
G	08-Nov-60	Am	1	Fixing commencement of legislators term	L	579,022	92,187	T
G	08-Nov-60	Am	2	Financing urban redevelopment projects	L	335,792	312,187	T
G	08-Nov-60	Am	3	Permitting prosecution by information or indictment	L	306,190	340,197	F
G	08-Nov-60	Am	4	Authorizing legislature to propose revised constitution	L	358,367	289,895	T

G	08-Nov-60	Am	5	State bonds for higher education facilities	L	467,557	233,759	T
G	08-Nov-60	Am	6	Voter qualification amendment	L	508,108	183,977	T
G	08-Nov-60	Am	7	Authorizing bonds for state building program	L	232,250	433,515	F
G	08-Nov-60	Am	8	Compulsory retirement for judges	L	578,471	123,283	T
G	08-Nov-60	Am	9	Elective office when to become vacant	L	486,019	169,865	T
G	08-Nov-60	Am	10	Financing improvements in home rule counties	L	399,210	222,736	T
G	08-Nov-60	Am	11	Continuity of government in enemy attack	L	578,266	88,995	T
G	08-Nov-60	Am	12	War veterans bonding and loan amendment	L	415,931	266,630	T
G	08-Nov-60	St	13	Daylight savings time	L	357,499	393,652	F
G	08-Nov-60	St	14	Personal income tax bill	R	115,610	570,025	F
G	08-Nov-60	St	15	Billboard control	P	261,735	475,290	F
P	18-May-62	Am	1	Six percent limitation amendment	L	141,728	262,140	F
P	18-May-62	Am	2	Salaries of state legislators	L	241,171	178,749	T
G	06-Nov-62	Am	1	Reorganize state militia	L	312,680	234,440	T
G	06-Nov-62	Am	2	Forest rehabilitation debt limit amendment	L	323,799	199,174	T
G	06-Nov-62	Am	3	Permanent road debt limit amendment	L	319,956	200,236	T
G	06-Nov-62	Am	4	Power development debt limit amendment	L	298,255	208,755	T
G	06-Nov-62	Am	5	State courts: creation and jurisdiction	L	307,885	193,487	T
G	06-Nov-62	Am	6	Constitutional six per cent limitation amendment	L	270,637	219,509	T
G	06-Nov-62	Am	7	Legislative apportionment constitutional amendment	P	197,322	325,182	F
G	06-Nov-62	St	8	Repeals school district reorganization law	P	206,540	320,917	F
G	06-Nov-62	St	9	Daylight saving time	L	388,154	229,661	T
S	15-Oct-63	St	1	Personal and Corporation Income tax bill	R	103,737	362,845	F
G	03-Nov-64	Am	1	Capital punishment bill	L	455,654	302,105	T
G	03-Nov-64	Am	2	Leasing property for state use	L	447,031	238,241	T
G	03-Nov-64	St	3	Amending State workmen's compensation law	P	205,182	549,414	F
G	03-Nov-64	St	4	Prohibiting commercial fishing for salmon, steelhead	P	221,797	534,731	F
P	15-May-64	Am	1	Authorizing bonds for education building program	L	327,220	252,372	T
P	24-May-66	St	1	Cigarette Tax Bill	L	310,743	181,957	T
P	24-May-66	Am	2	Superintendent of Public Instruction Constitutional Amendment	L	197,096	267,319	F

G	08-Nov-66	Am	1	Public Transportation System Employees Constitutional Amendment	L	468,103	123,964	T
G	08-Nov-66	Am	2	State Bonds for Educational Facilities	L	237,282	332,983	F
P	28-May-68	Am	1	Common school fund constitutional amendment	L	372,915	226,191	T
P	28-May-68	Am	2	Constitutional amendment changing initiative --referendum requirements	L	321,731	244,750	T
G	05-Nov-68	Am	1	Constitutional amendment broadening veterans loan eligibility	L	651,250	96,065	T
G	05-Nov-68	Am	2	Constitutional amendment for removal of judges	L	690,989	56,973	T
G	05-Nov-68	Am	3	Empowering legislature to extend ocean boundaries	L	588,166	143,768	T
G	05-Nov-68	Am	4	Constitutional amendment broadening county debt limitations	L	331,617	348,866	F
G	05-Nov-68	Am	5	Government consolidation city-county over 300,000	L	393,789	278,483	T
G	05-Nov-68	Am	6	Bond issue to acquire ocean beaches	P	315,175	464,140	F
G	05-Nov-68	Am	7	Constitutional amendment changing property tax limitation	P	276,451	503,443	F
S	03-Jun-69	Am	1	Property tax relief and sales tax	L	65,077	504,274	F
P	26-May-70	Am	1	Capital construction bonds for state government	L	190,257	300,126	F
P	26-May-70	Am	2	Repeals "White Foreigner" section of constitution	L	326,374	168,464	T
P	26-May-70	Am	3	Revised constitution for Oregon	L	182,074	322,682	F
P	26-May-70	Am	4	Pollution control bonds	L	292,234	213,835	T
P	26-May-70	Am	5	Lowers Oregon voting age to 19	L	202,018	336,527	F
P	26-May-70	Am	6	Local school property tax equalization measure	L	180,602	323,189	F
G	03-Nov-70	Am	1	Constitutional amendment concerning convening of legislature	L	261,428	340,104	F
G	03-Nov-70	Am	2	Automatic adoption, federal income tax amendments	L	337,976	269,467	T
G	03-Nov-70	Am	3	Constitutional amendment concerning county debt limitation	L	283,659	294,186	F
G	03-Nov-70	Am	4	Investing funds donated to higher education	L	332,188	268,588	T
G	03-Nov-70	Am	5	Veterans' loan amendment	L	481,031	133,564	T
G	03-Nov-70	Am	6	Limits term of defeated incumbents	L	436,897	158,409	T
G	03-Nov-70	Am	7	Constitutional amendment authorizing education bonds	L	269,372	318,651	F
G	03-Nov-70	St	8	Allows penal institutions anywhere in Oregon	L	352,771	260,100	T
G	03-Nov-70	St	9	Scenic Waterways Bill	P	406,315	214,243	T
G	03-Nov-70	Am	10	New property tax bases for schools	P	223,735	405,437	F
G	03-Nov-70	Am	11	Restricts governmental powers over rural property	P	272,765	342,503	F

S	18-Jan-72	St	1	Increases Cigarette Tax	R	245,717	236,937	T
P	23-May-72	Am	1	Eliminates literacy requirement; lowers voting age	L	327,231	349,746	F
P	23-May-72	Am	2	Repeals requirement for decennial state census	L	420,568	206,436	T
P	23-May-72	Am	3	Allows legislators to call special sessions	L	241,371	391,698	F
P	23-May-72	Am	4	Capital construction bonds for state government	L	232,391	364,323	F
P	23-May-72	Am	5	Irrigation and water development bonds	L	233,175	374,295	F
P	23-May-72	St	6	Enabling city-county vehicle regulation tax	R	120,027	491,551	F
G	07-Nov-72	Am	1	Eliminates location requirements for state institutions	L	594,080	232,948	T
G	07-Nov-72	Am	2	Qualifications for Sheriff set by legislature	L	572,619	281,720	T
G	07-Nov-72	Am	3	Amends county purchase and lease limitations	L	329,669	462,932	F
G	07-Nov-72	Am	4	Changes state constitution provision regarding religion	L	336,382	519,196	F
G	07-Nov-72	Am	5	Authorizes legislature to provide by law juries consisting of less than twelve members	L	591,191	265,636	T
G	07-Nov-72	Am	6	Broadens eligibility for Veterans' loans	L	736,802	133,139	T
G	07-Nov-72	St	7	Repeals Governor's Retirement Act	P	571,959	292,561	T
G	07-Nov-72	Am	8	Changes succession to Office of Governor	P	697,297	151,171	T
G	07-Nov-72	Am	9	Prohibits property tax for school operations	P	342,885	558,136	F
S	01-May-73	St	1	Property tax limitation; school tax revision	L	253,682	358,219	F
P	28-May-74	St	1	Income, corporate tax, school support increase	L	136,851	410,733	F
P	28-May-74	Am	2	Highway fund use for mass transit	L	190,899	369,038	F
P	28-May-74	Am	3	New school district tax base limitation	L	166,363	371,897	F
P	28-May-74	Am	4	Authorizes bonds for water development fund	L	198,563	328,221	F
P	28-May-74	Am	5	Increases Veterans' loan bonding authority	L	381,559	164,953	T
P	28-May-74	Am	6	Permits legislature to call special sessions	L	246,525	298,373	F
G	05-Nov-74	Am	1	Liquor licenses for public passenger carriers	L	353,357	384,521	F
G	05-Nov-74	Am	2	Opens all legislative deliberations to public	L	546,255	165,778	T
G	05-Nov-74	Am	3	Revises constitutional requirements for grand juries	L	437,557	246,902	T

G	05-Nov-74	Am	4	Governor vacancy successor age requirement eliminated	L	381,593	331,756	T
G	05-Nov-74	Am	6	Permits establishing qualifications for county assessors	L	552,737	146,364	T
G	07-Nov-74	Am	7	Tax base includes revenue sharing money	L	322,023	329,858	F
G	05-Nov-74	Am	9	Permits state employers to be legislators	L	218,846	476,547	F
G	05-Nov-74	Am	10	Revises Oregon voter qualifications requirements	L	362,731	355,506	T
G	05-Nov-74	Am	11	Right to jury in civil cases	L	480,631	216,853	T
G	05-Nov-74	Am	12	Community development fund bonds	L	277,723	376,747	F
G	05-Nov-74	St	13	Obscenity and sexual conduct bill	R	393,743	352,958	T
G	05-Nov-74	St	14	Public officials' financial ethics and reporting	L	498,002	177,946	T
G	05-Nov-74	St	15	Prohibits purchasing or sale of steelhead	P	458,417	274,182	T
P	25-May-76	Am	1	Expands Veterans' home-farm loan eligibility	L	549,553	158,997	T
P	25-May-76	Am	2	Discipline of judges	L	639,977	59,774	T
P	25-May-76	Am	3	Housing bonds	L	315,588	362,414	F
P	25-May-76	Am	4	Authorizes vehicle tax mass transit use	L	170,331	531,219	F
G	02-Nov-76	Am	1	Validates inadvertently superseded statutory amendments	L	607,325	247,843	T
G	02-Nov-76	Am	2	Allows changing city, county election days	L	376,489	536,967	F
G	02-Nov-76	Am	3	Lowers minimum age for legislative service	L	285,777	679,517	F
G	02-Nov-76	Am	4	Repeals emergency succession provision	L	507,308	368,646	T
G	02-Nov-76	St	5	Permits legislature to call special session	L	549,126	377,354	T
G	02-Nov-76	Am	6	Allows charitable, fraternal, religious organizations bingo	L	682,252	281,696	T
G	02-Nov-76	St	7	Partial public funding of election campaigns	L	263,738	659,327	F
G	02-Nov-76	St	8	Increase motor fuel, ton-mile taxes	R	465,143	505,124	F
G	02-Nov-76	St	9	Regulates nuclear power plant construction approval	P	423,008	584,845	F
G	02-Nov-76	St	10	Repeals land use planning coordination statues	P	402,608	536,502	F
G	02-Nov-76	St	11	Prohibits adding fluorides to water systems	P	419,567	555,981	F
G	02-Nov-76	St	12	Repeals intergovernmental cooperation, planning district Statues	P	333,933	525,868	F
S	17-May-77	Am	1	School operating levy measure	L	112,570	252,061	F
S	17-May-77	Am	2	Authorizes additional Veterans' fund uses	L	200,270	158,436	T

S	17-May-77	Am	3	Increases Veterans' loan bonding authority	L	250,783	106,953	T
S	08-Nov-77	Am	1	Water development loan fund created	L	124,484	118,953	T
S	08-Nov-77	Am	2	Development of non-nuclear natural energy resources	L	105,219	137,693	F
P	23-May-78	Am	1	Home rule county initiative-referendum requirements	L	306,506	156,623	T
P	23-May-78	Am	2	Open meetings rules for legislature	L	435,338	80,176	T
P	23-May-78	Am	3	Housing for low income elderly	L	291,788	250,810	T
P	23-May-78	Am	4	Domestic water fund created	L	148,822	351,843	F
P	23-May-78	St	5	Highway repair priority, gas tax increase	L	190,301	365,170	F
P	23-May-78	St	6	Reorganizes metropolitan service district, abolishes CRAG	L	110,600	91,090	T
G	07-Nov-78	Am	1	Appellate judge selection, running on record	L	358,504	449,132	F
G	07-Nov-78	Am	2	Authorizes senate confirmation of Governor's appointments	L	468,458	349,604	T
G	07-Nov-78	St	3	Vehicle and fee increase referendum	R	208,722	673,802	F
G	07-Nov-78	St	4	Shortens formation procedures for people's utility districts	P	375,578	471,027	F
G	07-Nov-78	St	5	Authorizes, regulates practice of denture technology	P	704,480	201,463	T
G	07-Nov-78	Am	6	Limitations on ad valorem property taxes	P	424,029	453,741	F
G	07-Nov-78	St	7	Prohibits state expenditures, programs, or services for abortion	P	431,577	461,542	F
G	07-Nov-78	St	8	Requires death penalty for murder under specified conditions	P	573,707	318,610	T
G	07-Nov-78	St	9	Limitations on public utility rate base	P	589,361	267,132	T
G	07-Nov-78	Am	10	Land use planning, zoning constitutional amendment	P	334,523	515,138	F
G	07-Nov-78	Am	11	Reduces property tax payable by homeowner and renter	L	383,532	467,765	F
G	07-Nov-78	Advisory	12	State advisory question, federal balanced budget amendment	L	641,862	134,758	T
P	20-May-80	Am	1	Constitutional amendment limits uses of gasoline and highway user taxes	L	451,695	257,230	T
P	20-May-80	Am	2	Amends liquor by the drink	L	325,030	384,346	F
P	20-May-80	Am	3	State bonds for small scale local energy project loan fund	L	394,466	278,125	T
P	20-May-80	Am	4	Veterans' home and farm loan eligibility changes	L	574,148	130,452	T
P	20-May-80	St	5	Continues tax reduction program	L	636,565	64,979	T
P	20-May-80	Am	6	Definition of multifamily low income elderly housing	L	536,002	138,675	T
G	04-Nov-80	Am	1	Repeal of constitutional provision requiring elected superintendent of public instruction	L	291,142	820,892	F

G	04-Nov-80	Am	2	Guarantees mentally handicapped voting rights, unless adjudged incompetent to vote	L	678,573	455,020	T
G	04-Nov-80	Am	3	Dedicates oil, natural gas taxes to common school fund	L	594,520	500,586	T
G	04-Nov-80	St	4	Increases gas tax from seven to nine cents per gallon	L	298,421	849,745	F
G	04-Nov-80	St	5	Forbids use, sale of snare, leghold traps for most purposes	P	425,890	728,173	F
G	04-Nov-80	Am	6	Constitutional real property tax limit preserving 85% of districts' 1977 revenue	P	416,029	711,617	F
G	04-Nov-80	St	7	Nuclear plant licensing requires voter approval, waste disposal facility existence	P	608,412	535,049	T
G	04-Nov-80	Am	8	State bonds for fund to finance correctional facilities	L	523,955	551,383	F
P	18-May-82	Am	1	Use of state bond proceeds to finance municipal water projects	L	333,656	267,137	T
P	18-May-82	Am	2	Multifamily housing for elderly and disabled persons	L	389,820	229,049	T
P	18-May-82	Am	3	State bonds for fund to finance corrections facilities	L	281,548	333,476	F
P	18-May-82	St	4	Raises taxes on commercial vehicles, motor vehicles fuels for roads	L	308,574	323,268	F
P	18-May-82	St	5	Governor to appoint Chief Justice of Oregon Supreme Court	L	129,811	453,415	F
G	02-Nov-82	Am	1	Increases tax base when new property construction increases district's value	L	219,034	768,150	F
G	02-Nov-82	Am	2	Lengthens governor's time for post-session veto or approval of bills	L	385,672	604,864	F
G	02-Nov-82	Am	3	Constitutional real property tax limit preserving 85% districts' 1979 revenue	P	504,836	515,626	F
G	02-Nov-82	St	4	Permits self-service dispensing of motor vehicle fuel at retail	P	440,824	597,970	F
G	02-Nov-82	R	5	People of Oregon urge mutual freeze on nuclear weapons development	P	623,089	387,907	T
G	02-Nov-82	St	6	Ends State's land use planning powers, retains local planning"	P	461,271	565,056	F
P	15-May-84	Am	1	State may borrow and lend money for public works projects	L	332,175	365,571	F
P	15-May-84	St	2	Increase fee for licensing and registration of motor vehicles	L	234,060	487,457	F
G	06-Nov-84	Am	1	Changes minimum requirement for recall of public officers	L	664,464	470,139	T
G	06-Nov-84	Am	2	Constitutional real property tax limit	P	599,424	616,252	F
G	06-Nov-84	St	3	Creates citizens' utility board to represent interests of utility consumers	P	637,968	556,826	T

G	06-Nov-84	Am	4	Constitutional amendment establishes state Lottery, commission; profits for economic development	P	794,441	412,341	T
G	06-Nov-84	St	5	Statutory provisions for state operated lottery if constitutionally authorized	P	786,933	399,231	T
G	06-Nov-84	Am	6	Exempts death sentences from constitutional guarantees against cruel, vindictive punishments	P	653,009	521,687	T
G	06-Nov-84	Am	7	Requires by statute death or mandatory imprisonment for aggravated murder	P	893,818	295,988	T
G	06-Nov-84	St	8	Revises numerous criminal laws concerning police powers, trials, evidence, sentencing	P	552,410	597,964	F
G	06-Nov-84	St	9	Adds requirements for disposing wastes containing naturally occurring radioactive isotopes	P	655,973	524,214	T
S	17-Sep-85	Am	1	Approves limited 5% sales tax for local education.	L	189,733	664,365	F
P	20-May-86	Am	1	Bans income tax on social security benefits.	L	534,476	118,766	T
P	20-May-86	Am	2	Effect on merger of taxing units on tax base	L	333,277	230,886	T
P	20-May-86	Am	3	Verification of signatures on initiative and referendum petitions	L	460,148	132,101	T
P	20-May-86	Am	4	Requires special election for United States Senator vacancy, removes constitutional provision	L	343,005	269,305	T
P	20-May-86	Am	5	$96 million bonds for state-county prison buildings	L	300,674	330,429	F
G	04-Nov-86	Am	1	Deletes constitutional requirement that Secretary of State live in Salem.	L	771,959	265,999	T
G	04-Nov-86	Am	2	Revising legislative district reapportionment procedures after federal census	L	637,410	291,355	T
G	04-Nov-86	Am	3	Allows charitable, fraternal, religious organizations to conduct raffles	L	736,739	302,957	T
G	04-Nov-86	Am	4	Replaces public utility commissioner with three member public utility commission	L	724,577	297,973	T
G	04-Nov-86	St	5	Legalizes private possession and growing of marijuana for personal use	P	279,479	781,922	F
G	04-Nov-86	Am	6	Prohibits state funding abortions. Exception: prevents mother's death	P	477,920	580,163	F
G	04-Nov-86	Am	7	Constitutional 5% sales tax, funds schools, reduces property taxes	P	234,806	816,369	F
G	04-Nov-86	St	8	Prohibits mandatory local measured telephone service except mobile phone service	P	802,099	201,918	T

G	04-Nov-86	Am	9	Limits property tax rates and assessed value increases	P	449,548	584,396	F
G	04-Nov-86	St	10	Revises many criminal laws concerning victims' rights, evidence, sentencing, parole	P	774,766	251,509	T
G	04-Nov-86	St	11	Homeowners', renters' property tax relief program; sales tax limitation measure	P	381,727	639,034	F
G	04-Nov-86	St	12	State income tax changes, increased revenue to property tax relief	P	299,551	720,034	F
G	04-Nov-86	Am	13	Twenty day pre-election voter registration cutoff	P	693,460	343,450	T
G	04-Nov-86	St	14	Prohibits nuclear power plant operation until permanent waste site licensed	P	375,241	674,641	F
G	04-Nov-86	St	15	Supersedes "Radioactive Waste" definition: changes energy facility study payment procedure	P	424,099	558,741	F
G	04-Nov-86	St	16	Phases out nuclear weapons manufactured with tax credits, civil penalty	P	400,119	590,971	F
S	19-May-87	St	1	State role in selection of high-level nuclear waste repository site	L	299,581	100,854	T
S	19-May-87	St	2	Continues existing levies to prevent school closures: tax base elections	L	223,417	178,839	T
P	17-May-88	Am	1	Authorizes water development fund loans for fish protection, watershed restoration	L	485,629	191,008	T
P	17-May-88	Am	2	Protective headgear for motorcycle operators and passengers and moped riders	L	486,401	224,655	T
G	08-Nov-88	St	1	Extends governor's veto deadline after legislature adjourns; requires prior announcement	L	615,012	520,939	T
G	08-Nov-88	St	2	Common school fund investments; Using income for state lands management	L	621,894	510,694	T
G	08-Nov-88	St	3	Requires the use of safety belts	L	528,324	684,747	F
G	08-Nov-88	St	4	Requires full sentence without parole, probation for certain repeat felonies	P	947,805	252,985	T
G	08-Nov-88	St	5	Finances intercollegiate athletic fund by increasing malt beverage, cigarette taxes	P	449,797	759,360	F
G	08-Nov-88	St	6	Indoor clean air law revisions banning public smoking	P	480,147	737,779	F
G	08-Nov-88	St	7	Oregon scenic waterway system	P	663,604	516,998	T
G	08-Nov-88	St	8	Revokes ban on sexual orientation discrimination in State executive branch	P	626,751	561,355	T
S	16-May-89	Am	1	Establishes new tax base limits on schools	L	183,818	263,283	F

S	27-Jun-89	Am	1	Removes constitutional limitation on use of property forfeited to state	L	340,506	141,649	T
S	27-Jun-89	Am	2	Prohibits selling/exporting timber from State lands unless Oregon processed	L	446,151	48,558	T
P	15-May-90	Am	1	Permits using local vehicle taxes for transit if voters approve	L	294,099	324,458	F
P	15-May-90	Am	2	Allows pollution control bond use for related activities	L	352,922	248,123	T
P	15-May-90	Am	3	Requires annual legislative sessions of limited duration	L	294,664	299,831	F
P	15-May-90	Local	4	Amends laws on organization of international Port of Coos Bay	L	4,234	4,745	F
P	15-May-90	Advisory	5A	Changing the school finance system	L	462,090	140,747	T
P	15-May-90	Advisory	5B	Income tax increase reducing homeowner school property taxes	L	177,964	408,842	F
P	15-May-90	Advisory	5C	Income tax increase eliminating homeowner school property taxes	L	128,642	449,725	F
P	15-May-90	Advisory	5D	Sales tax reducing school property taxes	L	202,367	385,820	F
P	15-May-90	Advisory	5E	Sales tax eliminating school property taxes	L	222,611	374,466	F
G	06-Nov-90	Am	1	Grants Metropolitan Service District electors right to home rule	L	510,947	491,170	T
G	06-Nov-90	Am	2	Allows merged school districts to combine tax bases	L	680,463	354,288	T
G	06-Nov-90	St	3	Repeals tax exemption, grants additional benefit payments for PERS retirees	R	406,372	617,586	F
G	06-Nov-90	St	4	Prohibits Trojan operation until nuclear waste, cost, earthquake standards met	P	446,795	660,992	F
G	06-Nov-90	Am	5	State constitutional limit on property taxes for schools, government operations	P	574,833	522,022	T
G	06-Nov-90	St	6	Product packaging must meet recycling standards or receive hardship waiver	P	467,418	636,804	F
G	06-Nov-90	St	7	Six county work in lieu of welfare benefits pilot program	P	624,744	452,853	T
G	06-Nov-90	Am	8	Amends Oregon constitution to prohibit abortion with three exceptions	P	355,963	747,599	F
G	06-Nov-90	St	9	Requires the use of safety belts	P	598,460	512,872	T
G	06-Nov-90	St	10	Doctor must give parent notice before minor's abortion	P	530,851	577,806	F
G	06-Nov-90	Am	11	School choice system, tax credit for education outside public schools	P	351,977	741,863	F
G	03-Nov-92	Am	1	Bonds may be used for state parks	L	653,062	786,017	F
G	03-Nov-92	Am	2	Future fuel taxes may go to parks	L	399,259	1,039,322	F

G	03-Nov-92	Am	3	Limits terms for Legislative, Statewide Offices, Congressional Offices	I	1,003,706	439,694	T
G	03-Nov-92	St	4	Bans operation of triple-truck trailer combinations on Oregon highways	I	567,467	896,778	F
G	03-Nov-92	St	5	Closes Trojan until nuclear waste, cost, earthquake, health conditions met	I	585,051	874,636	F
G	03-Nov-92	St	6	Bans Trojan power operation unless earthquake, waste storage conditions Met	I	619,329	830,850	F
G	03-Nov-92	Am	7	Raises tax Limit on Certain property: renter tax relief	I	362,621	1,077,206	F
G	03-Nov-92	St	8	Restricts lower Columbia fish harvests to most selective means available	I	576,633	828,096	F
G	03-Nov-92	Am	9	Government Cannot facilitate, must discourage homosexuality, other "behaviors"	I	638,527	828,290	F
S	09-Nov-93	Am	1	Should we pass a %5 sales tax for public schools with these exemptions...	L	240,991	721,930	F
P	17-May-94	Am	1	Allows new motor vehicle fuel revenue for dedicated purposes	L	158,028	446,665	F

BIBLIOGRAPHY

Books, articles and other material:

"12-minute time-out." The Register-Guard, 12 January 1993, __.

"1993 Legislature gets off to unfortunate start." Statesman-Journal, 12 January 1993, __.

"A modern crusade." City and State, 19 July 1993, 1.

Abbott, Carl, Deborah Howe and Sy Adler, ed. Planning the Oregon Way -- A Twenty Year Evaluation. Corvallis: Oregon State University Press, 1994.

Abraham, Henry J. Justices & Presidents - A Political History of Appointments to the Supreme Court, 2nd Ed. New York: Oxford University Press, 1985.

_____. The Judicial Process, 5th Ed. New York: Oxford University Press, 1986.

"Accused convicted in 1961 slaying." Statesman, 23 April 1975, 34.

"America on ice." The Economist, 5 February 1994, 27.

"An Interview with Bernie Jolles." Oregon State Bar Bulletin, October 1986, __.

"Anti-gay-rights ballots abuse initiative system." Statesman-Journal, 20 June 1993, 10A.

Aristotle, The Politics of Aristotle, trans. Ernest Baker. New York: Oxford University Press, 1958.

Bates, Stephen. "Fundamentally Out of Fashion." The Washington Post, 7 September 1993, A17.

Beehan, Brian. "Future Bleak for higher education." The Oregonian, 30 May 1993, A18.

Beggs, Charles. "At Capitol, judgment still mixed on term-limits law." The Oregonian, 27 July 1993, B4.

_____. "Oregon Supreme Court disbars former judge." The Oregonian, 2 May 1992, B1.

Blankenbaker, Ron. "Budget process gains new look." Statesman-Journal, 17 March 1993, __.

_____. "Senate ends stalemate, elects leader." Statesman-Journal, 16 January 1993, 1C."

Bockelman, Joanne. 'The 45th Legislative Session." Unpublished paper, Portland State University, 1987.

Boller, Paul F. Presidential Campaigns. New York: Oxford, 1984.

Bourgin, Frank. The Great Challenge -- The Myth of Laissez-Faire in the Early Republic. New York: George Braziller, Inc., 1989.

"Bowles admits Hunter murders, get two life terms." The Oregonian, 13 November 1975, Sec A, 1.

Burns, James MacGregor. Leadership. New York: Harper and Row, 1978.

Burton, Robert E. Democrats Of Oregon: The Pattern of Minority Politics, 1900-1956, Eugene: University of Oregon Press, 1970.

Cain, Brad. "Campbell blocking rights measure." The Oregonian, 15 June 1993, B4.

"Candidates Urge Repeal of Capital Punishment." The Oregonian, 11 October 1964, sec.,1, 3.

Carey, Charles H. A General History of Oregon. Portland: Metropolitan Press, 1935, vol. 1.

"Case tests Oregon justice: Brudos belongs in prison." Statesman, 1 April 1989, Sec. A, 8.

"Checks go out after day's wait." Statesman Journal, 1 August 1993, D1.

"Choice Politics." The Wall Street Journal, 15 October 1993, A12.

"Choice Reality." The Wall Street Journal, 21 September 1993, A22.

Church, Foster. "Goldschmidt apologizes to Bend for his 'nowhere' remark." The Oregonian, 22 August 1986, C 12.

_____. "Lutz may have lost, but he is still primary's big story." The Oregonian, 25 May 1986, B3.

City Club of Portland. City Club Bulletin Vol 74 No. 51, Tax reform in Oregon. Portland: City Club of Portland, 1993.

City of Portland. Mayor's Proposed Budget-City of Portland-Fiscal Year 1993-1994.

"Cowardice in the House." The Oregonian, 20 June 1993, J2.

Crankshaw, Edward. Bismarck. New York: The Viking Press, 1981.

Danks, Holly. "Autopsy shows man hit by five shots." The Oregonian, 3 June 1993, C1, C3.

_____. "Moose pins on chief's stars." The Oregonian, 30 June 1993, B1, B5.

Dann, Robert H. "Abolition and Restoration of the Death Penalty in Oregon," in The Death Penalty in America, ed. Adam Bedau. Chicago: Aldine, 1964.

Davis, Janet. "Marquette Admits Slaying third women." Statesman, 4 June 1975, 1.

_____. "Retiring state judge appeals for respect." Statesman-Journal, 31 December 1992, 1C., 2C.

Dees , Morris and Steve Fiffer. Hate on Trial. New York: Villard, 1993.

"Defender says judge prejudiced." The Oregonian, 6 July 1977, A10.

Dodds, Gordon B. and Craig Wollner. The Silicon Forest. Portland: The Oregon Historical Society Press, 1990.

Duin, Steve. "A frightenly close call with Dr. Death." The Oregonian , 11 May 1993, B5.

_____. "Armageddon and the 'dead sea scrolls.'" The Oregonian, 30 M7 1993, B7;

_____. "They're all bozos on the same bus." The Oregonian, 18 May 1993, B9.

_____. "Why legislate when you can waste time?" The Oregonian, 14 January 1993, __.

Durden, Robert F. The Climax of Populism: the Election of 1896. Louisville: ____, 1966. Quoted in Paul Boller. Presidential Campaigns. New York: Oxford, 1984 .

Eaton, Allan H. The Oregon System - -The Story of Direct Legislation in Oregon. Chicago: A.C. McClurg & Co., 1912.

Edsall, Thomas. "Buchanan Warns GOP Of Schism on Abortion --Christians Told Not to Abandon 'Culture War.'" The Washington Post, 12 September 1993, A8.

Egan, Timothy. "150 Years Later, Indians Cope With Bitter Results of White's Arrival." The New York Times, 1 June 1993, A11.

_____. "Eastward Ho! The Great Move Reverses - Forsaken Frontier." The New York Times, 30 May 1993, 1, 12.

_____. "Voters in Oregon Back Local Anti-Gay Rules." The New York Times, 1 July 1993, A6.

"Ex-lobbyist relates car, home dealings involving Groener." The Oregonian, 29 March 1981, A1.

"Field becomes district judge." The Oregonian, 15 July 1972, C3.

"French and Indian Word Wars." New York Times, 15 March 1992, A-16.

Friedman, Lawrence M. History of American Law, 2nd Ed. New York: Touchstone, 1985.

Galvani, William H. "Reflections of J.F. Stevens and J.H. Mitchell." Oregon Historical Quarterly, LVII, no. 3 (September, 1943), 320-321.

Gardner, James. "The Competitive Advantage of Cascadia." The New Pacific, Winter 1992/1993, 12-13.

Godley, Elizabeth. "View from the edge." The New Pacific, Issue # 9, 12-15.

Goodwyn, Lawrence. Democratic Promise - The Populist Moment in America. New York: Oxford University Press, 1976.

_____. The Populist Moment - A Short History of the Agarian Revolt in America. New York: Oxford University Press, 1978.

Gordon, Diana R. The Justice Juggernaut. New Brunswick: Rutgers University Press, 1990.

Gould, Steven J. "Leadership vacuum will sink state." The Oregonian, 19 May 1993, B11.

Hallman, Tom. "Harrington: I had to start a new life." The Oregonian, 2 May 1993, D1, D6.

Hamburg, Ken. "Forecast." The Oregonian, 2 May 1993, K-1

Hamilton, Don and Alan Ota. "Oregon Remains in basement for military spending." The Oregonian, 27 June 1993, A18.

Hardeman, D.B. and Donald C. Bacon. Rayburn - A Biography. Austin: Texas Monthly Press, 1987.

Haynes, Dana. "Cornelius: newest name in gay-rights battle." The Oregonian, 20 May 1993, A20.

Haynes, Richard W. An analysis of the timber situation in the United States 1989 -2040, Gen. Tech. Rep. RM-199. Ft. Collins, CO: U.S. Department of Agriculture, Forest Service, Rocky Mountain Forest and range Experiment Station, 1990.

Hill, Gail Kinsey. "Activist, legislator clash publicly over tax." The Oregonian, 21 October 1993, E1, E9.

_____. "House OKs big school funding cut." The Oregonian, 5 March 1993, A1, A22.

_____. "It's Salem's lot: The winners - the losers & the snoozers." The Oregonian 16 May 1993, B6.

_____. "Johnson may face reprimand in Senate." The Oregonian, 23 June 1993, C1, C4.

_____. "Lawmaker accused of sexual harassment." The Oregonian, 26 March 1993, C4.

_____. "Legislature sets out on hard road to accord." The Oregonian, 12 January 1993, A1, A10.

_____. "Now its up to you." The Oregonian 4 August 1993, A1, A12.

_____. "Harassment panelist tries to quit." The Oregonian, 10 April 1993, D3.

Hogan, Dave. "Judge admits forgery, bigamy - Robert L. Kirkman says he should be left on his job because his trouble didn't affect his rulings." The Oregonian, 15 September 1990, A1.

_____. "Oregonians appointed to top-level legal posts." The Oregonian, 20, November 1993, D1, D8.

Holmes, Oliver Wendell Jr. The Common Law. Boston: Little Brown, 1881.

Horner, John B. Oregon. Corvallis: Press of the Gazette Times, 1919.

Hortsch, Dan. "Del Parks to plan gay-rights session." The Oregonian, 27 June 1993, D4.

_____. "Emotions run high in race for District 11 House seat." The Oregonian, 21 October 1992, B4.

_____. "Gay-rights hearing passionate but civil." The Oregonian, 30 June 1993, B9.

_____. "House Approves truce on gay rights." The Oregonian, 7 July 1993, A1, A11.

_____. "Metzger loses Oregon Appeal." The Oregonian, 18 November 1993, D5.

_____. "Partisan politics commands the stage." The Oregonian, 25 July 1993, C4

Hosticka, Carl. "Financial Provisions of the Oregon Constitution." Oregon Law Review, 67 (1988): 116.

"Initiative Primer." The Oregonian, 2 October 1993, A11.

Johnson. Dirk. "Colorado's Anti-Gay Measure Set Back." The New York Times, 20 July 1993, A6.

Kantor, Stephen. "Brief Against Death." 17 Willamette Law Review 629(1981).

Keisling, Phil. "Big Bucks for Small Offices." The New York Times, 16 February 1993, __.

Kendrick. "The Initiative and Referendum and How Oregon Got Them." McClures, July, 1911, 234-48 in Thompson, Cecil T. The Origin of Direct Legislation in Oregon. Master's thesis, University of Oregon, 1929. 16.

Kesey, Ken. Sometimes a Great Notion. New York: Penguin, 1964.

"Kidnapping Assault Charged to Bowles." The Oregonian, 18 June 1975, 2.

Kinney, Terry. "Gay-rights issues hot across U.S.." The Oregonian, 15 October 1993, A20.

Kiyomura, Cathy and Hortsch, Dan. "Legislators tackle gay rights, sales tax." The Oregonian, 1 July 1993, A1, A15.

Kiyomura, Cathy. "Long walk on the low road." The Oregonian, 23 July 1993, C8.

_____. "Session ends: politics linger." The Oregonian, 6 August 1993, A1, A17.

_____. "House bill to protect gays may do opposite." The Oregonian, 4 July 1993, E6.

_____. "House will hold hearings on gay-rights bill." The Oregonian, 24 June 1993, A1, A20.

_____. "Quake hazards shift legislators." The Oregonian, 31 March 1983, A1, A14.

Koenig, Louis. Bryan - A Political biography of William Jennings Bryan. New York: G.P. Putnam Son, 1971, 197.

Kosmin, Barry A. and Seymour P. Lachman. One Nation Under God, New York: Harmony Books, 1993; cited in Kenneth L. Woodward. "The Rites of Americans." Newsweek, 29 November 1993, 80-82.

Lang, William L. "Creating the Columbia: Historians and the Great River of the West." <u>Oregon Historical Quarterly</u> , 93 (Fall 1992), 237.

LaPalombara, Joseph G. <u>The Initiative and Referendum in Oregon: 1938-1948</u>, Corvallis, Oregon: Oregon State College Monograph, 1950.

Leeson, Fred. "Bored county judge says he's returning to private practice." <u>The Oregonian</u>, 7 July 1993, B-4.

_____. "Kirkman to resign Multnomah County Judgeship." <u>The Oregonian</u>, 4 January 1991, A1.

_____. "Police pressure fails to sway judge's sentence." <u>The Oregonian</u>, 16 June 1993, D2.

_____. "Public service takes a new direction." <u>The Oregonian</u>, 30 November 1993, B-5.

_____. "The other Supreme Court." <u>The Oregonian,</u> 27 June 1993, B1, B4.

"Legislator Pleads Guilty in Sex Abuse." <u>The Oregonian</u>, 13 October 1987, B2.

Lent, John A. <u>Newhouse, Newspapers, Nuisances</u>. New York: Exposition Press, 1966.

Linde, Hans A. "When Initiative Lawmaking Is Not 'Republican Government: The Campaign Against Homosexuality." <u>Oregon Law Review</u>, Vol. 72 (1993) 20.

Lindsay, Vachel. <u>Collected Poems</u>, New York: Macmillan, ___.

Lindstrom, Carl. <u>The Fading American Newspaper</u>, New York: Doubleday, 1960.

Long, James. "Of Grants and geed." <u>The Oregonian,</u> 23 may 1993, A1, A16-17.

Lowenstein, Steven. <u>The Jews of Oregon 1850 - 1950</u>. Portland: Jewish Historical Society of Oregon, 1987.

MacColl, E. Kimbark. <u>The Growth of a City - Power and Politics in Portland, Oregon 1915 to 1950</u>. Portland: Georgian Press, 1979.

MacKenzie, Bill. "Campaign funds make nice nest egg." <u>The Oregonian</u>, 4 September 1993, B1, B4.

_____. "Lobbyists' cry: 'Give me a (tax) break." <u>The Oregonian</u>, 19 May 1993, B4.

Mapes, Jeff. "Compromise bill on gays may bring confusion." <u>The Oregonian</u>, 8 July 1993, B1.

_____. "East County voters recall Rep. Gillis." <u>The Oregonian</u>, 27 March 1985, B1.

_____. "GOP chief won't lead OCA fight." <u>The Oregonian</u>, 7 May 1993, C6.

_____. "House seats Gillis, approves censure." <u>The Oregonian</u>, 19 January 1988, C1.

_____. "Jury Clears Gillis of Lying in Voters' Pamphlet." <u>The Oregonian</u>, 30 May 1985, A1.

_____. "Measure 1 is like a crystal ball." <u>The Oregonian</u>, 31 October 1993, E3.

_____. "OCA creates activists." <u>The Oregonian</u>, 22 June 1993, B12.

_____. "Signatures filed seeking recall of Gillis." <u>The Oregonian</u>, 5 March 1985, A1.

_____. "Turns, twists of Gillis story enliven Oregon politics." <u>The Oregonian</u>, 24 March 1985, B4.

_____. "Upfront-Verbatim-Drug Wars." <u>The Oregonian</u> , 22 March 1993, B-1.

Mason, Paul. <u>Mason's Manual of Legislative Procedure</u>. St. Paul: West Publishing Co. 1989.

Mason, Thomas L. "A Conversation with the Master." Oregon State Bar Bulletin, October, 1985.

_____. "Partisan Voting in the Oregon Legislature." Master's thesis. Portland State University, 1973.

McCall, Tom and Steve Neal. Tom McCall: Maverick, Portland: Binford & Mort, 1977, 190.

McCarthy, Nancy. "Charter provision aside, Collier conducts campaign." The Oregonian, May 7, 1993, C-2.

McFetridge, Scott. "Governor stumps some legislators." Statesman-Journal, 12 January 1993, 2C.

McLagagan, Elizabeth. A Peculiar Paradise. Portland: The Georgian Press, 1980, 116.

Meador, Daniel. American courts, St. Paul, Minn.: West Publishing, 1991, 19.

Morgan, Kenneth O. Ed. The Oxford History of Britain. New York: Oxford University Press, 1988, 172.

Morrison, Samuel Elliot. The Oxford History of the American People, New York: Oxford University Press, 1965, 542.

Myers, Donald P. "Parole Board to Review Freeman case." Journal, 5 March 1979, 1, 10.

Neuberger, Richard. Adventures in Politics. New York: Oxford University Press, 1954.

O'Callaghan, Jerry A. "Senator Mitchell and the Oregon Land Frauds, 1905." Pacific Historical Review, (August, 1952).

O'Donnell, Terence. "Oregon History;" in Oregon, Secretary of State, Oregon Blue Book 1993-1994, Salem: Secretary of State, 1991, 3788.

_____. That Balance So Rare -- The Story of Oregon. Portland: Oregon Historical Society Press, 1988.

"Olson Refuses to Resign." The Oregonian, 23 October 1987, C4.

Oregon School Board Association. Covering Education - A Reporters Guide to Education. Salem: Oregon School Board Association, 1986.

Oregon State Bar. "One-half century-An illustrated time-line of significant of the Bar." Undated pamphlet.

Oregon, Oregon Legislative Assembly. Form and Style Manual for Legislative Measures - 1992 Edition, Salem: Legislative Administration Committee, 1992.

_____. Oregon Legislative Assembly, Legislative Research. "Report 83:026." Salem: Legislative Research, 1983.

_____. Oregon Legislative Assembly. House Journal, 19 March 1993.

_____. Oregon Legislative Assembly, Legislative fiscal Office. Budget Highlights, Legislatively Approved 1993-95 Budget, Salem: Legislative Fiscal Office, 1993.

_____. Oregon Legislative Assembly, Legislative Revenue Office. Basic Tax Packet --Research Report , Salem OR: Legislative Revenue Office, 1993.

_____, Oregon Legislative Assembly, Oregon State Senate. Senate Journal 1987-1988.

_____. Oregon Legislative Assembly. Rules of the House. Salem: Committee on Rules and Reapportionment, 1991.

_____. Oregon Legislative Assembly. Rules of the Senate. Salem: Committee on Rules, 1991.

_____. Oregon Legislative Assembly. <u>Senate Legislative Calendar</u>. 5 August 1993.

_____. Oregon Legislative Assembly. <u>Session Laws 1987</u>.

_____. Port of Portland. <u>1993-1994 Budget</u>. Portland, OR: Port of Portland, 1993.

_____. Secretary of State. <u>1992 General Voters' Pamphlet</u>.

_____. Secretary of State. <u>Oregon Blue Book 1949-1950</u>. Salem: Secretary of State, 1949.

_____. Secretary of State. <u>Oregon Blue Book 1991-1992.</u> Salem: Secretary of State, 1991.

_____. Secretary of State. <u>Oregon Blue Book 1993-1994</u>. Salem: Secretary of State, 1993.

_____. Secretary of State. <u>Summary of Campaign Contributions and Expenditures - 1992 General Election</u>. Salem: Secretary of State, 1993.

Ota, Alan. "South emerges as No. 1 wood-products region." <u>The Oregonian</u>, 18 December 1991, A1, B1.

"Ousted Judge Field has brain tumor surgery." <u>The Oregonian</u>, 26 April 1979, B1.

Painter, John. "News Analysis: Fitness panel comes of age." <u>The Oregonian</u>, 20 September 1977, B1.

_____. "Removal of Judge Field recommended." <u>The Oregonian</u>, 20 September 1977, A1.

Peterson, Todd A. and Jack A. Collins. "Years of Growth," in <u>The First Duty - A History of the US. District Court in Oregon</u>, ed. Carolyn M. Buam. Portland: US. District Court Historical Society, 1993, 133-138.

"Petition hucksterism." <u>The Register-Guard</u>, 10 October 1993, 2B.

Pierce, Walter M. <u>Oregon Cattleman/Governor, Congressman</u>, Edited and expanded by Arthur H. Bone. Portland: Oregon Historical Society, 1981.

Pintarich, Dick and J. Kingston Pierce. "The Achievement of Oregon's Statehood," in <u>Great Moments in Oregon History</u>. Win McCormack and Dick Pintarich Ed. Portland: New Oregon Publishers, 1987, 48.

Prosser, William L. <u>Law of Torts</u>, 4th Ed St. Paul: West Publishing, 1971.

"Roberts' First Judicial Appointment - Janice Wilson sworn in." <u>The Oregonian</u>, 11 April 1991, C4.

Rollins, Michael. "Retiring Portland police chief's career hit some highs, and lows." <u>The Oregonian</u>, 27 June 1993, D1, D8.

Rubenstein, Sura. "All anti-gay-rights measures pass." <u>The Oregonian</u>, 30 June 1993, A1, A18.

_____. "Cornelius seen as a 'turning point,'" <u>The Oregonian</u>, 20 May 1993, A1, A20.

_____. "High court backs political petitioners." <u>The Oregonian</u>, 24 March 1993, B1, B4.

_____. "Increasingly, Christian right becomes a power in politics." <u>The Oregonian</u>, 20 June 1993, A1, A22.

_____. "Mabon, OCA wield political power." <u>The Oregonian</u>, 28 July 1991, A1.

_____. "New anti-gay rights measure filed." <u>The Oregonian</u>, 7 May 1993, A1, A18.

_____. "OCA's rise meteoric since start-up in 1986." <u>The Oregonian</u>, 21 June 1993, B1, B4.

Sarasohn, David. "In Salem, 'gridlock' too nice a word." <u>The Oregonian</u>, 1 July 1993, J2.

_____. "Joe Lutz running for nabob of normal." <u>The Oregonian</u>, 15 December 1991, C8.

_____. "On Higher Ed, not quite high enough." <u>The Oregonian</u>, 30 May 1993, B-8.

Schama, Simon. <u>Citizens</u>. New York: Alfred A. Knopf, 1989.

Schimdt, David D. <u>Citizen Lawmakers</u>. Philadelphia: Temple University Press, 1989.

Scott, Harvey W. <u>History of the Oregon Country</u>, vol. 5. Cambridge: Riverside press, 1924.

Schrag, John. "Postponed Promises." <u>The Willamette Week</u>, 18 November 1993, 9.

"Session yields a bumper crop of lobbyists." <u>Statesman Journal</u>, 29 March 1993, 2C.

"Slayer Says Law Invited Crime." <u>The Oregonian</u>, 2 October 1919, sec. 1, 1.

Smith, Jill "Devil's Dictionary - The Oregon Citizens' Alliance from A to Z." <u>Willamette Week</u>, 8 August 1991, 1,11-14.

Stanford, Phil. "Michael Francke - the case that won't go away." <u>The Oregonian</u>, 6 April 1993, C1, C4.

Starr, Paul. <u>The Social Transformation of American Medicine</u>. New York: Basic Books, 1982.

"State Warden Backs Death Penalty Ban." <u>The Oregonian</u>, 16 October 1964, sec. 1, 33.

<u>Statistical Abstract of the United States 112th Ed</u>. Washington DC: Government Printing Office, 1993.

Steeves, David. "Senate rejects education cuts." <u>Statesman-Journal</u>, 10 March 1993, 1A, 2A.

Sullivan, Robert. "Meet the Adkissons." <u>The New York Times Magazine</u>, 25 April 1993,__.

"Texas Meets School-Financing Deadline." <u>The New York Times</u>, 1 June 1993, A8.

<u>The Book of States 1988-89 Edition</u>. Lexington, Kentucky: The Council of State Governments, 1988.

<u>The Economist Diary 1993</u>. London: The Economist Newspapers Ltd, 1993 85. 97.

<u>The O & C Lands</u>. Eugene OR: University of Oregon, Bureau of Governmental Research, 1981.

<u>The Oregonian</u>. "Trivia and Visitor's Guide -- Pamphlet," 1993.

"The Race is On and She's off." <u>Willamette Week</u>, 2 September 1993,__.

<u>The West Comes of Age: Hard Times, Hard Choices</u>. Lexington: The Council of State Governments, 1993.

Thompson, Cecil T. <u>The Origin of Direct Legislation in Oregon</u>. Master's thesis, University of Oregon, 1929.

Turnbull, George S. <u>History of Oregon Newspapers</u>. Portland: Binford & Mort, 1939.

Turner, Frederick Jackson. <u>Frontier and Section - Selected essays of Frederick Jackson Turner</u>, with a Introduction by Ray Allen Billington. Englewood Cliffs, New Jersey: Prentice-Hall, 1991.

_____. <u>The Frontier in American History</u>. New York: Henry Holt, 1948.

"Up Front - Call to Order." <u>The Oregonian</u>, 22 June 1993, B1.

"Upfront -Verbatim." <u>The Oregonian</u>, 12 July 1993, B-1.

"Upfront-McIntire Tapped." <u>The Oregonian</u>, 18 August 1993, B1.

Van Caenegem, R.C. <u>The Birth of the English Common Law</u>, 2d Ed. Cambridge: Cambridge University Press, 1988.

Walth, Brent. "Gridlock in Legislature leaves lawmakers glum." <u>The Register-Guard</u> (Eugene), 26 April 1993, 1A, 4A.

"Warden told to explain killer's escape." <u>The Oregonian</u>, 22 May 1974, 1.

Waterwoman, Ariel. "Stuck between a rock and a hard place - Rep. Gail Shibley takes us on a guided tour of the death of SB-34 and the birth of HB 3500." <u>Just Out</u>, (Portland), 15 July 1993, 9.

_____. "Waiting for the dust to settle on HB 3500." <u>Just Out</u>. (Portland), 15 July 1993, 8.

Wermiel, Stephen. "State Supreme Courts Are Feeling Their Oats About Civil Liberties." <u>The Wall Street Journal</u>, 16 June 1988, 1,__.

West, Cornel. <u>Race Matters</u>, Boston: Beacon Press, 1993.

West, Oswald. "Reminiscences and Anecdotes." <u>Oregon Historical Quarterly</u>, LI, Number 1 (March 1950), 96.

Wilkerson, Isabel. "Tiring of Cuts, District Plans to Close Schools." <u>The New York Times</u>, 21 March 1993, 12.

Will, George. "Term-limits success vexes politicians vexes politicians." <u>The Oregonian</u>, 24 June 1993, C7.

_____. <u>Restoration</u>. New York: Freepress, 1992.

Wong, Peter. "Johnson locks horns with speaker, loses post." <u>Medford Mail Tribune</u>, 31 January 1993, __.

Woodward, Steve. "Books, Bucks and Ballots." <u>The Oregonian</u>, 2 May 1993, L1, L3.

Zeigler, Harmon and Michael Baer. Lobby <u>Interaction and Influence in State Legislatures</u>, Belmont California: Wadsworth, 1969.

Zusman, Mark. "Manchild in the Promised Land." <u>Willamette Week</u>, 11 April 1985, 9.

Cases:

<u>12 Hen. VII</u>, Keilwey 3b, 72 Eng. Rep. 156.

<u>Apodaca v. Oregon</u>, 406 U.S. 356 (1972).

<u>Brown v. Board of Education of Topeka</u>, 347 U.S. 483 (1954).

<u>Buchana v. Wood</u>, 79 Or App 722, 720 P 2d 1285 (1986).

<u>Buckley v. Valeo</u>, 424 U.S. 1, 96 S. Ct. 612 (1976).

<u>Burch v. Louisiana</u>, 99 S. Ct. 1623 (1979).

<u>Cook v. Corbett</u>, 251 OR 263, 446 P.2d 179 (19680>

<u>Dept. of Revenue v. County of Multnomah</u>, 4 OR 133 (1970).

<u>Deras v. Myers</u>, 272 OR 47, 535 P. 2 d 541 (1975).

<u>Dred Scott v. Sandford</u>, 60 U.S. 383 (1857).

<u>Eckles v. Oregon</u>, 306 OR 380, 760 P 2d 846 (1988).

<u>Fidanque v. Paulus</u>, 297 OR 711, 688 P 2d 1303 (1984).

<u>Higgins v. Hood River County</u>, 245 OR 135, 420 P 2d 634 (1966).

<u>In re Bernard Jolles</u>, 235 Or. 262, 277 (1963).

In the Matter of Sawyer, 286 OR 594 (1979).

Marbury v. Madison, 1 Cranch 137, 2 L. Ed. 60 (1803).

OEA v. Roberts, 301 OR 228, 721 P 2d 837 (1986).

Merrick v. Board of Education, 116 Or App. 293 (1993).

Pacific Power and Light v. Paulus, 289 OR 31, 609 P 2d 813 (1980);

Pierce v. Society of Sisters, 268 U.S. 510 (1925).

State of Oregon v. John Wayne Quinn 290 OR 383 (1981).

State v. Cargill, 100 Or App 336, 786 P 2d 208 (1990), Sup Ct review allowed; State v. Dameron,
  101 Or App 237, 789 P 2d 707 (1990).

The Libertarian Party of Oregon et al v. Norma Paulus, et al, No. 82-521FR United States District
    Court of Oregon, 1982.

United States F. & G. Co. v. Bramwell, 109 OR 261, 217 Pac. 332 (1923).

Zemprelli v. Scranton, 519 A2d 518 (1986).

SUBJECT INDEX

C

C & D Lumber, 131
C&E's, 61
Cabrillo, 3
California, 4
Californian, 164
call, 89, 92
call of the House, 89
call of the Senate, 89
Callenbach, Ernest, 8
"Camel's nose," 96
campaign contributions, 21
campaign spending limits, 129
Campaigners, 9
Campbell, Larry, 36, 39, 40, 42, 54, 77, 99,
    102, 103, 131
Campbell, Craig, 102
Canada, 2
Canby, 41
Capital Construction Sub-Committee, 61
Capitol, 35
Capitol Club, 138
Capitol Coffee Shop, 10
Capitol Press, 165
Carmen Miranda, 9
carrying bills, 91
"Carrying water," 96
Carson, Wallace, 110
Carter, Jimmy, 54, 145
Carter, Margaret, 40
Cascade Mountains, 2
Castagna, Bob, 136
caucus rules, 73
caucuses, 71
Caudle, Joan, 179
Cease, Jane, 8
Cease, Ron, 8
Cecil Edward's Archives Building, 62
central committees, 143
Chamberlain, George, 142
Champoeg, 3
Chancellor,higher ed, 61
check fiasco, 103
Cherriots, 161
Cherry, Howard, 136

chief elections officer, 9, 61
chief investment officer, 63
Chief Judge, 111
Chief Justice, 110
chief of staff, 52
chief purpose of the measure, 32
chiropractors, 134
Church, Frank, 145
cigarette taxes, 56
circuit court, 111, 112, 114
city dog, 150
city incorporation, 155
civil rights, 65
Clackamas County, 154
Clark, Bud, 157
Clark, Don, 153
CLE, 119
clean government, 20
clemency, 18
clerk of the House, 74, 94
Clinton, Hillary Rodham, 134
coalition, 6, 99
Coast Range, 2
Code of Professional Responsibility, 119
Colorado, 37, 39, 119, 191
COLT, 133
Columbia County, 154, 155
Columbia Rediviva , 3
Columbia Region Association of
    Governments, 160
Columbia Ridge, 161
Columbia River, 3, 130, 159, 176
commercial fishing, 30
Commission on Judicial Fitness &
    Disability, 114
commissioner of labor and industries,
    50, 65
commissioner of labor and industries,
    pay, 65
commissioner of labor and industries,
    staff, 65
committee appointments, 74
committee jurisdiction over a bill, 75
committees, relating clause, 82
committee assignment, 72
Committee on Political Education, 135

committees, chair votes last, 82
committees, ending work, 101
committees, hearings, 81
committees, jurisdiction, 80
committees, majority report, 88
committees, minority report, 88
committees, minority reports, 82
committees, personalities, 79
committees, power of the chair, 81
committees, report, 88
committees, rules, 81
committees, voting, 83
committees, work sessions, 83
Common Cause, 129
common law, 108, 109
common law, Oregon, 109
common school system, 192
Communications Workers, 135
community colleges, 64
commutations, 18, 51, 53
Compulsory Education Bill, 188
Concerned Oregon Lawyers Trust, 133
Concurrent Resolution, 79
conference committee, 76
conflict of interest, 21, 93
Congress, 70, 74, 79, 83, 87, 89, 109, 186
Conkling, Gary, 133
Constitutional law, 13
constitutional offices, 65
construction liens, 131
continuing legal education, 119
contributory negligence, 180
control, majority party, 99
Conversation with Oregon, 54
Cook, Vern, 76, 147
Cooter, John, 99
COPE, 135
Corbett, Alice, 146
Cornett, Marshall, 4, 52
corporate law, 87
corporate taxes, 56
corrections, 54, 100, 178
Corrections Division, 62
corruption, 10
Corvallis, 43, 177
Council on Court Procedures, 123

county boundaries, 30
county court, 152
county dog, 150
county issues, 153
county politics, 154
coup d'etat, 89
Court of Appeals, 35, 111, 114, 116
Court of Appeals, number of cases, 111
court of general jurisdiction, 112
courts of record, 111
courts, finance, 121
courts, number of, 110
courts, personalities of, 114
courts, trial, 111
"Cowardice in the House," 40
Craven, Jim, 133
Credentials Committee, 28
credit unions, 131
criminal defense bar, 117
Cronin, Thomas, 184
Crooked River Gorge, 53
"Cross of Gold," 27
culture wars, 24, 37
Cusma, Rena, 160
cut targets, 85

D

Daily Barometer, 165
Daily Emerald, 165
Danielson, John, 135
DAS, 55, 57, 59, 60, 61, 66
Davis, Jim, 157
daylight savings time, 30
Dayton Tribune, 165
Des Moines Register, 165
de Tocqueville, 1
Deady, Mathew, 15
death certificates, 150
death march, 101
death penalty, 18, 51, 52, 53, 137, 178,
  188
death penalty, last Oregon execution, 52
debate, 92
decision packages, 58
decisiveness, 54

home schooling, 32
homosexuality, 38
honoraria, 20
House Appropriations Committee, 102, 103
House Democratic Caucus, 73
House Democrats, 71
house district, 71
House District-20, 36
House Journal, 94
House Judiciary Committee, 40, 87, 100
House Judiciary, sub-committees, 88
House of Commons, 87
House Republicans, 71
House Revenue, 103
Housekeeping bill, 97
Hudson's Bay Company, 3
Human Resources Department, 101
husbands and wives, 8
Huss, Walter, 144

I

I&R, 26, 28
ice water, 146
immigration, 4
imprisonment for debt, 16
incumbent, judges use, 115
indigent defense, 121, 153
Ingram, Genoa, 134
initiative, 7, 25
initiative and referendum, 19, 29, 70, 184
initiative and referendum, assumptions, 29
initiative and referendum, number of, 29
initiative and referendum, original intent, 29
initiative and referendum, progressive instruments, 29
initiative and the referendum, 26, 29, 32
initiative, court cases, 32
initiative, drafting, 32
initiative, expense of, 34
initiative, one subject rule, 32
innovation, 7
insurance companies, 132

insurance defense, 117
insurance taxes, 56
integrated bar, 118
Intel, 5
International Paper, 131
International Workers of the World, 178
Investor Owned Utilities, 130
"IOU," 130
Ivancie, Frank, 157

J

Jackson, William, 179
James G. Blaine Society, 8
Japan, 2
Johnson, Cecil, 179
Johnson, Clarence, 179
Johnson, Lyndon, 55
Johnson, Rod, 100
Jolin, Peg, 17
Jolles, Bernie, 120
Jones, Delna, 103
Joseph, George, 91
Joseph, George M., 111
Josephine County, 41
Journal, 160, 166
judges' terms of office, 18
judges, incumbent, 117
judges, pay, 112
judges, state, 110
judiciary committees, 87
judicial appointments, 116
judicial budget, 51
judicial review, 110
judicial selection, 115
Judiciary, 72, 77
Junction City, 41
juries, size, 112
jury, power to determine fact, 18
Justice Endorsed by Women Lawyers, 116
justices of the peace, 113
juvenile law, 87

K

L

standard time, 30
standing committees, 72
star system, 143
stare decisis, 109
Stassen, Harold, 144
State Accident Insurance Fund, 53
state bank, 18
State Board of Education, 64
State Board of Higher Education, 60
State Board of Medical Examiners, 119
State Capitol, 90
State Capitol, rotunda, 102
state constitutions, 13, 15
State Fair, 146
state functions, 14
state income tax, 56
State Industrial Accident Commission, 180
state owning stock, 18
State Senate confirmation, 50
state treasurer, 63
State v. Quinn, 179
state wine cellar, 7
state's bond rating, 63
state's credit, 19
Statements of Economic Interest, 20
Statesman, 165
Statesman-Journal, 10, 165, 166
statewide elected officials, 50
statutory offices, 65
steelhead, 30
stereotypers' union, 166
Stevenson, Adlai, 171
Still, Ron, 157
Straub, Robert, 53, 55
Streich, Dedi, 179
Streisinger, Cory, 116, 159
stricter state standard, 15, 114
subject of the measure, 32
subsequent referral, 81
substantive bills, 86
substantive" committees, 88
succession, 18
suffrage, 29
Sunriver, 155
sunshine laws, 21

superintendent of public instruction, 50, 64, 65
support document, 86
Supreme Court, 18, 34, 35, 110, 111, 114, 115, 116, 118, 119, 120, 121, 129, 179, 180
Supreme Court Building, 110
switchblades, 15
Sykes, Michael, 155

T

talk radio, 167
tavern and saloon owners, 30
tax and spend Democrats, 93
tax base, 19, 172
Tax Revolt, 174, 186
taxes, 19, 30, 86
teachers, 16, 135
Tektronix, 5, 133
Telegraph, 166
Tent Show, 9
term limit on the commissioners, 153
term limits, 186
Territorial Assembly, 14
the "call," 89
The Christian Science Monitor, 165
The Ethics Commission, 20
"the fat lady sings," 100
The Gay Agenda, 41
The Minority Status and Child Protection Act, 39
The New York Times, 41, 165
The Oregonian, 14, 26, 39, 40, 41, 103, 134, 160, 164, 165, 167, 168, 179
The Oregonian, strike, 166
The Oregonian, no Indian names, 166
The Oregonian, opposed to initiative, 26
the people of the state of Oregon, 70
The San Francisco Chronicle, 165
The Supremes, 110
The Wall Street Journal, 165, 192
Third House, 138
third readings, 91
Thorne, Mike, 159
Timber Carnival, 34

Ways and Means Committee, 16, 57, 59,
60, 72, 73, 79, 81, 83, 85, 86, 101, 102,
159, 186
ways and means, co-chairs, 83, 102
Ways and Means, sub-committees, 84
weak governor, 50
weapons, 16
Weaver, Jim, 144
wedge issues, 129
West, Cornell, 190, 191
West, Oswald, 142, 178
West-Side Light Rail, 161
Western Frontier, 188
Wheeler County, 152
Whig, 14, 142, 165, 166
whips, 71
White Aryan Resistance, 113
Wilhelms, Gary, 131
Willamette Industries, 131
Willamette Valley, 2, 4, 164, 165, 177
Willamette Week, 104, 165, 167
Willamette University, 3
Williams, George, 122
Withycombe, James, 178
Wolfer, Curt, 8
Wolfer, Martin, 8
women lobbyists, 131
workers' compensation, 133, 180
World War II, 4

X

xenophobia, 8

Y

Yamhill County, 165
Yih, Mae, 39, 102
Younts, Dick, 38

Z

Zeigler, Harmon, 138
zoning, 151